AF841019

THE CHOICE OF LAW CONTRACT

This book offers a contractual framework for the regulation of party autonomy in choice of law. The party autonomy rule is the cornerstone of any modern system of choice of law; embodying as it does the freedom enjoyed by parties to a cross-border legal relationship to agree on the law applicable to it. However, as this study shows, the rule has a major shortcoming because it fails to give due regard to the contractual function of the choice of law agreement. The study examines the existing law on choice of law agreements, by reference to the law of both common and civil law jurisdictions, and international instruments. Moreover, it suggests a new coherent approach to party autonomy that integrates both the law of contract and choice of law. This important new study should be read with interest by private international law scholars.

Volume 18 in the series Studies in Private International Law

Studies in Private International Law

Recent titles in the series

Volume 6: International Child Abduction: The Inadequacies of the Law
Thalia Kruger

Volume 7: Mediating International Child Abduction Cases
Sarah Vigers

Volume 8: International Antitrust Litigation: Conflict of Laws and Coordination
Edited by Jürgen Basedow, Stéphanie Francq and Laurence Idot

Volume 9: The Governing Law of Companies in EU Law
Justin Borg-Barthet

Volume 10: Intellectual Property and Private International Law: Comparative Perspectives
Edited by Toshiyuki Kono

Volume 11: Child Abduction within the European Union
Katarina Trimmings

Volume 12: International Surrogacy Arrangements: Legal Regulation at the International Level
Edited by Katarina Trimmings and Paul Beaumont

Volume 13: The Hague Child Abduction Convention: A Critical Analysis
Rhona Schuz

Volume 14: Interregional Recognition and Enforcement of Civil and Commercial Judgments: Lessons for China from the US and EU Law
Jie Huang

Volume 15: The Recovery of Maintenance in the EU and Worldwide
Paul Beaumont, Burkhard Hess, Lara Walker and Stefanie Spancken

Volume 16: Australian Private International Law for the 21st Century: Facing Outwards
Edited by Andrew Dickinson, Thomas John and Mary Keyes

Volume 17: Maintenance and Child Support in Private International Law
Lara Walker

The Choice of Law Contract

Maria Hook

• HART •
OXFORD • LONDON • NEW YORK • NEW DELHI • SYDNEY

HART PUBLISHING
Bloomsbury Publishing Plc
Kemp House, Chawley Park, Cumnor Hill, Oxford, OX2 9PH, UK

HART PUBLISHING, the Hart/Stag logo, BLOOMSBURY and the Diana logo are trademarks of Bloomsbury Publishing Plc
First published in Great Britain 2016

First published in hardback, 2016
Paperback edition, 2019

A catalogue record for this book is available from the British Library.

Library of Congress Cataloging-in-Publication Data

Names: Hook, Maria (Law teacher), author.

Title: The choice of law contract / Maria Hook.

Description: Oxford ; Portland, Oregon : Hart Publishing, an imprint of Bloomsbury Publishing Plc, 2016. | Series: Studies in private international law ; v. 18 | Based on author's thesis (doctoral - Victoria University of Wellington, 2014). | Includes bibliographical references and index.

Identifiers: LCCN 2016012641 (print) | LCCN 2016013057 (ebook) | ISBN 9781849467643 (hardback : alk. paper) | ISBN 9781509901029 (Epub)

Subjects: LCSH: Conflict of laws. | Liberty of contract.

Classification: LCC K7068 .H66 2016 (print) | LCC K7068 (ebook) | DDC 340.9—dc23

LC record available at http://lccn.loc.gov/2016012641

ISBN: HB: 978-1-84946-764-3
PB: 978-1-50992-680-0
ePDF: 978-1-50990-101-2
ePub: 978-1-50990-102-9

Series: Studies in Private International Law, volume 18

Typeset by Compuscript Ltd, Shannon

SERIES EDITORS' PREFACE

In this work, Dr Maria Hook writes with great authority on a core aspect of private international law: the extent to which parties should be able to exercise their autonomy to choose the law to govern various aspects of their lives. The book is not just concerned with the private international law of contract. The author ranges across party autonomy in contract, tort, divorce, maintenance, matrimonial property and succession. She regards the exercise of party autonomy to choose the law applicable to their relationship in any area of law as falling within the law of contract in the sense that the parties must agree to a 'choice of law contract'. Dr Hook argues that the characterisation of the exercise of party autonomy in agreeing the law applicable to a relationship or a dispute as 'contractual' is helpful in enabling a sophisticated and clear regime to be developed for analysing whether the parties have lawfully agreed on the law to govern a particular relationship or dispute.

This book builds and develops upon the author's previous work (see 'The concept of modal choice of law rules' (2015) 11 *Journal of Private International Law* 185–211). This monograph, in its detailed and careful unpacking of how choice of law contracts should be dealt with, argues that the contractual characterisation must be augmented by a significant body of modal choice of law rules if party autonomy is to be sufficiently well regulated to create the legal certainty and predictability that are meant to be the hallmarks of a system based on party autonomy. The author expresses the hope that more of these modal choice of law rules might be agreed universally through the work of the Hague Conference on Private International Law. She cites the Hague Maintenance Protocol 2007 as the best international example so far of modal choice of law rules being agreed to regulate party autonomy in applicable law.

This is a sophisticated work of scholarship showing the benefits of the comparative method (the author considers material from Australia, England and Wales, the European Union, France, Germany, Hague Conference on Private International Law, Switzerland and USA). The author draws upon academic literature published in English, French and German and demonstrates a command of a range of private international law concepts and theories, as well as the ability to conduct a detailed legal analysis of conventions, EU instruments, national codifications, statutes and case law. The book is written with enormous confidence.

The range, depth and originality of the analysis of complex and intricate aspects of party autonomy in applicable law make this a must read for anyone engaged in research in this field.

Paul Beaumont, University of Aberdeen

Jonathan Harris, King's College, London

ACKNOWLEDGEMENTS

Many people have contributed to this book, which is based on a PhD thesis completed at Victoria University of Wellington. I am especially grateful to my doctoral supervisor, Campbell McLachlan, for his intellectual guidance and support over the years; to Tony Angelo, Richard Garnett and Mary Keyes for their helpful comments; to Jack Wass, for our many conversations about all things 'private international law'; and to my colleagues at the University of Otago Faculty of Law. The project greatly benefited from financial assistance offered by Victoria University of Wellington and the Max Planck Institute for Comparative and International Private Law in Hamburg, Germany, where I was able to undertake research from September to November 2012.

Maria Hook
December 2015

CONTENTS

TABLE OF CASES

Australia

France

Germany

New Zealand

United Kingdom

United States

Switzerland

Other

TABLE OF LEGISLATION

Australia

European Union

France

Germany

International

New Zealand

Switzerland

United Kingdom

Other

1

Introduction

I. The Contractualisation of Choice of Law

A manufacturer of model trains, whose business is located in Germany, orders screws from a multinational company incorporated in Canada. Due to a design fault, the screws damage the manufacturer's machinery. He brings proceedings in negligence in a German court. These proceedings are governed by the law of Texas, based on a choice of law clause in the parties' contract that submits contractual and non-contractual claims to the law of Texas. The effect of this choice of law is that the court will not hold the supplier liable for the damage.

A New Zealand consumer places a large order for model trains through the manufacturer's website. On delivery, he discovers that the trains do not work properly because they have been built with the Canadian company's faulty screws. He wants his money back and brings proceedings for breach of contract in the New Zealand court. The manufacturer argues successfully that his terms and conditions evidence an implied choice of German law, because they refer to German legislation. The New Zealand plaintiff cannot afford to plead and prove his claim pursuant to German law and discontinues the proceedings.

The manufacturer declares insolvency because he has no funds to repair his expensive machinery. This prompts the manufacturer's wife to bring matrimonial property proceedings in Switzerland, where she lives separated from her husband. The manufacturer is a citizen of Germany, and the wife is a citizen of Kenya; but before the parties separated they lived together in Switzerland. The parties chose to submit their matrimonial property relationship to the law of Kenya, where they got married. As a result of this choice, the wife's legal position is less favourable than it would be under Swiss (or German) law.

Each of these scenarios is an example of the rule of party autonomy—the power enjoyed by litigants to choose the law applicable to their cross-border legal relationship. By selecting the applicable law, parties are able to opt out of the objective choice of law rules of the forum—those choice of law rules that would apply in default of their choice—and submit their relationship to the chosen legal system. Typically, the parties' choice is subject only to overriding mandatory rules or the public policy of the forum.[1] Party autonomy is becoming more and more popular. It is firmly established in the area of contract, and has spread to other matters such as divorce, maintenance, matrimonial property and tort.

This book provides an account of the contractual nature of the party autonomy rule. It argues that the rise of party autonomy—the growing contractualisation of choice of law—has been unduly divorced from the principles and the law of contract. Parties are given the power to opt out of choice of law rules by agreeing on the applicable law. But unlike conventional contracts, the choice of law agreement sits in a regulatory twilight zone. It is a creature of the law of contract, placed in the service of the conflict of laws, fulfilling the unique contractual function of identifying the applicable law: it is a choice of law contract. Current approaches to regulating party autonomy are often out of tune with this unique contractual function. For example, a New Zealand court may infer that the German manufacturer and the New Zealand consumer made a choice of German law even if, according to the law of contract, there was no implied choice of law agreement.

It is submitted that a better, more principled approach would be to confront the dual nature of the party autonomy rule head-on. The party autonomy rule operates through a choice of law contract. Thus, it requires an integrated approach to regulation that merges the laws and policies of choice of law and contract. This book adopts such an integrated approach. It uses the existing infrastructure of the conflict of laws—in particular, the law governing the choice of law agreement, and contractual rules of the conflict of laws, so-called modal choice of law rules, that regulate the choice of law agreement directly and specifically; and it uses these tools to give effect to the unique function of the choice of law contract.

A. Extent of the Contractualisation of Choice of Law

Because party autonomy is a global phenomenon, the work draws on sources from a range of jurisdictions, which may be split into four groups: common law jurisdictions (England, Australia and New Zealand); civil law jurisdictions (France, Germany and Switzerland); the United States; and international instruments (European Regulations on choice of law and the work of the Hague Conference on Private International Law). The conflict of laws has long relied on the comparative method as a natural ally.[2] The purpose of choice of law rules is to respond to foreign elements in international private relationships and, where possible, to achieve uniform outcomes across borders. It is important, therefore, that the party

[1] See, eg, Arts 9 and 21, Reg (EC) 593/2008 on the law applicable to contractual obligations [2008] OJ L177/6 (Rome I).

[2] See B Fauvarque-Cosson, 'Comparative Law and Conflict of Laws: Allies or Enemies? New Perspectives on an Old Couple' (2001) 49 *American Journal of Comparative Law* 407; AT von Mehren, 'The Contribution of Comparative Law to the Theory and Practice of Private International Law' (1977–1978) 26 *American Journal of Comparative Law (Supplement)* 31.

autonomy rule is not developed in isolation from foreign norms and practices, or in a way that will increase the risk of inconsistent choice of law outcomes.

The international scope of this work goes hand in hand with the topical breadth of its inquiry. The central theme is the bilateral exercise of the power to choose the applicable law—that is, the choice of law agreement—whether it applies to contractual, non-contractual or family relationships.[3] Unilateral party autonomy (such as the power to choose the law applicable to one's will) and forum selection agreements fall outside of the scope of the work, which is not to say that it would be wrong to draw parallels between these different areas of the conflict of laws.

i. Common Law Jurisdictions

In England, Australia and New Zealand, courts have been giving effect to party autonomy when determining the proper law of an international contract. In *Vita Food Products Inc v Unus Shipping Co Ltd*, Lord Wright held that the parties' intention to select the applicable law was enforceable 'provided the intention expressed is bona fide and legal, and provided there is no reason for avoiding the choice on the ground of public policy'.[4] While, in England, this rule has been largely superseded by European instruments, the common law approach continues to be applicable in Australia and New Zealand. Despite recommendations by the Australian Law Reform Commission on the reform of party autonomy in contract,[5] no attempts have been made to codify the rule in Australia.

In some areas, overriding mandatory rules have been enacted to exclude the party autonomy rule from certain contracts. The Credit Contracts and Consumer Finance Act 2003 (NZ), for example, provides that the Act applies to a credit contract, guarantee, lease or buy-back transaction if it 'would be governed by the law of New Zealand but for a choice of law provision';[6] and the Competition and Consumer Act 2010 (Aust) provides that, if the proper law of a consumer contract for the supply of goods or services 'would be the law of any part of Australia but for a term of the contract that provides otherwise', then the consumer guarantees provisions of the Australian Consumer Law apply despite that term.[7]

Common law has also recognised the party autonomy rule in relation to matrimonial property contracts and, it seems, in relation to the effect of marriage on property more generally.[8] However, in England and Australia, matrimonial

[3] Previous works on party autonomy have typically focused on party autonomy in contracts: see, eg, P Nygh, *Autonomy in International Contracts* (Oxford, Oxford University Press, 1999); J-M Jacquet, *Principe d'autonomie et contrats internationaux* (Paris, Economica, 1983); J Püls, *Parteiautonomie* (Berlin, Duncker & Humblot, 1995).

[4] *Vita Food Products Inc v Unus Shipping Co Ltd* [1939] AC 277 (PC) 290.

[5] Australian Law Reform Commission, *Choice of Law* (Report 58, 1992) ch 8.

[6] Credit Contracts and Consumer Finance Act 2003 (NZ), s 137(b).

[7] Competition and Consumer Act 2010 (Aust), sch 2, s 67.

[8] L Collins (ed), *Dicey, Morris and Collins on the Conflict of Laws* 15th edn (London, Sweet & Maxwell, 2012) paras 28R-031 and 28-020; see *Re Egerton's Will Trusts* [1956] Ch 593.

matters that fall under the Matrimonial Causes Act 1973 and the Family Law Act 1975, respectively, are now largely governed by the law of the forum.[9] In New Zealand, on the other hand, section 7A of the Property (Relationships) Act 1976 provides that the Act applies in any case where the spouses or partners agree that it is to apply, and that it does not apply to any relationship property if the spouses or partners have agreed that the law of a country other than New Zealand is to apply.

None of these three jurisdictions has paid much attention to the legal nature of the parties' intention to choose the applicable law. This may be because, under the common law concept of the proper law, a contract becomes 'embedded' in, or 'naturalised' by, the agreed proper law:[10] it becomes one with the choice of law agreement.

ii. Civil Law Jurisdictions

As in England, much of the German and French law on choice of law is now contained in European instruments. Although German courts had already been giving effect to party autonomy in relation to contracts for several decades,[11] the rule was not codified until 1986, as part of a wider reform of private international law.[12] Articles 14 and 15 of the German Einführungsgesetz zum Bürgerlichen Gesetzbuch (EGBGB) also provide for the freedom to choose the law governing the general effects of marriage and matrimonial property, but the parties' choice is limited to a number of pre-selected connecting factors. In 1999, lawmakers introduced limited party autonomy for non-contractual obligations, which allowed parties to choose the applicable law after the event giving rise to the dispute had occurred.[13] The parties' agreement on the applicable law is commonly referred to as a choice of law contract.[14]

In France, on the other hand, scholars have been critical of the concept of a choice of law contract. One author even suggested that the choice of law contract has been the victim of a 'triple conspiracy':[15] it was incompatible with *la thèse de l'incorporation*, popular at the beginning of the twentieth century, which allowed parties simply to incorporate applicable laws into their contract by converting them into contractual stipulations; with Batiffol's theory of localisation, which provided that the parties' intentions were relevant only to the localisation

[9] See ch 3, s II.B.iii for more detail.

[10] FA Mann, 'The Proper Law in the Conflict of Laws' (1987) 36 *ICLQ* 437, 448.

[11] U Magnus (ed), *Staudingers Kommentar zum Bürgerlichen Gesetzbuch: Rom I-VO Art 3* (Berlin, Sellier, 2011) para 27, citing RGZ 120, 70 (1928); BGHZ 52, 239 (1969); BGHZ 73, 391 (1979).

[12] Gesetz zur Neuregelung des Internationalen Privatrechts (IPRNG) (BGBl 1986 I 1142); Einführungsgesetz zum Bürgerlichen Gesetzbuch (EGBGB), Art 27.

[13] Gesetz zum IPR für außervertragliche Schuldverhältnisse und für Sachen (BGBl 1999 I 1026); EGBGB, Art 42.

[14] Magnus (n 11) para 36.

[15] J Foyer, 'Le Contrat d'Electio Juris à la Lumière de la Convention de Rome du 19 Juin 1980' in *L'Internationalisation du Droit: Mélanges en l'Honneur de Yvon Loussouarn* (Paris, Dalloz, 1994) 169, 169.

of the contract;[16] and with the *méthode unilatérale*, which sought to identify the law to which the parties had voluntarily submitted.[17] More generally, the choice of law contract has been criticised as an artificial construct, a *faux problème*.[18] Nevertheless, French courts have long given effect to party autonomy both in the areas of contract[19] and matrimonial property.[20] In 1979, France ratified the Hague Convention on the Law Applicable to Matrimonial Property Regimes (Hague Convention 1978), which came into effect in 1992.[21]

Switzerland has a strong tradition of party autonomy. Now codified in the Bundesgesetz über das Internationale Privatrecht (IPRG),[22] Swiss courts started giving effect to party choice in international contracts in the nineteenth century;[23] and they have developed a comparatively sophisticated understanding of the choice of law contract.[24] Consumer contracts are excluded from the rule;[25] but employment contracts are open to a choice of law (though the choice is limited to the law of the place of the employee's habitual residence and the laws of the employer's place of business, domicile or habitual residence).[26] The IPRG also provides for party autonomy in relation to matrimonial property (with a choice between the law of common domicile or the law of nationality of either spouse),[27] movable property (with a choice between the law of the place of departure, the law of the place of destination, or the law of the underlying transaction),[28] and civil delicts (with the choice being limited to the law of the forum, after the event causing the damage occurred).[29]

iii. United States

US courts have also given effect to the party autonomy rule since the nineteenth century;[30] yet the first Restatement of Conflict of Laws was critical of the rule

16 H Batiffol, *Les conflits de lois en matière de contrats: Etude de droit international privé comparé* (Paris, Recueil Sirey, 1938) 41, as cited by Foyer (n 15) 170.

17 P Gothot, 'La méthode unilatéraliste face au droit international privé des contrats' (1975–1977) *Travaux du Comité Français de Droit International Privé* 201.

18 Batiffol (n 16) 46; see also V Heuzé, *La réglementation française des contrats internationaux* (Paris, Joly éditions, 1990) paras 275ff.

19 Cass civ, 5 December 1910, Sirey 1911.1.129 (*American Trading Co v Quebec Steamship Co*).

20 Based initially on the spouses' presumed intention, as developed by C Dumoulin in his *Consultation aux époux de Ganay* in 1525: see D Bureau and H Muir Watt, *Droit international privé* 2nd edn (Paris, Presses Universitaires de France, 2010) vol 2, 202–05.

21 Hague Convention on the Law Applicable to Matrimonial Property Regimes (1977) 16 ILM 14 (opened for signature 14 March 1978, entered into force 1 September 1992).

22 Bundesgesetz über das Internationale Privatrecht (IPRG), Art 116.

23 See H Honsell et al (eds), *Basler Kommentar* 3rd edn (Basel, Helbing Lichtenhahn, 2013) Art 116, para 3.

24 See ibid, 994–95.

25 IPRG, Art 120.

26 IPRG, Art 121.

27 IPRG, Art 52.

28 IPRG, Art 104.

29 IPRG, Art 132.

30 See, eg, *Arnold v Potter* 22 Iowa 194 (1867).

and did not adopt it.[31] It now finds expression principally in section 187(2) of the Restatement (Second) of Conflict of Laws and section 1-301 of the Uniform Commercial Code (UCC).[32] Both these provisions deal with choice of law for contracts.

Section 187(2) confers party autonomy subject to two conditions. First, the chosen state must have a 'substantial relationship' to the parties or the transaction, or there must be another 'reasonable basis' for the choice.[33] Second, application of the chosen law cannot be 'contrary to a fundamental policy' of the *lex causae* that would otherwise be applicable, provided the state of the *lex causae* has a 'materially greater interest than the chosen state in the determination of the particular issue'.[34] This safeguard is wider than the traditional public policy (or ordre public) exception.[35] Section 187 is used in almost all US states.[36] It has even been applied to surrogacy contracts.[37]

The UCC has allowed party autonomy since 1952. Section 1-301(a) provides that parties may select a law that bears a 'reasonable relation' to the transaction, but it is subject to a number of exceptions for specified transactions.[38] The section applies to contracts that fall within the scope of the UCC. The American Law Institute introduced significant changes to the rule in 2001. In particular, it abolished the 'reasonable relation' requirement and placed restrictions on party autonomy in consumer contracts. But when states refused to adopt the 2001 version of the rule, the American Law Institute re-introduced the old approach in section 1-301.

The Restatement (Second) does not address the question of party autonomy in relation to non-contractual obligations. However, in a 'sizeable number' of cases US courts have held that the parties intended to encompass tort claims in their choice of law agreements, treating the question 'as a matter of contractual *intent* (rather than contractual *power*)'.[39] The Restatement also seems to provide for party autonomy in relation to matrimonial property (or at least matrimonial property contracts).[40]

iv. International Instruments

On the international plane, the party autonomy rule has received particularly strong support in the European Union's regulations on choice of law and in the instruments of the Hague Conference on Private International Law.

[31] American Law Institute, *Restatement of Conflict of Laws* (1934).
[32] American Law Institute, *Restatement (Second) of Conflict of Laws* (1971); American Law Institute, *Uniform Commercial Code* (2008).
[33] s 187(2)(a).
[34] s 187(2)(b).
[35] s 187, cmnt (g).
[36] P Hay, P Borchers and S Symeonides, *Conflict of Laws* 5th edn (St Paul, West Academic Publishing, 2010) 1088.
[37] See ibid, 1127–28.
[38] s 1-301(c).
[39] Symeon C Symeonides, *Codifying Choice of Law Around the World* (New York, Oxford University Press, 2014) 101; Hay, Borchers and Symeonides (n 36) 1141–46.
[40] *Restatement (Second)* (n 32) Art 258 and see Hay, Borchers and Symeonides, ibid 684.

a. European Union

In the European Union, large areas of choice of law have been unified (or 'communitarised') in the name of removing obstacles to 'the proper functioning of the internal market' and creating an 'area of freedom, security and justice'.[41] There are currently four European regulations on choice of law that give effect to (bilateral) party autonomy.

Regulation (EC) 593/2008 on the law applicable to contractual obligations (Rome I) applies to 'contractual obligations in civil and commercial matters' and provides, in Article 3, that a contract shall be governed by the law chosen by the parties.[42] Rome I replaced the Rome Convention on the law applicable to contractual obligations (Rome Convention),[43] which entered into force in 1991. Consumer and employment contracts are not excluded from Article 3, but certain consumer and employment contracts are subject to the 'principle of the more favourable law', which disapplies rules of the chosen law if these deprive the weaker party 'of the protection afforded to him by provisions that cannot be derogated from by agreement' under the objective law.[44]

Regulation (EC) 864/2007 on the law applicable to non-contractual obligations (Rome II) applies to 'non-contractual obligations in civil and commercial matters',[45] including tort or delict, unjust enrichment, *negotiorum gestio* and *culpa in contrahendo*. Article 14 provides that parties may agree to submit non-contractual obligations to the law of their choice once the event giving rise to the damage has occurred, unless all the parties are pursuing a commercial activity. In that latter case, the parties may choose the applicable law 'by an agreement freely negotiated before the event giving rise to the damage occurred'.

Article 5 of Regulation (EU) 1259/2010 implementing enhanced cooperation in the area of the law applicable to divorce and legal separation (Rome III) provides that spouses may agree to designate the law applicable to divorce and legal separation, provided that it accords with one of a number of pre-selected connecting factors.[46] The Regulation applies to Germany and France, but not the United Kingdom.[47]

Regulation (EC) 4/2009 on jurisdiction, applicable law, recognition and enforcement of decisions and cooperation in matters relating to maintenance obligations (Maintenance Regulation) provides,[48] in Article 15, that the law applicable

[41] See Recital 1 of, eg, Rome I (n 1).

[42] Rome I (n 1).

[43] Convention 80/934/ECC on the law applicable to contractual obligations [1980] OJ L266/1 (opened for signature 19 June 1980, entered into force 1 April 1991) (Rome Convention).

[44] Rome I, Arts 6(2) and 8(1).

[45] Reg (EC) 864/2007 on the law applicable to non-contractual obligations [2007] OJ L199/40 (Rome II).

[46] Reg (EU) 1259/2010 implementing enhanced cooperation in the area of the law applicable to divorce and legal separation [2010] OJ L343/10 (Rome III).

[47] ibid, Recital 6.

[48] Reg (EC) 4/2009 on jurisdiction, applicable law, recognition and enforcement of decisions and cooperation in matters relating to maintenance obligations [2009] OJ L7/1 (Maintenance Reg).

to maintenance obligations shall be determined in accordance with the Hague Protocol on the Law Applicable to Maintenance Obligations (Hague Maintenance Protocol) in the Member States that are bound by the Protocol.[49] The Protocol has been ratified by the European Union, but the United Kingdom is not bound by the ratification. Article 7 of the Protocol provides for party choice of the law of the forum 'for the purpose of a particular proceeding', and Article 8 provides for a choice of law in accordance with one of a number of pre-selected connecting factors.

Article 16 of the Proposal for a Council Regulation on jurisdiction, applicable law and the recognition and enforcement of decisions in matters of matrimonial property regimes (Proposal for a Regulation on matrimonial property) allows spouses to choose the law applicable to their matrimonial property, provided that the choice accords with one of a number of pre-selected connecting factors.[50] Conversely, parties to registered partnerships did not receive the power to select the applicable law in the parallel Proposal for a Council Regulation on jurisdiction, applicable law and the recognition and enforcement of decisions regarding the property consequences of registered partnerships;[51] but the new compromise text of the Proposal provides for party choice in accordance with pre-selected connecting factors in Article 15-03.[52] The Council of the European Union has been unable to reach a unanimous political agreement on the Proposals.[53]

Finally, Regulation (EU) No 650/2012 on jurisdiction, applicable law, recognition and enforcement of decisions and acceptance and enforcement of authentic instruments in matters of succession (Succession Regulation) provides for party autonomy in relation to succession agreements.[54] Parties may choose the law(s) of nationality of the person 'whose estate is involved';[55] and the choice applies

[49] Hague Protocol on the Law Applicable to Maintenance Obligations (opened for signature 23 November 2007, entered into force 1 August 2013) (Hague Maintenance Protocol). The European Community declared the Protocol to be provisionally applicable from 18 June 2011 pursuant to Art 24 of the Protocol: see Council Decision 2009/941/EC on the conclusion by the European Community of the Hague Protocol of 23 November 2007 on the Law Applicable to Maintenance Obligations [2009] OJ L331/17.

[50] Proposal for a Council Reg on jurisdiction, applicable law and the recognition and enforcement of decisions in matters of matrimonial property regimes (COM 2011, 126, 16 March 2011) (Proposal for a Reg on Matrimonial Property).

[51] Proposal for a Council Reg on jurisdiction, applicable law and the recognition and enforcement of decisions regarding the property consequences of registered partnerships (COM 2011, 127, 16 March 2011).

[52] The compromise text is annexed to Council of the European Union, 'Proposal for a Council Regulation on jurisdiction, applicable law and the recognition and enforcement of decisions regarding the property consequences of registered partnerships—Political agreement' (Note, 14652/15, Brussels, 26 November 2015).

[53] Council of the European Union, Justice and Home Affairs, Meeting No 3433, 2/4 December 2015.

[54] Reg (EU) No 650/2012 on jurisdiction, applicable law, recognition and enforcement of decisions and acceptance and enforcement of authentic instruments in matters of succession and on the creation of a European Certificate of Succession [2012] OJ L201/107, Art 25(3). cp Art 11, Hague Convention on the Law Applicable to Succession to the Estates of Deceased Persons (opened for signature 1 August 1989, not yet in force).

[55] Arts 25(3) and 22.

to the admissibility, substantive validity and 'binding effects' of the succession agreement.

b. Hague Conference on Private International Law

The principal instruments by the Hague Conference on Private International Law to grant party autonomy in choice of law are the Hague Maintenance Protocol, which has already been referred to,[56] the Principles on Choice of Law in International Commercial Contracts (Hague Principles)[57] and the Hague Convention 1978.[58]

The Hague Principles, which are intended to serve as a model for national, regional, supranational or international instruments, affirm the party autonomy rule for international contracts 'where each party is acting in the exercise of its trade or profession'.[59] They are a non-binding instrument. Their primary purpose is to promote the party autonomy rule in international commercial contracts, and they do not provide for choice of law rules in the absence of choice.

The Hague Convention 1978, which entered into force in 1992, provides that matrimonial property is governed by the internal law designated by the spouses.[60] However, the parties' choice is limited to a number of pre-selected connecting factors. Of the jurisdictions discussed in this book, France is the only state to have entered into this Convention.

B. Contractualisation—But Divorced from the Law of Contract

Because it is based on an agreement to choose the applicable law, the party autonomy rule has had the effect of 'contractualising' choice of law rules in those areas where it is applicable. The applicable law is no longer derived from objective factors but selected by the parties by consent. The problem is that this contractualisation of choice of law has been unduly divorced from the principles and the law of contract. Although the choice of law agreement sits at the junction of the law of contract and choice of law, the two areas of law do not always work in harmony.

i. Closed Approach to Party Autonomy and its Consequences

A fundamental manifestation of this problem is the failure, in legal scholarship and practice, to engage with the contractual nature of the parties' agreement on choice

[56] See text at n 49.

[57] Hague Conference on Private International Law, *Principles on Choice of Law in International Commercial Contracts* (approved on 19 March 2015).

[58] Hague Convention on the Law Applicable to Matrimonial Property Regimes (n 21).

[59] Art 1(1).

[60] Arts 3 and 6.

of law. This is particularly true of common law jurisdictions. While the choice of law agreement has been variously characterised as a 'factual' agreement,[61] a 'true contract',[62] a bargain,[63] a promise,[64] and a 'declaratory' act,[65] little effort has been made to justify these labels on a principled basis, or to evaluate the implications that would arise from these respective characterisations for the operation of the party autonomy rule. Rather, discussion of the choice of law agreement is typically framed by a narrow focus on its scope and effect as a connecting factor.[66]

This normatively closed approach to party autonomy has had a number of consequences. The first is that there has been no principled approach to the granting of party autonomy—that is, the question whether party autonomy ought to be available in relation to a particular claim or issue (for example, should parties like the German manufacturer and the Canadian company be free to choose the law applicable to their non-contractual obligations?). It is often assumed that party autonomy ought to be linked to the degree of freedom that the parties enjoy at a substantive level in the ordering of their relations. But there is no basis for this view in the law of contract. In fact, it seems to misunderstand the contractual effect of the party autonomy rule. The effect of the party autonomy rule is *not* to contract out of the *lex causae* (ie tort law), but to contract out of the choice of law rules that would otherwise be applicable.

The second consequence of the closed approach to party autonomy is that courts rarely consider whether there is a proper agreement on the applicable law, based on the governing law of contract, before applying the chosen law.[67] Courts either fail to apply the governing rules of contract law, or they apply these rules in a manner that misconstrues the function of the choice of law agreement. For example, courts often give effect to the choice of law agreement on a putative basis—they apply the 'chosen law' to determine the existence of a contract even if the grounds of challenge logically extend to the agreement on the applicable law. The German manufacturer may argue that he is not bound by the Canadian company's terms and conditions, including the choice of Texas law, because they were not incorporated into the sales contract; and the court, if it relies on putative reasoning, would apply the law of Texas to determine whether the terms and conditions formed part of the contract, without determining first whether the clause came into existence as a matter of contract.

[61] AE Anton, *Private International Law: a Treatise from the Standpoint of Scots law* (Edinburgh, Green, 1967) 189.

[62] E Rabel, *The Conflict of Laws* 2nd edn (Ann Arbor, University of Michigan Law School, 1960) 368–69.

[63] *Akai Pty Ltd v People's Insurance Co Ltd* [1998] 1 Lloyd's Rep 90 (QB) 100.

[64] A Briggs, *Agreements on Jurisdiction and Choice of Law* (Oxford, Oxford University Press, 2008) para 11.43.

[65] *Ace Insurance Ltd v Moose Enterprise Ltd* [2009] NSWSC 724, 15 ANZ Ins Cas 61-818 [47].

[66] See, eg, the current edition of *Dicey, Morris and Collins* (n 8), which dedicates two paragraphs to the existence and validity of the parties' consent as to choice of law (paras 32-066–32-067).

[67] cp, from a US perspective, W Woodward, 'Finding the Contract in Contracts for Law, Forum and Arbitration' (2006) 2 *Hastings Business Law Journal* 1.

Where courts give effect to the choice of law agreement on a putative basis, the agreement becomes virtually irrelevant.[68] This lack of interest in the existence and validity of the choice of law agreement is matched by an equal appetite for pragmatism in legal scholarship, which recently culminated in renewed support for a 'factual' approach to party autonomy.[69] Thus, while choice of law agreements have been described as an 'elaborate exercise of personal autonomy' that promote the increasing 'contractualization of the conflict of laws',[70] they have also been described as constituting mere 'data' for the purposes of the party autonomy rule.[71]

Thirdly, there has been limited engagement with the role of modal choice of law—as opposed to the law of contract—in regulating the existence and validity of choice of law agreements. Modal choice of law rules are rules of the conflict of laws that, instead of identifying the applicable law, regulate elements of choice of law rules. They may define the meaning of a choice of law element, or they may place conditions on its operation. That modal choice of law rules do play a role in the regulation of choice of law agreements is free from doubt. For example, the rule that a choice of law agreement need not be express in order to be valid is a modal choice of law rule. However, it seems that lawmakers do not fully appreciate the contractual function of such modal choice of law rules, or their interrelationship with the law of contract.

One way in which this lack of engagement manifests itself is that modal choice of law often appears to be lagging behind modern policies of contract law. For example, there is currently no modal choice of law rule in New Zealand that would require choice of law agreements in consumer contracts to be express and in writing, or to be written in a way that is accessible to consumers. A New Zealand court would uphold a German choice of law clause in the German manufacturer's terms and conditions in the same way that it would uphold a choice of law clause in a commercial contract between professionals.

ii. Freedom of Contract at all Costs?

It is difficult to avoid the impression that the party autonomy rule has been developed in accordance with a 'contractarian' approach—a 'single-minded pursuit of individualism'[72] that leaves little scope for a normative assessment of the choice

[68] eg *Compania Naviera Micro SA v Shipley International Inc (The Parouth)* [1982] 2 Lloyd's Rep 351 (CA) 353; see ch 4. cp jurisdiction and arbitration agreements: *Fiona Trust Holding Corp v Privalov* [2007] UKHL 40, [2008] 1 Lloyd's Rep 254 [17] (Lord Hoffmann); *Deutsche Bank AG v Asia Pacific Broadband Wireless Communications Inc* [2008] EWCA Civ 1091, [2008] 2 Lloyd's Rep 619 [24]–[25].

[69] eg R Plender and M Wilderspin, *European Private International Law of Obligations* 3rd edn (London, Sweet & Maxwell, 2009) paras 29-011–29-014; but cp R Plender and M Wilderspin, *European Private International Law of Obligations* 4th edn (London, Sweet & Maxwell, 2015) paras 29-010–29-013; see ch 2, s II.

[70] Briggs (n 64) paras 13.27 and 1.05.

[71] Anton (n 61) 189; ibid, paras 13.26 and 1.23.

[72] J Braucher, 'Contract versus Contractarianism: The Regulatory Role of Contract Law' (1990) 47 *Washington and Lee Law Review* 697, 699.

of law agreement. One author has thus noted that 'it is often forgotten amidst the euphoria generated by eloquent rhetoric about individual and contractual freedom, and other majestic generalities' that 'party autonomy presupposes the *free will of both parties freely expressed*'.[73] This seems to have several (over-lapping) causes: mischaracterisation of the functions of the choice of law agreement; a historic (and out-dated) attachment to laissez-faire policies, which no doubt shaped the rise of the party autonomy rule in the nineteenth and early twentieth century; and conflation of objective choice of law rules, and choice of law rules based on presumed intent, with party autonomy, resulting from a failure to treat the choice of law agreement as 'institutive' of the parties' choice of applicable law.[74]

The problem with such a contractarian approach to the contractualisation of relationships is that it takes an unduly one-sided (or even fictional) view of the law of contract.[75] A contract is both a tool and a subject of regulation. Championing freedom of contract, or free choice, without also considering the attendant normative questions that must define the purpose, the meaning and the limits of that freedom ignores the regulatory role of the law of contract. Choice of law agreements ought not to replace, but ought to serve the aims and policies of choice of law, in a way that satisfies the normative standards considered necessary for such agreements. This requires a shift in focus, from party autonomy as an almost self-validating rule, to party autonomy as a power-conferring rule that fuses the law of choice of law and contract.

II. A New Perspective: The Choice of Law Contract

This book analyses the party autonomy rule within a contractual framework. It argues that the party autonomy rule does, in fact, rest on a contract to choose the applicable law—albeit a peculiar contract (see chapter two). The primary function of the choice of law agreement is to bind the parties to a choice of applicable law and to dispense with the applicable objective choice of law rule. This characterisation of party autonomy has implications for the way in which it ought to be regulated: because the party autonomy rule is based on a contract, it ought to be shaped by a framework that fuses principles of choice of law and contract. This proposed framework builds on existing choice of law processes, which include the application of the law governing the choice of law agreement, and the application of modal choice of law rules. But it uses these processes in a manner that reflects the unique nature of the choice of law contract (see section A below), giving effect

[73] S Symeonides, 'The Hague Principles on Choice of Law for International Contracts: Some Preliminary Comments' (2013) 61 *American Journal of Comparative Law* 873, 878.

[74] On contract as an '*institution*' as opposed to a 'legal *response* to particular events', see D Nolan, 'The Classical Legacy and Modern English Contract Law' (1996) 59 *MLR* 603, 604.

[75] Braucher (n 72); see H Collins, *Regulating Contracts* (Oxford, Oxford University Press, 1999) ch 4.

to the idea that the choice of law contract—just like any other contract—ought to be subject to adequate regulation (see section B below).

The framework covers three fundamental questions. First, when should parties be granted the freedom to choose the applicable law (see chapter three)? Second, what is the interrelationship between the choice of law contract and any substantive contract that it purports to govern (see chapter four)? Third, what sources should determine the existence and validity of choice of law contracts, and what is the role of modal choice of law (see chapter five)? The answers to these questions, which are often surprising, provide a set of principles to evaluate—and, where necessary, reform—existing rules on the existence and validity of choice of law contracts (see chapters six to eight).

A. Understanding the Choice of Law Contract

The choice of law contract is not an ordinary contract. Rather than binding parties to a future course of conduct, its effect is limited to the operation of the forum's choice of law rules. As will be explained in chapter two, the characterisation of the choice of law agreement as a contract does not necessarily conform with conventional definitions of contract but follows logically if the purpose of the party autonomy rule is to be upheld: the party autonomy rule is triggered where the parties had a mutual intention as to the applicable law, but only a legally binding agreement—or contract—is able to give direct effect to a mutual intention to choose the applicable law.

It follows that the choice of law contract is not only a connecting factor, because it designates the law applicable pursuant to the party autonomy rule, but also an object of connection, because it is itself an international contract whose existence and validity must be determined (see subsection i below). It is independent from any underlying relationship to which the chosen law is applied, because the sole function of the choice of law contract is to opt out of the applicable objective choice of law rule and select the law governing the underlying relationship (see subsection ii below). As an independent contract, the choice of law contract must have its own applicable law (see subsection iii below); but in addition, it must be regulated by rules that are specific to the choice of law contract—by 'modal choice of law rules' (see subsection iv below).

i. An International Contract …

The party autonomy rule forms part of the forum's choice of law rules. The choice of law contract, unlike a substantive contract governed by foreign law, is given effect pursuant to a choice of law rule of the forum. It is the law of choice of law that is responsible for its enforcement. Nevertheless, the choice of law contract clearly has an international element. Like all choice of law rules, the party autonomy rule is charged with the regulation of cross-border relationships. The choice of law contract is an international contract. Consequently, the question arises which rules should apply to determine its existence and validity.

ii. … that is Independent of the Parties' Underlying Relationship …

Because the determination of the parties' choice is a logically anterior step to the application of the chosen law to the dispute, the choice of law contract must operate as an independent contract.[76] It sits apart from the relationship that the chosen law is intended to govern, as a contract whose sole function is to deselect the applicable choice of law rule and to allocate a new applicable law in substitution. This is not generally appreciated, which has consequences for the determination of choice of law contracts.

The conclusion that choice of law agreements are contractually independent necessarily requires that the choice of law contract not be given effect—that is, that the chosen law not be applied to the underlying relationship—before the existence and validity of the choice of law contract have been established. In other words, the independence of the choice of law contract requires the rejection of putative reasoning: the chosen law cannot be applied on the assumption that the choice of law contract is valid. This means that there is no necessary synchronisation between the existence and validity of the choice of law contract and the existence and validity of any underlying contract. Even where the choice of law contract is physically included in the underlying contract, it is a legally separate agreement.

iii. … and whose Existence and Validity is Determined by the Law Applicable to the Choice of Law Contract …

The choice of law contract requires its own applicable law. In most jurisdictions, the choice of law contract is submitted to the putative chosen law—the law that was allegedly chosen.[77] The reason why the putative chosen law is applicable is not that the parties intended the law to be applicable, because the parties' agreement on the applicable law is precisely what is in dispute. It is that, due to its subject-matter, there is no other law that could more appropriately be applied to the choice of law contract. The effect of the putative chosen law is to ensure that the choice of law contract is enforced only if it is valid under its own chosen law. So while application of the putative chosen law to the underlying relationship, under the guise of the party autonomy rule, must be rejected, there is no reason in principle why the putative chosen law ought not to be applicable to the choice of law contract. More specifically, it is the law of contract of the putative chosen law that is needed to establish the existence and validity of the choice of law contract.

[76] See ch 4.

[77] eg Rome I (n 1) Art 3(5); see ch 5, s III.C.

Because choice of law contracts are independent agreements, they should not be treated as if they were implied terms of other contracts; and they should not be inferred on the basis of putative jurisdiction or arbitration agreements. Courts often infer choice of law clauses as if they were implied terms, failing to appreciate that choice of law agreements are contractually independent contracts and that the gap-filling rationale that informs the law on implied terms does not, therefore, apply to choice of law agreements. For example, a New Zealand court might well impute to the German manufacturer and the New Zealand consumer an implied intention to select the law of Germany, on the basis of the references to German legislation in the manufacturer's terms and conditions, even though a joint imputed intention would not be enough to found a contract.

Choice of law contracts also should not, like ordinary contracts, be submitted to rules of contract that are concerned with the content of parties' rights and obligations. For example, the New Zealand consumer might rely on the German law of contract to argue that the choice of law agreement is 'unfair' or 'unreasonable' in substance. But such contractual rules control the parties' rights and obligations—the fairness of the parties' bargain. They can have no application to choice of law agreements, which fail to give rise to *inter partes* rights or obligations. Choice of law contracts are concerned exclusively with the determination of the applicable law. More generally, the particular nature of the choice of law contract means that the law of contract is not always an effective or sufficient source of regulation; and that it is also necessary, therefore, to rely on contractual rules that are specific to the choice of law contract.

iv. … as well as by Modal Choice of Law Rules

These rules are described as modal choice of law rules, because they prescribe *how* a particular choice of law rule is to be applied.[78] Not all rules that form part of the system of choice of law are choice of law rules—that is, rules that, like the party autonomy rule, identify the applicable law by reference to a particular connecting factor and produce a choice-of-law effect. In determining what is the law that is designated by a particular connecting factor, it may also be necessary to rely on additional rules that define the meaning of the connecting factor. Thus, rules that define the meaning of, for example, 'domicile'[79] or 'habitual residence'[80] or 'characteristic performance of the contract'[81] do not directly result in the application of a particular law but simply regulate the way in which choice of law rules based on domicile, habitual residence or the place of characteristic performance are to be applied. These rules may be judge-made or created by legislation.

[78] M Hook, 'The Concept of Modal Choice of Law Rules' (2015) 11 *Journal of Private International Law* 185; cp P Stankewitsch, *Entscheidungsnormen im IPR als Wirksamkeitsvoraussetzungen der Rechtswahl* (Frankfurt, Peter Lang, 2003); see ch 5, s IV.

[79] eg Domicile Act 1976 (NZ).

[80] Rome I (n 1) Art 19.

[81] See *Print Concept GmbH v GEW (EC) Ltd* [2001] EWCA Civ 352, [2002] CLC 352 [3]–[6].

Modal choice of law rules are particularly relevant to the operation of the party autonomy rule, because here they function as contractual rules. They are needed to regulate any matters that are specific to the choice of law contract—for example, whether the choice of law contract needs to be in writing; or whether spouses, when choosing the law governing their matrimonial property relationship, are required to obtain legal advice. The drafting of modal choice of law rules requires careful consideration of their interrelationship with the law of contract, conflicts policies and the international context within which they operate (see chapter five).

B. Regulating Freedom of Contract

The party autonomy rule operates through a choice of law contract; and contracts require regulation. It is not sufficient to grant freedom of contract without a body of rules and principles to define the meaning and the limits of that freedom. The choice of law contract should be no exception to this. To achieve normative consistency between the law of contract and choice of law, the party autonomy rule should be regulated in a way that reflects the modern law of contract. This goes beyond submission of the choice of law agreement to the general law of contract. We should also rely on principles of contract to shape the scope of party autonomy, and to shape the content of modal choice of law for party autonomy. What is needed, in other words, is a fusion of the law of contract and choice of law to regulate the freedom to choose the applicable law.

i. The Law of Contract as a Tool of Regulation

There is no unitary theory of contract that runs through the modern law of contract—whether within the jurisdictions that are examined here, or across their legal systems.[82] Nevertheless, the position may, very generally, be stated as follows: the law of contract defines the meaning of contract and facilitates the process of contracting; and while freedom of contract remains the starting point for the regulation of private relationships, the law of contract delimits freedom of contract by public policies aimed at the protection of the parties, of third parties, or of society and the legal order as a whole.[83] There has been a move away from the classic theory of contract, which viewed the role of the law of contract as largely facilitative and treated the parties as 'sovereign',[84] towards a 'materialisation' of the law of contract, which recognises that contracting parties do not always make

[82] Collins (n 75) 32. On pluralism in contract law more generally, see L Trakman, 'Pluralism in Contract Law' (2010) 58 *Buffalo Law Review* 1031.

[83] See H Kötz and A Flessner, *European Contract Law* (Oxford, Clarendon Press, 1997) 11–13; J Beatson and D Friedman, 'Introduction: From "Classical" to Modern Contract Law' in J Beatson and D Friedman (eds), *Good Faith and Fault in Contract Law* (Oxford, Clarendon Press, 1995) 3.

[84] M Chen-Wishart, *Contract Law* (Oxford, Oxford University Press, 2007) 12.

free, rational and informed decisions; and that their decisions sometimes give rise to externalities.[85] The modern law of contract, whose sources range beyond the general law of contract, is a system of competing values.

ii. Regulating the Freedom to Choose the Applicable Law

Party autonomy must be shaped by these competing values. Choice of law agreements, just like other contracts, should depend on external standards of contracting; and the conflict of laws should lend its power of enforcement to only those agreements that do not undermine personal autonomy or harm the public good. There are three principal steps that must be taken to achieve this.

First, the availability of party autonomy ought to depend on the policies of choice of law, in the same manner that freedom of contract more generally depends on the area of law that is the subject of the contract. In particular, it is the role of objective choice of law that must be evaluated, because the function of the party autonomy rule is to contract out of the applicable objective choice of law rule. The question that ought to be asked is this: should the parties be free, by entering into a choice of law agreement, to contract out of the choice of law rule that would otherwise be applicable? Should the German manufacturer and the Canadian company be free to displace the objective choice of law rule on product liability, or does the rule serve a 'mandatory' purpose? Should the Kenyan wife and the German manufacturer be free to displace the law of their common habitual residence?

Second, choice of law contracts ought to be submitted to the general law of contract, in a manner that recognises their peculiar function; and choice of law contracts will not properly benefit from the law of contract unless courts recognise their independent nature.

Third, modal choice of law ought to provide contractual rules specific to the choice of law contract where the general law of contract is not a sufficient or appropriate source of regulation. By way of analogy, modal choice of law rules are to choice of law contracts what consumer, employment and family law are to matrimonial property, employment and consumer contracts. It is necessary to do for choice of law contracts what has already been done for those contracts: to supplement the general law of contract with a specialist regime applicable only to the choice of law contract. For example, New Zealand modal choice of law could require that choice of law agreements in consumer contracts be expressed clearly and in writing, to reflect a more general concern of the law of contract with consumer protection. The flipside of this argument is that modal choice of law should not *replace* the law of contract without substituting adequate regulation.

[85] See generally PS Atiyah, *The Rise and Fall of Freedom of Contract* (Oxford, Clarendon Press, 1979); V Ranouil, 'L'Autonomie de la Volonté: Naissance et Évolution d'un Concept' (Paris, Presses Universitaires de France, 1980) 33.

iii. Fusing the Law of Contract and Choice of Law

The proposed framework differs from scholarship on the party autonomy rule that has sought to adopt a more ideological methodology for its evaluation, based, for example, on economic theory, or on political liberalism. It has been argued that party autonomy can be justified on grounds of efficiency and general economic analysis;[86] or that it is an expression of the forum's more limited state power over private cross-border disputes;[87] or that it is simply a human right.[88] The proposed framework, on the other hand, seeks to ground the party autonomy rule in the law of contract. While efficiency, political liberalism and human rights may all form part of the ideological make-up of the law of contract (or, for that matter, of choice of law), they offer only a narrow snapshot of the kinds of regulatory questions that, from a properly contractual perspective, ought to be raised about the party autonomy rule.

[86] G Rühl, 'Party Autonomy in the Private International Law of Contracts: Transatlantic Convergence and Economic Efficiency' in E Gottschalk et al (eds), *Conflict of Laws in a Globalized World* (Cambridge, Cambridge University Press, 2007) 153.

[87] J Basedow, 'Theorie der Rechtswahl oder Parteiautonomie als Grundlage des Internationalen Privatrechts' (2011) 75 *Rabels Zeitschrift für ausländisches und internationales Privatrecht* 32; JA Pontier, 'The Justification of Choice of Law: A Liberal-Political Theory as a Critical and Explanatory Model, and the Field of International Consumer Transactions as an Example' (1998) 45 *Netherlands International Law Review* 388.

[88] E Jayme, 'L'autonomie de la volonté des parties dans les contrats internationaux entre personnes privées' (1991) 64-I *Annuaire de l'Institut de Droit International* 7, 147.

2

Selection of the Applicable Law by Contract

I. A Mutual Intention to Choose the Applicable Law

When parties exercise the power conferred by the party autonomy rule to select the applicable law, do they enter into a contract? The answer to this question is an emphatic but qualified 'yes'. Emphatic, because there is no label that better communicates the legally binding nature of choice of law agreements; but qualified, because unlike ordinary contracts choice of law contracts are not directly concerned with *in personam* rights and obligations. Their function is to contract out of objective choice of law rules. This chapter sets out the reasoning behind these conclusions and explains why, contrary to some authors' views, choice of law agreements are not of mere 'factual' value.

Whether a choice of law agreement is legally binding or factual, whether it creates rights and obligations or not—these are questions that ought to be crucial to the way the party autonomy rule is regulated. If the party autonomy rule requires no more than a 'factual' agreement, then—depending on one's view of what a 'factual' agreement entails—a court may enforce a choice of law agreement that does not comply with the law of contract (for example, because it does not meet the rules on offer and acceptance); it may uphold a choice of law agreement that is not based on an 'agreement' in the legal sense, but on mere expectations or understandings; or it may even refuse to enforce a choice of law agreement because it considers another law to be more appropriate. On the other hand, if the choice of law agreement is a legally binding agreement, there would have to be a good reason not to treat it like a contract. It would have to be submitted to the kinds of rules and principles that are relevant to contracts of its kind, and the court's discretion to refuse enforcement would have to be limited. If the choice of law contract is promissory in nature, a party would be able to bring a claim in breach of contract; and a court would have to apply all those rules of contract that inquire into the rights and obligations created by the contract. If the choice of law contract is non-promissory, such rules may not apply. Although the questions raised in this chapter are of a highly theoretical nature, they have far-reaching practical implications for regulating and enforcing choice of law agreements.

The starting point for this chapter is the party autonomy rule itself, and its requirement that the parties mutually intended—or agreed—to select the chosen law. Section I.B relies on first principles to demonstrate that this requirement is for a legally binding agreement. Section II dissects, and ultimately rejects, arguments that the party autonomy rule requires choice of law agreements of mere factual effect. Having demonstrated that choice of law agreements are legally binding, the chapter concludes in section III by examining their unusual contractual nature.

A. The Party Autonomy Rule

One of the first legal uses of the term 'autonomy', which is derived from the Greek 'auto-' (self) and 'nomos' (law), was to describe the freedom that certain corporations and noble families enjoyed in Germany to regulate their own affairs through private legislation.[1] Modelled on this concept, the term 'party autonomy' gained some currency in German legal science in the nineteenth century in relation to choice of law. But it was the Italian jurist Pasquale Mancini who, in 1874, founded the theory of party autonomy as we know it today, by submitting the question of choice of law to the free choice of the parties.[2] While earlier writers such as Dumoulin and Savigny contributed to the development of the theory, they did not understand the parties' intention as an independent connecting factor, but rather used the concept to justify the application of the *lex loci contractus* or,[3] in Savigny's case, the localisation of the relationship within a given legal system more generally.[4] In fact, Savigny criticised 'modern authors' for their use of the term 'autonomy' to refer to the 'very general influence of the free will' on the applicable law.[5]

The theory of party autonomy was the subject of intractable theoretical criticism, which at first slowed its rise to the firmly entrenched principle that it is today.[6] Critics complained that it was logically impossible to elevate the will of the parties above the law, as there was no law outside legal systems that could give effect to it. Proponents of party autonomy rejected this argument. They reasoned

[1] FK von Savigny, *System des heutigen römischen Rechts*, vol 8 (Berlin, Veit, 1849) 112–13; J Kropholler, *Internationales Privatrecht* 6th edn (Tübingen, Mohr Siebeck, 2006) 292.

[2] PS Mancini, 'De l'utilité de rendre obligatoires pour tous les États, sous la forme d'un ou de plusieurs traités internationaux, un certain nombre de règles générales du droit international privé pour assurer la décision uniforme des conflits entre les différentes législations civiles et criminelles' (1874) 1 *Journal du Droit International Privé* 221, 295. However, Mancini seemed to consider that, at least in theory, party autonomy was to be exercised within the mandatory bounds of the law of contract: Y Nishitani, *Mancini und die Parteiautonomie im Internationalen Privatrecht* (Heidelberg, Winter, 2000) 220–22, 246.

[3] P Nygh, *Autonomy in International Contracts* (Oxford, Oxford University Press, 1999) 4–6.

[4] V Ranouil, 'L'Autonomie de la Volonté: Naissance et Évolution d'un Concept' (Paris, Presses Universitaires de France, 1980) 27.

[5] Savigny (n 1) 112: 'Die neueren Schriftsteller pflegen … diese sehr allgemeine Einwirkung des freien Willens als Autonomie zu bezeichnen' (author's translation).

[6] Ranouil (n 4) 99–129; M Giuliano, 'La Loi Applicable aux Contrats: Problèmes Choisis' (1977) 158 *Recueil des Cours* 183, 206–08; O Lando, 'Contracts' in K Lipstein (ed), *International Encyclopaedia of Comparative Law: Private International Law* (Tübingen, Mohr Siebeck, 1977) 14–33.

that the parties' choice did not place them within a lawless vacuum because it operated as a connecting factor given effect to by the forum.[7] This is now generally considered to be an appropriate answer to the claim that the party autonomy rule is logically deficient.[8] The parties are free to choose the law applicable to their relationship because it is the choice of law rule of the forum that prescribes that effect be given to the choice.

The rule finally gained a strong foothold in the courts in the early twentieth century, following on from the rise of laissez-faire philosophy in the nineteenth century.[9] 'Autonomy' was then heralded as a principle of self-ordering that gave parties the freedom to regulate their own affairs, and focus shifted to the intention of individuals as a source of obligation or legal effect, whether in the law of obligations, property or probate.[10] The gradual espousal of the party autonomy rule was a clear manifestation of the liberal values that gained acceptance in those days.[11] So in 1910, the French Cour de Cassation held that 'the law governing contracts, be it in relation to their formation, their effects or their conditions, is the law chosen by the parties';[12] and having already been foreshadowed by Lord Mansfield in 1760,[13] party autonomy was cemented in English common law by the Privy Council 180 years later, when it stated:

> [W]here the English rule that intention is the test applies, and where there is an express statement by the parties of their intention to select the law of the contract, it is difficult to see what qualifications are possible, provided the intention expressed is bona fide and legal, and provided there is no reason for avoiding the choice on the ground of public policy.[14]

It is generally accepted now that what is needed to effect a choice of law is a manifest intention to choose the applicable law. Where the choice of law is to govern a legal relationship of two or more parties, this intention to choose the applicable law must be a 'common intention', or an 'agreement', or a 'contract'; or it must be based on 'consent'.[15] Thus, Lord Diplock in *Amin Rasheed Shipping Corp v Kuwait Insurance Co* required 'a common intention as to the system of law by reference to which [the parties'] mutual rights and obligations under it are to

[7] W Haudek, *Die Bedeutung des Parteiwillens im internationalen Privatrecht* (Berlin, Springer, 1931).

[8] Lando (n 6) para 63; Nygh (n 3) 32.

[9] Nygh (n 3) 3–14.

[10] See generally Ranouil (n 4); PS Atiyah, *The Rise and Fall of Freedom of Contract* (Oxford, Clarendon Press, 1979).

[11] See Nygh (n 3) 8; H Yntema, '"Autonomy" in Choice of Law' (1952) 1 *American Journal of Comparative Law* 341, 342–43.

[12] Cass civ, 5 December 1910, Sirey 1911.1.129 (*American Trading Co v Quebec Steamship Co*): 'la loi applicable aux contrats, soit en ce qui concerne leur formation, soit quant à leurs effets et conditions, est celle que les parties ont adoptée' (author's translation); see P Mayer and V Heuzé, *Droit international privé* 10th edn (Paris, LGDJ, 2014) 517ff.

[13] *Robinson v Bland* (1760) 1 Bl W 234 (KB); see Nygh (n 3) 5.

[14] *Vita Food Products Inc v Unus Shipping Co Ltd* [1939] AC 277 (PC) 290 (Lord Wright); see Nygh (n 3) 10–11.

[15] See Lando (n 6) para 81.

be ascertained'.[16] US courts frequently refer to an 'agreement' on choice of law.[17] Swiss courts routinely require a 'contract'.[18] Article 3 of Regulation (EC) 593/2008 on the law applicable to contractual obligations (Rome I) provides that the contract 'shall be governed by the law chosen by the parties' and refers to 'the consent of the parties as to the choice'.[19] Article 7 of the Hague Convention on the Law Applicable to Matrimonial Property Regimes similarly refers to the 'consent' of the parties to the designated law;[20] and section 1-301 of the Uniform Commercial Code (UCC),[21] Article 6 of the Hague Principles on Choice of Law in International Commercial Contracts,[22] Article 14 of Regulation (EC) 864/2007 on the law applicable to non-contractual obligations (Rome II),[23] Article 5 of Regulation (EU) 1259/2010 implementing enhanced cooperation in the area of the law applicable to divorce and legal separation (Rome III),[24] Articles 7 and 8 of the Hague Protocol on the Law Applicable to Maintenance Obligations,[25] and section 7A of the Property (Relationships) Act 1976 (NZ) all refer to an 'agreement' on choice of law. Despite the inconsistencies in terminology, all these rules appear to share the same basic requirement: an agreement, or a mutual or common intention, to select the applicable law.

B. The Choice of Law Agreement as a Legally Binding Agreement

But what is a common intention, or agreement, to choose the applicable law?[26] Are choice of law agreements a non-legal form of agreement; are they legally

[16] *Amin Rasheed Shipping Corp v Kuwait Insurance Co* [1984] 1 AC 50 (HL) 61. Lord Wilberforce, at 69, referred to a 'mutual intention'. In *Compagnie d'Armement Maritime SA v Compagnie Tunisienne de Navigation SA* [1971] AC 572 (HL), Lord Morris and Lord Diplock both referred to an 'agreement' on the applicable law (at 585 and at 604), and so did Lord Reid in *James Miller and Partners Ltd v Whitworth Street Estates (Manchester) Ltd* [1970] AC 583 (HL) at 603.

[17] eg *Town of Smyrna, Tenn v Municipal Gas Authority of Georgia* 723 F 3d 640 (6th Cir Tenn 2013) 646; in *Benicorp Insurance Co v National Medical Health Card Systems Inc* 447 F Supp 2d 329 (SDNY 2006), the Court referred to a requirement of 'mutual assent'.

[18] eg BGE 91 II 248.

[19] Reg (EC) 593/2008 on the law applicable to contractual obligations [2008] OJ L177/6 (Rome I).

[20] Hague Convention on the Law Applicable to Matrimonial Property Regimes (1977) 16 ILM 14 (opened for signature 14 March 1978, entered into force 1 September 1992).

[21] American Law Institute, *Uniform Commercial Code* (2008).

[22] Hague Conference on Private International Law, *Principles on Choice of Law in International Commercial Contracts* (approved on 19 March 2015).

[23] Reg (EC) 864/2007 on the law applicable to non-contractual obligations [2007] OJ L199/40 (Rome II).

[24] Reg (EU) 1259/2010 implementing enhanced cooperation in the area of the law applicable to divorce and legal separation [2010] OJ L343/10 (Rome III).

[25] Hague Protocol on the Law Applicable to Maintenance Obligations (opened for signature 23 November 2007, entered into force 1 August 2013).

[26] cp A Briggs, *Agreements on Jurisdiction and Choice of Law* (Oxford, Oxford University Press, 2008) para 2.05 and KFK Low, 'Choice of Law in Formation of Contracts' (2004) 20 *Journal of Contract Law* 167, 169, who do not treat these terms as interchangeable: see below, s II.C.

binding; or are they contracts, even? It is submitted that a choice of law agreement is a legally binding agreement; *and* that it is best described as a contract, although it does not feature some of the usual hallmarks of a contract. In other words, when parties agree to select the applicable law, and the party autonomy rule gives effect to this agreement, the parties have entered into a legally binding agreement, or—for want of a better term—a contract. The purpose of the present chapter is to make good on this argument.

What is a legally binding agreement? Broken down into its basic components, a legally binding agreement is a bilateral legal act. A legal act is a declaration of will whose purpose and function is to produce a legal effect, while a bilateral legal act is a common declaration of will with the same purpose and function.[27] The bilateral legal act allows individuals 'to regulate their mutual relations ... by norms created by way of legal transactions'.[28] It is a manifestation of autonomy.[29] The choice of law agreement is a bilateral legal act because it consists of mutual declarations of intention to produce a legal effect—namely the application of the chosen law; and this intention is given effect by the party autonomy rule.

Use of the 'bilateral legal act' as an ordering principle is well established in some civil law jurisdictions.[30] It is also not entirely foreign to common law legal theory.[31] Its attraction, for present purposes, lies in its capacity to distil the choice of law agreement to its most basic function: the mutual selection of the applicable law with binding effect. The agreement is 'binding' in that it is both effective as a connecting factor and revocable only by agreement. It is a legal construct. This is true whether or not the concept of the 'legal act' is formally recognised in the forum's private law: the purpose of the party autonomy rule is to confer on parties the power to choose the applicable law and, subject to some limitations, to give effect to the choice.[32] If party X and party Z enter into an agreement to submit their contractual relationship to the law of Y, and a dispute arises that requires judicial resolution, the party autonomy rule will hold the parties to their agreement, requiring the court to apply the law of Y to determine the dispute.

[27] For a discussion of 'juristic acts', see G Whitecross Paton, *A Text-book of Jurisprudence* 4th edn (Oxford, Oxford University Press, 1972) 315ff, 433–34; G Sartor, 'Legal Reasoning: A Cognitive Approach to the Law' in E Pattaro, *A Treatise of Legal Philosophy and General Jurisprudence*, vol 5 (Dordrecht, Springer, 2005) 589ff.

[28] H Kelsen, *Pure Theory of Law* (Berkeley, University of California Press, 1978) 257; JW Salmond, *Jurisprudence or The Theory of Law* 2nd edn (London, Stevens and Haynes, 1907) 31 to similar effect, in relation to agreements.

[29] H Kelsen, *General Theory of Law and State* (New Jersey, The Lawbook Exchange, 2009) 137.

[30] AA Levasseur, *Comparative Law of Contracts* (Durham, Carolina Academic Press, 2008) 13–15.

[31] eg Salmond (n 28) 306; Paton (n 27) 319.

[32] See C Gialdino, 'La volonté des parties en droit international privé' (1972) 137 *Recueil des Cours* 743, 763, 769–70 and Giuliano (n 6) 207, who both describe party autonomy as a 'power' conferred by the forum. On the significance of power-conferring rules more generally, see Paton (n 27) 317; G Klass, 'Three Pictures of Contract: Duty, Power, and Compound Rule' (2008) 83 *New York University Law Review* 1726, 1730ff; see also Salmond (n 28) 194.

The conclusion that the choice of law agreement is a legal and binding construct does not sit well with those views that have sought to paint the choice of law agreement as a largely extra-legal, or factual, concept. These views will now be addressed—and rejected—in section II, which will leave one final question to be resolved in section III: if the choice of law agreement is a bilateral legal act, does this mean that it is also a contract? Every contract is a bilateral legal act, and as 'the main form of normative self-organisation', it is the most important legal act.[33] A consent-based theory of contract thus treats as the core of contract a manifest intention to be legally bound.[34] However, unlike ordinary contracts, choice of law agreements do not create rights or obligations *in personam*.[35]

II. The Factual View: Choice of Law as an Extra-legal Agreement

The view that choice of law agreements are based on a form of extra-legal, or factual, agreement has found some favour with both civil and common law scholars. This view denies that party choice is based on a legally binding agreement, or at least that a legally binding agreement is needed for the purposes of the party autonomy rule. Implicit in the factual approach, therefore, is the conclusion that an effective choice of law is not produced by the mutual exercise of a legal power to choose the applicable law. Naturally, this begs the question of what is the source of the choice, or the content of the party autonomy rule, if not a legally effective power to choose the applicable law by agreement.

There are three broad, often overlapping conceptualisations of the factual approach. In essence, it is argued that party choice does not rely on a legally effective agreement because: the choice is a mere 'factor' in the determination of the applicable law (see section A below); agreement on the applicable law is determined purely as a matter of fact (section B below); and the party autonomy rule requires nothing more than a 'common intention' as to the applicable law, which is said to differ from an agreement to choose the applicable law (section C). It is submitted that these arguments do not properly reflect the function of the choice of law agreement for the purposes of the party autonomy rule.

A. Party Choice as a Mere Factor in the Choice of Law Process

The first, most basic form of opposition to a 'binding' understanding of the choice of law agreement is the proposition that the agreement on the applicable law must

[33] Sartor (n 27) 591.
[34] See R Barnett, 'A Consent Theory of Contract' (1986) 86 *Columbia Law Review* 269.
[35] See Salmond (n 28) 307; see also Paton (n 27) 319.

be treated as a mere factor in the determination of the applicable law. It is wrong, therefore, to look at choice of law 'as constituting an independent "subsidiary agreement" or as anything more than factual data relevant to the application of one of the connecting factors of the *lex fori*'.[36] The underlying justification is that parties do not have the power to regulate the operation of choice of law by private binding agreement (see subsection i below). But this argument fails to appreciate the power-conferring nature of the party autonomy rule (see subsection ii below).

i. The Non-delegable 'Public' Function of Choice of Law

The view that party choice is a mere factor in the determination of the applicable law rests on the premise that parties have 'no legal power to dictate' the outcome of the choice of law process, and that they therefore 'cannot create primary rules of … choice of law'.[37] In other words, '[j]urisdictions adopting the autonomy doctrine simply predicate certain legal consequences (the application of the chosen law) upon the factual conduct of the parties (the making of the choice)'.[38]

The argument replicates, on a different plane, concerns about party autonomy by objective theorists such as Batiffol, who were concerned that the party autonomy rule made the parties 'masters of the law', and that party autonomy could therefore only be a factual connecting or localising element in the court's determination of the proper law.[39] In effect, Batiffol reversed the rationale behind the party autonomy rule by treating party choice as a crucial factor in the objective localisation of the contract:

> It follows from this analysis that the parties merely localise their contract; from which the judge infers the applicable law. … Despite their terms, express choice of law clauses are to be interpreted as a simple intention to localise the contract … the judge is not strictly bound by the express choice of law clause, as if it literally provided the legal solution: it is only one element—certainly a crucial one—in the localisation of the contract, but is not absolutely binding in law because this localisation remains a question of fact.[40]

The argument is not confined to choice of law contracts. Procedural agreements, too, are considered by some authors to be mere factual agreements

[36] AE Anton, *Private International Law: a Treatise from the Standpoint of Scots Law* (Edinburgh, Green, 1967) 189.

[37] Briggs (n 26) paras 1.26 and 1.28.

[38] J Prebble, 'Choice of Law to Determine the Validity and Effect of Contracts: A Comparison of English and American Approaches to the Conflict of Laws' (1973) 58 *Cornell Law Review* 433, 495.

[39] See the overview by Lando (n 6) 18–19; for a similar view, see W Mincke, 'Die Parteiautonomie: Rechtswahl oder Ortswahl?' [1985] *Praxis des Internationalen Privat- und Verfahrensrechts* 313.

[40] H Batiffol and P Lagarde, *Droit international privé* 7th edn (Paris, LGDJ, 1981) 266, 268: 'Cette analyse entraîne que les parties localisent seulement leur contrat; le juge en déduit la loi applicable. … les clauses de choix exprès de la loi applicable sont à interpréter, malgré leurs termes, comme une simple volonté de localisation du contrat … le juge n'est pas strictement lié par la clause de choix exprès comme si elle constituait, selon sa lettre, le principe de la solution de droit: elle n'est qu'un élément—capital assurément—de la localisation du contrat, mais non absolument obligatoire en droit parce que cette localisation reste une question de fait' (author's translation).

because of their procedural (or 'public') effect. It has accordingly been argued that a jurisdiction agreement is a mere 'statement of consent to the jurisdiction of the selected court, which the selected court may take into account', because '[w]hen private parties attempt to regulate public law issues one is taken out of the usual contractual sphere'.[41] It was this procedural character of jurisdiction and arbitration agreements that meant that they were ultimately excluded from the Rome Convention on the law applicable to contractual obligations,[42] with the *Giuliano-Lagarde Report* commenting that 'rules on jurisdiction are a matter of public policy and there is only marginal scope for freedom of contract'.[43]

ii. The Power-conferring Nature of the Party Autonomy Rule

The problem with this argument—that parties do not hold the power to decide what is the applicable law—is that it does not appreciate the power-conferring nature of the party autonomy rule. The choice of law agreement is not merely one of several factors to be taken into account in determining the applicable law. As the Privy Council concluded in *Vita Food Products Inc v Unus Shipping Co Ltd*, under the party autonomy rule, it is the determinative factor.[44] It is the party autonomy rule of the forum that sanctions the parties' choice of law agreement. The court is bound by the parties' choice, pursuant to the forum's choice of law rules, in the same way that it would be bound to enforce a contract.[45] Neither the localisation theory nor the analogy with procedural agreements offers a viable explanation for the factual approach to party choice.

The paradox inherent in the objective localisation theory is glaring: while it accepts that, in effect, it is the parties' choice that renders applicable the chosen law, it attributes to the parties a fictitious intention to localise the contract that, in turn, is a crucial factor in the court's (factual) localisation of the contract.[46] Although the localisation approach may better reflect the traditional notion of what constitutes a 'connecting factor', which was that the applicable law had to be derived from an assessment of relevant facts (such as the place of performance or the place with the closest connection),[47] it has long been accepted that 'the exigencies of

[41] CJS Knight, 'The Damage of Damages: Agreements on Jurisdiction and Choice of Law' (2008) 4 *Journal of Private International Law* 501, 507; see also LC Ho, 'Anti-Suit Injunctions in Cross-Border Insolvency: A Restatement' (2003) 52 *ICLQ* 697, 707–08.

[42] Convention 80/934/ECC on the law applicable to contractual obligations [1980] OJ L266/1 (opened for signature 19 June 1980, entered into force 1 April 1991).

[43] M Giuliano and P Lagarde, *Report on the Convention on the Law Applicable to Contractual Obligations* [1980] OJC 282/1 (*Giuliano-Lagarde Report*).

[44] *Vita Food Products Inc v Unus Shipping Co Ltd* [1939] AC 277 (PC) 290.

[45] I Schwander, 'Subjektivismus in der Anknüpfung im internationalen Privatrecht' in C Dominicé et al (eds), *Etudes de droit international en l'honneur de Pierre Lalive* (Basel, Helbing & Lichtenhahn, 1993) 181, 182, who even considers that the failure of a Swiss court to give effect to the parties' choice when required to do so may, in extreme cases, lead to an obligation of compensation by the state (at 185).

[46] Gialdino (n 32) 827.

[47] Mincke (n 39) 317; see also the references in Gialdino (n 32) 862, fn 221.

logic' of the party autonomy approach 'are fully satisfied by the argument ... that the party reference acquires its legal sanction by the conflict rules of the *forum*'.[48] Rabel accordingly concluded:

> An agreement of the parties to subject their contract to New York law is itself a perfectly serious contract that cannot be degraded into a mere 'localization' or disposal of the center of gravity. Why should this contract be a simple element for the finding by a court, instead of a binding transaction legalized by the conflicts rule, as all recognized contracts are sanctioned by law?[49]

By the same logic, procedural agreements cannot be treated as mere factual agreements. An agreement is not deprived of its binding nature simply because it has procedural effect. The law thus distinguishes between 'the jurisdiction agreement as a contract, which is a matter of substance, and the effect of the contract on the jurisdiction of the forum, which is a matter of procedure'.[50] Whether a jurisdiction agreement is also capable of substantive effect by supporting a cause of action for damages is a separate issue. The German Bundesgerichtshof has fittingly described jurisdiction agreements as a 'contract about procedural relationships'.[51]

There is nothing unusual about parties agreeing to modify dispositive rules of procedure and courts giving effect to these agreements.[52] Depending on the applicable rules of procedure, the parties may be able to agree on such matters as the burden of proof to be applied, the nature of evidence to be adduced, indemnification of litigation costs or discontinuance of an action. The choice of law agreement is not concerned with regulating procedure; but when it comes to the party autonomy rule, the parties are equally free to contract out of the choice of law rule that would otherwise be applicable.

B. Ascertaining the Choice of Law Agreement as a Matter of Fact

Another justification for the view that choice of law agreements are not legally binding is based on the assertion that they need not be established in accordance

[48] Lando (n 6) para 63; FA Mann, 'The Proper Law of the Contract' (1950) 3 *International Law Quarterly* 60, 62; see above, s I.A.

[49] E Rabel, *The Conflict of Laws* 2nd edn (Ann Arbor, University of Michigan Law School, 1960) 368 (footnotes omitted).

[50] TM Yeo, 'The Contractual Basis of the Enforcement of Exclusive and Non-Exclusive Choice of Court Agreements' (2005) 17 *Singapore Academy of Law Journal* 306, para 17; see also K Takahashi, 'Damages for Breach of a Choice-of-Court Agreement' (2008) 10 *Yearbook of Private International Law* 57, 67.

[51] eg BGHZ 59, 23 (1972): 'Vertrag über prozessrechtliche Beziehungen' (author's translation).

[52] G Wagner, *Prozessverträge: Privatautonomie im Verfahrensrecht* (Tübingen, Mohr Siebeck, 1998) 57ff; see also H Noyes, 'If You (Re)Build It, They Will Come: Contracts to Remake the Rules of Litigation in Arbitration's Image' (2006–2007) 30 *Harvard Journal of Law and Public Policy* 579; J Resnik, 'Procedure as Contract' (2004–2005) 80 *Notre Dame Law Review* 593.

with the law of contract. It has thus been argued that 'the parties' choice of law does not require agreement which is valid in accordance with any legal system'.[53] The parties' choice of law is 'mere fact',[54] requiring a purely 'empirical assessment'[55] of the parties' intentions. There are two different rationales for this approach, neither of which is justifiable in principle. The first is that the choice of law agreement cannot be established in law because it is applied on a putative basis. The second is that the existence and validity of choice of law agreements may be regulated exclusively by the party autonomy rule itself.

i. The Putative Nature of the Choice of Law Agreement

Where the choice of law agreement forms part of an underlying contract, putative reasoning is relied upon to apply the 'chosen' law to the underlying contract in circumstances where the grounds of challenge to the underlying contract would equally affect the choice of law agreement. Because, here, the choice of law agreement is not established in accordance with the law, it is considered by some to be only an agreement in fact.[56] However, as will be argued in chapter four, the party autonomy rule is incompatible with a putative application of the choice of law agreement. Putative reasoning does not give effect to a common intention to choose the applicable law.

ii. The Party Autonomy Rule as a Source of Exclusive Regulation

Yet another manifestation of the factual approach is the argument that the choice of law agreement must be determined on a purely factual basis where it is not expressly submitted to its own choice of law rule. This view is not reconcilable with most rules of party autonomy.[57] The common law, for example, requires that the choice of law agreement is founded on 'real consent', which is 'effective consent given in accordance with the standards of a particular legal system';[58] and Rome I submits the existence and validity of the choice of law agreement to the putative chosen law.[59]

[53] H Stoll, 'Das Statut der Rechtswahlvereinbarung—eine irreführende Konstruktion' in I Meier and K Siehr (eds), *Rechtskollisionen: Festschrift für Anton Heini zum 65. Geburtstag* (Zurich, Schulthess, 1995) 429, 436, 440–41: 'Die Rechtswahl in Schuldverträgen erfordert …, um kollisionsrechtlich zu wirken, keine Einigung, die nach dem materiellen Recht irgendeiner Rechtsordnung wirksam wäre' (author's translation); M Wolff, 'The Choice of Law by the Parties in International Contracts' (1937) 49 *Juridical Review* 110, 129.

[54] H Marti, 'Die Bedeutung des Parteiwillens im IOR' (1942) 77 *Zeitschrift des bernischen Juristenvereins* 97, 100–01: 'blosse Tatsache' (author's translation); C Baldoni, 'Il contratto di lavoro nel diritto internazionale privato italiano' (1932) 24 *Rivista di diritto internazionale* 1, 355–56, as cited by Gialdino (n 32) 862.

[55] Gialdino (n 32) 861: 'une recherche empirique' (author's translation).

[56] Stoll (n 53) 435; BA Marshall, 'Reconsidering the Proper Law of the Contract' (2012) 13 *Melbourne Journal of International Law* 1, 12; see Low (n 26) 170.

[57] See ch 5.

[58] Nygh (n 3) 94.

[59] Arts 3(5), 10(1) (n 19).

There are some party autonomy rules that do not expressly submit the choice of law agreement to its own applicable law. Rome II, for example, simply provides that 'the court has to respect the intentions of the parties' in establishing an agreement on choice of law.[60] It has been argued that the drafters' use of the word 'agreement' was meant to avoid the legal connotations of the word 'contract'; and that identification of an 'agreement' merely requires the court to determine whether the parties were in fact *ad idem*.[61] Similar arguments have been made in relation to jurisdiction agreements under Article 23 of Regulation (EC) 44/2001 on jurisdiction and the recognition and enforcement of judgments in civil and commercial matters (Brussels I),[62] which has since been amended, however, to provide that such agreements are enforceable unless they are 'null and void as to [their] substantive validity' under the law of the chosen Member State.[63]

Even if it were true that Rome II treats the question of 'agreement' as a question divorced from any applicable law,[64] this would not mean that the agreement is not legally binding. Rather, Article 14 would have to be understood as prescribing an autonomous rule of agreement whose meaning would have to be developed by the courts over time. Submission of the choice of law agreement to a general rule of agreement rather than to an existing body of contractual rules changes neither its nature nor its function: the agreement's effect on choice of law is both determinative and direct.[65]

C. Common Intention—A Qualitative Difference?

The factual approach does not exhaust itself in the view that party choice is a mere factor in the determination of the applicable law, or that it is not to be tested in accordance with an applicable law. The non-binding conceptualisation of choice of law agreements has broader application, with a further distinction being drawn between a 'common intention' on the applicable law, as established in fact and

[60] Recital 31, Art 14 (n 23).

[61] R Plender and M Wilderspin, *European Private International Law of Obligations* 3rd edn (London, Sweet & Maxwell, 2009) paras 29-011–29-014; but cp R Plender and M Wilderspin, *European Private International Law of Obligations* 4th edn (London, Sweet & Maxwell, 2015) paras 29-010–29-013; contrast A Dickinson, *The Rome II Regulation: The Law Applicable to Non-Contractual Obligations* (Oxford, Oxford University Press, 2010) 550.

[62] Reg (EC) 44/2001 on jurisdiction and the recognition and enforcement of judgments in civil and commercial matters [2001] OJ L12/1 (Brussels I); R Fentiman, *International Commercial Litigation* (Oxford, Oxford University Press, 2010) para 2.36, but cp R Fentiman, *International Commercial Litigation* 2nd edn (Oxford, Oxford University Press, 2015); L Merrett, 'Article 23 of the Brussels I Regulation: A Comprehensive Code for Jurisdiction Agreements?' (2009) 58 *ICLQ* 545, 550; cp J Kuipers, 'Party Autonomy in the Brussels I Regulation and Rome I Regulation and the European Court of Justice' (2009) 10 *German Law Journal* 1505, 1512; contrast U Magnus and P Mankowski (eds), *Brussels I Regulation* 2nd edn (Munich, Sellier, 2012) 476, para 80.

[63] Reg (EU) 1215/2012 on jurisdiction and the recognition and enforcement of judgments in civil and commercial matters (Brussels I Recast) [2012] OJ L351/1, Art 25(1).

[64] But see ch 5, s III.A.

[65] See Gialdino (n 32) 826–27.

(it seems) in law, and a legally binding agreement. It has thus been argued that recognition of the party autonomy rule does not require the choice of law agreement to be 'itself embodied in a legally binding agreement', as the rule is 'predicated on the manifestation of intent alone'.[66]

Two reasons have been advanced to justify this purported qualitative difference between a 'common intention' and a 'legally binding agreement'. The first is that, unlike an agreement, a requirement of 'common intention' does not require the parties to have communicated their intentions. A common 'understanding' that a particular law will govern is sufficient. The second is that a 'common intention' to choose the applicable law has mere declaratory, rather than promissory, effect.

i. *Intentions that Happen to Coincide*

It has been suggested that the party autonomy rule is not based on an agreement to choose the applicable law because the concept of 'common intention' requires no communication or acknowledgement of the parties' respective intentions.[67] Pursuant to this view, the rule requires nothing more than two independently held intentions that happen to coincide. The view is based on a much broader principle that 'Where there is no agreement to point to, those who enter into a form of relationship, or otherwise interact, may also expect to be held to a common understanding if there was one'.[68] This, in turn, is achieved through equitable or common law doctrines, 'which have at their root the duty to act in relation to another consistently with such shared understandings or otherwise in accordance with what conscience demands'.[69] If party A knows that party B expects the law of state A to be applicable even though the objective applicable law would be that of state B, their shared understanding might be sufficient to amount to a 'common intention' as to the law of state A.

It is submitted that this position is not borne out by authority. The concept of 'common intention' is usually employed in the law of contract to signify the meeting of the minds that is needed to form a contract. Independently held but common intentions are not generally sufficient, on their own, to trigger legal effects; and neither is a shared 'understanding' or expectation that a particular state of affairs will prevail, as opposed to an intention to effect that state of affairs.[70] It is not enough that party B expects the law of state A to be applicable—he has to

[66] D Cavers, *The Choice of Law Process* (Ann Arbor, University of Michigan Press, 1966) 196; Briggs (n 26) paras 2.05 and 1.24–1.26; Low (n 26); Marshall (n 56) 10–12.

[67] Low (n 26) 184–85; see Wolff (n 53) 130; contrast A Steiner, *Die stillschweigende Rechtswahl im Prozess im System der subjektiven Anknüpfung im deutschen Internationalen Privatrecht* (Frankfurt, Peter Lang, 1998) 35. However, Low also argues that the parties' intentions should be objectively ascertained: at 176–77; see ch 6, s III.

[68] Briggs (n 26) para 2.05.

[69] Briggs (n 26) para 2.05, referring to *CSR Ltd v Cigna Insurance Australia Ltd* (1997) 189 CLR 345, 392; cp Low (n 26) 177.

[70] See ch 6, s II.

intend to bring about the application of the law of state A; and it is not enough that party A knows that party B intends to select the law of state A, party A has to communicate to party B his own intention that the law of state A be applicable. Otherwise there is no 'common intention' at all.

One of the few examples where the concept of 'common intention' is relied upon outside of the law of contract is the 'common intention constructive trust' in relation to family homes. This area of law, which 'engages the law of contract, land and equity',[71] continues to be a source of confusion. In particular, the meaning of a 'common intention' to share ownership of the family home has proved to be somewhat elusive.[72] The better view is that the common intention constructive trust has always been based on an agreement to share ownership, rather than on mere expectations or on intentions that happen to coincide.[73] Thus, Lord Diplock in *Gissing v Gissing* stated:

> As in so many branches of English law in which legal rights and obligations depend upon the intentions of the parties to a transaction, the relevant intention of each party is the intention which was reasonably understood by the other party to be manifested by that party's words or conduct notwithstanding that he did not consciously formulate that intention in his own mind or even acted with some different intention which he did not communicate to the other party.[74]

Moreover, it is now accepted that an imputed common intention—that is, an intention that the parties would have had if they had turned their minds to the question—is only relevant for the purposes of quantification of the respective shares, but cannot form the basis of the parties' agreement to share ownership.[75]

In any case, the common intention constructive trust is a creature of the law of equity, and it is primarily concerned, therefore, with implementing an agreement that is otherwise unenforceable to prevent the unjust enrichment of the legal owner.[76] The courts' tendency to 'fictionalise' the parties' common intention, or to adopt a lower threshold than agreement, when determining a party's beneficial interest, must be viewed within this context. This is the case particularly where courts rely on notions of proprietary estoppel to justify their reasoning,[77] because proprietary estoppel is concerned with reliance on expectation rather than intention.

[71] *Stack v Dowden* [2007] UKHL 17, [2007] 2 AC 432 [101] (Lord Neuberger).

[72] ibid.

[73] See J Smithdale, 'Inference, Imputation, or Both? Confusion Persists over Beneficial Interests in the Family Home' (2011) 7 *Cambridge Student Law Review* 74; K Gray and S Gray, *Elements of Land Law* 4th edn (London, Oxford University Press, 2005) paras 10.92–10.99.

[74] *Gissing v Gissing* [1971] AC 886 (HL) 906. The point is made even more clearly by the Court of Appeal in *Lightfoot v Lightfoot-Brown* [2005] EWCA Civ 201, [2005] 2 P&CR 22 [27], where it held that communication of the common intention was an essential ingredient of a common intention constructive trust. See also *Springette v Defoe* (1993) 65 P&CR 1 (CA) 6 (Dillon LJ), 8 (Steyn LJ), 10 (Sir Christopher Slade).

[75] *Jones v Kernott* [2011] UKSC 53, [2012] 1 AC 776; cp ch 6, s IV.

[76] MP Thompson, 'Constructive Trusts, Estoppel and the Family Home' [2004] *Conveyancer and Property Lawyer* 496, 506.

[77] See *Oxley v Hiscock* [2004] EWCA Civ 546, [2004] 3 WLR 715 [66] (Chadwick LJ).

The party autonomy rule is not, of course, concerned with rectifying the harshness of objective choice of law. It confers an outright power to choose the applicable law by agreement.[78] Consequently, there are no helpful parallels that can be drawn between the party autonomy rule and equitable doctrines such as the common intention constructive trust. Whether equitable principles are available to enforce a choice of law agreement that does not fulfil the requirements of the party autonomy rule is an entirely separate matter.

ii. The Declaratory Effect of Choice of Law Agreements

Because choice of law agreements result in courts applying the chosen law, their effect is sometimes described as 'declaratory'. This declaratory effect is contrasted, in turn, with a legally binding agreement—on the basis, it seems, that any legally binding agreement would have to be promissory in nature and be capable of founding a cause of action for breach of contract.

Briggs has argued, for example, that consent, 'as something essentially distinct from agreement', explains how the court takes into account the parties' intentions when applying the rules of conflict of laws.[79] Accordingly, the question of choice of law is 'distinct from the proposition that an agreement between parties to a contract should be enforceable between them in private law',[80] because 'a common intention that something shall happen is not the same as an agreement that it will happen.'[81] A distinction must be drawn between 'recording and informing the court of the parties' common intention as to governing law' on the one hand, and 'recording and informing each other of their mutual agreement that the contractual relationship shall, when adjudicated, be governed by the chosen law' on the other.[82] It follows that, although a parties' choice of law is accompanied in many cases by a legally binding agreement,[83] it is only the parties' common intention that is relevant for choice of law purposes.

As will be explored further in the following section, the party autonomy rule does not require a promissory agreement to choose the applicable law. Contrary to Briggs' argument, choice of law agreements are inherently non-promissory. When party A and party B agree that their relationship be governed by the law of state A, they do not have to do anything to honour that agreement. It is the court that has to give effect to it. However, the fact that choice of law agreements are primarily 'declaratory' in nature does not impel the conclusion that they are not legally

[78] It is more akin, therefore, to the power of co-owners to declare a trust over land in accordance with the Law of Property Act 1925 (UK).

[79] Briggs (n 26) para 1.25; see also *Ace Insurance Ltd v Moose Enterprise Ltd* [2009] NSWSC 724, 15 ANZ Ins Cas 61-818 [47].

[80] Briggs (n 26) para 1.25.

[81] ibid, para 11.32.

[82] ibid, para 11.25.

[83] ibid, paras 1.24, 11.16–11.32.

binding. There is no denying the fact that it is the parties' mutual intention to choose the applicable law, expressed in a bilateral legal act, that causes the chosen law to be applied.

It follows that there is neither room nor need for 'extra-legal constructs' like factual agreements.[84] The next question to be determined is whether choice of law agreements can also be described as contracts, even though they do not fit the conventional understanding of what constitutes a contract.

III. The Choice of Law Agreement as a Contract

The conventional understanding of contract, both in civil and in common law jurisdictions, is founded on obligation: a contract creates rights and duties between the parties.[85] This concept is so ingrained in contract theory that it hardly warrants elaboration. Justinian considered civil obligations to be 'vinculum juris', a 'legal bond, with which we are bound by a necessity of performing some act according to the laws of our State'.[86] The French Code Civil provides that 'A contract is an agreement by which one or several persons bind themselves, towards one or several others, to transfer, to do or not to do something'.[87] And Blackstone, in his *Commentaries on the Laws of England*, wrote: 'A contract, which usually conveys an interest merely in action, is thus defined: "an agreement, upon sufficient consideration, to do or not to do a particular thing"'.[88] More particularly, the common law understanding of contract is based on 'The basic principle … that a person who makes a promise to another ought to keep his promise'.[89]

The sole function of the choice of law agreement, however, is to opt out of the forum's objective choice of law rules and to select the applicable law. It is not, as has been variously suggested, a promise or a bargain (see section A below); or even a contract in the nature of a 'disposition of rights' (see section B below). In other words, the choice of law agreement is not an agreement that creates, transfers,

[84] R Moser, *Vertragsabschluss, Vertragsgültigkeit und Parteiwille im internationalen Obligationenrecht* (St Gallen, Verlag der Fehr'schen Buchhandlung, 1948) 231: 'außerrechtliche Gebilde' (author's translation); Gialdino (n 32) 863; V Heuzé, *La réglementation française des contrats internationaux* (Paris, Joly éditions, 1990) 127.

[85] The term 'right' is to be understood here in its narrow sense, as 'an interest recognised and protected by a rule of rights … respect for which is a duty, and the disregard of which is a wrong': Salmond (n 28) 182.

[86] JB Moyle, *The Institutes of Justinian* 5th edn (Oxford, Clarendon Press, 1913) 106, Book III, Title XIII.

[87] Code Civil, Art 1101 (translation taken from http://www.legifrance.gouv.fr/).

[88] William Blackstone, *Commentaries on the Laws of England, Book the Second* 16th edn by JT Coleridge (London, printed by A Strahan for T Cadell and J Butterworth & Son, 1825) ch XXX, IX.

[89] *Lep Air Services v Rolloswin Ltd* [1973] AC 331 (HL) 346 (Lord Diplock).

modifies or extinguishes *in personam* rights or obligations. The question arises, therefore, whether it ought to be labelled a contract at all and, more importantly, whether it ought to be treated as one (see section C below).

A. Does the Choice of Law Agreement Create Rights and Obligations?

There have been some suggestions in English common law that the choice of law agreement could amount to a 'bargain', indicating an exchange of value by the parties, or even mutual promises. In *Akai Pty Ltd v People's Insurance Co Ltd*, for example, Thomas J refused to grant a stay of proceedings on the basis that the court 'should give effect to the bargain of the parties and their freely negotiated choice of law and jurisdiction';[90] and Briggs, in particular, has embraced the idea of party choice as a promissory agreement:

> For the purposes of determining whether the parties agreed upon the law to be applied to disputes, a court should ask whether the parties agreed that the law which they identify was to be applied by the court or tribunal, as the case may be. If the answer to the last question is affirmative, the parties' agreement on the resolution of disputes will have, as a term, mutual promises as to the application of that law. The parties will therefore have bound themselves, and each other, to that result.[91]

This characterisation of the choice of law agreement as a bargain or a mutual promise is misconceived. If the choice of law agreement gives rise to any obligations, these are merely of an ancillary nature (see subsection i below). A side effect of the non-promissory nature of choice of law agreements is that, even in common law jurisdictions, they need not be supported by additional consideration beyond the agreement on the applicable law: the reciprocal nature of the choice of law agreement is sufficient consideration (see subsection ii). The only possible exception is a choice of law agreement contained in an arbitration agreement, to the extent that it may impose on the arbitrator a contractual duty to comply with the parties' choice of law (see subsection iii).

i. An Obligation to Do What?

The principal function of the choice of law agreement is not to create rights and obligations between the parties, but to choose the norms applicable to the parties'

[90] *Akai Pty Ltd v People's Insurance Co Ltd* [1998] 1 Lloyd's Rep 90 (QB) 100, approved in *OT Africa Line Ltd v Magic Sportswear Corp* [2005] EWCA Civ 710, [2005] 2 Lloyd's Rep 170 [27]; see also *Vita Food Products Inc v Unus Shipping Co Ltd* [1939] AC 277 (PC) 290, 300; *Horn Linie GmbH & Co v Panamericana Formas e Impresos SA* [2006] EWHC 373, [2006] 2 Lloyd's Rep 44 [9], [20], [32].

[91] Briggs (n 26) para 11.43, see also para 3.02; cp Fentiman, 2nd edn (n 62) paras 3.15–3.17.

legal relationship by stipulating the governing law.[92] When party A and party B enter into an agreement to select the law of state A, neither party A nor party B are required to do anything to perform the contract. The agreement, which is effective from the time of conclusion, does not require execution and cannot be breached. It does not impose obligations on the parties. Its sole effect is to opt out of the objective choice of law rule that would have applied in its absence. The chosen law may, in turn, create or otherwise affect the parties' rights and obligations—by determining, for example, how an underlying contract is to be performed, or what the consequences are for its breach. But it is not the choice of law agreement that produces these effects—it is the chosen law.[93] The rules of the chosen law are not 'incorporated' into the choice of law agreement as contractual rights and obligations.[94]

It does not necessarily follow that the choice of law agreement cannot produce obligations that are ancillary to its principal function of selecting the applicable law. Briggs argues, for example, that a choice of law agreement is capable of founding a promise not to do anything that would defeat the choice. He refers to two obligations in particular: a promise not to argue, before court, that a law other than the chosen law governs the dispute; and a promise not to bring proceedings in a forum that will not recognise the choice, on the basis of mandatory rules or public policy.[95]

It is difficult to envision circumstances in which a party could successfully make out an implied promise not to impugn the choice of law contract. This would require a court to infer an agreement that is tantamount to a covenant not to sue, with the result that parties could no longer contest the validity or effect of the choice of law agreement.[96] If this reasoning were followed to its logical conclusion, the possibility of such an implied promise would be present in most ordinary contracts, which is not the case.

More plausible is the argument that a choice of law agreement may create an implied promise not to bring proceedings in a forum that will disregard the parties' choice of law. It has long been accepted that the governing law is a relevant factor in the exercise of the court's jurisdictional discretion where there is 'evidence of relevant differences in the legal principles or rules applicable to

[92] Gialdino (n 32) 871; see comments made by J-M Jacquet at the colloquium 'Le règlement communautaire "Rome I" et le choix de loi dans les contrats internationaux' (Dijon, 9–10 September 2010) as transcribed in S Corneloup and N Joubert (eds), *Le Règlement Communautaire 'Rome I' et le Choix de Loi dans les Contrats Internationaux* (Paris, LexisNexis, 2011) 55, 58–59; see also *Heyman v Darwins Ltd* [1942] AC 356 (HL) 373–74 (Lord Macmillan), in relation to arbitration agreements.

[93] But cp Heuzé (n 84) para 238.

[94] BGE 91 II 248.

[95] Briggs (n 26) paras 11.53 and 11.30; cp Fentiman, 2nd edn (n 62) paras 3.15–3.17; cp Schwander (n 45) 184–85.

[96] See also Jacquet (n 92) 60; D Henry, *Kollisionsrechtliche Rechtswahl—eine Untersuchung ihrer Wirkungen und Grenzen* (Zurich/St Gallen, Dike Verlag, 2009) 258–59; but cp Fentiman, 2nd edn (n 62) para 3.15.

[issues of law] in the two countries in contention as the appropriate forum'.[97] In particular, English courts have been open to the argument that the choice of law agreement should not be defeated simply by a unilateral choice of jurisdiction.[98] But this does not necessarily mean that a choice of law agreement could also give rise to an implied agreement to exclude choice-defeating jurisdictions, or even an implied obligation or promise that the parties refrain from bringing proceedings in such jurisdictions. In fact, this argument was rejected in two relatively recent cases.

In *Ace Insurance Ltd v Moose Enterprise Pty Ltd*,[99] the New South Wales Supreme Court concluded that an Australian choice of law clause did not amount to a promissory agreement to exclude the jurisdiction of the Californian courts. The plaintiff, Ace Insurance Ltd, was an Australian insurance company that had issued a legal liability policy to Moose Enterprise Pty Ltd (Moose), an Australian toy company. The policy covered personal injury or property damage arising from products exported to the United States, where a class action litigation had been brought against Moose alleging that its toys contained a toxic substance. Moose commenced proceedings in the Californian courts, seeking a declaration that Ace Insurance was obliged to defend the class action. In commencing the proceedings in California, Moose apparently wished to avail itself of certain advantages that Californian law conferred on an insured. The insurance policy included an express choice of Australian law and jurisdiction, but the jurisdiction clause was not expressed to be exclusive.

In the New South Wales Supreme Court, Ace Insurance argued that Moose should be restrained from pursuing the Californian proceeding because the parties' express choice of Australian law founded an implied negative stipulation not to sue in a jurisdiction that would not apply Australian law, and that instituting proceedings in California would amount to a breach of this implied negative stipulation. It submitted that the proceeding was in breach of a contractual term implied by law that a party will not do anything to deprive the other party of the benefit or efficiency of the contractual 'bargain', here the choice of law clause.[100]

Brereton J disagreed, concluding that choice of law was about 'ascertaining the intention of the parties' as to the applicable law, and not 'about covenants or promises that a particular legal system will apply', and that making a choice of law clause promissory would 'require very clear language':

[97] *VTB Capital Plc v Nutritek International Corp* [2013] UKSC 5, [2013] 1 All ER 1296 [46] (Lord Mance, obiter).

[98] *Seashell Shipping Corp v Mutualidad de Seguros del Instituto Nacional de Industria (The Magnum)* [1989] 1 Lloyd's Rep 47 (CA) 53; *Cadre SA v Astra Asigurari SA* [2005] EWHC 2626, [2006] 1 Lloyd's Rep 560 [18]; *Stonebridge Underwriting Ltd v Ontario Municipal Insurance Exchange* [2010] EWHC 2279, [2010] 2 CLC 349 [36], but cp [44]; cp *Golden Ocean Group Ltd v Salgaocar Mining Industries Pvt Ltd* [2011] EWHC 56, [2011] 2 All ER (Comm) 95 [143]; *Navig8 Pte Ltd v Al-Riyadh Co* [2013] EWHC 328 [28] and [35]. For criticism, see M Hook, 'The Choice of Law Agreement as a Reason for Exercising Jurisdiction' (2014) 63 *ICLQ* 963.

[99] *Ace Insurance Ltd v Moose Enterprise Ltd* [2009] NSWSC 724, 15 ANZ Ins Cas 61-818.

[100] ibid, [41]ff.

> [T]here is a well-established distinction between a choice of jurisdiction clause, which imposes contractual obligations on the parties, and a choice of law clause, which is merely declaratory of their intent as to the applicable legal system. Not being promissory in effect, a choice of law clause does not found implied negative stipulations.[101]

A similar conclusion was reached by the English High Court in *Navig8 PTE Ltd v Al-Riyad*, on an application for an injunction restraining the respondent's proceedings in Jordan and equitable damages.[102]

If it is accepted that choice of law agreements are legally binding agreements, then this reasoning is not entirely convincing. Under common law rules on implied terms, an intention may be imputed to the parties to a contract that they undertake not to incapacitate themselves from performing their contractual obligations: 'if I grant a man all the apples growing upon a certain tree, and I cut down the tree, I am guilty of a breach'.[103] Although, by bringing proceedings in California, Moose did not technically incapacitate itself from 'performing' the choice of law contract, its actions were clearly inconsistent with the purpose of the choice of law agreement.[104] So unless it is assumed that the parties intended their choice of law agreement to be subject to conflicting choice of law rules or overriding mandatory rules in a choice-defeating forum, the choice of law agreement does not seem to be inherently incompatible with the idea of an 'implied negative stipulation' as to jurisdiction.

However, the argument faces a different challenge. Because the alleged agreement on jurisdiction is an ancillary agreement arising from the choice of law agreement, the claimant would need to be able to establish both a valid choice of law agreement and a valid (exclusionary) agreement on jurisdiction. Pursuant to ordinary rules of jurisdiction, it is unlikely that an implied (and probably imputed) agreement on jurisdiction would be given effect.[105] Thus, the last remaining option would be to enforce the implied agreement by way of a claim for damages, which would succeed only if the court did not consider itself bound by the validity requirements that would have been applicable for the purposes of jurisdiction (or 'specific performance').[106]

[101] ibid, [51], [53].

[102] *Navig8 Pte Ltd v Al-Riyadh Co* [2013] EWHC 328. The Court did, however, grant permission to serve out of the jurisdiction a claim for declaratory relief, on the basis that the foreign proceedings would defeat the English choice of law agreement.

[103] *M'Intyre v Belcher* (1863) 14 CBNS 654, 664 (Willes J), cited in *Secretary of State for Employment v Associated Society of Locomotive Engineers and Firemen* [1972] 2 QB 455 (CA) 492 (Lord Denning MR).

[104] cp Briggs (n 26) para 11.52; but see K Takahashi, 'Damages for Breach of a Choice-of-Court Agreement: Remaining Issues' (2009) 11 *Yearbook of Private International Law* 73, 101.

[105] On the need for an express agreement, see *New Hampshire Insurance Co Ltd v Strabag Bau AG* [1992] 1 Lloyd's Rep 361 (CA) 371–72; L Collins (ed), *Dicey, Morris and Collins on the Conflict of Laws* 15th edn (London, Sweet & Maxwell, 2012) para 14-079.

[106] cp Collins, ibid para 12-160 ('it is plainly no answer to a claim for damages for breach of contract that a court declined to grant specific or other procedural relief to the victim of the breach'). English courts have previously construed jurisdiction agreements as actionable promises (see, eg, *Union Discount Co Ltd v Zoller* [2001] EWCA Civ 1755, [2002] WLR 1517; *Donohue v Armco Inc* [2001] UKHL 64, [2002] 1 Lloyd's Rep 425 [36]; *Sunrock Aircraft Corp Ltd v Scandinavian Airlines System Denmark-Norway-Sweden* [2007] EWCA Civ 882, [2007] 2 Lloyd's Rep 612 [37]). But in relation to German law, it has been

In these circumstances, it seems unlikely that a choice of law agreement would be capable of founding an implied negative stipulation as to jurisdiction. But even if it were, this would not affect the more fundamental point, which has already been made, that the primary function of the choice of law agreement is non-promissory in nature.

ii. Consideration

At first sight, the non-promissory nature of the choice of law agreement does not seem to sit easily with the common law doctrine of consideration. The function of this doctrine is to 'put some legal limits on the enforceability of agreements' by ensuring that the parties exchange 'something of value'.[107] Consideration is an essential element in the formation of contracts in common law jurisdictions: it is not sufficient that the promisor intends to bind himself by the promise, the promise must also be supported by consideration to be legally binding. The doctrine has a long history, having first been formulated as a general principle by Coke in 1588:

> [E]very consideration that doth charge the defendant in an assumpsit must be to the benefit of the defendant or charge of the plaintiff, and no case can be put out of this rule.[108]

Does this mean that the choice of law agreement, which does not create rights or obligations, may in some cases fall foul of the requirement of consideration with the result that it should not be considered legally binding?

It is submitted that consideration does not pose any obstacles to the enforceability of choice of law agreements as legally binding agreements. Because every choice of law agreement consists of mutual declarations of intent with reciprocal effect, the requirement of consideration is satisfied by definition. Both parties may rely on the agreement to insist on the application of the chosen law to a dispute; and where the choice of law agreement is relied upon, both parties forego the application of the objective applicable law. It is immaterial whether the chosen law is, in fact, beneficial to each party's case; and it is also unnecessary to look for consideration outside of the choice of law agreement (for example, in the parties' underlying substantive transaction): the mere possibility that both parties will benefit is sufficient.[109]

The doctrine of consideration is not recognised in civil law jurisdictions. The French and the German laws of contract employ more nuanced rules to limit

suggested that any jurisdictional promises could be expected to have been expressly made: P Mankowski, 'Ist eine vertragliche Absicherung von Gerichtsstandsvereinbarungen möglich?' [2009] *Praxis des Internationalen Privat- und Verfahrensrechts* 23, 26ff and references there cited.

[107] H Beale (ed), *Chitty on Contracts* 31st edn (London, Sweet & Maxwell, 2012) paras 3-001–3-002.

[108] *Stone v Wythipol* (1588) Cro Eliz 126, as cited by MP Furmston, *Cheshire, Fifoot and Furmston's Law of Contract* 16th edn (Oxford, Oxford University Press, 2012) 9.

[109] See, in a different context, PS Atiyah, *An Introduction to the Law of Contract* 5th edn (Oxford, Clarendon Press, 1995) 144, stating that 'The bare possibility that both sides will benefit is enough' where a contract is discharged at a time when some duties remain outstanding on both sides.

the enforceability of contracts,[110] none of which are relevant to choice of law agreements.

iii. The Arbitrator's Contract

The only situation in which a choice of law contract may impose direct contractual obligations is when it is contained in an arbitrator's contract. Unlike a judge, the arbitrator is tied to the parties by a contractual relationship.[111] The arbitrator is required to determine the parties' dispute in accordance with his or her mandate, including the parties' stipulation as to the applicable law.[112] There is considerable support for the view that an arbitration award may be set aside, or that it may not be recognised, where the arbitrator has failed to give effect to a choice of law contract, provided that there was no legitimate basis for the arbitrator's decision to ignore the choice.[113] Because the arbitrator is also required, for example, to render an award that is enforceable, he or she must still be free to apply overriding mandatory rules and public policy where this will aid in the enforceability and recognition of the award.[114]

However, whether an arbitrator's failure to give effect to a choice of law contract could found an action for breach of contract would depend largely on the view that is adopted of the arbitrator–party relationship more generally: is it primarily a contractual relationship that creates *in personam* rights and obligations; or does the arbitrator's quasi-judicial status protect him or her from personal liability for breach of contract?[115] This question—which would, in any case, be unlikely to assume much practical relevance because a failure to apply the chosen law may well be covered by immunity[116]—is beyond the scope of this book.

B. The Choice of Law Agreement as a 'Contract of Disposition'?

Because choice of law agreements do not give rise to obligations, it has been argued that they must instead be contracts that modify or extinguish existing

110 AT von Mehren, 'Civil-law Analogues to Consideration: an Exercise in Comparative Analysis' (1959) 72 *Harvard Law Review* 1009.

111 G Born, *International Commercial Arbitration* 2nd edn (Alphen aan den Rijn, Kluwer, 2014) paras 13.02–13.03; see *K/S Norjarl A/S v Hyundai Heavy Indus Co Ltd* [1992] 1 QB 863 (CA).

112 See Born, ibid 1997–98 and 2001.

113 See L Silbermann and F Ferrari, 'Getting to the Law Applicable to the Merits in International Arbitration and the Consequences of Getting it Wrong' in F Ferrari and S Kröll (eds), *Conflict of Laws in International Arbitration* (Munich, Sellier, 2011) 257, 312ff.

114 See Born (n 111) 1997–98.

115 See generally ML Smith, 'Contractual Obligations Owed by and to Arbitrators: Model Terms of Appointment' (1992) 8 *Arbitration International* 17; J Gal, *Die Haftung des Schiedsrichters in der internationalen Handelsschiedsgerichtsbarkeit* (Tübingen, Mohr Siebeck, 2009); T Clay, *L'arbitre* (Paris, Dalloz, 2001) paras 931–32.

116 On arbitrators' immunity generally, see Born (n 111) para 13.06[C].

rights or obligations (see subsection i below). However, this argument relies on the same mistaken assumption as the proposition that the choice of law agreement is a promise: namely, that the choice of law agreement has a direct effect on the parties' rights and obligations (see subsection ii). The agreement's function may more fittingly be described as a disposition of norms (see subsection iii).

i. The Concept of Disposition of Rights

Contracts that transfer, alter or extinguish rights are known, in German law, as 'contracts of disposition'.[117] The contract of disposition can be traced back to Savigny, who was convinced that the more conventional notion of contract was too narrowly conceived.[118] In particular, Savigny focused on real contracts, which had as their purpose the transfer of property rather than the creation of *in personam* rights and obligations. Contracts of disposition produce immediate legal effects by virtue only of a declaration of common intent. By analogy with such contracts, it has hence been argued that the choice of law agreement 'disposes the [underlying] contract' to the applicable law from the time of agreement:

> The agreement on the applicable law is of a different nature [from promissory contracts]. … The choice of law contract achieves its effect at the time of agreement. It is therefore like a disposition: it disposes the contract to one of several hundred legal systems in the world.[119]

It is true that, just like a contract of disposition, the choice of law agreement does not require any further action to be taken by the parties once it has been concluded. But the choice of law agreement does not modify or extinguish rights to which it applies.

ii. Is the Choice of Law Agreement a Disposition of Rights?

The problem with conceptualising the choice of law agreement in this way is that the agreement's 'object' of disposition is not, in fact, the parties' underlying relationship (with all the rights and obligations that may, or may not, form part of it),

[117] The German term is 'Verfügungsvertrag': see B Markesinis, H Unberath and A Johnston, *The German Law of Contract: A Comparative Treatise* 2nd edn (Oxford, Hart Publishing, 2006) 27ff; cp the conceptualisation of contract as transfer by P Benson, 'The Unity of Contract Law' in P Benson (ed), *The Theory of Contract Law: New Essays* (Cambridge, Cambridge University Press, 2001) 118 and the argument in favour of an abstraction principle by WJ Swadling, 'Rescission, Property and the Common Law' (2005) 121 *LQR* 123.

[118] FK von Savigny, *System des heutigen römischen Rechts*, vol 3 (Berlin, Veit, 1840) 309–14.

[119] J Basedow, 'Theorie der Rechtswahl oder Parteiautonomie als Grundlage des Internationalen Privatrechts' (2011) 75 *Rabels Zeitschrift für ausländisches und internationales Privatrecht* 32, 53: 'Die Vereinbarung über die Rechtswahl hat eine ganz andere Natur [als der Verpflichtungsvertrag]. … [Der Rechtswahlvertrag] hat mit seinem wirksamen Zustandekommen seine Wirkung schon erreicht. Ihm ist also gleichsam eine Verfügungswirkung zu eigen: Er verfügt die Zuweisung des Vertrages an eine einzige von mehreren hundert auf der Welt vorfindbaren Rechtsordnungen' (author's translation). cp, in relation to jurisdiction agreements, Mankowski (n 106) 27; and, in relation to arbitration agreements, E Bucher, 'Was macht den Schiedsrichter?' in B Bachmann et al (eds), *Grenzüberschreitungen: Beiträge zum Internationalen Verfahrensrecht und zur Schiedsgerichtbarkeit—Festschrift für Peter Schlosser* (Tübingen, Mohr Siebeck, 2005) 97, 99.

but the forum's choice of law rules. The choice of law agreement disposes of the parties' right to have their dispute determined in accordance with the objective applicable law, but this is not a right between the parties. The power to choose the applicable law is not derived from the law of obligations, in the way that an assignment of contract or a release of obligations would be; and the choice of law agreement does not describe the power of rights-holders to dispose of or modify their rights.[120] Although the choice of law agreement can ultimately affect the parties' rights, it is the chosen law, and not the power to choose the law, that directly modifies the parties' underlying relationship, and that may give rise to rights and obligations between the parties.

In other words, the choice of law agreement does not create, modify or extinguish rights and obligations; and, more fundamentally, it would be wrong to equate the function or effect of the rules of the chosen law with that of the choice of law agreement. If the choice of law agreement did create, modify or extinguish rights and obligations that are part of the chosen law, it would not be a choice of law but an agreement to 'incorporate' foreign laws as terms into the underlying contract.[121]

iii. The Choice of Law Agreement as a Disposition of Norms

As an agreement whose function is to opt out of the forum's objective choice of law rules and substitute a chosen applicable law, the choice of law agreement is truly nothing more than its name suggests. It is a bilateral legal act that selects a law to govern the underlying relationship. On that basis, the term 'disposition of norms', which has been used in German literature in relation to procedural contracts,[122] seems apt to describe the choice of law agreement—the relevant norms here being the forum's objective choice of law rules. Choice of law rules are mere 'rules about rules', rules that allocate the applicable law to international relationships; and the party autonomy rule allows parties to contract out of these default 'secondary' rules.[123] When party A and party B enter into an agreement to select the applicable law, they agree to opt out of a norm—the objective choice of law rule.

C. The Choice of Law Contract

So if the choice of law agreement is not a contract of obligation because its sole function is the selection of the applicable law, ought it nonetheless to be described

[120] See C von Bar, *Internationales Privatrecht*, vol 2 (Munich, Ch Beck, 1991) para 416; in relation to procedural agreements more generally, see Wagner (n 52) 220–24.

[121] On incorporation, see Collins (n 105) paras 32-056–32-057.

[122] Wagner (n 52) 224.

[123] cp Mills' categorisation of private international rules as 'secondary rules', based on HLA Hart's distinction between primary rules that impose duties and are rules of conduct, and secondary rules that confer powers and create, extinguish, modify or control primary rules: A Mills, *The Confluence of Public and Private International Law* (Cambridge, Cambridge University Press, 2009) 19–20.

as a contract? In some legal systems, the definition of 'contract' is sufficiently wide to include all forms of bilateral legal acts,[124] and the choice of law agreement is thus referred to as a *Verweisungsvertrag*.[125] In most legal systems, however, the choice of law agreement would not have obviously 'contractual' characteristics because it does not create, modify or extinguish rights or obligations.[126]

The alternative to labelling party choice as a contract would be to refer to it simply as an agreement:

> Bilateral acts in the law are called *agreements* in the wide and generic sense of that term. There is, indeed, a narrow and specific use, in which agreement is synonymous with contract, that is to say, the creation of rights *in personam* by way of consent.[127]

The drawback to this approach is that the term 'agreement' is not clearly understood as a legal concept and may give the impression that the choice of law agreement is not legally binding. Because contracts are known in all legal systems, this description would '[have] the advantage of a certain form of universality'.[128]

More fundamentally, choice of law agreements share the same legal and philosophical underpinnings as the law of contract.[129] Whether the rationale is to increase efficiency and certainty in commercial transactions, or to respect the right of individuals to self-ordering, the party autonomy rule, as well as the principle of freedom of contract more generally, perceive parties as 'private legislators' who are best left to regulate their own relations. The meaning of contract may thus be understood as a fluid concept, serving to identify transactions that are best explained by the freedom of individuals to regulate their own relations.[130] A mutual intention to be bound is at the heart of both the law of contract and the party autonomy rule—and it is the law of contract, therefore, that must provide many of the principles and rules that determine the scope, existence and validity of choice of law agreements. There is no separate regime of rules that deals only with legally binding agreements that are not, strictly speaking, contracts. For these reasons, choice of law agreements are best treated as contracts, and they will be referred to as 'choice of law contracts' in this book.

A number of key points have led to this final conclusion that the party autonomy rule relies on a choice of law contract. First, the choice of law agreement is not

[124] See, eg, for Germany: Markesinis (n 117) 25–27.

[125] U Magnus (ed), *Staudingers Kommentar zum Bürgerlichen Gesetzbuch: Rom I-VO Art 3* (Berlin, Sellier, 2011) para 36; H Honsell et al (eds), *Basler Kommentar* 3rd edn (Basel, Helbing Lichtenhahn, 2013) Art 116, para 32.

[126] But see Rabel (n 49) 368–69, who describes the choice of law agreement as a 'true contract'; and Gialdino (n 32) 863, who refers to the choice of law agreement as 'pactum de lege utenda'.

[127] Salmond (n 28) 307.

[128] V Brulhart, *Le choix de la loi applicable—questions choisies* (Bern, Stämpfli, 2004) para 746: 'présente par conséquent l'avantage d'une certaine forme d'universalité' (author's translation); Moser (n 84) 231–32.

[129] See Nygh (n 3) 7–8; S Leible, 'Parteiautonomie im IPR—Allgemeines Anknüpfungsprinzip oder Verlegenheitslösung?' in HP Mansel (ed), *Festschrift für Erik Jayme* (Munich, Sellier, 2004) 485, 485; von Bar (n 120) 308.

[130] See A Corbin, *Corbin on Contracts* (St Paul, West Pub Co, 1952) para 3.

a mere factor in the determination of the applicable law, or a 'factual agreement' that produces no legal effect. Based on a mutual intention to choose the applicable law, the choice of law agreement is a bilateral legal act, or a legally binding agreement. Second, the function of this agreement is not to create or modify rights and obligations: it is to opt out of the forum's objective choice of law rules and to choose the applicable law. Third, the fact that the choice of law agreement serves this peculiar function does not mean that it is not, or should not be, described as a contract. Although it is not a contract of obligation, party choice is firmly grounded in principles of autonomy that permeate much of private law, and the law of contract in particular. The party autonomy rule, although anchored in private international law, seeks to give parties the freedom to organise their own relations by contract. This conclusion ought to be crucial to the regulation of party autonomy and the enforcement of choice of law agreements. If choice of law agreements are contracts—or are at least *like* contracts—then they should be regulated and enforced accordingly.

3

The Scope of Party Autonomy

I. Party Autonomy as Freedom of Contract

A German and a Frenchman, both resident in the United Kingdom, decide to get married, adopting London as their matrimonial home. But the German, an heiress of an extremely rich family, insists on the execution of a pre-nuptial agreement in order to protect her wealth. The agreement contains a choice of law clause, which states that the effects of the parties' marriage are to be subject to German law, and provides for separation of the spouses' property during and upon termination of the marriage. The marriage breaks down eight years later.[1] Should the parties' choice of law contract be given effect to?

A New Zealander who is working for the subsidiary of an Australian company in New Zealand contracts mesothelioma as a result of his exposure to raw asbestos fibre in the course of his employment.[2] The employment contract submits the parties' relationship, including any non-contractual disputes, to the law of New South Wales. Should such an agreement be enforceable in relation to the employee's personal injury claim?

This chapter examines the considerations that should determine whether the party autonomy rule is an appropriate solution to a choice of law problem. An argument that is often made is that party autonomy ought to be linked to the degree of freedom that the parties enjoy at a substantive level in the ordering of their relations. On that basis, it has been suggested that party choice should only be permissible in contracts or, alternatively, in relationships that *could* form the subject of an agreement, including settlement agreements.[3] But where there is no such substantive freedom, as might be the case in areas like family law, party

[1] This is a simplified summary of the facts of *Radmacher v Granatino* [2010] UKSC 42, [2011] AC 534.

[2] cp *James Hardie & Co Pty Ltd v Hall* (1998) 43 NSWLR 554 (NSWCA) (there was no choice of law clause in this case).

[3] See, eg, J Kropholler, *Internationales Privatrecht* 6th edn (Tübingen, Mohr Siebeck, 2006) 296; ThM de Boer, 'Party Autonomy and its Limitations in the Rome II Regulation' (2007) 9 *Yearbook of Private International Law* 19, 20; PH Neuhaus, *Die Grundbegriffe des Internationalen Privatrechts* 2nd edn (Tübingen, Mohr Siebeck, 1976) 257; T Kadner Graziano, 'Freedom to Choose the Applicable Law in Tort—Articles 14 and 4(3) of the Rome II Regulation' in W Binchy and J Ahern (eds),

autonomy has still been considered justifiable on pragmatic grounds.[4] This is not the approach adopted here, which is to equate the question of party autonomy with the question of freedom of contract. If party autonomy is the freedom to contract out of the objective choice of law rule, what are the considerations that should determine whether this freedom is granted?

A. Freedom of Contract

Freedom of contract seems to require consideration of three broad questions. The first question concerns the function of the rule that is to be contracted out of. Does the rule pursue public policies that the parties should not be free to set aside? The second question concerns the possible effects of contractualisation of the rule. Are parties capable of entering into a free and informed agreement about the matter? Are there downsides to its commodification? This, too, is a question about 'public policy' in a broad sense. The final question is whether there are mechanisms to *reconcile* freedom of contract with the public policy concerns that it may engender. Only then is it possible to determine whether the rule to be contracted out of should be a default rule or a mandatory rule.

Mandatory rules seek to promote policies that cannot be left to private agreement.[5] These policies, which may be broadly characterised as 'public policy',[6] generally serve one of two goals: to protect public and third-party interests—that is, interests 'external' to those of the parties—or to protect the parties themselves, because 'the best way to promote a *public* policy may be to confer rights on private citizens'.[7] Contractual freedom ends where negative externalities and paternalism begin; or, more fundamentally, 'L'action du pouvoir social s'arrête là où elle rencontre la liberté inoffensive et dès lors légitime des particuliers'.[8] Default rules, on the other hand, are merely facilitative in nature and can be opted out of.

The Rome II Regulation on the Law Applicable to Non-Contractual Obligations: A New Tort Litigation Regime (Leiden, Martinus Nijhoff, 2009) 113, 115; J Harris, 'Contractual Freedom in the Conflict of Laws' (2000) 20 *OJLS* 247, 267; cp A Briggs, *Agreements on Jurisdiction and Choice of Law* (Oxford, Oxford University Press, 2008) para 10.48.

[4] See E Jayme, 'Party Autonomy in International Family and Succession Law: New Tendencies' (2009) 11 *Yearbook of Private International Law* 1, 3.

[5] The different concept of internationally mandatory rules, which is unique to choice of law and refers to substantive rules of the forum that are applicable regardless of the governing law, will be dealt with below at s IV.C.ii. There is a vast body of US literature on default and mandatory rules: see, eg, I Ayres and R Gertner, 'Filling Gaps in Incomplete Contracts: An Economic Theory of Default Rules' (1989) 99 *Yale Law Journal* 87.

[6] B Rudden, 'Ius Cogens, Ius Dispositivum' (1980) 11 *Cambrian Law Review* 87, 88.

[7] ibid, 90; see also generally HC Grigoleit, 'Mandatory Law: Fundamental Principles' in J Basedow et al (eds), *Max Planck Encyclopaedia of European Private Law* (Oxford, Oxford University Press, 2011); RH Youngs, 'Compulsory and Voluntary Law: Lessons in Categorization for English Law from Continental Models' (2012) 33 *Statute Law Review* 84.

[8] PS Mancini, 'De l'utilité de rendre obligatoires pour tous les États, sous la forme d'un ou de plusieurs traités internationaux, un certain nombre de règles générales du droit international privé pour assurer la décision uniforme des conflits entre les différentes législations civiles et criminelles'

This classification of law into default and mandatory rules generally serves to delineate the freedom enjoyed by private persons as a matter of substantive private law. In family law, for example, couples wishing to enter into a matrimonial property agreement may be held to mandatory standards because such agreements run counter to a public interest in upholding marriage; or because the spouses' agreement may not reflect the morals and values of the community within which they live; or because the agreement may not adequately cater for the interests of third parties, such as children of the relationship; or the law is simply considered to provide the fairest solution, particularly for an economically vulnerable spouse.[9]

B. Freedom of Contract in Choice of Law

It is submitted that these three questions are equally applicable to party autonomy. In order to evaluate the scope of party autonomy it is necessary to determine whether choice of law can appropriately be dealt with by contract, or whether there are public policy interests that militate against such an approach. This question must be resolved by reference to the objective choice of law rule that the parties' choice of law contract would seek to render inapplicable. Party autonomy ought to be evaluated against the purposes of objective choice of law, because it is the objective choice of law rule that the choice of law contract seeks to set aside. It has already been argued in chapter two that the subject of the choice of law contract is not the underlying relationship but the applicable law; and that the source of this power to choose the applicable law is not substantive law or the law of contract, but the forum's choice of law rules.[10]

In other words, it is necessary to determine whether the objective choice of law rule is mandatory in nature. Should the French-German couple be able to set aside the English rule that would submit their matrimonial property dispute to the law of the forum,[11] or the German rule that would designate the law of the couple's place of common residence?[12] Should the New Zealand employee and his Australian employer be able to set aside the Australian rule that submits tortious

(1874) 1 *Journal de Droit International Privé* 221, 292: 'The exercise of social power stops where it meets the harmless and hence justifiable freedom of individuals' (author's translation). Art 6 of the Code Civil similarly provides that 'On ne peut déroger, par des conventions particulières, aux lois qui intéressent l'ordre public et les bonnes moeurs' ('Statutes relating to public policy and morals may not be derogated from by private agreements'; translation taken from http://www.legifrance.gouv.fr/).

[9] See J Scherpe (ed), *Marital Agreements and Private Autonomy in Comparative Perspective* (Oxford, Hart Publishing, 2012).

[10] See also D Einsele, 'Rechtswahlfreiheit im Internationalen Privatrecht' (1996) 60 *Rabels Zeitschrift für ausländisches und internationales Privatrecht* 417, 418; Y Nishitani, *Mancini und die Parteiautonomie im Internationalen Privatrecht* (Heidelberg, Winter, 2000) 318; J Basedow, 'Theorie der Rechtswahl oder Parteiautonomie als Grundlage des Internationalen Privatrechts' (2011) 75 *Rabels Zeitschrift für ausländisches und internationales Privatrecht* 32, 58.

[11] In the context of an ancillary application to divorce proceedings under the Matrimonial Causes Act 1973: see below, s II.B.iii.

[12] Einführungsgesetz zum Bürgerlichen Gesetzbuch (EGBGB), Arts 14(1)(2) and 15.

claims to the *lex loci delicti*,[13] or the New Zealand double actionability rule, which requires tortious claims to be actionable both under the *lex loci delicti* and the law of the forum?[14] Or are these rules mandatory rules?

C. Default and Mandatory Rules of Choice of Law

The existence of default and mandatory choice of law rules has been described as 'doubtful', on the basis that all choice of law rules are mandatory because 'parties cannot replace them by a rule of their own making'.[15] But there is no need for such a formalistic interpretation of mandatory rules. A mandatory rule is simply a rule that cannot be set aside by the will of the parties.[16] In exercising their freedom to choose the applicable law, the parties necessarily set aside the objective choice of law rule. It is immaterial that they rely on the party autonomy rule to do so and that this rule is not a 'rule of their making'. After all, party autonomy simply embodies the very contractual freedom that is needed to set aside the objective rule. If the objective choice of law rule is *ius cogens*, the parties do not have the freedom to set it aside, and their choice produces no juridical effect.[17] There is no reason in principle why the distinction between default and mandatory rules in substantive law should not be equally applicable to the conflict of laws.

A more interesting question, perhaps, is whether the distinction is also relevant to objective choice of law rules that may be better described as choice of law 'approaches' because they involve a largely discretionary and fluid assessment of a range of factors. For example, section 145 of the Restatement (Second) of Conflict of Laws[18] requires a court to identify the law applicable to tort by reference to a catalogue of principles set out in section 6, as well as a list of physical 'contacts'. Section 6 includes such factors as the 'relative interests' of states in the determination of the issue, and 'the basic policies underlying the particular field of law'. Is it still possible, in this context, to speak of a default or mandatory choice of law *rule*? The answer must surely be 'yes'. One may wish to substitute a more fitting description for the word 'rule',[19] but a discretionary assessment of choice of law factors can be just as 'mandatory' as an ordinary choice of law rule.

By focusing on the policies of choice of law, and on whether these are in harmony with or contrary to party choice, the proposed contractual approach frees the

[13] *Regie Nationale des Usines Renault SA v Zhang* (2002) 210 CLR 491.

[14] *Baxter v RMC plc* [2003] 1 NZLR 305 (HC).

[15] ThM de Boer, 'Facultative Choice of Law: The Procedural Status of Choice-of-Law Rules and Foreign Law' (1996) 257 *Recueil des Cours* 223, 348–49.

[16] Rudden (n 6) 87.

[17] cp M Whincop and M Keyes, 'Putting the "Private" Back into Private International Law: Default Rules and the Proper Law of the Contract' (1997) 21 *Melbourne University Law Review* 515, 520–21, treating as mandatory statutory choice of law rules which preclude a choice by the parties.

[18] American Law Institute, Restatement (Second) of Conflict of Laws (1971).

[19] See S Symeonides, 'A New Conflicts Restatement: Why Not?' (2009) 5 *Journal of Private International Law* 383, 389–91.

party autonomy rule from the substantive straitjacket within which it has traditionally been evaluated. What matters is whether objective choice of law rules pursue public policy goals, to protect the parties or interests external to the parties;[20] not whether the parties' substantive freedom in any given area of law ought to translate into party autonomy, or whether choice of law is to be characterised as forming part of public law and thus as immune to private ordering.[21]

This is not to suggest that substantive law is of no relevance to party autonomy. As will be seen in this chapter, objective choice of law is not isolated from substantive influences. But this inquiry into the relationship between substantive law and objective choice of law, and how it might impact on the availability of party choice, is essential to a principled approach to party autonomy and should not be cut short. Thus, in order to determine whether a particular objective choice of law rule ought to be mandatory or dispositive in character, it is necessary to consider the function of the objective choice of law rule (see section II below) and the effects of its contractualisation (see section III). Only then is it possible to attempt a reconciliation of the party autonomy rule with these potentially competing considerations (see section IV), and to assess the proper scope of the party autonomy rule (see section V).

II. Functions of Objective Choice of Law

Choice of law comes into play only when a legal relationship falls outside the boundaries of a single country. The function of choice of law rules is to allocate a governing law to a particular legal issue or relationship involving a foreign element. When determining whether parties should be free to contract out of an objective choice of law rule, it is relevant whether the objective choice of law rule raises issues of public policy. Because public policy, as it is here understood, can consist of either external or protective interests, there are two overarching questions that must be considered.

The first question is whether the choice of law rule serves (potentially foreign) external interests, of the state or the community or of third parties connected to the applicable law;[22] or whether it is firmly wedded to a 'private law

[20] cp J Carruthers, 'Party Autonomy in the Legal Regulation of Adult Relationships: What Place for Party Choice in Private International Law?' (2012) 61 *ICLQ* 881, 884–85; H Yntema, '"Autonomy" in Choice of Law' (1952) 1 *American Journal of Comparative Law* 341, 356 ('Neither the sovereign state, nor its law, is an end in itself').

[21] See ch 2, pt II.A.i.

[22] For a more general discussion of the regulatory weakness of the conflict of laws in relation to international commercial actors, see H Muir Watt, '"Party Autonomy" in International Contracts: from the Makings of a Myth to the Requirements of Global Governance' (2010) 6 *European Review of Contract Law* 250; R Wai, 'Transnational Liftoff and Juridical Touchdown: The Regulatory Function of Private International Law in an Era of Globalization' (2001–2002) 40 *Columbia Journal of Transnational Law* 209.

paradigm'[23] that only takes account of the parties' interests. If the choice of law rule is concerned with the parties' interests, the second question is to what extent it fulfils a protective or paternalistic function by designating the law that is most likely to reflect the interests of the parties, or of one of the parties. Both external and protective interests may reflect public policies that are inconsistent with party autonomy.

Broadly speaking, there are three types of choice of law rules: choice of law rules based on localising connecting factors that are concerned with 'conflicts justice'; choice of law rules based on substantive connecting factors that are concerned with substantive justice; and mixed choice of law rules (or 'approaches') that combine both of these concerns, often in a fluid case-by-case assessment. The question is whether these different types of choice of law rules pursue external or protective interests.

A. Localising Connecting Factors

The predominant method of allocation continues to be based on Savigny's theory of the natural seat and aims to subject relationships to the law with which they are most closely connected. Thus, contracts are usually submitted to either a flexible connecting factor designating the law that is most closely connected to the contract, or a connecting factor setting up a presumption of closest connection;[24] rights in rem are mostly determined by the *lex situs*;[25] torts are generally submitted to the *lex loci delicti* or the *lex loci damni*;[26] and in civil law jurisdictions, disputes involving matrimonial property and applications for divorce are commonly decided by either the law of the spouses' common habitual residence or the law of the spouses' common nationality.[27] Because these choice of law rules are designed to take account of localising factors rather than substantive policies, they

[23] H Muir Watt, 'European Integration, Legal Diversity, and the Conflict of Laws' (2004–2005) 9 *Edinburgh Law Review* 6, 14.

[24] Reg (EC) 593/2008 on the law applicable to contractual obligations [2008] OJ L177/6 (Rome I), Art 4; Bundesgesetz über das Internationale Privatrecht (IPRG), Art 117; see L Collins (ed), *Dicey, Morris and Collins on the Conflict of Laws* 15th edn (London, Sweet & Maxwell, 2012) paras 32-071–32-073.

[25] IPRG, Art 99–100; EGBGB, Art 43; Code Civil, Art 3; Collins, ibid paras 23R-062–24R-001.

[26] Reg (EC) 864/2007 on the law applicable to non-contractual obligations [2007] OJ L199/40 (Rome II), Art 4; *Regie Nationale des Usines Renault SA v Zhang* (2002) 210 CLR 491; IPRG, Art 133(2), but see Art 133(1).

[27] Where neither of these connecting factors is established, additional connecting factors are relied upon, including the law with the closest connection to the relationship: Hague Convention on the Law Applicable to Matrimonial Property Regimes (1977) 16 ILM 14 (opened for signature 14 March 1978, entered into force 1 September 1992) (Hague Convention 1978), Art 4; EGBGB, Arts 14(1) and 15(1); Reg (EU) 1259/2010 implementing enhanced cooperation in the area of the law applicable to divorce and legal separation [2010] OJ L343/10 (Rome III), Art 8; see generally Consortium Asser-UCL, *Étude sur les régimes matrimoniaux des couples mariés et sur le patrimoine des couples non mariés dans le droit international privé et dans le droit interne des États membres de l'Union* (Offre n JAI/A3/2001/03) (*Asser Report*); see also IPRG, Arts 54 and 61(2).

are neutral as to the content of the applicable law, striving instead for 'conflicts justice'.[28] They are concerned with 'choice-of-law interests'.[29] But are these choice of law interests external or protective interests that are likely to be inconsistent with party autonomy?[30]

i. Uniformity of Outcome

Insofar as conflicts justice is a matter of uniformity of outcome and certainty,[31] it might not matter whose interests these goals are meant to serve. Whether they are private or 'systemic'[32] in nature, or whether they support such general aims as cross-border mobility of persons,[33] it is difficult to see why they would be inconsistent with the party autonomy rule, which is more likely than localising choice of law rules to achieve uniform and predictable choice of law results. In the first of the introductory examples, the party autonomy rule would ensure that German law is applied to the matrimonial property dispute, regardless of whether proceedings are brought in Germany, France or England.

Even where the party autonomy rule is not internationally established, and the capacity for uniformity is thus limited in practice, it would be strangely self-defeating to disallow the parties' choice of law simply on the basis that other countries have not yet recognised the rule. In theory, at least, party autonomy is the most suitable choice of law rule to avoid forum shopping and to achieve uniform outcomes across borders.

ii. External Interests

Most scholars would accept that conflicts justice consists of more than uniformity of outcome. The conflict of laws may be understood as a system of allocation of regulatory authority, advancing the 'objective interest' of states to regulate relationships with which they are closely connected.[34] Based on this 'public' view of the conflict of laws, reliance on connecting factors such as nationality, domicile

[28] G Kegel, 'Paternal Home and Dream Home: Traditional Conflict of Laws and the American Reformers' (1979) 27 *American Journal of Comparative Law* 615, 625; A Mills, *The Confluence of Public and Private International Law* (Cambridge, Cambridge University Press, 2009) 16–17.

[29] de Boer (n 15) 292; or 'objective' interests: Mills (n 28) 261.

[30] See Kegel (n 28) 621 (referring to 'party-interests', 'community-interests' and 'interests of order').

[31] See de Boer (n 15) 283ff.

[32] Mills (n 28) 17.

[33] See, eg, Explanatory Memorandum to the Proposal for a Council Regulation on jurisdiction, applicable law and the recognition and enforcement of decisions in matters of matrimonial property regimes (COM 2011, 126, 16 March 2011) para 1.2.

[34] See Mills (n 28) 261–64; more doubtful is ThM de Boer, 'Living Apart Together: The Relationship between Public and Private International Law' (2010) 57 *Netherlands International Law Review* 183, 206 (concluding that 'the choice-of-law perspective has shifted from the vindication of sovereign rights to the facilitation of international legal transactions between private parties'); cp H Muir Watt, 'The Challenge of Market Integration for European Conflicts Theory' in AS Hartkamp and EH Hondius (eds), *Towards a European Civil Code* 3rd revised edn (The Hague, Kluwer, 2004) 191.

or residence, and territoriality can all be traced to public international law. Consequently, their application to disputes involving contract, property, tort or matrimonial matters is dictated by considerations of sovereignty or comity, and has little to do with private justice.[35] For example, an Australian court would apply New Zealand law to the employee's personal injury claim, as the *lex loci delicti*, not because it considers this to be the fairest solution for the parties, but because it recognises New Zealand's regulatory authority over torts occurring within its territory.[36] This need for comity would be particularly pronounced in the context of trans-Tasman disputes (as it would between countries of the European Union), in light of the growing legal integration that is taking place between Australia and New Zealand.[37]

Localising connecting factors could also be considered to serve communitarian interests, requiring an evaluation of the interests of connected private persons or communities.[38] The law of the French-German couple's habitual residence could be applied, for example, 'to give consideration to the interests of others with whom [the parties are] living, that is, to the interests of the local society in which [the foreigners have] established [their] domicile'.[39] Such interests may include those of individual third parties whose legal rights are affected by the parties' dispute, including purchasers of the spouses' matrimonial property.

If localising choice of law rules seek to allocate authority over private relationships, on the basis that the state or the community with which the relationship is closely connected has an objective interest in the application of its law, they have little functional overlap with the party autonomy rule.

iii. The Parties' Interests

With the exception of the *lex situs* rule for claims in rem,[40] it is private justice rather than external interests that is often understood as the prevailing rationale for most localising choice of law rules.[41] What matters are the parties' expectations,

[35] On the public international law ideas of 'territoriality' and 'personality' as organising principles in private international law, see Mills (n 28) 234ff.

[36] See *Tolofson v Jensen* [1994] 3 SCR 1022 [37] (La Forest J); this passage by La Forest J was cited in *Regie Nationale des Usines Renault SA v Zhang* (2002) 210 CLR 491 [64] (Gleeson CJ, Gaudron, McHugh, Gummow and Hayne JJ).

[37] See Agreement between the Government of Australia and the Government of New Zealand on Trans-Tasman Court Proceedings and Regulatory Enforcement (signed 24 July 2008, entered into force 11 October 2013).

[38] See G Kegel, 'The Crisis of Conflict of Laws' (1964) 112 *Recueil des Cours* 92, 186.

[39] ibid, 186.

[40] See generally R Westrik and J van der Weide (eds), *Party Autonomy in International Property Law* (Munich, Sellier, 2011).

[41] AJE Jaffey, 'The Foundations of Rules for the Choice of Law' (1982) 2 *OJLS* 368; F Vischer, 'General Course on Private International Law' (1992) 232 *Recueil des Cours* 9, 30–31; Collins (n 24) para 1-005; J Fawcett and JM Carruthers, *Cheshire, North & Fawcett: Private International Law* 14th edn (Oxford, Oxford University Press, 2008) 37; A Flessner, *Interessenjurisprudenz im Internationalen Privatrecht* (Tübingen, JCB Mohr, 1990) 100; E Jayme, 'Identité culturelle et intégration: le droit international privé postmoderne' (1995) 251 *Recueil des Cours* 9, 80.

and their presumed preference to be subject to a system of law with which their relationship is closely connected and with which they are more likely to be familiar. *Dicey, Morris and Collins on the Conflict of Laws* accordingly states that 'The main justification for the conflict of laws is that it implements the reasonable and legitimate expectations of the parties to a transaction or an occurrence';[42] Kirby J in *Regie Nationale des Usines Renault SA v Zhang* noted that the *lex loci delicti* 'has "sure foundations in human psychology" … [because] [t]he ordinary expectations of most parties are … that the law of the place of the wrong will govern the rights and duties of the parties';[43] and in relation to matrimonial property, it has been said that 'the justification for applying the law of the domicile is that it is likely to reflect the values, attitudes and expectations of the parties'.[44]

Pursuant to this private law paradigm of choice of law, localising choice of law rules would be (potentially) incompatible with party autonomy only if their function was paternalistic or protective in nature as opposed to facilitative. A protective choice of law rule would apply the law most closely connected to the relationship because, objectively, it offers the fairest solution to the choice of law problem. For example, English law would apply to the matrimonial property relationship of the French-German couple, as the law of the couple's place of habitual residence, because this is the most significant common denominator between the parties to that relationship, and there is thus a legitimate basis for submitting the rights of both the French husband and the German wife to the authority of English law. It has been argued accordingly that party autonomy in family law is restricted in the interest of 'legal security';[45] and Vischer has argued more generally that, outside of the area of contract, it is 'preferable to limit the authority of the parties to choose a law with which they are supposedly especially familiar' because 'it cannot be presumed that parties are always well instructed about the consequences of a choice of law'.[46]

But because localising choice of law rules are decoupled from substantive considerations, the grounds for such paternalism seem rather tenuous. While localising choice of law rules clearly serve to protect the parties' expectations, they offer no more security or certainty than the party autonomy rule, provided the choice of law contract is based on free and informed agreement. For example, the French-German couple would have a legitimate expectation, in the absence of a choice of law contract, that English law would apply to their relationship; but this

[42] Collins (n 24) para 1-005.

[43] *Regie Nationale des Usines Renault SA v Zhang* (2002) 210 CLR 491 [130] (Kirby J, footnotes omitted).

[44] T Hartley, 'Matrimonial (Marital) Property Rights in Conflict of Laws: A Reconsideration' in J Fawcett (ed), *Reform and Development of Private International Law: Essays in Honour of Sir Peter North* (Oxford, Oxford University Press, 2003) 215, 225; see also CMV Clarkson, 'Matrimonial Property on Divorce: All Change in Europe' (2008) 4 *Journal of Private International Law* 421, 424.

[45] Nishitani (n 10) 314: 'Rechtssicherheit' (author's translation).

[46] Vischer (n 41) 127.

expectation could hardly be said to be defeated by the application of German law if the parties had entered into a German choice of law contract.

B. Substantive Choice of Law Rules

The second method of allocation reflects a trend towards the 'materialisation' or 'socialisation' of choice of law rules, and designates the law that is most likely to give effect to certain substantive policies.[47] Substantive choice of law rules include rules that call for the application of the law most closely connected to only one of the parties (usually a structurally weak party such as a consumer), on the basis that application of that law is likely to be in the party's interest (see subsection i below);[48] rules that designate the applicable law on the basis of a desired outcome (such as the validity of a contract, or the degree of protection offered to one of the parties) (see subsection ii);[49] and, in its most extreme form, unilateral rules calling for the application of the law of the forum (see subsection iii). Substantive choice of law rules are capable of pursuing both external and protective interests, so there is an obvious tension between party autonomy and substantive choice of law rules.

i. Designating the Law Most Closely Connected to the Weaker Party

Increasingly common are choice of law rules that seek to protect vulnerable parties, such as maintenance creditors or consumers, by applying the law of the vulnerable party's place of habitual residence.[50] This law is applied on the assumption that vulnerable parties would always prefer (and often expect) their own law to be applicable, with which they are most likely to be familiar, and perhaps also on the basis that they could not legitimately complain about the level of protection afforded to them under their own law.

Even localising choice of law rules may, in some cases, serve a hidden substantive purpose if they are likely to lead to the application of a law that is closely connected to a vulnerable party. For example, Article 8(2) of Regulation (EC) 593/2008 on the law applicable to contractual obligations (Rome I) submits

[47] See HU Jessurun d'Oliveira, 'The EU and a Metamorphosis of Private International Law' in J Fawcett (ed), *Reform and Development of Private International Law: Essays in Honour of Sir Peter North* (Oxford, Oxford University Press, 2002) 111, 116; de Boer (n 15) 293ff; K Zweigert, 'Some Reflections on the Sociological Dimensions of Private International Law or What is Justice in the Conflict of Laws?' (1972–1973) 44 *University of Colorado Law Review* 283.

[48] de Boer (n 15) 295.

[49] S Symeonides, 'Material Justice and Conflicts Justice in Choice of Law' in PJ Borchers and J Zekoll (eds), *International Conflict of Laws for the Third Millenium: Essays in Honor of Friedrich K Juenger* (New York, Transnational Publishers, 2001) 125; Vischer (n 41) 116–18.

[50] eg, Rome I (n 24) Art 6(1); Hague Protocol on the Law Applicable to Maintenance Obligations (opened for signature 23 November 2007, entered into force 1 August 2013) (Hague Maintenance Protocol), Art 3(1) (but see Art 5).

individual employment contracts to the law of the employee's habitual place of work,[51] which is also likely to be the employee's place of residence; and the *lex loci delicti* rule, when applied to employment relationships, would often achieve a similar effect. If the employee in the introductory example was an Australian working for a New Zealand company in Australia, then the Australian employee could rely on his own law to seek damages for torts occurring in the course of his employment in Australia, which would also relieve him of the burden of proving foreign law when bringing proceedings in the courts of his own jurisdiction.

Like localising choice of law rules more generally, choice of law rules that seek to apply a law that is closely connected to the vulnerable party are not necessarily inconsistent with the party autonomy rule. A consumer might have a legitimate expectation that the law of his place of habitual residence will apply to the purchase of a product that has been marketed to him in his country by a foreign retailer; but this does not mean that the consumer should not be able to agree to the application of a foreign law, which may even be more favourable than the law of the consumer's place of habitual residence.

ii. Designating the Applicable Law on the Basis of a Desired Outcome

A greater tension between objective choice of law and party autonomy is present in choice of law rules that seek to designate the applicable law on the basis of a desired outcome. A good example is the *favor creditoris* rule in the Hague Protocol on the Law Applicable to Maintenance Obligations, which provides for alternative connecting factors to ensure that certain maintenance creditors are able to obtain maintenance.[52] In the case of maintenance obligations of parents towards children, or children towards parents, Article 4 of the Protocol applies the law of the forum (or, alternatively, the law of common nationality) if the creditor is unable to obtain maintenance from the debtor pursuant to the law of the creditor's habitual place of residence.

Choice of law rules that deal with the property consequences of registered partnerships, as a matter separate from matrimonial property, also seem to pursue a substantive outcome. For example, Article 15 of the Proposal for a Council Regulation on jurisdiction, applicable law and the recognition and enforcement of decisions regarding the property consequences of registered partnerships provides for the law of the state of registration;[53] and the principal purpose of this rule appears

[51] Rome I (n 24).

[52] Hague Maintenance Protocol (n 50) Art 4; see also Hague Convention on the Law Applicable to Maintenance Obligations 1056 UNTS 204 (opened for signature 2 October 1973, entered into force 1 October 1977) Arts 5 and 6.

[53] Proposal for a Council Regulation on jurisdiction, applicable law and the recognition and enforcement of decisions regarding the property consequences of registered partnerships (COM 2011, 127). See, for an exception to this rule, Art 15(2) of the new compromise text of the Proposal, annexed to Council of the European Union, 'Proposal for a Council Regulation on jurisdiction, applicable law and the recognition and enforcement of decisions regarding the property consequences of registered partnerships—Political agreement' (Note, 14652/15, Brussels, 26 November 2015).

to be to ensure the application of a law that recognises such partnerships.[54] Similar provisions can be found in German[55] and French law.[56] The German rule also provides, however, that the consequences of foreign registered partnerships cannot go beyond German substantive law,[57] which is similar in effect to the forum rule.

Examples of substantive choice of law rules that are focused on external interests are Articles 6 and 7 of Regulation (EC) 864/2007 on the law applicable to non-contractual obligations (Rome II).[58] Article 6(1), on the law applicable to acts of unfair competition, provides for the law of the country 'where competitive relations or the collective interests of consumers are, or are likely to be, affected', with the result that 'all participants in that particular market will be treated equally, regardless of any foreign connection';[59] and Article 7, on environmental damage, provides for the *lex loci damni* in the first instance, but gives the person seeking compensation the option of choosing the law of the country in which the event giving rise to the damage occurred, which is meant to increase environmental protection.[60]

iii. The Forum Rule

The forum rule is comparatively well established in common law jurisdictions. For example, England, New Zealand and Australia all seem to rely on unilateral forum rules to determine applications under the Matrimonial Causes Act 1973 (UK), the Family Law Act 1975 (Aust) and the Property (Relationships) Act 1976 (NZ).[61] The New Zealand Act is the only one to also provide for party autonomy. Divorce, too, is governed by the law of the forum.[62] While the application of domestic law may lead to efficiency gains, because the parties need not determine the content of foreign law, and also to improved decision-making, because the court will always be better equipped to apply its own rather than foreign law,[63] the real rationale behind this rule is usually that the relevant issue is considered so fundamental to the public interest that it could not be appropriately dealt with by foreign law.[64]

The forum rule is thus an extreme version of a substantive choice of law rule. Rather than rely on exceptions to the application of foreign law, in the form of

[54] ibid, para 5.3.
[55] EGBGB, Art 17b.
[56] Code Civil, Art 515-7-1.
[57] EGBGB, Art 17(b)(4).
[58] Rome II (n 26). See ThM de Boer, 'The Purpose of Uniform Choice-of-Law Rules: the Rome II Regulation' (2009) 56 *Netherlands International Law Review* 295, paras 5.3 and 5.4.
[59] de Boer (n 58) 323.
[60] ibid, 325.
[61] See *Radmacher v Granatino* [2010] UKSC 42, [2011] AC 534 [103]; *Marriage of Hannema* (1981) 7 Fam LR 542 (FC) (but see Mary Keyes, 'Financial Agreements in International Family Litigation' (2011) 25 *Australian Journal of Family Law* 167, 183 that the provisions of the Family Law Act should not be interpreted to apply to foreign financial agreements); Property (Relationships) Act 1976 (NZ), s 7.
[62] Collins (n 24) para 18R-032. cp IPRG, Art 61.
[63] See Clarkson (n 44) 430.
[64] See Vischer (n 41) 123.

overriding mandatory rules or public policy, the forum rule excludes the application of foreign law altogether. But it is important to appreciate that the effect of the rule is usually tempered by limitations on the court's subject-matter jurisdiction. Because the court has limited jurisdiction to hear family law matters with foreign elements, it is not every divorce or family law claim that is subject to the law of the forum. Subject-matter jurisdiction may require, for example, that at least one of the parties is domiciled or habitually resident in the forum.[65] This does not change the fact that the forum rule is driven by substance. But the limitations on subject-matter jurisdiction ensure that the forum has at least *some* connection with the case before these substantive concerns become operative.

Confusingly, the common law choice of law rules on matrimonial property, which continue to be applicable in limited circumstances,[66] display no such substantive policies. On the contrary, common law rules apply the party autonomy rule to matrimonial property contracts and, it seems, to the effect of marriage on property more generally.[67] In the absence of choice, the applicable law is the proper law of the matrimonial property contract,[68] the law of the matrimonial domicile[69] or the *lex situs*.[70] Where the parties have not entered into a matrimonial property contract, courts have even resorted to imputing an implied matrimonial contract on the basis of the parties' choice of matrimonial property regime, in order to give effect to the law that the parties expected to be applicable at the time.[71] There is a real disconnect, therefore, between the common law and the statutory approach to choice of law in matrimonial matters. In English law, for example, matrimonial property and maintenance disputes are determined as ancillary applications to divorce proceedings under the Matrimonial Causes Act 1973. In *Radmacher v Granatino*, the Supreme Court held that English law applied to an application under the Act, and that the parties' choice of German law was relevant only to the extent that it indicated an intention by the parties to be bound by their prenuptial agreement, such agreements generally being enforceable under German law.[72] Under common law rules, the choice of German law would have been given effect.

A variation on the forum rule is the double actionability rule, which still applies to torts in New Zealand, and which requires that a tort committed abroad must be actionable both under New Zealand law and under the *lex loci delicti*.[73] The rule, which has been abolished in England and Australia, is 'intended to operate as a

[65] See Matrimonial and Family Proceedings Act 1984, s 15.

[66] See Collins (n 24) ch 28; Keyes (n 61) 18; *Murakami v Wiryadi* [2010] NSWCA 7, (2010) 268 ALR 377; R Fisher (ed), *Fisher on Matrimonial and Relationship Property* (online looseleaf ed, Butterworths) paras 1.55, 1.61.

[67] Collins (n 24) paras 28R-031 and 28-020; see *Re Egerton's Will Trusts* [1956] Ch 593.

[68] ibid, 28R-031.

[69] ibid, 28R-001.

[70] But see *Murakami v Wiryadi* [2010] NSWCA 7, (2010) 268 ALR 377; ibid, paras 28-028–28-029.

[71] See *Murakami v Wiryadi* (n 70); discussed in more detail in ch 6, s II.A.

[72] *Radmacher v Granatino* [2010] UKSC 42, [2011] AC 534 [103]–[108]. Lady Hale, who gave a dissenting judgment, adopted similar reasoning on this point at [182].

[73] *Baxter v RMC plc* [2003] 1 NZLR 305 (HC).

technique of forum control' and may be explained by a now outdated 'perception of the law of civil delict as intimately connected with the criminal law'.[74] Even if the *locus delicti* of the New Zealand employee's personal injury claim was Australia, on the basis that the asbestos-contaminated material that caused the employee's injury was supplied from Australia,[75] a New Zealand court would be required to test the employee's case under New Zealand and Australian law (unless it can invoke the exception to the double actionability rule).[76] By way of a side note, this conclusion rests on the assumption that the *lex loci delicti* rule is, in fact, applicable to personal injury claims. The Accident Compensation Act 2001 appears to provide for a unilateral forum rule for all personal injury claims falling within the scope of the Act.[77] The Act excludes, in return for compensation,[78] a claimant's right to sue for personal injuries that occur to anyone in New Zealand[79] or that occur anywhere to a person ordinarily resident in New Zealand.[80]

C. Mixed Choice of Law Rules

The third 'category' of choice of law rules are rules that combine conflicts and substantive concerns, typified by the Restatement (Second) of Conflict of Laws (1971). Most substantive choice of law rules, with the exception of the forum rule, have an indirect interest in conflicts justice, because they identify a law that is closely—but not necessarily most closely—connected to the dispute.[81] Similarly, some localising rules may have a hidden substantive purpose.[82] But the Restatement makes its double agenda explicit. Section 6 instructs the court to consider a number of factors when determining the applicable law, which include: the relevant policies of the forum as well as of other interested states, and the relative interests of those states in the determination of the particular issue; the protection of justified expectations; the basic policies underlying the particular field of law; and certainty, predictability and uniformity of result. These factors are meant to assist in the identification of the law with the 'most significant' relationship, which is a concept that is more multi-faceted than 'close connection'.[83]

[74] *Regie Nationale des Usines Renault SA v Zhang* (2002) 210 CLR 491 [60] and [46] (Gleeson CJ, Gaudron, McHugh, Gummow and Hayne JJ).

[75] This, and similar arguments, were rejected in the Australian courts: for references, see R Mortensen, 'Woodhouse Reprised: Accident Compensation and Trans-Tasman Integration' (2012) 9 *Journal of Private International Law* 1 at 22–23.

[76] *Red Sea Insurance Co Ltd v Bouygues SA* [1995] 1 AC 190 (PC).

[77] But see R Tobin and E Schoeman, 'The New Zealand Accident Compensation Scheme: The Statutory Bar and the Conflict of Laws' (2005) 53 *American Journal of Comparative Law* 493; cp Mortensen (n 75) fn 112, noting the possibility that application of the Act to cases involving New Zealand plaintiffs may be mandatory.

[78] Accident Compensation Act 2001, s 317.

[79] s 20.

[80] s 22.

[81] See above, ss B.i.

[82] ibid.

[83] Symeonides (n 19) 388.

Section 6 clearly incorporates external interests and, depending on the issue in question, is wide enough to give effect to protective interests. State interests appear to be systemic rather than focused on the outcome of individual cases. States are interested in the application of their law because 'the policies, purposes, and values embodied in a state's law *can* be adversely affected when that law is *not* applied to a case the law was intended to reach'.[84] These policies, purposes and values may include protection of the parties or of one of the parties. Whether a law was 'intended to reach' a case depends on substantive considerations, as well as on the degree of connection between the state and the case.

For example, a plaintiff in state A suffers loss after relying on an audit report that was prepared negligently by the defendant in state B.[85] Section 145 of the Restatement calls for the application of the law with the most significant relationship to the tort. Relevant contacts, set out in subsection (2), include the place where the injury occurred (state A); the place where the conduct causing the injury occurred (state B) and the residence or place of business of the parties (state A and state B). The action could not succeed under the law of state B, which seeks to protect accountants from indeterminate claims; but the action could succeed under the law of state A, which seeks to protect innocent investors and to encourage accountants to exercise care. Thus, both states have an interest in protecting or regulating state B's accountants who cause loss to plaintiffs in state A; and a court would have to weigh state A's and state B's respective interests in the application of their laws.

The problem with such a fluid approach to determining the applicable law is that, depending on the case in question, party autonomy may or may not be an appropriate option. If the predominant interest of state A is to protect investors, and the predominant interest of state B is to protect accountants, these protective interests may well be incompatible with party autonomy. But a different torts case involving different groups of parties may raise entirely different considerations. This problem does not arise where the Restatement pre-selects the law with the most significant relationship; and it arises to a lesser extent where the Restatement provides a presumptive law with the most significant relationship. But even here, the range of possible public policy concerns that would have gone into the formulation of the rule makes an assessment of party autonomy difficult.

III. The Risks and Benefits of Contractualisation

The previous section considered whether objective choice of law rules pursue public policies. This is the first of three questions that ought to be asked when

[84] S Symeonides, 'The American Choice-of-Law Revolution in the Courts: Today and Tomorrow' (2003) 298 *Recueil des Cours* 9, 364.

[85] See *Performance Motorcars of Westchester Inc v KPMG Peat Marwick* 643 A2d 39 (NJAD 1994), on which this example is based.

determining the appropriate scope of party autonomy. The second question is whether the contractualisation of objective choice of law would have undesirable implications. If the freedom of parties to regulate their own affairs is of inherent value, party autonomy may amount to a powerful counterweight when balanced against competing public policies. But there may also be risks associated with the contractualisation of choice of law that go beyond the public policy concerns that have already been addressed, namely the risk that parties would be unable to reach a free and informed agreement on the applicable law, and dangers resulting from a 'commodification' of the applicable law.

A. Value of Party Autonomy

It has already been noted that party choice is a useful tool for achieving some of the purposes of objective connecting factors, such as uniformity of outcome, certainty, and giving effect to the parties' expectations.[86] But party autonomy may also be understood as a rule of inherent value—a rule that should be given effect simply because it embodies the parties' right to self-determination and establishes the individual as an independent actor on the international plane.[87] Once a relationship assumes international or cross-border dimensions and has become detached from any one legal system, the usual reasons for restricting autonomy by reference to substantive law no longer hold true.

It is immaterial for present purposes whether this principle of autonomy is grounded in domestic or in international law,[88] and how it is best explained as part of political-liberal theory.[89] The important point is that a decision to grant or refuse party autonomy must weigh any competing considerations of public policy against the interference, by mandatory choice of law, with the parties' right to self-determination. A possible manifestation of this approach is the Property (Relationships) Act 1976 (NZ), which, in section 7, provides for a unilateral choice of law rule predicating the application of the Act on comparatively generous connecting factors, but also provides for party autonomy in section 7A.[90]

[86] See J Schmeding, 'Zur Bedeutung der Rechtswahl im Kollisionsrecht: Ein Beitrag zur funktionalen Methode nach von Mehren/Trautman' (1977) 41 *Rabels Zeitschrift für ausländisches und internationales Privatrecht* 299 for a functional explanation of party autonomy based on Governmental Interest Analysis.

[87] See, eg, Jayme (n 41) 147ff; S Leible, 'Parteiautonomie im IPR—Allgemeines Anknüpfungsprinzip oder Verlegenheitslösung?' in HP Mansel (ed), *Festschrift für Erik Jayme* (Munich, Sellier, 2004) 485, 488; Flessner (n 41) 106; Nishitani (n 10) 325; cp Basedow (n 10) 50–54; TM Yetano, 'The Constitutionalisation of Party Autonomy in European Family Law' (2010) 6 *Journal of Private International Law* 155, 157ff and 191.

[88] See Mills (n 28) 291ff.

[89] See JA Pontier, 'The Justification of Choice of Law: A Liberal-Political Theory as a Critical and Explanatory Model, and the Field of International Consumer Transactions as an Example' (1998) 45 *Netherlands International Law Review* 388.

[90] Another explanation is that s 7A was intended to reflect a corresponding degree of substantive freedom that allows parties to enter into relationship property agreements (s 21): see above, s I.

B. Capacity to Enter into a Free and Informed Choice of Law Contract

Relationships that involve non-commercial parties are often characterised by power imbalances, bounded rationality and a corresponding potential for exploitation, and unpredictability. In these circumstances, there could be concerns that parties such as spouses, consumers or employees are not capable of exercising their choice in a free and informed manner. In particular, it is true that party choice may lead to injustice because the choice can be tailored to suit the stronger party's needs, and may even be used as a tool of exploitation. Such concerns are especially relevant where objective choice of law rules serve a protective purpose.

If party autonomy is considered to have inherent value, then often these concerns may not in themselves be a reason against party autonomy.[91] Instead, it would be necessary to determine whether there are appropriate safeguards that can be relied upon to ensure contractual justice while retaining a meaningful degree of freedom for the parties. The party autonomy rule might have to be regulated to take account of the likely vulnerability of certain parties. Such regulation can take different shapes and forms. One of these forms of regulation—namely rules on the existence and validity of choice of law contracts—will be explored more generally in subsequent chapters.[92] Lawmakers may also restrict the scope of party autonomy—by placing limitations on the reach of the chosen law, by limiting the parties' choice to laws that are closely connected, or by imposing overriding mandatory rules.

There is a link here between substantive autonomy and party choice, because parties who are thought to be capable of private ordering by substantive law may also be trusted with choice of law. The inverse reasoning does not apply necessarily. It may not be unprincipled for a legal system to rely on the party autonomy rule in relation to matrimonial relationships even if it did not give spouses the freedom to regulate their own affairs at a substantive level. This is merely a reiteration of the point that has already been made. Party autonomy may still be appropriate because of the relative substantive vacuum of objective choice of law, which, unlike family law, does not usually seek to ensure an outcome that is fair in substance. Coming back to the introductory example, even if German family law consisted almost exclusively of mandatory rules, this resistance against private ordering at a substantive level would not translate into a need to exclude the party autonomy rule, because the objective law applicable to the French-German couple's relationship would be English law, which might not contain any of the protections offered by the mandatory rules of German family law.

[91] But cp Vischer (n 41) 127.
[92] See chs 6–8.

C. Commodification of the Applicable Law

It has been said that the party autonomy rule turns '[the applicable law] into a commodity that private parties can demand and need not even pay for'.[93] Is there something wrong with this 'commodification' of the applicable law, which allows parties to treat it as a product that they can choose to suit their needs? The French-German couple might wish to choose the law of Belgium, even though their relationship has no connection at all with Belgium, because both spouses once lived in that country and consider the law to best reflect their interests. Would such a choice of law be inappropriate?

Unless party autonomy interferes with the public policies of objective choice of law,[94] or a limitation on the choice of applicable laws is intended to reduce the risk of unfairness,[95] it is not clear why the parties' freedom of choice ought to be restricted on the ground that the parties may otherwise base their choice on the content of the chosen law.[96] In these circumstances, a forum that is willing to apply the party autonomy rule should also be prepared to relinquish control over the subject of the parties' choice. If, in the absence of choice, a German court would apply English law to the French-German couple's relationship because this is the law that they would have expected to be applicable, there would be just as much reason, in principle, to recognise a choice of Belgian law as there would be to recognise a choice of German law.

Indeed, the ability to choose the law that best reflects the parties' needs is one of the factors that is usually cited in support of the party autonomy rule in contracts.[97] Party choice in this context has even been described as *délocalisateur*.[98] This same reasoning should also apply to non-commercial parties. It would be wrong, for example, to reject party autonomy for the property consequences of registered partnerships on the basis of 'the differences between the national laws of those [states] that make provision for registered partnerships'.[99] On the contrary, party autonomy 'might be even more relevant against a background that offers a

[93] F Rödl, 'Private Law Beyond the Democratic Order? On the Legitimatory Problem of Private Law "Beyond the State"' (2008) 56 *American Journal of Comparative Law* 743, 749.

[94] See above, s II.

[95] See above, s III.B.

[96] See also ch 8, s III; cp J Fawcett, 'Evasion of Law and Mandatory Rules in Private International Law' (1990) 49 *CLJ* 44, 50 (for the proposition that a desire to evade the law is not 'in itself morally reprehensible').

[97] See, eg, *Beximco Pharmaceuticals Ltd v Shamil Bank of Bahrain* [2004] EWCA Civ 19, [2004] 1 WLR 1784 [54], where Potter LJ said that 'English law is a law commonly adopted internationally as the governing law for banking and commercial contracts, having a well-known and well developed jurisprudence in that respect'. The parties in that case had no connection to England.

[98] J-M Jacquet, 'La Théorie de l'Autonomie de la Volonté' in S Corneloup and N Joubert (eds), *Le Règlement Communautaire 'Rome I' et le Choix de Loi dans les Contrats Internationaux* (Paris, LexisNexis, 2011) 1, 11.

[99] Proposal for a Reg on the property consequences of registered partnerships (n 53) para 5.3.

higher degree of diversity compared to one where the applicable laws differ to a lesser degree'.[100]

The commodification of the applicable law would be of concern only if it were to lead to a race to the bottom through the creation of a law market.[101] With party choice, a market for the applicable law does not depend on the physical exit by parties from states whose law they consider unfavourable.[102] States could therefore more easily compete for the application of their own law; and party autonomy might in turn result in the application of the law that is least restrictive, because states, as the suppliers of the applicable law, would have an incentive to produce a regulatory framework that meets the perceived needs of its consumers.

While there has been a veritable 'battle of the brochures' between the governments of the United Kingdom, France and Germany to advertise their legal systems to international commercial actors,[103] there is only very limited evidence that party autonomy gives rise to such regulatory competition.[104] This may be due to the fact that parties often choose the applicable law for reasons other than its content; as well as to a certain degree of apathy on the part of lawmakers to reform their legal systems in accordance with the needs of international parties.[105] In fact, it is not entirely clear what incentives there may be for lawmakers to engage in such regulatory competition,[106] particularly in relation to non-commercial matters.[107]

All in all, party autonomy is unlikely to lead to a race to the bottom. The only example of such an approach, it seems, is the Unfair Contract Terms Act 1977, whose protective provisions on exclusion of liability clauses do not apply to contracts that, but for an English choice of law clause, would not be subject to English law.[108] In 2005, the Law Commission recommended that this exemption be retained 'on the grounds that where foreign commercial parties choose English or Scots law to govern their relationship, their background understanding is that it is a law where freedom of contract prevails'.[109]

[100] European Union Agency for Fundamental Rights, *Opinion on the Proposal for a regulation on jurisdiction, applicable law and the recognition and enforcement of decisions regarding the property consequences of registered partnerships* (1/2012) para 2.2.1. See the new compromise text of the Proposal (n 53), which now provides for party autonomy.

[101] See G Rühl, 'Regulatory Competition in Contract Law: Empirical Evidence and Normative Implications' (2013) 9 *European Review of Contract Law* 61, who argues that regulatory competition in contract law will generally lead to a 'race to the top', but that it may lead to a 'race to the bottom' where choice of law does not account for the interests of third parties.

[102] See EA O'Hara and LE Ribstein, *The Law Market* (New York, Oxford University Press, 2009); H Eidenmüller, 'Recht als Produkt' (2009) 64 *Juristenzeitung* 641; cp H Muir Watt, 'Concurrence d'ordres juridiques et conflits de lois de droit privé' in *Le droit international privé: esprit et méthodes, Mélanges en l'honneur de Paul Lagarde* (Paris, Dalloz, 2005) 616.

[103] S Vogenauer, 'Regulatory Competition through Choice of Contract Law and Choice of Forum in Europe: Theory and Evidence' (2013) 21 *European Review of Private Law* 13, 30ff.

[104] ibid, 35ff; but see Rühl (n 101).

[105] Vogenauer (n 103) 53 and 60ff.

[106] See ibid, 27–29.

[107] See O'Hara and Ribstein (n 102) ch 8.

[108] Unfair Contract Terms Act 1977, s 27; see Vogenauer (n 103) 67.

[109] Law Commission, *Unfair Terms in Contracts* (Law Com No 292, 2005) para 7.28.

IV. Reconciling Party Choice with Public Policy

The party autonomy rule may conflict with public policies of objective choice of law; and the contractualisation of objective choice of law, too, may give rise to public policy concerns. Depending on the significance of these public policies, they may be a reason to refuse parties the power of party autonomy. It is trite to observe that the freedom to choose the applicable law should not come at all costs. But as in substantive law, party autonomy need not always be a blunt instrument that is either granted or refused.[110] When balancing party autonomy with conflicting considerations of public policy, account should be taken of restrictions on party autonomy and overriding mandatory rules. Such limitations may be able to provide a regulatory framework that provides for party autonomy while safeguarding important public policies.

There are three ways in which the scope of party autonomy may be limited to protect conflicting public policies: through restrictions on the choice of applicable laws (see section A), through specific exclusions to the party autonomy rule (see section B), or through restrictions on the effect of the chosen law, particularly in the form of overriding mandatory rules (see section C). These regulatory tools sit alongside protective rules on the existence and validity of choice of law contracts,[111] which will be discussed in subsequent chapters.

A. Restrictions on the Choice of Applicable Laws

Where objective choice of law rules serve a protective function, it may be appropriate to restrict party choice to a selection of applicable laws in order to reduce the risk that vulnerable parties are disadvantaged through their choice of a particularly unfavourable law.[112] An example of this technique is Article 8 of the Hague Protocol on the Law Applicable to Maintenance Obligations,[113] which provides that parties may select the law of either party's nationality or habitual residence, the law applicable to the parties' property regime, or the law applicable to their divorce or separation. As a result, the French-German couple in the introductory example would be limited to a choice of English, French or German law to govern their maintenance obligations. The rich German wife would not be able to insist on the application of an entirely unconnected law that would have the effect of significantly limiting the French husband's right to maintenance. This, in turn, would be consistent with the protective function of the objective choice of law

[110] See also Leible (n 87) 488.

[111] On the need to take account of the interrelationship between these approaches, see ch 5.

[112] This rationale is adopted by Carruthers (n 20) 912 (in relation to matrimonial matters). See also ch 8, s III.

[113] Hague Maintenance Protocol (n 50).

rule in Article 3, which calls for application of the law of the creditor's place of habitual residence.

There are many other apparent examples of this technique.[114] Even in New Zealand, where the Property (Relationships) Act does not impose any limitations on the parties' choice unless application of the law would be 'contrary to justice or public policy', the High Court has noted that insufficient connection by the parties to the chosen law may be a relevant factor in determining whether the choice is enforceable.[115]

In some circumstances, it may even be possible to confine the parties' choice on the basis of certain substantive criteria. If registered partnerships are submitted to the law of the state of registration to ensure application of a law that recognises such partnerships,[116] then arguably parties ought to be free to choose the applicable law as long as the applicable law recognises such partnerships. Article 15-03 of the new compromise text of the Proposal for a Regulation on the property consequences of registered partnerships thus provides that parties may choose the applicable law 'provided that that law attaches property consequences to the institution of the registered partnership' (and provided the choice satisfies one of a number of pre-selected connecting factors).[117] The wholesale exclusion of party autonomy from the original Proposal for a Regulation on the property consequences of registered partnerships (as well as from Article 515-7-1 of the French Civil Code) seems unjustified.[118]

It is also conceivable that restrictions on the choice of applicable laws could be used to uphold a localising function of objective choice of law. If the objective choice of law rule designates the law with the closest connection, and there is more than one law that could be considered to be most closely connected, then there is no harm in letting the parties select one of these laws. For example, spouses could be granted a choice between the law of the parties' common habitual residence and the law of their common nationality.

More problematic are general restrictions on the choice of applicable laws that do not reflect any obvious public policy concerns. Section 187 of the Restatement (Second) requires that the chosen law have a 'substantial relationship to the parties or the transaction', or (alternatively) that the parties have a 'reasonable basis' for their choice.[119] These restrictions do not safeguard the aims of the functional

[114] Art 5 of Rome III (n 27); Art 16 of the Proposal for a Reg on matrimonial property (n 33); Art 5 of Rome I (n 24) on contracts of carriage; and Art 7 of Rome I (n 24) on insurance contracts; EGBGB, Art 15(2); Hague Convention 1978 (n 27) Art 3; but see the French approach prior to the coming into force of the Hague Convention 1978, as described in M Revillard, 'Premier bilan de la Convention de La Haye du 14 mars 1978 sur la loi applicable aux régimes matrimoniaux' in A Borrás et al (eds), *E Pluribus Unum. Liber Amicorum Georges AL Droz* (The Hague, Martinus Nijhoff, 1996) 369, 372; cp Collins (n 24) para 28-034.

[115] *Bergner v Nelis* HC Auckland CIV-2004-404-149, 19 December 2005 [27].

[116] See above, s II.B.ii, III.C.

[117] Compromise text of the Proposal (n 53).

[118] But cp S Davis, 'Same-sex Couples and the Harmonisation of EU Matrimonial Property Regimes: Unjustifiable Discrimination or Missed Opportunities?' (2013) 25 *Child and Family Law Quarterly* 19.

[119] See also s 1-301(a), American Law Institute, *Uniform Commercial Code* (2008).

choice of law approach of section 188. They do not ensure that the chosen law is that of a state interested in the application of its law. They also do not seem to be concerned—at least not primarily—with protecting parties from unfavourable choice of law agreements. Parties are free to select an unconnected law on the basis, for example, that the law is particularly familiar to them, or that it has the value of neutrality.[120] Even a state with a 'substantial relationship'—which seems to describe a close connection in the localising sense—is not necessarily a state that is particularly interested in the application of its law.[121] If, as has been suggested, the purpose of the limitations is to avoid choices of law in relation to 'essentially local transactions', then this purpose could be achieved by a less restrictive requirement of internationality.[122]

B. Specific Exclusions to the Party Autonomy Rule

Public policies of objective choice of law rules may also be protected by specific exclusions to the reach of the party autonomy rule. An example of this is Article 8(4) of the Hague Maintenance Protocol, which provides that, notwithstanding any choice of law by the parties, the question of whether the creditor can renounce his or her right to maintenance is to be determined by the law of the creditor's place of habitual residence; and by Article 6 of Rome II, which submits acts of unfair competition to the law of the country where competitive relations are likely to be affected, and which specifically excludes the party autonomy rule.[123]

Exclusions to party autonomy can also operate to accommodate third party interests. Article 14 of Rome II, for example, provides that the parties' choice 'shall not prejudice the rights of third parties'.[124] To the extent that third party interests may be the main reason why, in international property law, the *lex situs* rule is generally considered mandatory, such exclusions could provide a basis for increasing reliance on the party autonomy rule in relation to inter partes rights in rem.[125] Rights to intangible property, in particular, might well fall within the private justice paradigm of choice of law.[126] In the context of matrimonial property disputes, it has been suggested that the *lex situs* should determine the spouses' matrimonial property when third parties are involved;[127] or that, in certain circumstances, the

[120] P Hay, P Borchers and S Symeonides, *Conflict of Laws* 5th edn (St Paul, West Academic Publishing, 2010) 1090.

[121] ibid, 1092.

[122] ibid, 1091.

[123] See also Rome III (n 27) Art 10.

[124] cp Rome I (n 24) Art 3(2), which states that a change in the applicable law must not adversely affect the rights of third parties.

[125] See generally Westrik and van der Weide (n 40).

[126] See, eg, Art 14 of Rome I (n 24), which submits the relationship between assignor and assignee to the law governing the parties' contract (including the 'property aspects' of the assignment: Recital 38); and the possibility of party autonomy in intellectual property: R Matulionyte, 'Calling for Party Autonomy in Intellectual Property Infringement Cases' (2013) 9 *Journal of Private International Law* 77.

[127] Hartley (n 44) 233.

law applicable to a matrimonial property regime may not be relied on by a spouse in dealings with a third party if that party did not have constructive knowledge of the applicable law.[128]

C. Restrictions on the Effect of the Chosen Law

A third option for reconciling party autonomy with conflicting public policies is to impose restrictions on the effect of the chosen law by deferring to the objective applicable law where this serves an external or protective interest.

i. Reliance on Simple Mandatory Rules of the Objective Applicable Law

Rome I subjects certain consumer and employment contracts to the mandatory rules of the objective law where these offer more protection than the chosen law. These mandatory rules of the objective law are simple mandatory rules that 'cannot be derogated from by agreement' as a matter of substantive law.[129] The 'principle of the more favourable law' thus combines the benefits of party autonomy with a need to give effect to the protective policies of objective choice of law rules, by converting the pursuit of substantive choice of law interests—such as the protection of consumers through the application of the law of the consumer's habitual place of residence—into a direct application of substantive law where this is of benefit to the consumers.

ii. Internationally Mandatory Rules/Public Policy of the Objective Applicable Law

It is a general rule of the conflict of laws that internationally mandatory rules of the forum override the applicable law, and that the applicable law applies only to the extent that it does not infringe fundamental public policies of the forum. Mandatory rules or public policies *of the forum* do not respond to public policies pursued by objective choice of law rules (unless the objective choice of law rule is the *lex fori* rule)—but in some circumstances, mandatory rules or public policies of the objective applicable law may.[130] Thus, another means of reconciling party autonomy with public policies of objective choice of law rules is to give effect to

[128] See Proposal for a Reg on matrimonial property (n 33) Art 35(2), as well as Art 20 b of the compromise text of the Proposal, annexed to Council of the European Union, 'Proposal for a Council Regulation on jurisdiction, applicable law and the recognition and enforcement of decisions in matters of matrimonial property regimes—Political agreement' (Note, 14651/15, Brussels, 26 November 2015). cp Hague Convention 1978 (n 27) Art 9; EGBGB, Art 16; IPRG, Art 57.

[129] Rome I (n 24) Arts 6(2) and 8(1).

[130] cp overriding mandatory rules of the forum that apply only if the *lex fori* is also the objective applicable law: see ch 5, s V.

internationally mandatory rules or fundamental public policies of the objective applicable law.

For example, if Australian courts apply the *lex loci delicti* to give effect to a regulatory interest by the state on whose territory the tort occurred, then party autonomy might still be appropriate if application of the state's overriding mandatory rules was sufficient to meet that interest. In that case, an Australian court would be able to decline application of Australian law to the personal injury claim of the New Zealand employee by giving effect to New Zealand's Accident Compensation Act (provided the Act is treated as an overriding mandatory rule).[131]

The Restatement (Second) relies heavily on this approach. Section 187(2)(b) provides that the chosen law will not be given effect if its application 'would be contrary to a fundamental policy of [the objective applicable law]', provided the state has a 'materially greater interest than the chosen state in the determination of the particular issue'.[132] This safeguard is consistent with the public policies pursued by section 188. For example, in a case involving a New York telephone company and its Washington customers, a choice of New York law allowing waivers of class actions was contrary to a fundamental policy of Washington to support the use of class actions for small consumer claims.[133] The objective applicable law would have been the law of Washington, and 'Washington's interest in protecting large classes of its consumers materially outweigh[ed] New York's limited interest in this matter'.[134]

With the exception of the United States, most jurisdictions currently do not have regard to the fundamental public policies or internationally mandatory rules of foreign states (unless they are concerned with an issue of illegality of performance).[135] Article 19 of the Swiss Bundesgesetz über das Internationale Privatrecht (IPRG) calls for the application of foreign overriding mandatory rules where such rules have a close connection to the issue and protect an overriding interest of one of the parties. But Article 19 is not limited to circumstances in which parties have chosen the applicable law.

Perhaps this reluctance to use overriding rules of the objective applicable law lends support to the view that most choice of law rules are, in fact, firmly wedded to a non-paternalistic private justice paradigm, seeking to give effect to the parties' expectations rather than external or protective interests. In these circumstances, the rationale for restricting party autonomy would fall away, as would the principal reason for mandatory choice of law.

[131] See above at n 77.

[132] cp s 1-301, American Law Institute, *Uniform Commercial Code* (2008).

[133] *McKee v AT & T Corp* 164 Wash 2d 372 (2008).

[134] ibid, [21].

[135] Rome I (n 24) Art 9(3); see J Harris, 'Mandatory Rules and Public Policy under the Rome I Regulation' in F Ferrari and S Leible (eds), *Rome I Regulation: The Law Applicable to Contractual Obligations in Europe* (Munich, Sellier, 2009) 269, 274ff; but cp A Chong, 'The Public Policy and Mandatory Rules of Third Countries in International Contracts' (2006) 2 *Journal of Private International Law* 27; P Mayer and V Heuzé, *Droit international privé* 10th edn (Paris, LGDJ, 2014) paras 131ff.

iii. Classification as Internationally Mandatory Rule/Public Policy

Linked to this previous issue is the question of classification: what counts as an internationally mandatory rule or as fundamental public policy? Traditionally the concept of overriding mandatory rules has been confined to 'semi-public' or public law rules;[136] and the *ordre public* exception has been reserved for the most serious principles of justice.[137] Under a more functional approach, overriding mandatory rules and public policy serve as a regulatory backstop to protect all those 'mandatory' aims of choice of law that would otherwise be threatened by the parties' agreement. The concept of 'fundamental policy' in section 187 of the Restatement is broader than the traditional notion of *ordre public*,[138] extending to such matters as non-compete covenants in employment contracts[139] and the regulation of franchises.[140] However, it is not enough that the chosen law simply differs from the objective applicable law—otherwise the point of party autonomy would be defeated.[141]

This functional approach could also be relevant to other choice of law rules pursuing public policies, particularly the forum rule. In the family context, overriding mandatory rules could include rules for the protection of the family home,[142] or rules providing for a no-fault divorce. Section 7A(3) of the Property (Relationships) Act (NZ) may well be an example of this, providing that the chosen law will not be applied if it is 'contrary to justice or public policy'. The concept of 'justice or public policy' seems to impose a higher threshold than rules and policies that would be considered mandatory in a domestic context, while imposing a lower threshold than internationally overriding mandatory rules and public policy as these concepts are traditionally understood. The Family Court has thus relied on section 7A(3) to strike down a South-African pre-nuptial agreement because the agreement amounted to unjust enrichment under New Zealand common law.[143]

[136] This seems to be particularly true of civil law countries: F Maultzsch, 'Rechtswahl und ius cogens im Internationalen Schuldvertragsrecht' (2011) 75 *Rabels Zeitschrift für ausländisches und internationales Privatrecht* 60, 82–92. Yetano (n 87) 177 considers that there is 'No such thing as internationally mandatory rules' in family law; but see G Rühl, 'Rechtswahlfreiheit im europäischen Kollisionsrecht' in D Baetge et al (eds), *Die Richtige Ordnung: Festschrift für Jan Kropholler* (Tübingen, Mohr Siebeck, 2008) 187, 206.

[137] *Loucks v Standard Oil Co of New York* (1918) 120 NE 198, 202.

[138] *Restatement (Second)* (n 18) s 187, cmnt (g).

[139] Hay, Borchers and Symeonides (n 120) para 18.6.

[140] ibid, para 18.7.

[141] *Restatement (Second)* (n 18) s 187, cmnt (g).

[142] See Proposal for a Reg on matrimonial property (n 33) Art 22 and the Explanatory Memorandum, para 5.3; *Asser Report* (n 27) 159–60.

[143] *Pretorius v Pretorius* [2000] NZFLR 72 (FC) 77. The High Court has left open the question whether a 'materially different outcome' under the chosen law would be sufficient to satisfy s 7A(3): *Bergner v Nelis* HC Auckland CIV-2004-404-149, 19 December 2005 [26].

V. Scope of the Party Autonomy Rule

It is obvious by now that the proper scope of party autonomy depends on many variables. A determinative assessment of party autonomy would require an in-depth analysis of these variables and is beyond the confines of this work. But it is still possible to hazard a rough evaluation of the status quo of the party autonomy rule, as well as of its potential.

A. Contract

Party autonomy is well-established in relation to commercial contracts.[144] This makes sense if the predominant purpose of objective choice of law rules is to facilitate private interests. Where objective choice of law pursues no public policies, parties should be free to choose the applicable law unless the risks of contractualisation are unmanageable. It is quite possible that most localising choice of law rules on contract serve neither external nor protective public policies. Section 188 of the Restatement is the obvious exception here; but balanced against the value of party autonomy and the safeguard of the 'fundamental public policy' exception, section 188 clearly need not be a mandatory rule. On the other hand, the additional requirement of a substantial relationship/reasonable basis seems out of place, because it does not appear to serve a well-defined choice of law interest.[145]

Party autonomy is less well established in relation to specific contracts that involve imbalances in bargaining power. This seems to be consistent with public policies pursued by corresponding objective choice of law rules, and it may also be a response to the obvious risks associated with contractualising choice of law in this area. The Swiss IPRG excludes party autonomy for consumer contracts[146] and limits the choice of laws applicable to employment contracts;[147] and Rome I imposes restrictions on party autonomy in contracts of carriage, consumer contracts, insurance contracts and employment contracts.[148]

Conversely, jurisdictions like New Zealand and Australia that subject all contracts to simple localising choice of law rules do not tend to regulate party autonomy in relation to particular types of contracts. With the exception of some specific exclusions to party autonomy,[149] the only mechanisms to keep this power

[144] This is reflected in Hague Conference on Private International Law, *Principles on Choice of Law in International Commercial Contracts* (approved on 19 March 2015).

[145] See above, s IV.A.

[146] IPRG, Art 120.

[147] Art 121(3).

[148] Rome I (n 24) Arts 5–8.

[149] eg, s 137(b) of the Credit Contracts and Consumer Finance Act 2003 (NZ) and sch 2, s 67 of the Competition and Consumer Act 2010 (Aust).

in check are the forum's overriding mandatory rules and *ordre public*. Given the (presumably) private and facilitative nature of localising choice of law rules for contracts, this hands-off approach is not surprising. But it does raise the question whether rules on the existence and validity of choice of law contracts are enough to address the obvious risks of contractualisation.

B. Tort

The European Union is at the forefront of recognising party autonomy for non-contractual obligations. Article 14 of Rome II provides that parties may agree to submit non-contractual obligations to the law of their choice once the event giving rise to the damage has occurred, unless all the parties are pursuing a commercial activity. The general choice of law rule for torts is a localising choice of law rule, the *lex loci damni*.[150] If the predominant purpose of this rule is to facilitate private interests, Article 14 is consistent with it. The limitation to post-tort party choice is clearly designed to mitigate the risks of contractualisation for non-commercial parties. Where objective choice of law is perceived to serve external interests—for example, in the case of actions for the infringement of intellectual property rights—party autonomy is excluded.

The Swiss IPRG also allows for party autonomy in relation to non-contractual obligations, but the parties' choice is limited to the law of the forum after the event causing the damage occurred.[151] The general choice of law rule for non-contractual obligations is localising in nature, calling for application of the law of common habitual residence, the *lex loci delicti* or the *lex loci damni*.[152] Localising choice of law rules serve only a tenuous protective function.[153] So limiting the parties' choice to the *lex fori* is arguably incongruous, unless this rule is concerned with external interests and the choice of forum law is offered for the sake of convenience.

A similar tension exists in the choice of law rules of Australia, which subjects tortious obligations to the *lex loci delicti*,[154] and does not appear to recognise the party autonomy rule for torts. It is not clear whether the *lex loci delicti* is applied as a matter of comity,[155] or whether its main function is to achieve justice between the parties.[156] If the rule does not serve a public policy function, and if parties are able to enter into a free and informed choice of law contract to choose the law governing their non-contractual obligations, then party autonomy should be available as a matter of principle. For example, if the *lex loci delicti* is not applied

150 Rome II (n 26) Art 4(1).
151 IPRG, Art 132.
152 Art 133.
153 See above, s II.A.iii.
154 See generally *Regie Nationale des Usines Renault SA v Zhang* (2002) 210 CLR 491.
155 ibid, [64] (Gleeson CJ, Gaudron, McHugh, Gummow and Hayne JJ), citing *Tolofson v Jensen* [1994] 3 SCR 1022 [37] (La Forest J). See above, s II.A.ii.
156 ibid, [130] (Kirby J, footnotes omitted).

to personal injury claims in order to give effect to public policies, the New Zealand employee and his employer[157] should be free to choose Australian law pursuant to Australian choice of law rules, which, in this case, would enable the employee to 'evade' the Accident Compensation Act and bring his claim for personal injury. Where the *lex loci delicti* does pursue public policies, reliance on the overriding mandatory rules of the objective applicable law (here, New Zealand law) may still leave room for party autonomy.

Finally, the Restatement (Second) does not address the question of party autonomy in relation to non-contractual obligations. But in a 'sizeable number' of cases, US courts have held that parties did intend to encompass tort claims in their choice of law agreements, treating the question 'as a matter of contractual *intent* (rather than contractual *power*)'.[158] To the extent that the Restatement's choice of law rules for contract and tort cover similar interests, party autonomy may be equally appropriate in contract and tort.

C. Family Matters

There are many different permutations of party autonomy in the area of family law. Article 5 of Rome III, for example, provides that spouses may agree to designate the law applicable to divorce and legal separation, provided that it accords with one of a number of pre-selected connecting factors.[159] A similar approach is taken by the Hague Maintenance Protocol, the Proposal for a Regulation on matrimonial property, the new compromise text of the Proposal for a Regulation on the property consequences of registered partnerships, the Hague Convention 1978, Articles 14 and 15 of the German Einführungsgesetz zum Bürgerlichen Gesetzbuch (EGBGB) on the general effects of marriage and matrimonial property, Article 52 of the IPRG on matrimonial property, and Article 25(3) of Regulation (EU) No 650/2012 on jurisdiction, applicable law, recognition and enforcement of decisions and acceptance and enforcement of authentic instruments in matters of succession (in relation to succession agreements).[160]

Consistent with the grant of party autonomy, most of the corresponding objective choice of law rules are localising in nature.[161] But what is the rationale in those cases for limiting party autonomy to pre-selected connecting factors? The choice of connecting factors—including, for example, the law of each party's nationality—is too wide-ranging to be concerned with external interests.[162] More

[157] See the introductory example at the beginning of this chapter.

[158] Symeon C Symeonides, *Codifying Choice of Law Around the World* (New York, Oxford University Press, 2014) 101; Hay, Borchers and Symeonides (n 120) 1141–46.

[159] Rome III (n 27).

[160] Reg (EU) No 650/2012 on jurisdiction, applicable law, recognition and enforcement of decisions and acceptance and enforcement of authentic instruments in matters of succession and on the creation of a European Certificate of Succession [2012] OJ L201/107.

[161] But cp choice of law on the property consequences of registered partnerships: above, ss II.B.ii and IV.A.

[162] See above, s IV.A.

generally, the institutional character of family law is no reason why spouses should not, in principle, be able to choose a law that most properly reflects their cultural identity[163] or even their own idea of matrimonial justice.[164] The best explanation is that the restrictions are designed to reduce risks of contractualisation, which is a particular concern in family relationships.[165] Parties who are restricted to a limited choice of applicable laws have less opportunity to seek out a law that favours one of the parties disproportionately. Compared to the scope of party autonomy for contracts, this approach may be unduly paternalistic. Limiting international parties to a choice of pre-selected connecting factors is a significant infringement of their cultural autonomy. Perhaps a less restrictive—and equally effective—approach would be to rely on protective requirements for the existence and validity of choice of law agreements.[166]

Common law and US courts have recognised the party autonomy rule in relation to matrimonial property contracts and, it seems, in relation to the effect of marriage on property more generally.[167] However, in England and Australia, family matters that fall under the Matrimonial Causes Act 1973 (and the Matrimonial and Family Proceedings Act 1984) and the Family Law Act 1975, respectively, are now largely governed by the law of the forum.[168] New Zealand, too, relies heavily on the *lex fori* rule, but still provides for party autonomy in relation to claims that would otherwise fall under the Property (Relationships) Act 1976. A more functional approach to overriding mandatory rules might enable England, Australia and New Zealand to extend the reach of the party autonomy rule in relation to matrimonial matters.

In the United States, some courts have given effect to choices of law in surrogacy contracts, relying on an extension of the party autonomy rule for contracts generally.[169] This may seem like an extreme example, but in light of the exception of fundamental public policy, it is difficult to see how party autonomy for surrogacy arrangements would undermine the policies of objective choice of law rules.

D. Property

Outside of matrimonial relationships and succession agreements, parties are not usually free to select the law applicable to their property rights, which tend to

[163] On the relevance of cultural identity in private international law more generally, see Jayme (n 41) ch 7.
[164] See above, s III.C.
[165] See above, s III.B.
[166] See chs 7–8, and s III of ch 8 in particular.
[167] Collins (n 24) paras 28R-031 and 28-020; *Re Egerton's Will Trusts* [1956] Ch 593. For a recent US example, see *Hussemann ex rel Ritter v Hussemann* 847 NW2d 219 (Iowa 2014); and on party autonomy in relation to matrimonial property more generally, see *Restatement (Second)* (n 18), Art 258 and Hay, Borchers and Symeonides (n 120) 684.
[168] See above, s II.B.iii.
[169] Hay, Borchers and Symeonides (n 120) 1127–29.

be governed by the *lex situs*.[170] This is understandable to the extent that the *lex situs* reflects external interests, although a rule on the third party effects of party autonomy might loosen the grip of the *lex situs* rule on inter partes rights in rem. Article 104(2) of the IPRG, for example, provides parties with a limited choice of the law governing the acquisition and loss of movable property, but specifies that this choice of law is not effective against third parties. Some forms of property rights are also inherently 'local' in nature and cannot be divorced from the law that has created them. This is true in particular of intellectual property rights that are registered and managed by domestic agencies.

E. Choice of Non-national Rules

Objective choice of law rules designate the law of a sovereign state rather than a body of non-national rules. While a choice of non-national rules is generally permitted in arbitral proceedings,[171] courts have given effect to such rules by way of incorporation only.[172] Concerns have been voiced that the ability to choose non-national rules may 'lead to a proliferation of unfair unilateral rules of law, articulated by the party with greater bargaining power'; or that it would 'reduce the certainty of outcome' for the parties.[173] It might be possible to address these concerns by restricting the kinds of rules that parties are able to choose. Thus, Article 3 of the Hague Principles on Choice of Law in International Commercial Contracts provides that 'The law chosen by the parties may be rules of law that are generally accepted on an international, supranational or regional level as a neutral and balanced set of rules, unless the law of the forum provides otherwise'.[174]

Aside from these protective interests, there is the more fundamental question whether application of a national system of law is mandated by external interests of choice of law, including the state's interest in 'maintain[ing] its own legal monopoly' by recognising only the lawmaking power of other states.[175] At this stage, it seems unlikely that courts will recognise a general power to choose non-national rules.

[170] IPRG, Arts 99–100; EGBGB, Art 43; Code Civil, Art 3; Collins (n 24) paras 23R-062–24R-001.

[171] Code de Procédure Civile (Fr), Art 1496(1); Zivilprozessordnung (Ger), Art 1051; Arbitration Act 1996 (UK), s 46(1)(b); Arbitration Act 1996 (NZ), sch 1, Art 28; International Arbitration Act 1974 (Aust), sch 2, Art 28; IPRG, Art 187.

[172] See Collins (n 24) para 32-049.

[173] Hague Conference on Private International Law, *Report of the November 2012 Special Commission Meeting on the Choice of Law in International Contracts* (Prelim Doc No 6, February 2013) para 13.

[174] *Hague Principles on Choice of Law in International Commercial Contracts* (n 144) Art 3.

[175] See R Michaels, 'The Re-*state*-ment of Non-State Law: The State, Choice of Law, and the Challenge from Global Legal Pluralism' (2005) 51 *Wayne Law Review* 1209, 1235 and 1248.

VI. Practical Implications

The purpose of this chapter was to identify the kinds of considerations that should inform an evaluation of the party autonomy rule. Whether party choice ought in fact to be available is a balancing decision that will depend to a considerable degree on the functions accorded to objective choice of law, and on the value attributed to party autonomy. What is needed, therefore, is a renewed examination of the purposes of choice of law. If choice of law rules operate within a private justice paradigm, the current approach to party autonomy may be too conservative. If choice of law rules serve important external or protective interests, we may have taken the party autonomy rule too far.

The varied scope of party autonomy has practical implications for the way in which international parties may wish to structure the resolution of their disputes. Forum selection, in particular, can determine whether party autonomy is available and the chosen law is given effect. If parties are particularly concerned to enjoy as wide a power to choose the applicable law as possible, international arbitration could be the most suitable option. In any case, parties would be wise to combine their choice of law agreement with a forum selection agreement that complements their choice of law needs. Lone choice of law agreements are capable of producing unwanted jurisdictional effects, by 'excluding' the jurisdiction of fora that will not give effect to them.[176]

Just as important as a workable combination of party autonomy and forum selection, is a choice of law agreement whose scope is clearly defined. It is not enough to agree that the law applicable to a contract be the law of France, if French law is also intended to cover any non-contractual obligations arising between the parties. If the choice of law agreement exceeds the available scope of party autonomy, the chosen foreign law may still be incorporated into the contract as a matter of substantive law, depending on the intention of the parties and subject to the mandatory rules of the *lex causae*. But the chosen law will not be the applicable law in a choice of law sense.

It is a remarkable feat of the conflict of laws that parties enjoy such wide powers to select the applicable law. To many thinkers in the nineteenth and early twentieth centuries, the very idea of party autonomy was heretic.[177] We have come a long way since then. But party autonomy is explicable by an even stranger phenomenon: the relative normative vacuum of objective choice of law rules. There is much uncertainty about the values or interests that shape our search for the objective applicable law. On reflection, it is not surprising that party autonomy would thrive in such circumstances.

[176] M Hook, 'The Choice of Law Agreement as a Reason for Exercising Jurisdiction' (2014) 63 *ICLQ* 963.

[177] See V Ranouil, *L'Autonomie de la Volonté: Naissance et Évolution d'un Concept* (Paris, Presses Universitaires de France, 1980) 99–129 for an overview.

4

Independence of the Choice of Law Contract

I. Choice of Law in Contract—By Contract

Party choice is the exercise of a contractual power whose function is not to create or modify rights and obligations but to select the law applicable to the parties' relationship. It follows that the choice of law contract sits apart from the relationship to which it relates: it is a contract about the relationship, a contract in its own right. As such, the choice of law contract is not tied to the fate of any underlying contract that it purports to govern. It serves a dual role of connecting factor and object of connection, whose existence and validity need to be determined independently from the underlying contract.

However, the relationship between the choice of law contract and its underlying contract has long been misunderstood, which has led courts to rely on putative reasoning in giving effect to party choice. Putative reasoning assumes the existence and validity of the choice of law contract for the purpose of determining challenges to the existence and validity of the underlying contract, in circumstances in which the choice of law contract would ordinarily be struck down by these same challenges.

This chapter begins by providing a more principled analysis of the relationship between the choice of law contract and the underlying contract, before evaluating in more detail the shortcomings of the putative approach (see section II). It will then be necessary to address the implications that would arise from the rejection of putativity, both for the choice of law contract (see section III) and the underlying contract (see section IV). It is submitted that party autonomy without putativity is a feasible alternative.

A. A Distinct Rather than a Separable or Severable Contract

The argument advanced in this chapter is that the choice of law contract is self-sufficient and does not depend on the existence or validity of an underlying contract. Hence, where the parties' choice relates to a contractual relationship, or is made in the course of a contractual relationship, the existence or validity of this contract is not in itself determinative of the existence or validity of the choice of law contract. Serving an entirely separate function from the main contract, the parties' choice does not legally form part of the underlying bargain or contractual relationship.

On the contrary, the choice of law contract would lose its purpose if its existence and validity were not independently assessed because it would no longer satisfy the party autonomy rule, which requires that the law be applied that the parties jointly intended to govern. As a meta-contract that regulates the parties' contractual relationship by providing the applicable law, the choice of law contract is logically anterior in application to the main contract. It is similar, in this respect, to jurisdiction and arbitration agreements,[1] except that the choice of law contract cannot be submitted to the same applicable law as the underlying contract to determine challenges that may affect them both.

In these circumstances, the terms 'separability' or 'severability'[2] do not adequately describe the relationship between the choice of law contract and the underlying contract—implying, as they do, that there is one contract, components of which may be severed to ensure their survival.[3] Rather, the choice of law contract is a distinct contract that is factually related to the underlying contract:[4] while the two contracts may form part of the same act of agreement, and may thus be challenged on the same factual grounds, the choice of law contract is not legally one with the main contract. As Lord Hoffmann said in *Fiona Trust & Holding Corp v Privalov*, albeit in relation to arbitration agreements:

> The arbitration agreement must be treated as a 'distinct agreement' and can be void or voidable only on grounds which relate directly to the arbitration agreement. Of course there may be cases in which the ground upon which the main agreement is invalid is identical with the ground upon which the arbitration agreement is invalid. For example, if the main agreement and the arbitration agreement are contained in the same document and one of the parties claims that he never agreed to anything in the document and that his signature was forged, that will be an attack on the validity of the arbitration agreement. But the ground of attack is not that the main agreement was invalid. It is that the signature to the arbitration agreement, as a 'distinct agreement', was forged.[5]

The validity of the arbitration agreement in *Fiona Trust* fell to be determined under section 7 of the Arbitration Act 1996, but the common law position is

[1] See A Briggs, *Agreements on Jurisdiction and Choice of Law* (Oxford, Oxford University Press, 2008) para 3.19.

[2] Hague Conference on Private International Law, *Principles on Choice of Law in International Commercial Contracts* (approved on 19 March 2015), Art 7; Briggs, ibid paras 3.20ff.

[3] cp L Collins (ed), *Dicey, Morris and Collins on the Conflict of Laws* 15th edn (London, Sweet & Maxwell, 2012) para 12-129; but see P Mayer, 'Les Limites de la Séparabilité de la Clause Compromissoire' [1998] *Revue de l'arbitrage* 359, in relation to arbitration agreements.

[4] cp the concept of collateral contracts: see Briggs (n 1) para 3.13, citing *Kreglinger v New Patagonia Meat* [1914] 1 AC 25 (HL).

[5] *Fiona Trust Holding Corp v Privalov* [2007] UKHL 40, [2008] 1 Lloyd's Rep 254 [17]; cp P Schlosser, 'The Separability of Arbitration Agreements—a Model for Jurisdiction and Venue Agreements?' in T Einhorn and K Siehr (eds), *Intercontinental Cooperation Through Private International Law: Essays in Memory of Peter E Nygh* (The Hague, Asser Press, 2004) 305, 315ff.

the same, both for arbitration agreements and jurisdiction agreements.[6] In fact, section 7 simply codified the common law rule on the separability of arbitration agreements.[7]

It is wrong to ask, therefore, whether the choice of law contract 'survives' the voidness or invalidity of the main contract. The real issues are: (a) whether the choice of law contract is void or voidable, on grounds that would also affect the underlying contract, and if the choice of law contract is valid, (b) whether the validly concluded choice of law contract is sufficiently wide in scope to determine the existence or validity of the underlying contract.

B. Putativity as an Excuse for Unilateral Choice

That this is so becomes clear if the idea of the indivisible contract is taken to its logical conclusion. If the choice of law contract depended on the existence and validity of the main contract, as a mere term of the contract, application of the 'chosen' law to determine these very questions would occur putatively, and the (in)existence or (in)validity of the contract would then extend to the choice itself on a retrospective basis. As a result, only a putative choice rendering the contract valid could be considered effective, with invalidating choices setting off a potentially endless loop of choice of law, because there is no logical basis on which to give effect to a retrospectively invalid choice in order to determine the existence or validity of the contract.

But at the same time, it could not realistically be suggested that parties would never intend to choose a law under which the contract turns out to be void or invalid.[8] Thus, tying the parties' choice to the underlying contract does not accord with party autonomy, as it is logically impossible to grant parties the freedom to choose the law applicable to their relationship while making that freedom dependent on the very relationship it is supposed to regulate.

This is where the factual approach discussed in chapter two comes full circle: putativity will require effect to be given to what may, in law, be a unilateral choice of law. The parties' choice turns into an agreement outside of the law, with the result that 'The parties' choice is effective if it constitutes a "concurring idea or conception" of the applicable law [which] need not be effective as a contract (with all that that entails)'.[9] It has thus been suggested that 'autonomous' standards, rather than a governing law, be applied to assess the effectiveness of the choice of law agreement; and that it is not (only) the parties' intention, but 'the fact of

[6] *Harbour Assurance Co (UK) Ltd v Kansa General International Insurance Co Ltd* [1993] QB 701 (CA).

[7] *Fiona Trust Holding Corp v Privalov* [2007] EWCA Civ 20, [2007] 2 Lloyd's Rep 267 [23].

[8] cp the concept of the *lex validitatis*: M Abend, *Die lex validitatis im internationalen Vertragsrecht* (Heidelberg, Winter, 1994); ch 6, s IV.C.iii.

[9] A Thomson, 'A Different Approach to Choice of Law in Contract' (1980) 43 *MLR* 650, 652; H Stoll, 'Das Statut der Rechtswahlvereinbarung—eine irreführende Konstruktion' in I Meier and K Siehr (eds), *Rechtskollisionen: Festschrift für Anton Heini zum 65. Geburtstag* (Zurich, Schulthess, 1995) 429, 436 and 440; cp KFK Low, 'Choice of Law in Formation of Contracts' (2004) 20 *Journal of Contract Law* 167.

the overall conclusion of the contract, taking place in the context of a mutually wanted applicable law', that is the relevant connecting factor.[10]

There is no good reason for squeezing a bilateral choice of law into the strait-jacket of an indivisible contract, by relying on a factual interpretation of the party autonomy rule that is contrary to principle.[11] This, however, is the approach that has overwhelmingly been taken, in numerous manifestations, and that will be explored in section II.

C. A Residual Role for the Putative Chosen Law

Even though the putative application of the 'chosen' law to the underlying contract must be rejected, there is nothing wrong, in principle, with reliance on the putative chosen law to determine the existence and validity of the distinct choice of law contract. This is because, unlike the underlying contract, the choice of law contract is not governed by the party autonomy rule. Here, the putative chosen law is applied not because the parties have agreed to it, but because it is the law that the parties appear to have chosen,[12] and because there is a certain logic to upholding only those choice of law contracts that have been validly formed under their own chosen law.[13]

For example, if a buyer disputes that a choice of English law was validly incorporated into the seller's terms and conditions, then it is English law, as the putative chosen law, which will best apply to determine the existence and validity of the choice of law contract. If, under English law, the seller did not reasonably attempt to bring the standard terms to the buyer's attention, then the parties made no choice of English law. There is no harm in relying on a putative (and ultimately invalid) choice of English law to determine this question. The seller could hardly complain about rejection of a choice of law contract that was not validly formed pursuant to its own stipulated law. The choice of law contract and the putative chosen law are intrinsically linked. It is here, in the context of determining the law applicable to the choice of law contract, that the factual approach finds legitimate application.[14]

[10] Stoll, ibid 441.

[11] R Moser, *Vertragsabschluss, Vertragsgültigkeit und Parteiwille im internationalen Obligationenrecht* (St Gallen, Verlag der Fehr'schen Buchhandlung, 1948) 230–31.

[12] U Magnus (ed), *Staudingers Kommentar zum Bürgerlichen Gesetzbuch: Rom I-VO Art 3* (Berlin, Sellier, 2011) para 171 and references there cited.

[13] cp B Haftel, 'Pour en finir avec le cercle vicieux du principe d'autonomie (ou presque)' in L d'Avout, D Bureau and H Muir Watt, *Mélanges en l'honneur du Professeur Bernard Audit: les relations privées internationales* (Paris, LGDJ, 2014) 409. But see V Heuzé, *La réglementation française des contrats internationaux* (Paris, Joly éditions, 1990) para 234 and fn 75; V Brulhart, *Le choix de la loi applicable—questions choisies* (Bern, Stämpfli, 2004) para 265.

[14] cp Briggs (n 1) para 3.05 and fn 9, who says that the choice of law clause is 'the only provision of the contract which is not tested for its validity by reference to the law which governs the contract' because application of the *lex contractus* would 'allow the principle of renvoi into choice of law for contracts'; see also at para 3.65.

The same reasoning cannot be extended to the underlying contract. The buyer could not rely on English law to argue that the remainder of the seller's standard terms was not validly incorporated into the parties' agreement. As a separate contract, the underlying contract is not tied to the putative chosen law. If the parties have failed to make a valid choice of law, the underlying contract may still be valid under the objective applicable law, unless the underlying contract is conditional on the choice of law contract (see section IV.B below).

II. Putative Reasoning

Although putative reasoning is the very antithesis of contractual reasoning, it is commonly applied in private international law[15] and is particularly well established in choice of law. There are many different manifestations of putative reasoning, but their rationale is, ultimately, the same: the wish to apply the 'chosen' law to determine challenges to the existence and validity of the underlying contract, even if the grounds of challenge would equally affect the existence or validity of the choice of law contract.

It is this perceived need for pragmatism that has helped jurisdictions, which vary in their characterisation of the choice of law contract as an independent agreement, to unite in their embrace of putativity. Thus, putative reasoning has played an important role not only in English common law, which has traditionally thought of the choice of law agreement as a term that is dependent on the underlying contract, but also in jurisdictions like Germany, which has long recognised that, at least in principle, the choice of law contract is a distinct agreement. Possible outliers to this approach may be Switzerland and the United States, where putativity does not appear to be as well established. In the United States, the Restatement (Second) of Conflict of Laws may hold putativity in check by calling on the *lex fori* to determine whether the choice was obtained by improper means or mistake[16]—although the existence and general validity of the choice do not fall within the scope of this rule.[17]

Attempts have been made to justify putativity on grounds other than mere pragmatism and to clothe the putative approach with a cloak of contractual integrity. English common law, in particular, has sought to uphold its notion of the indivisible

[15] See generally E Crawford, 'The Uses of Putativity and Negativity in the Conflict of Laws' (2005) 54 *ICLQ* 829.

[16] American Law Institute, *Restatement (Second) of Conflict of Laws* (1971), s 187, cmnt (b) ('A choice-of-law provision, like any other contractual provision, will not be given effect if the consent of one of the parties to its inclusion in the contract was obtained by improper means … or by mistake. Whether such consent was in fact obtained by improper means or by mistake will be determined by the forum in accordance with its own legal principles'); eg *Dunes Hospitality LLC v Country Kitchen International Inc* 623 NW 2nd 484 (SD 2001) 488.

[17] See ch 5, s III.C.

contract in the face of putative reasoning, by relying on a concept of 'qualified putativity' (see section A below).[18] However, because 'qualified putativity' is born from a misunderstanding of the choice of law contract as an inherently dependent contract, it is, in some ways, more harmful to the purposes of party autonomy than the more generous approach to putativity that is now generally followed (see section B).

A. The Proper Law Approach and Qualified Putativity

In common law jurisdictions, the underlying contract and the choice of law contract have often been conceptualised as an entire contract that should, in theory, stand and fall as one. If the underlying contract is void or invalid, this must also logically be the case for the choice of law agreement included in it. But because this dependence of the choice of law contract on the underlying contract would deprive the parties' choice of any effect where the existence or validity of the underlying contract is disputed, the chosen law must be applied on a 'putative' basis. Pursuant to this view, the choice of law contract is not an independent contract.

i. The Proper Law Approach and Putativity

It is the concept of the 'proper law' that can in large part be blamed for this development. While Westlake first used the term to describe the law of the country 'with which the transaction has the most real connection',[19] it has long since become synonymous with the three-step approach to determining the applicable law that is still followed today—express choice, implied choice, or the law with the closest and most real connection.[20] The proper law of a contract is thus 'the system of law by reference to which the contract was made or that with which the transaction has its closest and most real connection'.[21]

More crucially, the proper law was thought to irrevocably ground the contract within its legal system, so that the contract '[became] embedded in or ... naturalised by the agreed proper law'.[22] There could not be a contract without a proper law.[23] But because the proper law was necessarily derived from the contract, the proper

[18] See also *John T Jones Construction Company v Hoot General Construction Company* 613 F 3d 778 (8th Circuit 2010) 782–83, where the Court applied the law with the most significant relationship to the transaction to determine whether a contract and its choice of law clause came into existence, treating the contracts as one: 'Once the existence of a contract is determined, the parties' intent as evinced in the choice-of-law provision controls ... and we will apply [the chosen law] to questions of interpretation or construction of the contract'.

[19] J Westlake, *A Treatise on Private International Law* 7th edn (London, Sweet & Maxwell, 1925) para 212.

[20] See FA Mann, 'The Proper Law in the Conflict of Laws' (1987) 36 *ICLQ* 437, 443–45.

[21] *Bonython v Commonwealth of Australia* [1951] AC 201 (PC) 219.

[22] Mann (n 20) 448.

[23] *Armar Shipping Co Ltd v Caisse Algérienne d'Assurance et de Réassurance* [1981] 1 WLR 207 (CA) 215 (Megaw LJ).

law was as dependent on its contract as the contract was on its proper law, creating the need for a 'putative' proper law.

Thus, in *Albeko Schuhmaschinen AG v Kamborian Shoe Machine Co Ltd*,[24] Salmon J suggested that the existence of a contract would have to be determined in accordance with the law that would be applicable if the contract had come into existence—in this case, the objective proper law. An Englishman had posted a letter to a person in Switzerland, offering to appoint him as his agent. The Swiss offeree claimed that he had accepted the offer. The English offeror, however, had never received the Swiss offeree's acceptance letter, and so it was necessary to determine whether the contract of agency had been formed. Salmon J was not satisfied that the letter had in fact been posted, but went on to conclude, obiter, that the objective proper law of the alleged contract would have been Swiss law and that, under Swiss law, postage of the offeree's letter would not have amounted to effective acceptance. Because there could be no proper law without a contract, Swiss law was applicable as the putative proper law. Although there was no choice of law clause in this case, it was the first time that an English court had made use of the concept of putativity in order to avoid the *circulus inextricabilis* of relying on the terms of a disputed contract in determining its existence or validity.[25]

ii. Qualified Putativity

Since then, there have been attempts to preserve the integrity of the parties' agreement by resorting to putative reasoning only where it is the validity, but not the existence, of the underlying contract that is in issue. This approach will be referred to here as 'qualified putativity'. The rationale for 'qualified putativity', it seems, is that only an existing agreement can (and must) have a proper law, but that an allegedly invalid contract is to have effect until it is avoided. The choice of law contract, as an ordinary term of the underlying contract, can be given effect to as long as the underlying agreement has been validly formed.

The Court of Appeal decision in *Mackender v Feldia* offers support for this approach.[26] In that case, the underwriters of an insurance policy had sought to serve the insured, a Belgian diamond merchant, out of the jurisdiction, on the basis that the Belgian jurisdiction and choice of law clauses in the policy were not effective because the policy was void for illegality and non-disclosure. The Court of Appeal concluded that both clauses remained unaffected by the plaintiffs' claims, but indicated that a different result might have obtained in the case of a claim of *non est factum*. Diplock LJ, the only judge to consider the issue in any detail, found that Belgian law was clearly applicable:

> Where acts done in England, in this case the oral negotiations between the assured's broker and the underwriters, the initialling of the slip and the signing of the policy, are

[24] *Albeko Schuhmaschinen AG v Kamborian Shoe Machine Co Ltd* (1961) 111 LJ 519.
[25] See Thomson (n 9) 653.
[26] *Mackender v Feldia* [1967] 2 QB 590 (CA).

> alleged not to have resulted in an agreement at all (ie, where there is a plea of non est factum) and the question is whether there was any real consensus ad idem, it may well be that this question has to be determined by English law and not by the law which would have been agreed by them as the proper law of the contract if they had reached an agreement. But that is not the position when underwriters seek to repudiate a contract upon discovering that material facts were not disclosed to them by their assured before the policy was entered into. … The fallacy in the argument to the contrary is that when what is said to be a 'voidable' contract is said to be 'avoided,' that does not mean that the contract never existed but that it ceases to exist from the moment of avoidance, and that upon its ceasing there may then arise consequential rights in respect of things done in performance of it while it did exist which may have the effect of undoing those things as far as practicable. … Whether one of the legal incidents or characteristics of the contract of insurance in the present case is that the underwriters are entitled to repudiate for the non-disclosure of the particular facts which they alleged have not been disclosed must be determined by the proper law of the policy, which is Belgian law and not English law.[27]

Russell LJ agreed that the parties had 'undoubtedly entered into a contract' and that they had 'in terms agreed that the law governing the contract is Belgian law'.[28] In these circumstances, there was no 'need to search for some other law', as 'To do so would seem to introduce a wholly unnecessary complication into the affair', and the case did not 'involve either non est factum or fraud or even innocent misrepresentation'.[29]

Lord Denning MR did not consider the validity of the choice of law clause, other than to say that the Belgian jurisdiction clause was a 'positive agreement by the underwriters that the policy is governed exclusively by Belgian law'.[30] But he too drew a distinction between *non est factum* and avoidance in relation to the jurisdiction clause:

> I can well see that if the issue was whether there ever had been any contract at all, as, for instance, if there was a plea of non est factum, then the foreign jurisdiction clause might not apply at all. But here there was a contract, and when it was made, it contained the foreign jurisdiction clause. Even if there was non-disclosure, nevertheless non-disclosure does not automatically avoid the contract. It only makes it voidable. It gives the insurers a right to elect. They can either avoid the contract or affirm it. If they avoid it, it is avoided in this sense, that the insurers are no longer bound by it. They can repudiate the contract and refuse to pay on it. But things already done are not undone. The contract is not avoided from the beginning but only from the moment of avoidance. In particular, the foreign jurisdiction clause is not abrogated.[31]

Even on the view adopted in this book, which is that the choice of law contract is an independent contract, the outcome of the Court of Appeal's decision cannot be faulted. In particular, it is difficult to see why the plaintiffs' claims of

[27] ibid, 602–04.
[28] ibid, 605.
[29] ibid, 605.
[30] ibid, 598.
[31] ibid, 598.

non-disclosure or illegality, which related to the insured's alleged practice of diamond smuggling in Italy, should have affected the validity of the choice of law contract. The underwriters' challenge was aimed at the substance of the parties' bargain, and was therefore incapable of impugning the parties' intention to choose the applicable law. It is also true that, had the underwriters attacked the existence of the policy, the choice of law contract could well have been challengeable on the same ground. Thus, an allegation that the insured never signed the policy would have put in doubt the existence of both the policy and the choice of law contract.

But it is submitted that this factual parallelism (or, as the case may be, incongruity) is not a symptom of any form of legal dependence by the choice of law contract on the underlying contract. At least Diplock LJ seemed to suggest exactly that:[32] the agreed proper law was effective as long as the contract had come into existence and had not yet been avoided. This reasoning ignores two things: on the one hand, that the very purpose of the choice of law contract—the application of the chosen law to the contractual dispute—is exhausted before the validity of the underlying contract is finally determined; and on the other hand, that an agreement on the applicable law is possible even though the main contract within which it is physically contained may not have come into existence.

The notion of qualified putativity does not appear to have had a lasting influence on the courts' approach to choice of law contracts.[33] It is, instead, in legal scholarship that the distinction between *non est factum* and avoidance has met with considerable success. It has thus been argued that the putative proper law ought to be applicable as long as the transaction satisfies: 'English requirements for classification as a contract', consisting of consensus ad idem and an intention to create legal relations;[34] or 'basic components of contractual agreement', consisting of offer and acceptance, consideration (even though this is 'less clear'), an intention to create legal relations, and 'the absence of any factor which renders the otherwise-contract void *ab initio*';[35] or a 'prima facie case of agreement to the existence of the "main" contract' as well as designation of a proper law.[36] If there is

[32] It has been suggested that *Mackender* supports the application of the putative chosen law to determine the validity of the choice of law contract: P Nygh, *Autonomy in International Contracts* (Oxford, Oxford University Press, 1999) 97; cp Collins (n 3) para 32-066. This is not strictly correct because the purpose of the distinction seems to be to ensure a contractual foundation for the proper law on the basis of the underlying contract; and the 'chosen' law would still be applied on a putative basis even if the challenge to the validity of the underlying contract was sufficiently wide to also affect the choice of law contract.

[33] But see the obiter dicta in *Oceanic Sun Line Special Shipping Co Inc v Fay* (1988) 165 CLR 197 by Gaudron J and Brennan J that the law of the forum applies to determine the existence of the contract and its terms: at 260–61 (Gaudron J), at 225 (Brennan J); cp also *John T Jones Construction Company v Hoot General Construction Company* 613 F 3d 778 (8th Circuit 2010) 782–83 (see n 18 above).

[34] DF Libling, 'Formation of International Contracts' (1979) 42 *MLR* 169, 172–73; see also P North, *Private International Law Problems in Common Law Jurisdictions* (Dordrecht, Martinus Nijhoff, 1993) 119.

[35] A Briggs, 'The Formation of International Contracts' [1990] *Lloyd's Maritime and Commercial Law Quarterly* 192, 198; cp Briggs (n 1) paras 3.64 and 10.28.

[36] J Harris, 'Contractual Freedom in the Conflict of Laws' (2000) 20 *OJLS* 247, 254.

such an agreement, the proper law must be applied to govern 'all issues of validity', because a voidable agreement is an agreement until it is avoided.[37]

The criticism remains, however, that any approach based on qualified putativity does not adequately grasp the independent nature of choice of law contracts, and thereby risks both their under- and over-enforcement. To the extent that the choice of law contract is said to depend on an existing agreement to the underlying contract, it denies parties the freedom of choosing a law to govern questions of formation.[38] And to the extent that the choice of law contract is treated as inviolable in the face of claims that the underlying contract is invalid, the approach assumes that choice of law contracts are unchallengeable once formed.

B. Putativity Unbound

Although there has, therefore, been some support for treating choice of law contracts as non-avoidable terms of the underlying contract, the more common approach is to rely on putative reasoning to determine both the existence and the validity of underlying contracts. This approach leads to potential over-enforcement of choice of law contracts, by giving effect to 'agreements' that have never been formed or that are otherwise defective. It has already been noted that this approach is similar in effect to the factual approach and thus fundamentally at cross-purposes with party autonomy.[39]

There is one striking inconsistency within the putative approach that sets it apart from the factual approach: even though it does not allow the parties' choice to be impugned on the same grounds as the underlying contract, it nevertheless inquires into the existence or validity of the choice of law contract where it is only the parties' choice, and not the underlying contract, that is in dispute.[40] The implicit aim of the putative approach, therefore, is to avoid an independent assessment of the choice of law contract on the same grounds that are also alleged to affect the underlying contract.[41]

Except for oblique references to a *circulus inextricabilis*, the rationale for this approach is rarely articulated. Putativity is accepted in common law jurisdictions, in the form of an unqualified putative proper law (see subsection i below), as well as in civil law jurisdictions, even if they purport to recognise the choice of law agreement as an independent contract (see subsection ii). It has been followed

[37] ibid, 252 and 255; Libling (n 34) 174; Briggs (n 35) 198; cp A Chong, 'Choice of Law for Void Contracts and Their Restitutionary Aftermath: The Putative Governing Law of the Contract' in P Giliker (ed), *Re-examining Contract and Unjust Enrichment* (Leiden, Martinus Nijhoff, 2007) 155, 161.

[38] But see Chong (n 37) 165.

[39] See above, s I.B.

[40] See, eg, *The Lanyka Abbaya* BGHZ 99, 207 (1986), where the legibility of the choice of law and jurisdiction clause was in dispute (but the Court also concluded that the validity of the jurisdiction clause was to be determined in accordance with the putative chosen law).

[41] See below, s IV.A.i.

under Regulation (EC) 593/2008 on the law applicable to contractual obligations (Rome I) (see subsection iii),[42] and no discernible effort has been made to depart from this approach in the Hague Principles on Choice of Law in International Commercial Contracts (see subsection iv).[43]

i. The Proper Law Approach and Putativity Unbound

It is likely that 'qualified putativity' no longer forms part of the English common law approach to party autonomy. The current edition of *Dicey, Morris and Collins* accordingly states that 'The effect of [Rome I] is to refer questions relating to the existence of a contract to the putative governing law', and that the 'Regulation rule is the same as the prior common law rule in England'.[44] The case law provides some authority for applying the putative chosen law to determine the existence of the underlying contract.

For example, in *Compania Naviera Micro SA v Shipley International Inc (The Parouth)*,[45] the English Court of Appeal held that England was the appropriate forum for the dispute because the existence of an alleged charterparty would be determined in accordance with its putative proper law—which, on the basis of a London arbitration clause contained within the alleged charterparty, was arguably English law. It is likely that the Court of Appeal considered English law to be applicable as the implied chosen law, as opposed to the objective law.

Similarly, in *Union Transport Plc v Continental Lines SA*,[46] Lord Goff noted that an alleged charterparty, which included a provision requiring payment of commission in London, a London general average clause and a London arbitration clause, would be governed by English law as the putative proper law of the contract, having already concluded that the English court had jurisdiction to determine a dispute regarding the existence of the charterparty. In neither of these cases did the court consider that it was, or would be, necessary to establish agreement on the proper law before applying the proper law to determine the existence of the charterparty.

To the extent that the proper law concept assumes that the proper law is, in principle, indivisible from its contract, it is not surprising that the common law does not subject the choice of law contract to an independent assessment in such circumstances. The putative chosen law is applied because, unless its effect was to be limited to the voidability of the underlying contract, there is no alternative to putativity.

[42] Reg (EC) 593/2008 on the law applicable to contractual obligations [2008] OJ L177/6 (Rome I).

[43] *Hague Principles on Choice of Law in International Commercial Contracts* (n 2).

[44] Collins (n 3) para 32-108; see also M Davies, AS Bell and PLG Brereton, *Nygh's Conflict of Laws in Australia* 9th edn (Chatswood NSW, LexisNexis, 2014) 463–66.

[45] *Compania Naviera Micro SA v Shipley International Inc (The Parouth)* [1982] 2 Lloyd's Rep 351 (CA).

[46] *Union Transport Plc v Continental Lines SA* [1992] 1 WLR 15 (HL) 23 (Lord Goff).

ii. A Notionally Independent but Putative Choice of Law Contract

Putativity is also accepted—albeit largely implicitly—in jurisdictions that purport to recognise the choice of law contract as an independent contract. Although German courts and scholars have long emphasised the independent nature of the choice of law contract,[47] they have not thought it necessary to draw a distinction between the choice of law contract and the underlying contract where the ground of challenge is the same,[48] highlighting instead the benefits of *Gleichlauf* (synchronisation) or *Akzessorietät* (the accessory nature) between the two contracts.[49] In fact, the putativity inherent in this approach is rarely acknowledged.[50] Greater attention is being paid instead to the question of whether it is justifiable to apply the putative chosen law to the choice of law contract,[51] which, as has already been explained, poses no logical difficulties.[52]

iii. Putativity Under Rome I

The Rome Convention 80/934/ECC on the law applicable to contractual obligations (and now Rome I) has generally been interpreted as providing for a putative approach.[53] In *Morin v Bonhams & Brooks Ltd*, for example, the Court held, on an application for service out of the jurisdiction, that the putative chosen law was applicable to determine whether conditions of sale, which included a choice of law clause, were incorporated into the parties' contract.[54] The claimant had bought a Ferrari at an auction in Monaco, but sought to rescind the contract when he found out that the odometer reading that had been provided in the auction catalogue

[47] eg, W Haudek, *Die Bedeutung des Parteiwillens im internationalen Privatrecht* (Berlin, Springer, 1931) 88; Magnus (n 12) para 36; C Reithmann and D Martiny, *Internationales Vertragsrecht* 7th edn (Cologne, Dr Otto Schmidt, 2010) pt I, para 88; M Kost, *Konsensprobleme im internationalen Schuldvertragsrecht* (Frankfurt, Peter Lang, 1995) 66.

[48] Haudek, ibid 92; BGH NJW 2007, 2036, discussed in ch 6, s IV.D. The position in Switzerland—a jurisdiction that has long emphasised the independent nature of the choice of law contract—is unclear.

[49] Magnus (n 12) paras 36 and 167; Reithmann and Martiny (n 47) pt II, para 263; Kost (n 47) 33; A Baumert, 'Abschlusskontrolle bei Rechtswahlvereinbarungen' [1997] *Recht der Internationalen Wirtschaft* 805, 806.

[50] But see W Lorenz, *Vertragsabschluss und Parteiwille im internationalen Obligationenrecht Englands* (Heidelberg, Winter, 1957) 203.

[51] eg, Kost (n 47) 29ff.

[52] See above, s I.C.

[53] Convention 80/934/ECC on the law applicable to contractual obligations [1980] OJ L266/1 (opened for signature 19 June 1980, entered into force 1 April 1991) (Rome Convention). Briggs (n 1) paras 10.32 and 10.33; Reithmann and Martiny (n 47) pt II, para 263; J Foyer, 'Le Contrat d'Electio Juris à la Lumière de la Convention de Rome du 19 Juin 1980' in *L'Internationalisation du Droit: Mélanges en l'Honneur de Yvon Loussouarn* (Paris, Dalloz, 1994) 169, 175; P Kaye, *The New Private International Law of Contract of the European Community* (Aldershot, Dartmouth Pub Co, 1993) 169; but see W Wengler, 'Rechtswahl unter Zwang' in C Dominicé et al (eds), *Études de droit international privé en l'honneur de Pierre Lalive* (Basel, Helbing & Lichtenhahn, 1993) 211, 212.

[54] *Morin v Bonhams & Brooks Ltd* [2003] EWHC 467, [2003] 2 All ER (Comm) 36, aff'd on different grounds [2003] EWCA Civ 1802, [2004] 1 Lloyd's Rep 702; see also *Midgulf International Ltd v Groupe Chimique Tunisien* [2010] EWCA Civ 66, [2010] 2 Lloyd's Rep 543 [56]; Cass soc, 24 November 2004, no 02-42660 (*Hoegaerden v Horphag Research (UK) Ltd*).

was incorrect. When attending the auction, the claimant was required to complete a bidder registration form, which stated that any sale was subject to the general conditions set out in the auction catalogue. The general conditions excluded any liability of the auctioneer for misdescription, and provided for a choice of Monegasque law. The claimant argued that he had not agreed to the conditions 'in any meaningful sense'.[55]

Referring to Article 8(1) (now Article 10(1)) of the Rome Convention, the Court found that, because 'the putative law of the contract [was] Monegasque, it would be a matter for that law whether the contract was concluded on the terms of the conditions'.[56] Because, under Monegasque law, the claimant's signature of the bidder registration form constituted an effective acceptance of the general conditions, the general conditions were incorporated into the contract of sale. Admittedly, the result would have been no different had the Court not relied on putative reasoning to establish incorporation of the general conditions and instead applied the putative chosen law to determine the existence of the choice of law contract. The choice of law clause having been validly incorporated under Monegasque law, that law would then have led to the remainder of the conditions being incorporated. Monegasque law was, in essence, a self-validating choice of law. But the position would not have been so straightforward under an invalidating choice of law.

Article 3(5) of Rome I provides that 'the existence and validity of the consent of the parties as to the choice of the applicable law shall be determined in accordance with the provisions of Articles 10, 11 and 13'. Article 10(1), in turn, provides that 'The existence and validity of a contract, or of any term of a contract, shall be determined by the law which would govern it under this Regulation if the contract or term were valid'.

Although Article 3(5) is generally understood to refer the choice of law contract to its putative chosen law pursuant to Article 10(1), Article 10(1) is also relied upon to refer the underlying contract to the putative chosen law[57]—unless, it seems, the relevant issue of formation or validity concerns only the choice of law contract, in which case the choice of law contract would be established prior to the chosen law being applied to the underlying contract. It has accordingly been noted that Article 10 provides for a 'unilateral' choice of law.[58] This interpretation does not necessarily follow from Articles 3(5) and 10(1), but neither is it excluded by the open-ended wording that is used in these provisions.

[55] *Morin v Bonhams*, ibid [21].

[56] ibid, [23].

[57] See references in n 53; cp also A Dickinson, 'A Note on the Autonomy of the Parties' Agreement on Choice of Law' (Legal Studies Research Paper No 12/83, Sydney Law School, October 2012) para 19.

[58] E Jayme, 'Choice-of-Law Clauses in International Contracts: Some Thoughts on the Reform of Art 3 of the Rome Convention' in L de Lima Pinheiro, *Seminário Internacional sobre a Comunitarização do Direito Internacional Privado* (Almedina, Coimbra, 2005) 53, 55, 60; cp J Fawcett and JM Carruthers, *Cheshire, North & Fawcett: Private International Law* 14th edn (Oxford, Oxford University Press, 2008) 707.

iv. Putativity Under the Hague Principles

Article 7 of the Hague Principles on Choice of Law in International Commercial Contracts provides that 'A choice of law cannot be contested solely on the ground that the contract to which it applies is not valid'. Pursuant to Article 6, the question of 'whether the parties have agreed to a choice of law is determined by the law that was purportedly agreed to'. These provisions could easily be read as a rejection of putativity; and the supporting commentary would seem to confirm this view, stating that the choice of law agreement 'is affected when the defect causing the invalidity of the main contract necessarily extends, by its very nature, to this clause',[59] and that 'the severability doctrine may apply only if a valid choice of law agreement is shown to exist'.[60]

On the other hand, the commentary seems to assume that defects affecting both the choice of law agreement and the underlying contract will be determined in one step, according to the putative chosen law. A choice of law agreement is invalid if the defect affecting the underlying contract 'extends' to the choice of law agreement;[61] or if a contract is found to be invalid, then this invalidity may—but does not necessarily—affect the choice of law agreement.[62] A complete rejection of putativity would require that the existence and validity of the *choice of law agreement* be determined first. Depending on the outcome of this determination, the court would then apply either the chosen law or the objective applicable law to determine the existence and validity of the underlying contract.

III. The Choice of Law Contract as an Independent Contract

It is relatively easy to identify putative reasoning, which involves application of the 'chosen law' to any agreement other than the choice of law agreement prior to determining the choice of law agreement's existence and validity. Proposing a feasible alternative, however, is more challenging. The purpose of this section is to identify the steps that ought to be followed before the chosen law is given effect. The case of *Hoegaerden v Horphag Research (UK) Ltd*[63] will serve as an example.

In this case, the French Cour de Cassation relied on Article 8 of the Rome Convention (now Article 10) to hold that, pursuant to a putative choice of Swiss law, an employment contract had not come into existence because it was

[59] *Commentary on the Hague Principles on Choice of Law in International Commercial Contracts* (n 2) para 7.11.
[60] ibid, para 7.3.
[61] ibid, para 7.11.
[62] ibid, Illustrations 7.2 and 7.4.
[63] Cass soc, 24 November 2004, no 02-42660 (*Hoegaerden v Horphag Research (UK) Ltd*).

not intended to be binding. On 20 June 2000, the prospective employer, a Swiss branch of Horphag Research (UK) Limited, had sent a letter to the plaintiff, Mr van Hoegaerden, with the stated aim of confirming an outline of the contract of employment that Horphag Research was going to offer to him. Along with the essential terms of the contract, such as salary, commencement and place of employment and Mr van Hoegaerden's role and duties, the outline also stipulated that the employment contract was to be governed by Swiss law. The letter further stated that Horphag Research would offer Mr van Hoegaerden a final contract once it had verified certain aspects related to cross-border employment contracts. Employment duties were to commence on 2 August 2000 and were to be carried out in France. On 27 July 2000, however, Horphag Research sent another letter to Mr van Hoegaerden, which was received on 2 August 2000, informing him that it would not offer him employment after all. Mr van Hoegaerden brought proceedings against Horphag Research for breach of contract, and was awarded damages at first instance.

The Court of Appeal overturned the decision.[64] It concluded that, pursuant to Article 8 of the Rome Convention, Swiss law was applicable as the putative chosen law. Article 16 of the Swiss Obligationenrecht (Code of Obligations) establishes a presumption that, where parties agree to make a contract subject to formal requirements, they do not wish to be bound until such time as those requirements are satisfied. The Court concluded that the letter by Horphag Research established such a presumption because it made clear that there was to be a final contract at a later stage. There was also no evidence to rebut the presumption.

Mr Hoegaerden appealed to the Cour de Cassation, arguing that the Court of Appeal contradicted itself in upholding the choice of Swiss law yet concluding that the parties had only intended to bind themselves by way of a final contract. He submitted that Horphag had bound itself to employ him subject only to the condition that it would need to verify certain aspects related to cross-border employment contracts; and that Horphag had thus breached Article 1134 of the French Code Civil. The Cour de Cassation rejected the appeal on the basis that Article 8 called for the application of the law that would have been applicable had the employment contract been formed, which, due to the choice of law clause included in the document, was Swiss law.

For the reasons identified in section I of this chapter, it is clear that the Court's application of the putative chosen law to determine the existence of the alleged employment contract must be rejected in principle, even though it accords with the orthodox interpretation of Articles 3(5) and 10(1). Before Swiss law could be applied, the Court should have determined whether the parties had intended Swiss law to be applicable.

It is now necessary to consider the implications that arise from an independent treatment of the choice of law contract for the purposes of establishing the chosen

[64] CA Paris, 19 February 2002, no 2001-36869.

law as well as the underlying contract. Insofar as the choice of law contract itself is concerned, there are four broad areas that are affected: characterisation of the choice of law contract (see section A below); the existence and validity of the choice of law contract (see section B); the applicability of the chosen law to the consequences of the nullity or inexistence of the underlying contract (see section C); and timing of the choice (see section D). Implications for the underlying contract will be discussed in section IV below.

A. Characterisation of the Choice of Law Contract

Because it is the party autonomy rule that requires there to be an independent choice of law contract, the issue of 'putativity' or 'separability', forming part of the process of characterisation, is for the law of the forum. The Cour de Cassation was right, therefore, to rely on the Rome Convention to determine whether the Cour d'Appel had been wrong to apply the putative chosen law. It is immaterial whether the law applicable to the choice of law contract, or the law applicable to the underlying contract, do not recognise the independence of the choice of law contract. This would not be the case if the starting-point of analysis was the contract as a whole. It has thus been argued, in relation to English law, that:

> [I]t is wrong to suppose that severability is a technique which operates without reference to a *lex causae*, or that the question is in some sense insulated from the ordinary control of choice of law, or that it will in every case be answered by the application of a principle of English law.[65]

However, it is the law applicable to the choice of law contract that determines (a) whether challenges made to the existence or validity of the main contract are equally applicable to the choice of law contract, and (b) whether the choice of law contract is sufficiently wide in scope to provide the law applicable to questions of existence or validity. It was for the law applicable to the choice of law contract to determine whether the parties intended the Swiss choice of law clause to be binding, and if so, whether the choice was intended to cover questions as to the formation of the alleged employment contract.

B. Determining the Existence and Validity of the Choice of Law Contract

The existence and validity of the choice of law contract must be determined as an antecedent question, prior to determining the existence and validity of the

[65] Briggs (n 1) paras 3.10 and 3.17, in relation to arbitration and jurisdiction agreements; see also A Chong, 'Void Contracts and the Applicability of Choice of Law Clauses to Consequential Restitutionary Claims' (2009) 21 *Singapore Academy of Law Journal* 54, para 32; J Harris, 'Does Choice of Law Make Any Sense?' (2004) 57 *Current Legal Problems* 305, 326.

underlying contract. There is no room for application of the putative chosen law to the underlying contract—the law that would be applicable if the underlying contract, including the choice of law contract, were valid. If the Swiss choice of law contract never came into existence because the parties did not intend to be bound by the clause, the Court could not apply Swiss law to determine the existence of the employment contract.

More generally, this means (i) that the choice of law contract must have its own applicable law; (ii) that, even though the challenge to both contracts is the same, different factual considerations may arise in relation to the choice of law contract; (iii) that the choice of law contract does not depend on the underlying contract for consideration; and (iv) that the choice of law contract cannot be established as a part or term of the underlying contract.

i. The Law Applicable to the Choice of Law Contract

The choice of law contract must have its own applicable law. Ordinarily the existence and validity of the choice of law contract is established in accordance with the putative chosen law, as well as with any applicable modal choice of law rules.[66] This means that the law applicable to the Swiss choice of law clause would have been Swiss law, as the putative chosen law.

Alternative choice of law rules for the choice of law contract include the place of residence of the party who claims not to have consented to the contract (provided application of the putative chosen law would be 'unreasonable');[67] or the law of the forum.[68] The downside to these choice of law rules is that they increase the likelihood that the choice of law agreement and the underlying contract are submitted to differing laws. A defect potentially affecting both contracts would have to be considered first in relation to the choice of law agreement, and if the choice of law agreement was valid based on the law of the forum (or the place of residence), it is the chosen law that would then apply to assess the defect in relation to the underlying contract. If the putative chosen law is applied, and the choice of law agreement is valid, then the choice of law agreement and the underlying contract are governed by the same law (the putative chosen law and the chosen law).

ii. Different Factual Considerations

An independent assessment of the choice of law contract also requires that account be taken of any factual considerations that are relevant only to the parties' intention to choose the applicable law and not to the underlying contract. It was not necessarily the case, despite Article 16 of the Swiss Obligationenrecht, that Horphag Research and Mr van Hoegaerden did not intend to be bound by the

[66] See ch 5.

[67] Art 6(2), *Hague Principles on Choice of Law in International Commercial Contracts* (n 2); Art 10(2), Rome I (n 42).

[68] *Restatement (Second)* (n 16) s 187, cmnt (b): see nn 16 and 17 above.

choice of Swiss law contained in the outline document. It seems at least arguable that the two parties would have intended their pre-contractual negotiations to be covered by the stipulated law, even though their employment contract was yet to be finalised.[69] (A factor that may speak against such an interpretation is the narrow wording of the clause, which was expressed to submit only the employment contract to Swiss law.)

Where there are no factual differences, and the choice of law contract is valid pursuant to the putative chosen law—as it would have been, for example, in *Morin v Bonhams & Brooks Ltd*—then the chosen law is, in effect, self-validating. It follows that it is only where the choice of law contract is as affected by the challenge as the underlying contract, and the challenge voids or invalidates the choice of law contract, that the proposed approach ultimately differs from the application of the putative chosen law to the underlying contract. This is because, if Horphag Research and Mr van Hoegaerden did not intend to be bound by the Swiss choice of law clause, then Swiss law would not have been the law applicable to the alleged employment contract.

iii. Consideration

It has been suggested that a choice of law made in the context of a contract unsupported by consideration could only be given effect to if 'some reason can be advanced for holding that the [choice of law agreement] is in itself binding as a contract, although there is obviously no consideration for it'.[70] The reason for 'holding that [the choice of law agreement] is in itself binding as a contract' is, of course, that the choice of law agreement is an independent, legally binding agreement. It is an independent contract that need not be supported by additional consideration beyond the agreement on the applicable law.[71]

iv. The Choice of Law Contract as a Term

Because the function of the choice of law contract is to select the law applicable to the underlying contract, the choice of law contract cannot be treated as a term of the underlying contract. This has certain implications for determining the existence and validity of the choice of law contract: implied choice of law contracts cannot be submitted to the rules on implied terms;[72] ascertainment of the parties' intention as to the applicable law cannot take place on the assumption that the underlying contract is valid—that is, the parties' intention cannot be grounded in putative factors;[73] and choice of law contracts must remain unaffected by

[69] cp also ch 7, s III.A.

[70] JHC Morris, 'The Proper Law of a Contract: A Reply' (1950) 3 *International Law Quarterly* 197, 200; cp Briggs (n 35) 203.

[71] See ch 2, s III.A.ii; cp Libling (n 34) 174–75.

[72] See ch 6, s IV.

[73] See ch 6, s IV.C.ii and D.

restrictions on the admissibility of evidence applicable to the underlying contract.[74] These matters will be discussed in chapters six and seven.

C. Nullity or Non-existence of the Underlying Contract

The independence of the choice of law contract enables the chosen law to apply to pre-contractual obligations, the existence and validity of the underlying contract, and any consequences of the nullity of the underlying contract. As long as the choice of law contract has been validly concluded, the nullity of the underlying contract, or the failure to enter into the underlying contract, should not in itself affect a party's ability to rely on the chosen law. Of course, the choice of law contract must still be sufficiently wide in scope to include such claims,[75] and parties must be free to choose the applicable law.[76]

Assuming, for example, that the choice of Swiss law had in fact been intended to govern pre-contractual negotiations as well as any matters arising from an ultimate failure to enter into an employment contract, and assuming that Horphag Research had already mistakenly paid out the first instalment of Mr van Hoegaerden's salary, then Horphag Research could have relied on Swiss law to claim repayment of that instalment.

Thus, the distinction that is sometimes drawn in common law jurisdictions—that it is only where a contract has come into existence that the law applicable to the contract will govern the obligation to make restitution—is ill-founded insofar as choice of law contracts are concerned.[77] It presumes, in accordance with qualified putativity, that parties are unable to choose a law governing the existence of the underlying contract.[78]

Article 12(1)(e) of Rome I, on the other hand, which provides that 'The law applicable to a contract by virtue of this Regulation shall govern … the consequences of nullity of the contract', is at risk of being interpreted on a putative basis, in line with Articles 3(5) and 10.[79] The same risk arises in relation to Article 12(1) of Regulation (EC) 864/2007 on the law applicable to non-contractual obligations (Rome II), which provides that the law applicable to a non-contractual obligation arising out of pre-contractual dealings 'shall be the law … that would have been

[74] See ch 7, s II.

[75] cp *Deutsche Bank AG v Asia Pacific Broadband Wireless Communications Inc* [2008] EWCA Civ 1091, [2008] 2 Lloyd's Rep 619 [25] and [31], holding that a jurisdiction agreement which had been found to have come into existence applied to restitutionary claims arising from the challenged contract.

[76] See Rome I (n 42) Art 12(1)(e); Reg (EC) 864/2007 on the law applicable to non-contractual obligations [2007] OJ L199/40 (Rome II), Arts 10(1) and 12(1).

[77] See generally Chong (n 37) 170ff; cp J Bird, 'Choice of Law' in F Rose (ed), *Restitution and the Conflict of Laws* (Oxford, Mansfield Press, 1995) 64, 125.

[78] eg, *Baring Bros & Co Ltd v Cunninghame DC* [1997] CLC 108 (Scot Ct Sess) 115ff (Lord Penrose).

[79] But see Collins (n 3) para 36-021; Kost (n 47) 69; cp *CIMB Bank Bhd v Dresdner Kleinwort* [2008] SGCA 36, [2008] 4 SLR 543.

applicable to [the contract] had it been entered into'.[80] Horphag Research would then have been able to rely on the Swiss choice of law clause to bring a claim in restitution or *culpa in contrahendo*, even if there was no intention to be bound by the choice.

D. Timing of the Choice

As the *Horphag Research* case demonstrates, parties would be wise to enter into a choice of law contract that governs pre-contractual negotiations.[81] Under the proper law approach, objections had been raised against the power to choose the applicable law prior to or following the formation of the underlying contract, or the power to vary the chosen law in the course of the relationship.[82] Because the choice of law contract is an independent contract, such objections are ill-founded.[83] Equally ill-founded is the argument that variation of the parties' choice of law necessarily entails novation or variation of the underlying contract,[84] because it conflates the function of the choice of law contract—which is the selection of the applicable law—with the effect of the chosen law on the parties' rights and obligations.[85]

IV. Implications for the Substantive Contract

Once the choice of law contract has been separately examined, it is possible to establish the existence and validity of the underlying contract—under the chosen law if the choice of law contract was valid, or under the objective law if the parties did not make an effective choice of law. The fact that the choice of law contract necessarily precedes an assessment of the underlying contract has two important implications.

[80] Rome II (n 76). See Collins (n 3) para 35-095.

[81] See I Schwander, 'Zur Rechtswahl im IPR des Schuldvertragsrechts' in P Forstmoser et al (ed), *Festschrift für Max Keller zum 65. Geburtstag* (Zurich, Schulthess, 1989) 473, 478.

[82] See *Armar Shipping Co Ltd v Caisse Algérienne d'Assurance et de Réassurance* [1981] 1 WLR 207 (CA) 215–16 (Megaw LJ); for an overview, see DP Pierce, 'Post-formation Choice of Law in Contract' (1987) 50 *MLR* 176; A Beck, 'Floating Choice of Law Clauses' [1987] *Lloyd's Maritime and Commercial Law Quarterly* 532; A Briggs, 'The Validity of "Floating" Choice of Law and Jurisdiction Clauses' [1986] *Lloyd's Maritime and Commercial Law Quarterly* 508; see more generally M Tomaszewski, 'La désignation, postérieure à la conclusion du contrat, de la loi qui régit' [1972] *Revue critique de droit international privé* 567.

[83] See now Rome I (n 42) Art 3(2); *Mauritius Commercial Bank Ltd v Hestia Holdings Ltd* [2013] EWHC 1328 [30].

[84] As claims Kaye (n 53) 156; see also Pierce (n 82) 199; Briggs (n 1) para 10.17; *BP Plc v National Union Fire Insurance Co* [2004] EWHC 1132 [31].

[85] See ch 2, s III.

The first is that, where the choice of law contract and the underlying contract are challenged on the same grounds, an assessment of the underlying contract may well involve a reconsideration of these grounds of challenge (see section A below). The second is that the underlying contract may stand and fall with the choice of law contract, where the parties' intention to enter into the underlying contract is conditional on the effectiveness of their choice of law (see section B). These two implications are, in some respects, interrelated. Where the underlying contract is found to be conditional on the parties' choice of law, there is no longer a need to submit the underlying contract to a reconsideration of the same grounds of challenge that were already made out in relation to the choice of law contract.

Returning again to the *Horphag Research* case, if the choice of Swiss law was never intended to be binding under Article 16 of the Swiss Code of Civil Obligations, then the law applicable to the alleged employment contract would have been the objective applicable law, which was French law. Mr van Hoegaerden claimed that, pursuant to French law, the parties were bound by the company's outline of employment terms. Unless the alleged employment contract was conditional on a valid choice of Swiss law, the Court would thus have been required to re-determine the question of whether the parties intended to be bound, in relation to the alleged employment contract and pursuant to French law.

A. One Issue, Two Contracts

Independent determination of the choice of law contract inevitably creates the possibility of dépeçage—that the choice of law contract and the underlying contract are subjected to different applicable laws. While dépeçage is not, in principle, a problem, it seems to pose some difficulties where the choice of law contract and the underlying contract are challenged on the same ground, in relation to the same set of facts.

To the extent that this question has been considered, there seems to be agreement that the choice of law contract and the underlying contract must be submitted to the same applicable law when determining an issue that is equally relevant to both contracts. In other words, there must be 'synchronisation' of the two agreements, with the result that the issue is considered either under the putative chosen law or pursuant to objective choice of law rules (see subsection i below). It is submitted that this position is based on a mischaracterisation of the choice of law contract (see subsection ii).

i. One Issue, One Governing Law

Several authors have expressed the view that challenges that extend to both the underlying contract and the choice of law contract must be governed by only one applicable law.[86] The rationale for this view is not usually fully articulated, but the argument is broadly this: that, as a matter of logic and expediency, one legal system must determine whether parties have reached agreement on both contracts where there was one act of agreement on the same set of facts. Even Jaffey, who appeared to recognise the legal independence of the choice of law agreement, thought that application of two different laws could not be justified:

> The facts which bear on the issue whether the parties are to be held to have reached agreement on a governing law are the very same facts as bear on the issue whether they are to be held to have reached agreement on the contract itself. It is suggested, therefore, that there is no justification for using different, perhaps opposite, legal rules to determine these issues, which are in reality identical. ... As a matter of reality, the choice of law clauses and the substantive terms of the contract were equally agreed or not agreed.[87]

However, unless the alternative is reliance on an objective law to establish both the choice of law contract and the underlying contract,[88] this proposed need to synchronise the contracts will necessarily lead to an introduction of putativity through the backdoor. In fact, it is likely that the need for synchronisation has been the implicit driving force behind putativity.

It follows that the party autonomy rule is incompatible with synchronisation of the choice of law contract and the underlying contract pursuant to the chosen law. If the choice of law contract is governed by the putative chosen law, and the putative chosen law renders the choice of law contract void or invalid, the underlying contract cannot logically be governed by the chosen law. In the *Horphag Research* case, there was thus no way to synchronise the law applicable to the Swiss choice of law clause and the employment contract if, under Swiss law, the parties had not intended to be bound by the choice. It is only where the choice of law contract is valid pursuant to the (self-validating) putative chosen law, and the chosen law applies to also uphold the underlying contract, that there is no need to reconsider the issue.

ii. Two Contracts, Two Applicable Laws

This does not mean, however, that party autonomy can have no application to those issues that affect both the choice of law contract and the underlying contract. The case for synchronisation rests on the assertion that the question of agreement

[86] M Garner, 'Formation of International Contracts—Finding the Right Choice of Law Rule' (1989) 63 *Australian Law Journal* 751, 758; Stoll (n 9) 433; AJE Jaffey, 'Offer and Acceptance and Related Questions in the English Conflict of Laws' (1975) 24 *ICLQ* 603, 606–07; Lorenz (n 50) 203; Haudek (n 47) 92; P Gothot, 'La méthode unilatéraliste face au droit international privé des contrats' (1975–1977) *Travaux du Comité Français de Droit International Privé* 201, 209.

[87] Jaffey, ibid 606–07.

[88] See ibid, 609–11; Garner (n 86) 759; see *John T Jones Construction Company v Hoot General Construction Company* 613 F 3d 778 (8th Circuit 2010) 782–83 (see n 18 above) and *Farm & Ranch Services, Ltd v LT Farm & Ranch, LLC* 779 F Supp 2d 949 (SD Iowa 2011) 960 ('The choice of law provision in the contracts is not binding if there was no valid contract').

on either of these contracts must necessarily be construed as one and the same issue: because there is, in reality, only one act of agreement, it would be artificial to resort to separate applicable laws. However, even though the two contracts may arise from the same set of facts, or the same 'factual' act of agreement, they are two legal acts with separate functions;[89] and there is nothing wrong in principle, therefore, with reconsidering a (factual) act of agreement that has already been scrutinised in relation to the choice of law contract.

In particular, a (factual) act of agreement is not a legal category for the purposes of the conflict of laws. Following the ordinary process of characterisation, there are two relevant issues: the existence and validity of the choice of law contract, and the existence and validity of the underlying contract. In the *Horphag Research* case, it was not the alleged act of agreement—Horphag's letter with the outline of essential terms—that should have been in issue. Rather, the questions that needed to be answered were whether, as a result of that letter, there was (a) an intention to be bound by the choice of law clause and (b) an intention to be bound by the terms of employment. Because the contracts are not 'in reality identical',[90] it is the law applicable to each respective contract that must be relied upon to give meaning to the act of agreement.

If this solution is thought too cumbersome, the only principled alternative is to limit the scope of party autonomy to issues that do not arise in relation to both agreements. Parties would no longer have the freedom to select the law applicable to the existence and validity of their contract if the issue of existence/validity is equally relevant to the choice of law agreement. Instead, the court would rely on an objective law to determine the issue in relation to both the choice of law contract and the underlying contract.[91] Such an approach would amount to a significant limitation of party autonomy.

iii. Estoppel

At first sight, the proposed solution does not seem to sit well with the principle of estoppel.[92] Why should Mr van Hoegaerden be able to argue that there had been no intention to be bound by the Swiss choice of law clause, in order to rely on French law to establish an intention to be bound by the terms of employment? Or why should a party who claims to have entered into a contract under duress not be able to rely on the law stipulated in the contract to establish that duress? There are

[89] cp the so-called *Trennungsprinzip* in German property law: MPW van Vliet, 'Iusta Causa Traditionis and its History in European Private Law' [2003] *European Review of Private Law* 342, 377; S Habermaier, 'Das Trennungsdenken: Ein Beitrag zur europäischen Privatrechtstheorie' (1995) 195 *Archiv für die civilistische Praxis* 283; HC Grigoleit, 'Abstraktion und Willensmängel—Die Anfechtbarkeit des Verfügungsgeschäfts' (1999) 199 *Archiv für die civilistische Praxis* 379.

[90] Jaffey (n 86) 606.

[91] cp *Dunes Hospitality LLC v Country Kitchen International Inc* 623 NW 2nd 484 (SD 2001) 488; *John T Jones Construction Company v Hoot General Construction Company* 613 F 3d 778 (8th Circuit 2010): above, n 18.

[92] cp *CIMB Bank Bhd v Dresdner Kleinwort* [2008] SGCA 36, [2008] 4 SLR 543 [43].

two possible answers that go some way to addressing these concerns, but neither is founded on estoppel. Indeed, it is not evident why estoppel should apply at all where a party's only change in position is that the underlying contract and the choice of law agreement are not governed by the same law.

The first answer is that, as will be discussed in section B below, the underlying contract may be conditional on the choice of law contract, which will prevent parties from establishing the underlying contract, in reliance on the objective law, in circumstances where the choice of law contract is void or invalid. The second is that, where the challenge renders the contract only voidable, a party need not avoid both the choice of law contract and the underlying contract. A party who has coerced another to enter into a contract cannot complain that the law that is used to determine the allegations of duress is the law stipulated in the contract, if the coerced party has not sought to avoid the choice of law contract on that ground.

This point is nicely demonstrated by the House of Lords' decision in *Dimskal Shipping Co SA v International Transport Workers Federation*.[93] The claimants were the owners of a Panamanian ship. When the ship was in port in Sweden, agents of the International Transport Workers Federation (ITF) threatened that the vessel would be 'blacked' unless the claimants entered into ITF employment contracts with the crew and made certain payments to ITF. An undertaking entered into between the owners and ITF expressly provided for the application of English law. Having incurred losses as a result of the threats and the blacking of the vessel, the claimants sought to avoid the contracts on the ground of duress. The parties agreed that English law was the proper law of the claimants' contractual relationships with ITF, but ITF argued that the English courts should also have regard to the law of Sweden, as the place where the relevant pressure was exerted on the claimants. Under English law, blacking or a threat of blacking constituted illegitimate economic pressure, while Swedish law did not treat such pressure as unlawful.

The House of Lords rejected ITF's argument that Swedish law applied to the question of duress.[94] The parties were agreed that they had chosen English law as the proper law of the contracts, so the Court did not consider whether, like the underlying contracts, the choice of law was affected by the pressure exerted on the claimants. Because the threat of blacking the vessel caused the claimants to give in to ITF's demands, and the choice of law contract formed as much part of these demands as the contractual obligations that were imposed on the claimants, there seems to be no basis on which it could be argued that the choice of English law was not also the result of duress. It is likely that both the Court and the parties implicitly relied on putative reasoning to justify the application of English law to the underlying contracts. However, a more principled explanation would be that

[93] *Dimskal Shipping Co SA v International Transport Workers Federation* [1992] 2 AC 152 (HL) (Lord Templeman dissenting).

[94] ibid, 168 (Lord Goff).

the choice of English law was merely voidable, and that the claimants had not sought to avoid the choice of law contract.

B. Is the Underlying Contract Conditional on the Choice of Law Contract?

It is possible that another reason why there is such an aversion to an independent assessment of the choice of law contract is that, in some cases, there may be some degree of dependence by the underlying contract on the choice of law contract. That the choice of law contract is not dependent on the underlying contract has already been discussed at length;[95] but why should the underlying contract be equally sheltered from the fate of the choice of law contract, which after all has the potential to substantially affect the rights and obligations of the parties? That is, why should the employment contract that was alleged by Mr van Hoegaerden to have come into existence not be considered conditional on a valid choice of Swiss law?

i. Conditionality as an Explanation for Putative Reasoning

Although it is by no means a complete answer, the conditionality argument would go some way to justify the effect of putative reasoning. In *Midgulf International Ltd v Groupe Chimique Tunisien*, for example, the English Court of Appeal stated:

> Normally speaking, it is a well established principle of English private international law that questions relating to the existence and terms of a contract are governed by the putative proper law. This makes sense. Where, as in this case, a party makes an offer to enter into a contract which is explicitly to be governed by English law, only English law can determine whether the other party's conduct amounted to an acceptance so as to create an English law contract.[96]

Although the Court conflated the two contracts by equating an agreement to choose English law with an agreement on the underlying contract, the implication of the Court's reasoning is that the only possible contract between the parties was an 'English law contract' because the offeror's intention was for the contract to be governed by English law.[97]

[95] cp ch 8, s II.C on possible circumstances in which the choice of law contract might be conditional on a valid underlying contract.

[96] *Midgulf International Ltd v Groupe Chimique Tunisien* [2010] EWCA Civ 66, [2010] 2 Lloyd's Rep 543 [56]; see also KFK Low, 'Choice of Law in Formation of Contracts' (2004) 20 *Journal of Contract Law* 167, 170–71.

[97] Similarly, in *Navig8 Pte Ltd v Al-Riyadh Co* [2013] EWHC 328, the claimant argued that the dispute had to be considered on the basis that the parties had chosen English law to govern their relationship, even though it denied being a party to the bill of lading that included the English choice of law clause: at [21].

Translated into non-putative language, the real issue in this case was whether the party's conduct in *Midgulf* amounted to an acceptance of the English choice of law contract. If the English choice of law contract had not come into existence, this would also spell the end for the underlying contract—not because the underlying contract was governed by English law, but because it was dependent on an effective English choice of law contract.[98] Horphag Research could have similarly argued that it only ever intended to enter into an employment contract that was governed by Swiss law.

ii. Conditionality versus Severability

It seems that this potential relationship of dependency is best described as one of conditionality, to reflect the separate nature of the choice of law contract. The relevant question becomes, therefore, whether the parties (would have) intended the underlying contract to be operable even though they failed to come to an effective agreement on choice of law;[99] and not whether the underlying contract is severable from the choice of law contract.[100] Because parties' intentions as to the applicable law cannot be equated with their intentions to assume contractual obligations, it is particularly important that the content of the proposed law not simply be imported into an assessment of the parties' intentions to enter into the underlying contract. For example, the purported choice of Swiss law in the *Horphag Research* case could not be treated as an intention to negotiate the employment contract in accordance with Article 16 of the Swiss Code of Obligation. It was the Swiss choice of law contract that first needed to be established.

This approach based on conditionality is also preferable to Briggs' suggestion, made in relation to jurisdiction agreements, that there may be cases where it would be inequitable to impeach an agreement on jurisdiction (here: a choice of law agreement) while affirming the underlying contract, on the basis that a party should not be able to claim the benefit of the underlying contract while avoiding the burden of the jurisdiction agreement.[101] Because the choice of law contract does not form part of the parties' relationship of obligation, there can be little justification for treating the choice of law contract as the burden of the parties' underlying contract.

iii. A Case-by-case Assessment

It is not clear how far this argument of conditionality can be taken to justify the effect of putative reasoning. Successful challenges that relate only to the choice

[98] cp Stoll (n 9) 435, who argues that a failed choice of law agreement generally also invalidates the whole contract, but that this does not affect the parties' (factual) choice of law.

[99] On conditional contracts, see H Beale (ed), *Chitty on Contracts* 31st edn (London, Sweet & Maxwell, 2012) para 2-150.

[100] But see Beck (n 82) 532.

[101] Briggs (n 1) paras 3.44–3.48.

of law contract, or that are factually specific to the choice of law contract, are not usually considered to have an effect on the underlying contract;[102] and it is difficult to see why matters should be any different where the grounds of challenge would be the same for both contracts. It may be that, as an agreement to opt out of the default choice of law rules of any prospective forum state, the choice of law contract does not ordinarily have a sufficiently causal relationship with the parties' relationship of obligation to warrant a finding of conditionality;[103] and that any such intention would thus best be made express.[104]

Whether parties intended, or would have intended, their contract to be conditional on an effective choice of law contract can only be determined on a case-by-case basis, in accordance with the law applicable to the underlying contract. The fact that this argument is not ordinarily considered is not in itself an indication that it is not available.

V. Conclusion

The choice of law contract is an agreement that must be established independently from any underlying contract that it purports to govern. It is antecedent to the underlying contract, which may in turn be conditional on the choice of law contract. However, as demonstrated by the success of the putative approach, the independent nature of the choice of law contract is not generally appreciated. It is often suggested that putative reasoning is simply a necessary evil where legal certainty would otherwise be compromised:

> While the pursuit of intellectually logical solutions is commendable, this must never be at the expense of legal certainty. Therefore, use of the concept of the putative governing law of the contract in establishing voidness should not be anathema.[105]

But legal certainty is only enhanced by putative reasoning where the parties happen to have been in agreement on the (putative) chosen law, and not where it leads to enforcement of a choice of law contract that even under its own putative chosen law was not validly concluded. The whole point of the law of contract is to provide legal certainty by giving effect to the mutual, as opposed to the unilateral, intentions of the parties.

[102] Reithmann and Martiny (n 47) pt I, para 88; Kost (n 47) 67; cp Beck (n 82) 531–32.

[103] But cp Art 19(3) of the United Nations Convention on Contracts for the International Sale of Goods 1489 UNTS 3 (adopted 11 April 1980, entered into force 1 January 1988), dealing with the formation of contracts, which provides that 'Additional or different terms relating, among other things, to … the settlement of disputes are considered to alter the terms of the offer materially'.

[104] See D Czernich and H Heiss (eds), *EVÜ—Das Europäische Schuldvertragsübereinkommen* (Vienna, Orac, 1999) 55.

[105] Chong (n 37) 158; see also Crawford (n 15); Briggs (n 1) para 3.19.

What is more, rejection of putative reasoning appears to be more complex than it actually is. The following examples serve to demonstrate this.

(i) Party A seeks to enforce an alleged contract against party B. Party B claims that the contract did not come into existence because the person who purported to sign the contract on its behalf did not have authority to do so. The contract contains a choice of law clause. Pursuant to the putative chosen law, the third person had authority to contractually bind party B to the choice of law contract, with the result that the chosen law will be applied to determine whether the third person also had authority to bind party B to the underlying contract.

(ii) Party A seeks to enforce an alleged contract against party B. Party B claims that the contract did not come into existence because the person who purported to sign the contract on its behalf did not have authority to do so. The contract contains a choice of law clause. Pursuant to the putative chosen law, the third person did not have authority to contractually bind party B to the choice of law contract, with the result that the objective law will be applied to determine whether the third party also did not have authority to bind party B to the underlying contract.

It is true that, in those cases where the putative chosen law invalidates the choice of law contract (example ii), parties might be put to additional expense because they would be required to determine the content of both the putative chosen law and the objective applicable law. More generally, independent treatment of the choice of law contract would increase the number of cases in which courts have to deal with substantive issues concerning the existence and validity of the choice of law contract, which might make it more difficult to ascertain the applicable law at preliminary stages in the proceeding (for example, as part of an application concerning jurisdiction). But these inefficiencies are easily accommodated when they are evaluated against the overall effect of the proposed approach, which is that the underlying contract is given a second chance because it is not invalidated by a law that the parties did not intend to choose. If, under the putative chosen law, the choice of law contract is void because the defendant was not a party to it, then the plaintiff may still be able to argue that the defendant was a party to the underlying contract pursuant to the objective applicable law.

Unless provisions like Article 3 of Rome I are interpreted in a more principled fashion, and the common law rethinks its 'holistic' notion of a proper law, there may be cases, like the *Horphag Research* case, where putative reasoning leads to the potential under-enforcement of underlying contracts that would have been validly formed under the objective law. Admittedly, the number of such cases would be very small. This is because the objective law would not be applicable where the putative chosen law is self-validating, or where the choice of law contract is merely voidable and is not sought to be avoided; and even where these factors are not made out, it could still be argued that the underlying contract is conditional on an effective choice of law contract.

But if putativity is not rejected in favour of a more principled approach, this could have real implications for the long-term viability of the party autonomy rule. Mr van Hoegaerden was right to feel aggrieved by the reasoning of the Court of Appeal, which was then affirmed by the Cour de Cassation: that Horphag Research was able to rely on Swiss law to show that it had not intended to enter into the employment contract, on the basis that this was the law that the parties would have intended to be applicable had the employment contract come into existence. In *Navig8 Pte Ltd v Al-Riyadh Co*, the Court even relied on a putative choice of law contract to allow service out of the jurisdiction on the basis that the defendant's proceedings in Jordan would defeat the parties' agreement on English law.[106] Pursuant to Jordanian choice of law rules, the law governing the dispute was Jordanian law. The claimant's application was for a negative declaration that it was not a party to the alleged bills of lading, which included the English choice of law. Such reasoning makes a mockery of the party autonomy rule and will surely offend anyone who falls victim to it.

Even if independent treatment of the choice of law contract were, in fact, too difficult for the purposes of choice of law, then this would need to be expressly acknowledged in a clear qualification to the party autonomy rule, which, after all, calls for the application of the law that the parties intended to choose. But if the party autonomy rule can be reduced to unilateral choice of law, then no doubt its rationale is in need of re-examination.

[106] *Navig8 Pte Ltd v Al-Riyadh Co* [2013] EWHC 328; see ch 2, s III.A.i.

5

Regulating the Choice of Law Contract

I. Importance of a Cohesive Framework

The choice of law contract is a unique form of contract because it merges the law of contract and the conflict of laws.[1] It is a contract about choice of law. Consequently, the choice of law contract is subject to the principles and rules of *both* the law of contract and the conflict of laws. The purpose of this chapter is to analyse how these different sources fit together. How is the task of regulating choice of law contracts allocated between them, and why?

The reality is that choice of law contracts are subject to a patchwork of contract law, modal choice of law rules[2] and conflict of laws rules limiting the scope of party autonomy. Not all of these regulatory tools will be available or appropriate all the time, but there is the possibility of overlap. A choice of law contract might be submitted to the law of contract to determine whether the parties reached the necessary standard of agreement; or it might be submitted instead to a modal choice of law rule requiring 'real consent'. In these circumstances, the need for cohesiveness is obvious. There has to be a clear breakdown of functions or responsibilities between the law of contract, modal choice of law and conflict of laws limitations on party autonomy.

In analysing the functions of these different sources, the chapter will focus on the existence and validity of choice of law contracts, rather than the availability or scope of party autonomy—an issue already covered in chapter three of this book. By definition, the availability or scope of party autonomy is determined by conflict of laws rules on the scope of party autonomy. Examples of such rules are restrictions on the choice of applicable laws, and restrictions on the effect of the party autonomy rule via the objective applicable law (in the form of mandatory rules and public policy). The reason why these rules are still relevant to this chapter is that they affect the extent to which the existence and validity of choice of law

[1] See ch 2.

[2] M Hook, 'The Concept of Modal Choice of Law Rules' (2015) 11 *Journal of Private International Law* 185; see s IV below.

contracts ought to be regulated. For example, if party autonomy is limited to a small selection of applicable laws, or if mandatory rules of the objective applicable law override the parties' choice, there is reduced need to regulate the validity of one-sided choice of law contracts that are particularly unfavourable to the weaker party.

It follows that a cohesive framework for the regulation of choice of law contracts requires an understanding of the interplay between the law of contract, modal choice of law and conflict of laws rules limiting the availability or scope of party autonomy. The burden of ensuring a cohesive interplay between these sources falls on the conflict of laws. Proper regulation of the choice of law contract is, in essence, a conflict of laws problem. It is the conflict of laws that must ensure that choice of law contracts are submitted to their own applicable law (and hence, the law of contract); that, where application of the law of contract has reached its limits or is otherwise inappropriate, modal choice of law rules are devised to fill the gap or to offer tailored solutions; and that there is a balance between limitations on the scope of party autonomy and rules on the existence and validity of choice of law contracts. It has already been seen in chapter four that courts and legislators have displayed reluctance to embrace this important role of the conflict of laws; and chapters six to eight largely confirm this assessment. The present chapter aims to remove some of the barriers that have prevented the conflict of laws from taking ownership of the regulation of choice of law contracts.

Before we can turn to the task of dissecting the choice of law contract's regulatory matrix, it is necessary to raise one final but fundamental point. Why should we worry about regulating the existence, validity and interpretation of choice of law contracts at all? Why is this not an issue that can be resolved by courts as a matter of fact in their discretion? The system of choice of law has traditionally been understood as a normative lacuna that holds little interest in the regulation of substantive matters.[3] If the sole function of the party autonomy rule is the allocation of the applicable law, and choice of law is primarily value-neutral, then perhaps the choice of law contract is nothing more than a means to an end.[4] Contractual regulation may even be antithetical to the purposes of choice of law, which aims, above all, for predictability.[5]

The reason we need to worry about the regulation of choice of law contracts is that the decision to grant party autonomy is in itself a value judgment.[6] It is a value judgment that imports fundamental principles of the law of contract into the conflict of laws. So it would be wrong to argue that the conflict of laws is devoid of contractual values and hence relieved of the burden of regulating party

[3] For the classical view of the conflict of laws as a neutral system of allocation, see G Kegel, 'The Crisis of Conflict of Laws' (1964) 112 *Recueil des Cours* 92, 184–85.

[4] See A Briggs, *Agreements on Jurisdiction and Choice of Law* (Oxford, Oxford University Press, 2008) para 10.13, stating that 'the common law rule for choice of law in contracts took no specific account of … differences in the respective bargaining strengths of the parties'.

[5] See ch 3, s II.A.i.

[6] See ch 3.

choice. Like any contract, a choice of law contract can only be enforced if it is valid. Rules are needed, therefore, to determine whether the parties have agreed on the applicable law, and whether the agreement ought to be enforceable. Such rules must prescribe the necessary incidents of agreement and define the kinds of circumstances in which a choice of law is not the product of a free or informed decision.

This is not to say that conflicts principles—such as predictability or efficiency—are immaterial to the regulation of choice of law contracts. On the contrary, as a contract about choice of law, the choice of law contract must combine principles of the law of contract and the conflict of laws. But there has to be a balance. Giving courts free rein over the enforcement of choice of law contracts would undermine the very purpose of party autonomy. Moreover, it would be short-sighted to argue that the application of contractual rules necessarily interferes with the predictability or efficiency of choice of law. Not only is it the case that contractual efficiency depends, in large part, on the existence of free and informed agreement, and that the choice of law contract is no exception to this;[7] but a principled contractual regime would also alleviate some of the uncertainty that typically attaches to choice of law contracts.

II. Underlying Principles

The conflict of laws and the law of contract combine to provide comprehensive regulation of the party autonomy rule. It follows that the principles (or aims or policies) that underpin these areas of law must also underpin the party autonomy rule. For example, an important function of the law of contract is to create predictability and certainty for the parties; and the conflict of laws, too, strives to achieve choice of law outcomes that meet the legitimate expectations of the parties; so it is only natural that the party autonomy rule should operate in a way that supports these principles.

This example paints an admittedly simplistic picture. Whether a particular principle (or aim or policy) should shape the regulation of party autonomy may involve complex questions. Not *all* principles underpinning the law of contract and the conflict of laws will be relevant to choice of law contracts; and sometimes it will be necessary to balance conflicting principles. Some of these more difficult questions will be encountered at later points in this book. But for now, it will be useful to provide a brief overview of the principles that shape the law of contract and the conflict of laws, that may also be relevant to the regulation of party autonomy. Because these principles necessarily vary across borders, it is only possible to make the following general observations.

[7] See generally G Rühl, *Statut und Effizienz* (Tübingen, Mohr Siebeck, 2011) 204–06, 437ff.

A. Law of Contract

The law of contract is a form of regulation.[8] This proposition may seem counterintuitive, because after all the law of contract is all about *freedom* of contract—its primary function is to enable parties to self-regulate. But the principle of freedom of contract would be meaningless without rules that bind parties to their contractual obligations and define the meaning of contract; and it would be unjust without rules that impose certain conditions on the enforceability of contracts. In fact, the regulatory role of the law of contract has grown vastly since the days of laissez-faire in the nineteenth century. The law now draws on an amalgam of norms that goes far beyond a 'single-minded pursuit of individualism':

> Enforceable contract is a societal institution that sets the limits within which parties may exercise some degree of control over their legal liability. Contract law also defines parties' obligations to a large extent. Mediating between private ordering and social concerns, contract is a socioeconomic institution that requires an array of normative choices.[9]

People understand the term 'law of contract' to mean different things. In particular, it may refer to the general law of contract, that is, rules of contract that are of general application to all contracts; or it may encompass (often statutory) rules that are aimed at specific contracts. It is the latter, broader meaning of 'law of contract' that is adopted here. The law of contract includes any legal rule that purports to regulate a contractual issue: general rules on, for example, the formation of contract by offer and acceptance; and specific rules on, for example, the use of exclusion of liability clauses in consumer contracts. This broad understanding of the law of contract takes full account of the many different norms that may affect contracting parties.

The so-called 'classical' core principles of the law of contract may be succinctly stated. The principle of freedom of contract is the founding rationale of the law of contract, supported by the principle that contracts are binding and thus enforceable. In short, parties are free to enter into agreements with binding effect.[10] The law of contract facilitates the conclusion of contracts: it provides legal certainty by, for example, defining the meaning of offer and acceptance; and it gives effect to parties' reasonable expectations by, for example, taking account of common usages and practices to determine the parties' obligations.[11]

Today these principles remain at the core of the law of contract. But the modern law of contract has also become increasingly concerned with procedural and

[8] See H Collins, *Regulating Contracts* (Oxford, Oxford University Press, 1999) ch 4; J Braucher, 'Contract versus Contractarianism: The Regulatory Role of Contract Law' (1990) 47 *Washington and Lee Law Review* 697.

[9] Braucher (n 8) 699; see also Collins (n 8) ch 3.

[10] A typical statement to this effect can be found in H Beale (ed), *Chitty on Contracts* 31st edn (London, Sweet & Maxwell, 2012) paras 1-027–1-037.

[11] eg, O Lando and H Beale (eds), *Principles of European Contract Law (PECL): Parts I and II* (The Hague, Kluwer, 2000) Art 1:105.

substantive justice, engaging in 'general supervision over the process of contract formation and … intervention in the very contents of the contract'.[12] Such concerns are particularly prevalent where the parties are engaged in a relationship that would be prone to unequal bargaining power or information asymmetries. Consumers, employees and spouses are potentially vulnerable parties that are offered extra protection from improperly-concluded or ill-advised agreements. More generally, parties may be able to avoid or rescind a contract on the grounds of vitiating factors such as duress or mistake; and many jurisdictions recognise a general principle of good faith or fair dealing.[13]

Chapters six to eight will discuss in more detail the relevance of particular contract principles to determining the existence and validity of choice of law agreements. But where the underlying principles of the law of contract suggest that parties may be incapable of entering into a free and informed choice of law agreement, then the party autonomy rule should not be available, or it should be available only in limited form.[14]

B. Conflict of Laws

Chapter three contained a discussion of the often uncertain aims of choice of law rules. There is no need to repeat this discussion here, but it is worth reiterating that public policies of objective choice of law rules—in the form of external or protective interests—may be reflected in limitations on the scope of the party autonomy rule. Most choice of law rules are neutral as to the content of the applicable law. They strive instead for conflicts justice, or they seek to allocate regulatory authority to the state most closely connected to the dispute. The concept of conflicts justice is typically associated with choice of law rules that achieve uniformity of outcome and give effect to the parties' reasonable and legitimate expectations.

More generally, the conflict of laws must balance the often competing goals of certainty and flexibility.[15] Disputes about uncertain or complex choice of law rules can cause significant delays in the resolution of substantive disputes; but at the same time, choice of law rules must be sufficiently flexible to allow justice to be done in individual cases.

Finally, an obvious but crucial point is that the conflict of laws must retain a certain degree of normative openness to the principles, rules and practices of other jurisdictions. The founding rationale of the conflict of laws is to regulate cross-border aspects of private legal relationships, so it is imperative that its rules

[12] J Beatson and D Friedman, 'Introduction: From "Classical" to Modern Contract Law' in J Beatson and D Friedman (eds), *Good Faith and Fault in Contract Law* (Oxford, Clarendon Press, 1995) 3 at 12–13.

[13] See *PECL* (n 11) Art 1:201.

[14] See ch 3, ss III and IV.

[15] See H Gaudemet-Tallon, 'Le Pluralisme en Droit International Privé' (2005) 312 *Recueil des Cours* 9, 299–390.

be capable of communicating with other legal systems. Typical examples of the conflict of laws' ability to do so are the doctrine of renvoi and the process of characterisation, which must look beyond domestic classifications of legal issues.

III. Law of Contract

Party A and party B enter into a matrimonial property contract and, instead of making an express choice of law, stipulate that their obligations are to be determined by reference to certain provisions of country A's matrimonial property legislation. Party C and party D enter into a contract for the sale of goods, but there is an issue whether they agreed on party C's or party D's standard terms and conditions, which contain conflicting choice of law clauses. Party E seeks to avoid an express choice of law agreement with party F on the basis that party F misrepresented the content of the chosen law. Would a court apply the law of contract to determine the existence and validity of these choice of law agreements—and if so, whose law of contract? Chapters six to eight seek to provide specific answers to these questions, but the purpose of this section is to determine the relevance of the law of contract to choice of law agreements in principle. The focus is necessarily on the general law of contract.

The relationship between the law of contract and choice of law agreements is framed by the following three key propositions. Every choice of law contract must be submitted to a law of contract, which is needed to regulate fundamental questions about the existence, formation and validity of choice of law contracts (see section A below). However, because choice of law contracts do not give rise to rights and obligations, they are subject only to those rules of the law of contract that are not specific to relationships of obligations (see section B). The choice of law contract has one principal governing law, which is usually the putative chosen law; but the application of this connecting factor is subject to a number of exceptions (see section C).

A. Fundamental Role of the Law of Contract

Comprehensive regulation of the choice of law contract can be achieved only with the help of the law of contract.[16] It is the general law of contract that defines the meaning of 'agreement' and provides rules on the formation of agreements, as well as on their avoidance on the grounds of vitiating factors. In short, it establishes a regime for the ascertainment of the parties' mutual intention that is

[16] cp W Woodward, 'Finding the Contract in Contracts for Law, Forum and Arbitration' (2006) 2 *Hastings Business Law Journal* 1.

generally applied to all forms of contracts.[17] In *Hoegaerden v Horphag Research (UK) Ltd*,[18] for example, Article 16 of the Swiss Obligationenrecht (Code of Obligations) could have been applied to argue that the parties did not intend the Swiss choice of law clause to be binding until a final contract was drafted and signed.

Nevertheless, choice of law contracts are still sometimes said to be excepted from an application of the law of contract, either on the basis that they are 'factual' agreements (see subsection i below) or because general modal choice of law rules are thought to provide an exclusive source of regulation (see subsection ii). These arguments are not convincing.

i. Factual Approach

The factual approach to choice of law contracts has already been discussed at length in chapter two,[19] and it is not necessary to repeat this discussion here. If the conflict of laws requires the flexibility of a 'factual' agreement, which is subject only to the court's discretion and not the law of contract, then there would be little point in having a party autonomy rule at all.

It is true that there are codifications on choice of law that fail to identify a connecting factor for the law applicable to choice of law contracts;[20] and that some authors have interpreted this failure to identify a connecting factor as an endorsement of the factual approach.[21] But it would be wrong to assume that lawmakers intended to confer on the parties the power to choose the applicable law without also imposing the kinds of rules that would ordinarily apply to contracts. There are good reasons, after all, why we have a law of contract.

A more convincing view is that, where codifications are silent as to the law applicable to the choice of law contract, the putative chosen law acts as the default choice of law rule for choice of law contracts and need not be expressly

[17] The ability of non-national rules of law to provide such a regime may be one of the factors to be taken into account in determining whether parties are free to choose a non-national body of rules: see ch 3, s V.E.

[18] Cass soc, 24 November 2004, no 02-42660 (*Hoegaerden v Horphag Research (UK) Ltd*); see ch 4, s III.

[19] See ch 2, s II.

[20] eg Reg (EC) 864/2007 on the law applicable to non-contractual obligations [2007] OJ L199/40 (Rome II), Art 14; Property (Relationships) Act 1976 (NZ), s 7A; Einführungsgesetz zum Bürgerlichen Gesetzbuch (EGBGB), Arts 15(3) and 14(4); Proposal for a Council Reg on jurisdiction, applicable law and the recognition and enforcement of decisions in matters of matrimonial property regimes (COM 2011, 126, 16 March 2011) (Proposal for a Reg on matrimonial property), but see Art 19 a of the compromise text of the Proposal, annexed to Council of the European Union, 'Proposal for a Council Regulation on jurisdiction, applicable law and the recognition and enforcement of decisions in matters of matrimonial property regimes—Political agreement' (Note, 14651/15, Brussels, 26 November 2015).

[21] As did R Plender and M Wilderspin, *European Private International Law of Obligations* 3rd edn (London, Sweet & Maxwell, 2009) para 29-011 (in relation to Rome II); but cp R Plender and M Wilderspin, *European Private International Law of Obligations* 4th edn (London, Sweet & Maxwell, 2015) paras 29-010–29-013.

provided for.[22] To avoid confusion, future codifications ought to make express provision for the law applicable to the choice of law contract.

ii. Modal Choice of Law Rules as an Exclusive Source of Regulation

Similar considerations apply to the exclusive interpretation of those modal choice of law rules that provide for a general requirement of agreement for choice of law contracts. The scope of these rules is variously proposed to range from implied choice to manifestation of the parties' intentions more generally. Article 3 of Regulation (EC) 593/2008 on the law applicable to contractual obligations (Rome I) has thus been construed by some authors as a modal choice of law rule that regulates exclusively the existence of implied (and sometimes express) choice,[23] or the interpretation of the parties' intention to choose the applicable law.[24] A variation on this argument is that a putative choice of law, and hence also the choice of law contract, must satisfy a base level of mutuality. It has been argued, for example, that a unilateral declaration of intention would not be sufficient to constitute a putative choice of law because a putative choice requires at least an appearance of choice.[25]

The problem with this argument is that it tends to substitute a vague and general requirement, like a choice that is 'clearly demonstrated by the terms of the contract or the circumstances of the case',[26] for a set of specific rules of contract,

[22] A Dickinson, *The Rome II Regulation: The Law Applicable to Non-Contractual Obligations* (Oxford, Oxford University Press, 2010) paras 13.11–13.18; T Kadner Graziano, 'Freedom to Choose the Applicable Law in Tort—Articles 14 and 4(3) of the Rome II Regulation' in W Binchy and J Ahern (eds), *The Rome II Regulation on the Law Applicable to Non-Contractual Obligations: A New Tort Litigation Regime* (Leiden, Martinus Nijhoff, 2009) 113, 123; S Leible, 'Rechtswahl im IPR der außervertraglichen Schuldverhältnisse nach der Rom II-Verordnung' [2008] *Recht der Internationalen Wirtschaft* 257, 260; see C von Bar and P Mankowski, *Internationales Privatrecht*, vol 1 (Munich, CH Beck, 2003) 601, para 82; D Henrich (ed), *Staudingers Kommentar zum Bürgerlichen Gesetzbuch: Art 13–17b EGBGB* (Berlin, Sellier, 2011) Art 14, para 138 and Art 15, para 104.

[23] Reg (EC) 593/2008 on the law applicable to contractual obligations [2008] OJ L177/6 (Rome I); eg D Coester-Waltjen, 'Einige Überlegungen zur konkludenten Rechtswahl im europäischen Vertragsrecht' in M Coester, D Martiny and KA von Sachsen Gessaphe (eds), *Privatrecht in Europa—Festschrift für Hans Jürgen Sonnenberger* (Munich, CH Beck, 2004) 343, 348–50; T Rauscher (ed), *Europäisches Zivilprozess- und Kollisionsrecht* (Berlin, Sellier, 2011) Art 3 Rom I-VO, para 12; W-H Roth, 'Zur Stillschweigenden Rechtswahl in einem Künftigen EU-Gemeinschaftsinstrument über das Internationale Schuldvertragsrecht' in M Stathopoulos (ed), *Festschrift für Apostolos Georgiades* (Munich, CH Beck, 2006) 905, 914; F Vischer, L Huber and D Oser, *Internationales Vertragsrecht* 2nd edn (Berlin, Stämpfli, 2000) 85–87; C Reithmann and D Martiny, *Internationales Vertragsrecht* 7th edn (Cologne, Dr Otto Schmidt, 2010) pt I, para 114.

[24] L Collins (ed), *Dicey, Morris and Collins on the Conflict of Laws* 15th edn (London, Sweet & Maxwell, 2012) paras 32-047–32-048; *Egon Oldendorff v Libera Corporation* [1996] 1 Lloyd's Rep 380 (QB) 387; U Magnus (ed), *Staudingers Kommentar zum Bürgerlichen Gesetzbuch: Rom I-VO Art 3* (Berlin, Sellier, 2011) para 66; E Lorenz, 'Die Auslegung schlüssiger und ausdrücklicher Rechtswahlerklärungen im internationalen Schuldvertragsrecht' [1992] *Recht der Internationalen Wirtschaft* 697, 700; Rauscher, ibid Art 3 Rom I-VO, para 9.

[25] See references in C Rühl, 'Rechtswahlfreiheit und Rechtswahlklauseln in Allgemeinen Geschäftsbedingungen' (Baden Baden, Nomos, 1999) 51ff and 107ff; cp A Baumert, 'Abschlusskontrolle bei Rechtswahlvereinbarungen' [1997] *Recht der Internationalen Wirtschaft* 805, 806.

[26] Art 3(1), Rome I (n 23).

like the rules of offer and acceptance.[27] It fails to provide appropriate guidance to the court on what constitutes an 'agreement' on the applicable law, placing at risk the very thing that is often said to be its goal: certainty and consistent decision-making. One of the functions of modal choice of law rules is to replace rules of the law of contract where these do not meet the needs of the conflict of laws.[28] But the replacement of specific rules of contract with a vague and general modal choice of law rule would not usually be in the interest of the conflict of laws.

A related danger is that the party autonomy rule might then be manipulated to make up for perceived deficiencies of objective choice of law. For example, an expectation that a certain law would be applicable may suddenly qualify as an intention to choose the applicable law, because the objective choice of law rule points to a law that is considered less appropriate than the 'chosen' law in the circumstances.[29] Conversely, the need for an 'appearance' of an agreement on the applicable law would have the potential to be unduly restrictive, by ruling out a choice of law in cases where the general law of contract may have found such an agreement.

The better view, therefore, is that general modal choice of law rules in the nature of Article 3 of Rome I do not usually exclude the application of the law of contract to determine the parties' agreement on the applicable law.

B. Identification of Applicable Rules of Contract

Much of the law of contract is inapplicable to choice of law contracts because it is designed to apply to relationships of obligation, and choice of law contracts do not create relationships of obligation.[30] When submitting choice of law contracts to the law of contract it is necessary, therefore, to distinguish between rules that can apply only to relationships of obligation and rules that are of more general application. This task is inherently contractual in nature, and necessarily rule-specific. A court will have to inquire into the rationale for the particular rule and determine whether the rationale applies equally to choice of law contracts. Nevertheless, it is possible to make some generalised comments about the following broad 'categories' of contractual rules.

i. Rules on the Process of Agreement

Rules on the meaning, formation and vitiation of agreement are generally applicable to choice of law contracts to the extent that they are focused on the

[27] S Maire, *Die Quelle der Parteiautonomie und das Statut der Rechtswahlvereinbarung im internationalen Vertragsrecht* (Basel, Helbing & Lichtenhahn, 2011) 147; see von Bar and Mankowski (n 22) 601–02, paras 82–83.

[28] See below, s IV.B.

[29] See ch 6, s II.

[30] See ch 2; cp P Stankewitsch, *Entscheidungsnormen im IPR als Wirksamkeitsvoraussetzungen der Rechtswahl* (Frankfurt, Peter Lang, 2003) 95; Maire (n 27) 148.

process of agreement. For example, there may be a question whether parties reached an agreement by way of an effective offer and acceptance, or whether a party entered into the agreement under duress. Rules of contract that provide answers to these questions focus on the parties' conduct in the negotiation and conclusion of the contract; they may even impose obligations related to this process (for example, an obligation to negotiate in good faith). But they do not regulate—at least not directly—the rights and obligations created by the contract, which means that they will usually be applicable to choice of law contracts.

There is an important exception to this proposition. Some process-based rules of agreement are expressed to apply only to specific contracts like consumer or employment contracts.[31] For example, the enforcement of matrimonial property contracts may be subject to a requirement that the spouses obtained independent legal advice before entering into the contract. Because this requirement is expressed to apply specifically to matrimonial property contracts, a court could not apply it to a choice of law contract governing matrimonial obligations—at least not without wilfully distorting its meaning.[32]

Conversely, the fact that a particular rule of contract is *expressed* to apply to rights and obligations does not necessarily mean that it is not also applicable to agreements that do not give rise to rights and obligations. Article 16 of the Swiss Obligationenrecht, for example, which was relied upon by the employer in the *Horphag Research* case,[33] would probably have been applicable to the Swiss choice of law clause, even though the provision states that an agreement by the parties to make a contract subject to formal requirements will create a presumption 'that the parties do not wish to assume obligations until such time as those requirements are satisfied'.[34] The narrow drafting of this Article simply reflects the fact that the general law of contract has been developed with relationships of obligation in mind.

ii. Rules on the Content of Agreement

Different considerations apply to rules that regulate the content of the parties' contract. Most commonly, such rules determine the extent, fairness, reasonableness or conscionability of the parties' rights and obligations, and they will not be applicable to choice of law contracts. For example, a particular rule of contract may impose a mandatory limit of liability, voiding any agreement that purports to reduce the parties' maximum liability below the mandatory limit. Such a rule could not void a choice of law contract, even if the effect of the chosen law was to enforce the parties' exclusion of liability. It would be the underlying contract that reduced the defendant's liability, in conjunction with the chosen law—and not the choice of law contract.

[31] See Stankewitsch, ibid 96.

[32] See further ch 7, s VIII.B.

[33] Cass soc, 24 November 2004, no 02-42660 (*Hoegaerden v Horphag Research (UK) Ltd*); see ch 4, s III.

[34] Translation taken from www.admin.ch. The original uses the term 'verpflichtet'.

This distinction was lost on the House of Lords in *The Hollandia*,[35] where it decided that Article III(8) of the Hague Visby Rules invalidated a choice of Dutch law and jurisdiction, because Article III(8) rendered null and void any agreement purporting to lessen the maximum limit of liability provided for by the Rules. Under Dutch law, which still recognised an un-amended version of the Hague Visby Rules, the maximum limit of liability was lower than that provided for in the amended Hague Visby Rules.[36] Because the choice of law clause did not purport to limit the defendant's liability, the House of Lords should not have applied Article III(8) to void the choice of law contract, even if the ultimate effect of the choice of Dutch law was to lessen the maximum limit of liability. Instead, the House of Lords should have placed greater emphasis on Article X,[37] which expressly applied the Hague Visby Rules to every bill of lading issued in a contracting state, to conclude that the Rules were applicable to the carriage contract—and not the choice of law contract—in the form of overriding mandatory rules.[38]

'Content-controlling' rules should not usually be applicable to choice of law contracts because they do not provide content-controlling standards that are relevant to choice of law contracts.[39] A contract that is unfair in substance, for example, is unfair because of a mismatch in the parties' rights and obligations. The content of a choice of law contract is a choice of law: it does not create rights or obligations.[40] Besides, the content of the chosen law can hardly be subjected to a content-controlling rule.

There may be exceptions to this position. It is possible, for example, that burdens ancillary to a choice of law contract may fall within the scope of a content-controlling rule on unfairness. Where a chosen law is obscure and its rules are difficult to determine, it may be unfair, for the purposes of such a rule on unfairness, to put a party to the burden of determining the content of the chosen law.[41] More importantly, not all content-controlling rules are necessarily dependent on an obligation-based agreement. For example, a rule may invalidate terms if they are so unusual that a party need not expect their inclusion in a standard terms contract;[42] and a term may be unusual or surprising even if it has no direct effect on the parties' rights and obligations. But even then it would be difficult to apply this rule to choice of law contracts in a meaningful way, because the standards developed by the law of contract to define an unusual or surprising term would not translate easily to choice of law contracts. What is more, the rule might encroach on the regulatory scope of modal choice of law.[43]

[35] *The Hollandia* [1983] 1 AC 565 (HL).
[36] ibid, 573.
[37] ibid, 577.
[38] cp FA Mann, 'Uniform Statutes in English Law' (1983) 99 *LQR* 376, 396–97.
[39] Rühl (n 25) 204–05; see von Bar and Mankowski (n 22) 603, para 85; see ch 8, s III.
[40] See ch 2, s III.
[41] cp P Nygh, *Autonomy in International Contracts* (Oxford, Oxford University Press, 1999) 68.
[42] See ch 7, s VII and the references there cited.
[43] See below, s IV.

iii. Rules on the Performance and Breach of Contract

Obvious examples of rules that can be applied only to relationships of obligation are rules on performance and breach of contract, and on remedies for non-performance. A choice of law contract does not create obligations of performance, so it cannot be breached.[44]

C. The Putative Chosen Law and its Exceptions

With the exception of the United States, it is generally accepted that the principal connecting factor for choice of law contracts is the putative chosen law.[45] There is no consistent approach to this matter in the United States. The Restatement (Second) of Conflict of Laws does provide that the forum has to determine 'in accordance with its own legal principles' whether a choice of law was obtained by mistake or by improper means (such as undue influence, misrepresentation or duress).[46] But it is unclear what law applies to formation and validity generally. Some authors suggest it is the 'chosen law', based on sections 198, 199 and 200 of the Restatement (Second), which submit capacity, form and general validity to the law chosen by the parties 'if they have made an effective choice'.[47] But these provisions deal with the formation and validity of contracts generally and make no reference to the concept of the putative chosen law—on the contrary, they seem expressly to exclude the question of whether the choice is effective. In any case, US courts variously seem to apply the *lex fori*, the putative chosen law or the objective applicable law.

The putative chosen law has two main benefits. First, it increases the chance of synchronisation between the choice of law contract and any underlying contract where the contracts are challenged on the same grounds. As long as the putative

[44] See ch 2, s III.A.i.

[45] Rome I (n 23) Art 3(5); Reg (EU) 1259/2010 implementing enhanced cooperation in the area of the law applicable to divorce and legal separation [2010] OJ L343/10 (Rome III), Art 6(1); Hague Convention on the Law Applicable to Matrimonial Property Regimes (1977) 16 ILM 14 (opened for signature 14 March 1978, entered into force 1 September 1992), Art 10; Bundesgesetz über das Internationale Privatrecht (IPRG), Art 116; Hague Conference on Private International Law, *Principles on Choice of Law in International Commercial Contracts* (approved on 19 March 2015), Art 6(1); von Bar and Mankowski (n 22) 601–02, paras 82–83; Nygh (n 41) 94; but see the obiter dicta in *Oceanic Sun Line Special Shipping Co Inc v Fay* (1988) 165 CLR 197 by Gaudron J and Brennan J that the law of the forum applies to determine the existence of the contract and its terms: at 260–61 per Gaudron J, at 225 per Brennan J; cp *Evialis SA v SIAT* [2003] EWHC 863, [2003] 2 Lloyd's Rep 377 [38], where the Court concluded that the existence of an alleged choice of English law had to be determined in accordance with the law that would be applicable to the underlying contract in the absence of a choice by the parties, which was Italian law; cp Art 2 of the Preliminary Draft Convention on the Law Applicable to Contractual and Non-Contractual Obligations (Commission of the EC, XIV/398/72, Rev 1) which provided that 'Conditions governing the *validity* of the consent of the parties as to the applicable law shall be determined according to that law' (emphasis added); cp Collins (n 24) para 34-046.

[46] American Law Institute, *Restatement (Second) of Conflict of Laws* (1971), s 187, cmnt (b).

[47] P Hay, P Borchers and S Symeonides, *Conflict of Laws* 5th edn (St Paul, West Academic Publishing, 2010) 1129–30.

chosen law does not render the choice of law contract invalid, the same law will apply to determine the issue in relation to both contracts. Second, the choice of law contract is upheld only if it is valid under the chosen law, pre-empting the argument that a choice of law contract that the chosen law itself would have rendered void or invalid is contractually unsound.[48]

The flipside of this is that the putative chosen law is also the validating law, and a party challenging the choice of law contract might understandably object to the self-validating effect of the putative chosen law.[49] This problem is mitigated, however, by exceptions to the application of the putative chosen law, in the form of alternative connecting factors and overriding mandatory rules (see subsections i and ii below). Where the putative chosen law is not identifiable, it is necessary to rely on either modal choice of law rules or the *lex fori* (see subsection iii below). More generally, modal choice of law rules may reduce the need to rely on the putative chosen law (see section IV.B).

i. Alternative Connecting Factors

Just like an ordinary contract, the choice of law contract may be subject to more than one connecting factor. Article 10(2) of Rome I, for example, enables the challenging party to rely on the law of the place of its habitual residence to argue that it never agreed to the choice of law. The provision applies to contracts of obligation as well as to choices of law governing such contracts.[50] The scope of this rule is generally understood to be limited to questions of formation,[51] and it will apply only if 'it appears from the circumstances that it would not be reasonable to determine the effect of [the party's] conduct in accordance with the [putative chosen law]'.[52] Within these boundaries, however, the rule provides a valuable safety net, by ensuring that a challenging party may have recourse to a law other than the putative chosen law—a law to which it may have no connection at all.

Courts have also at times relied on the principle of the more favourable law for consumer contracts contained in Article 6(2) of Rome I to supplement the putative chosen law.[53] In 1996, for example, the Oberlandesgericht Düsseldorf struck down an English choice of law clause governing an agreement to conduct

[48] See ch 4, s I.C.

[49] See criticism by D Cavers, 'The Common Market's Draft Conflicts Convention on Obligations: Some Preventive Law Aspects' (1975) 48 *Southern California Law Review* 603, 609–10; V Heuzé, *La réglementation française des contrats internationaux* (Paris, Joly éditions, 1990) para 234 and fn 75.

[50] Arts 3(5) and 10(2), Rome I (n 23); Magnus (n 24) paras 171 and 173; see also *Hague Principles on Choice of Law in International Commercial Contracts* (n 45) Art 6(2); Rome III (n 45) Art 6(2); IPRG, Art 123 (but there is debate as to whether Art 123 would apply to choice of law contracts: H Honsell et al (eds), *Basler Kommentar* 3rd edn (Basel, Helbing Lichtenhahn, 2013) 1096).

[51] Collins (n 24) para 32-114. This includes rules on the incorporation of standard terms: Magnus (n 24) para 176.

[52] Art 10(2), Rome I (n 23).

[53] *Re Futures Transactions* [1998] ILPr 327 (OLG Düsseldorf); LG Bremen, 2 O 37-06 (7 December 2006); LG Krefeld, 5 O 502/04 (31 January 2006); LG Hamburg, 327 O 187/14 (2 September 2014).

futures transactions on behalf of a German plaintiff, on the basis that the plaintiff could not have reasonably expected the reference to English law.[54] The broker was located in England, but it was the broker's agent in Germany who had solicited the agreement with the plaintiff. The Court applied Article 6 (then Article 5) in order to invalidate the choice of law clause under the German law on standard terms. As a result, the law applicable to the substance of the dispute was German law, which in turn allowed the Court to conclude that the defendants had not met their disclosure obligations imposed by German law.

But the principle of the more favourable law was never intended to apply to choice of law contracts, because it requires a comparison between the chosen law and the law that would have applied to the consumer contract in the absence of choice. In other words, the rule requires a validly concluded choice of law contract.[55] This interpretation is also consistent with the purpose of the rule, which is to offer consumers the protection of the more favourable law, whether that is the chosen law or the law of habitual residence. Any added protection that a consumer stands to gain through the chosen law would be lost if the consumer's law already applied to strike down the choice of law contract.[56] It would have been more appropriate, therefore, had the Court relied on the consumer rule at the substantive stage of the proceeding, in order to apply the German disclosure provisions rather than the (less favourable) English law.

ii. Overriding Mandatory Rules

The application of overriding mandatory rules to choice of law contracts is not an issue that has received much attention. There are probably only few overriding mandatory rules that would be of relevance to choice of law contracts. An example might be the law of duress, where the pressure exerted on the party falls into 'a class of duress so unconscionable' that the law of the forum will 'override' the putative chosen law 'as a matter of public policy'.[57] There is no reason in principle why overriding mandatory rules should not be applicable to choice of law contracts[58]—even though a better, more direct approach may be to draft them as modal choice of law rules.

[54] *Re Futures Transactions* [1998] ILPr 327 (OLG Düsseldorf).

[55] P Mankowski, 'Unwirksame Vereinbarung englischen Rechts zwischen deutschen Anlegern und ausländischem Terminbroker' [1994] *Recht der Internationalen Wirtschaft* 420, 422; Rühl (n 25) 166–67.

[56] Mankowski (n 55) 423; Rühl (n 25) 166–67. But see W-H Roth, 'Rechtswahlklauseln in Verbraucherverträgen—eine schwierige Sache?' [2013] *Praxis des Internationalen Privat- und Verfahrensrechts* 515, 520–21.

[57] See *Royal Boskalis Westminster NV v Mountain* [1999] QB 674 (CA) 729 (Phillips LJ), on the application of the law of duress to a substantive contract (and not a choice of law).

[58] Stankewitsch (n 30) 85, fn 156; Collins (n 24) para 32-093 (but referring in support to *The Hollandia*, discussed above at s III.B.ii, where the House of Lords applied the forum's Hague Visby Rules to invalidate a Dutch choice of law clause even though the Rules were not contractually relevant to the choice of law contract); M Davies, AS Bell and PLG Brereton, *Nygh's Conflict of Laws in Australia* 9th edn (Chatswood (NSW), LexisNexis, 2014) para 19.10, fn 35.

iii. Identification of the Putative Chosen Law

Where the putative chosen law is not readily apparent because there are two or more potentially chosen laws, modal choice of law may be able to provide a solution. It may, for example, provide a rule on conflicting choice of law clauses.[59]

Where modal choice of law has not provided such a solution, the only viable alternative appears to be application of the *lex fori*.[60] In the past, common law courts have accorded the *lex fori* considerable weight in the determination of the parties' intentions as to the applicable law.[61] Because Article 3(5) of Rome I does not provide a connecting factor for the law governing the interpretation of choice of law contracts, the *lex fori* continues to be an option under the Regulation. For the reasons outlined above, it is submitted that use of the *lex fori* should be confined to those cases where, on the facts of the case, the putative chosen law is impossible to ascertain.

IV. Modal Choice of Law Rules

Modal choice of law rules are rules of choice of law that supplement the operation of choice of law rules. Although they are widely used, they have been neglected in theory.[62] This lack of oversight is particularly troublesome in the context of party autonomy, which, much more than most choice of law rules, is reliant on modal choice of law rules. It will be useful, therefore, to begin this section with some general comments about modal choice of law rules, before considering their relevance to choice of law contracts more specifically.

The choice of law process is commonly thought to involve three steps: characterisation of the claim or issue; selection of the applicable choice of law rule; and identification of the governing law on the basis of the relevant connecting factor provided by the choice of law rule.[63] The function of a choice of law rule is to identify the law applicable to an issue or claim with foreign elements. For example, choice of law rules provide that the existence and validity of contracts be governed by the law selected by the parties; or that liability in tort be submitted to the *lex loci delicti*, the place where the wrong was committed. They are allocative in nature.

Choice of law rules may give the impression of being largely self-sufficient, or self-contained. They provide for all of the elements necessary to identify the applicable law: the characterisation element, which identifies the scope of the choice of

[59] See ch 7, s III.B.

[60] Nygh (n 41) 90.

[61] Nygh (n 41) 90; *Compagnie d'Armement Maritime SA v Compagnie Tunisienne de Navigation SA* [1971] AC 572 (HL) 603 (Lord Diplock); cp *Oceanic Sun Line Special Shipping Co Inc v Fay* (1988) 165 CLR 197, 260–61 (Gaudron J), 225 (Brennan J).

[62] Hook (n 2). For related scholarship, see pt B3 of the article.

[63] See generally Collins (n 24) ch 2.

law rule (eg 'the existence and validity of contracts'); and the connecting factor (eg 'the law selected by the parties'), which may consist of multiple elements (eg 'characteristic performance' and 'habitual residence', in 'the country where the party required to effect the characteristic performance of the contract has his habitual residence').[64] But, often, these choice of law elements cannot—or do not—stand on their own. They may require definition or explanation; or they may be subject to extraneous policy considerations, in the form of qualifications or conditions.

This supplementary function can be served by the conflict of laws itself. The conflict of laws can provide, for example, that any agreement to select the applicable law be in writing;[65] or that a company's place of habitual residence is its place of central administration;[66] or that the *locus delicti* of a personal injury is the country where the individual was when he sustained the injury.[67] It is this supplementary function of the conflict of laws—the supplementary function of rules of choice of law that regulate choice of law elements—that is of particular relevance to choice of law contracts. Because it prescribes the 'modalities' of how choice of law rules operate, it is termed 'modal choice of law'.

Modal choice of law rules are easily spotted. They may apply to any choice of law element. For example, the common law choice of law rule for contracts is subject to a rule that includes in the term 'contract' agreements unsupported by consideration;[68] and the connecting factor of 'domicile' is identified by reference to a number of interconnected rules that distinguish between the domicile of origin, the domicile of choice and the domicile of dependence.[69] These rules serve a supplementary function to the identification of the applicable law: in the first example, the rule defines the characterisation element of 'contract'; and in the second example, the rules enable the working-out of the connecting factor of domicile.

Modal choice of law rules are of particular importance to the party autonomy rule because here they function as contractual rules, by regulating the exercise of party autonomy. They are contractual rules that are specific to choice of law agreements, sourced directly from the conflict of laws. The conflict of laws may require, for example, that a choice of law agreement be made expressly or that it be 'freely negotiated'.[70] Such rules are not choice of law rules, because they do not have the effect of identifying an applicable law; and they are not rules of the general law of contract. They are modal choice of law rules because they determine how the party autonomy rule—and specifically its connecting factor, the choice of law contract—is to be given effect.

As a contractual rule created by the conflict of laws, the modal choice of law rule is in a unique position to combine principles of both the law of contract and the

[64] Rome I (n 23) Art 4(2).
[65] Rome III (n 45) Art 7(1).
[66] Rome I (n 23) Art 19(1).
[67] Private International Law (Miscellaneous Provisions) Act 1995 (UK), s 11(2)(a).
[68] *Re Bonacina* [1912] 2 Ch 394.
[69] See Collins (n 24) ch 6.
[70] Rome II (n 20) Art 14.

conflict of laws. Different principles will be relevant to different modal choice of law rules. But a key principle of the conflict of laws is that cross-border relationships should not be submitted to legal systems with which they have little or no connection. Although modal choice of law rules are necessarily influenced by the law of contract of the forum, they must also reflect the international nature of the choice of law contract and the international environment within which it operates. An idiosyncratic modal choice of law rule is not an effective modal choice of law rule.

The principal function of contractual modal choice of law rules is to supplement, and also sometimes to replace, rules of the general law of contract that govern the choice of law contract (see sections A and B below). As *lex specialis*, they take precedence over the general law of contract, with the effect that any matter that is already regulated by modal choice of law rules need not be submitted to the law applicable to the choice of law contract. In some instances, courts may even apply foreign modal choice of law rules (see section C).

A. Supplement the General Law of Contract

The main purpose of contractual modal choice of law rules is to fill gaps that are left by the general law of contract. The general law of contract does not answer questions that are specific to choice of law agreements—for example, whether a choice of law must be express or may be implied; or whether a floating choice of law clause is permissible. Modal choice of law rules step in to resolve these questions. More specifically, modal choice of law rules supplement the law of contract by importing those of its principles that, although relevant to the exercise of party autonomy, do not give rise to general rules of contract that are also directly applicable to the choice of law contract.

For example, Article 14(1)(b) of Regulation (EC) 864/2007 on the law applicable to non-contractual obligations,[71] which states that a choice of law agreement relating to future non-contractual obligations must be 'freely negotiated', reflects a concern of the law of contract with unequal bargaining power between commercial parties.[72] This concern is particularly acute where parties rely on standard form contracts. The law of contract commonly offers extra protection to parties who have agreed to be bound by the other party's standard terms;[73] but these rules tend to target the rights and obligations created by the contract and are therefore inapplicable to choice of law contracts. Section 3 of the Unfair Contract Terms Act 1977 (UK), for example, restricts the use of exclusion of liability clauses where one of the contracting parties deals 'on the other's written standard terms of business'.

[71] Rome II (n 20).

[72] eg, Dickinson (n 22) para 13.41 (arguing that a choice of law clause in standard terms is valid under Art 14(1)(b) if 'every party had an opportunity to influence [it]').

[73] eg *PECL* (n 11) Art 2:104.

So if the law's concern about unequal bargaining power is to be addressed in relation to choice of law contracts, reliance on the general law of contract is not sufficient and modal choice of law has to step in.

Even though, usually, the primary purpose of supplementary modal choice of law rules is to give effect to contract principles, it goes without saying that modal choice of law rules should also be responsive to the needs of the conflict of laws. For example, a modal choice of law rule may require spouses to have obtained legal advice on the meaning and possible implications of their agreement on choice of law. This modal choice of law rule would give effect to a more general concern of the law of contract that family relationships are prone to power imbalances, information deficits and bounded rationality; and that contracts between family members should thus be subject to a requirement of legal advice.[74] But the modal choice of law rule should also be wide enough to reflect varying practices across borders on the provision of legal advice: for example, the requirement of independent legal advice in common law jurisdictions, and the requirement of notarisation in civil law jurisdictions.[75] In other words, the modal choice of law rule should impose an internationalised requirement that is sufficiently wide so as not to be unduly parochial, while still giving effect to the relevant concerns of the law of contract.

It is not always immediately obvious whether the general law of contract would leave a regulatory gap for modal choice of law to fill. A particular principle or concern of the law of contract that, at first sight, appears to be relevant to choice of law contracts may, on closer inspection, turn out to be irrelevant. For example, the principle of *favor negotii* or *favor contractus*, which provides that contracts ought to be interpreted so as to be valid,[76] is not usually relevant to implied choice of law contracts, which require more than a hypothetical intention to select the applicable law.[77] The boundary between the general law of contract and modal choice of law is particularly murky where a modal choice of law rule simply seems to clarify how the law of contract applies to choice of law agreements.

An illustration of this latter point is *BP Plc v National Union Fire Insurance Co*, which will be discussed in more detail in chapter seven, where the English High Court upheld a floating choice of law clause with retrospective effect on the basis that there was 'no doubt that parties to a contract can effectively agree to empower one of them to vary it without agreement of the other party or parties', as long as an option to vary the proper law 'is exercised in good faith … and with sufficient clarity'.[78] Another example is Article 4 of the Hague Principles on Choice of Law in International Commercial Contracts, which, instead of relying only on the operation of ordinary rules of contract to ascertain the parties' implied intentions,

[74] See ch 7, s VIII.B.
[75] ibid.
[76] eg *PECL* (n 11) Art 5:106.
[77] See ch 6, s IV.
[78] *BP Plc v National Union Fire Insurance Co* [2004] EWHC 1132 [35].

clarifies that 'An agreement between the parties to confer jurisdiction on a court or an arbitral tribunal to determine disputes under the contract is not in itself equivalent to a choice of law'.[79]

B. Replace the General Law of Contract

The second function of contractual modal choice of law rules is to replace rules of the general law of contract. In these circumstances, the choice of law contract *could* be governed by a rule of the law of contract but modal choice of law intervenes and imposes its own solution. The reason why modal choice of law may intervene in this manner is that application of the general law of contract would be inconsistent with the needs of the conflict of laws. For example, the law of contract might offer an idiosyncratic or parochial solution where the conflict of laws requires inclusiveness; the law of contract might be too difficult to apply, interfering with the speedy resolution of conflict of laws disputes; or the issue might be submitted to a uniform modal choice of law rule because application of the law of contract would lead to inconsistent choice of law outcomes.

An example of a modal choice of law rule that (arguably) has the effect of replacing the general law of contract is Article 3 of Rome I, which has been interpreted as doing away with substantive rules of contractual interpretation that exclude evidence of pre-contractual or subsequent conduct (on the basis that Article 3 requires the court to have regard to 'the terms of the contract or the circumstances of the case').[80] The rationale for this modal choice of law rule, presumably, is that the evidence rules of some *lex causae* may be too restrictive,[81] and that the rule produces a uniform approach to choice of law agreements generally.

Alternatively, modal choice of law may replace the law of contract because the issue is one that the forum wishes to control (but the applicable law is not the *lex fori*). For example, when the Privy Council in *Vita Food Products Inc v Unus Shipping Co Ltd* said that the parties' intention to choose the applicable law was to be ascertained objectively,[82] it probably relied on modal choice of law, and not on the law applicable to the choice of law agreement, to come to this conclusion, wishing to set down a rule for the enforcement of choice of law agreements generally.

In some cases, modal choice of law may be considered to regulate certain matters by omission.[83] It has been argued that rules of contract that would have the

[79] *Hague Principles on Choice of Law in International Commercial Contracts* (n 45).

[80] *Samcrete Egypt Engineers & Contractors SAE v Land Rover Exports Ltd* [2001] EWCA Civ 2019, [2002] CLC 533 [23], [29]; *Lawlor v Sandvik Mining and Construction Mobile Crushers and Screens Ltd* [2012] EWHC 1188, [2012] 2 Lloyd's Rep 25 [11]–[12], [47]; see Collins (n 24) para 32-037.

[81] Collins (n 24) para 32-037 ('[I]t would not be in keeping with the spirit of the Regulation to apply [the rule against subsequent conduct] so as to defeat the intention of the parties').

[82] *Vita Food Products Inc v Unus Shipping Co Ltd* [1939] AC 277 (PC) 290.

[83] But see above at s III.A.ii that general modal choice of law rules should not be understood to exclude an application of more detailed rules of the general law of contract.

effect of imposing restrictions on the content of the parties' choice are not applicable to choice of law contracts because they would amount to an undue interference with party autonomy.[84] Thus, the Oberlandesgericht Düsseldorf was criticised for applying a provision of the German law on standard terms to an English choice of law clause,[85] because the rule provided for the invalidity of any standard terms or conditions that unreasonably disadvantaged the non-drafting party. The concept of unreasonable disadvantage required an assessment of the parties' chosen law, but the Convention 80/934/ECC on the law applicable to contractual obligations (Rome Convention) had already implicitly regulated the matter by providing for free and unrestricted choice.[86] Modal choice of law thus provides another reason why content-controlling rules of contract are not generally applicable to choice of law contracts, in addition to the more general point explored in section III.B.ii that such rules are relevant only to relationships of obligation.

C. Foreign Modal Choice of Law Rules

The general position is that the conflict of laws rules of the *lex fori* apply to determine the scope of a choice of law rule and the meaning of its connecting factor.[87] Courts do not apply foreign modal choice of law rules unless they follow the doctrine of renvoi (or, in Australia, the principle of 'no advantage').[88] Thus, in *Re Annesley* the Court held that it would be wrong, in applying the English choice of law rule of domicile, to look to French rules prescribing certain formal requirements before a person could become domiciled there.[89] Mrs Annesley's domicile had to be 'determined by the English Court … according to those legal principles applicable to domicil which are recognised in this country and are part of its law'.[90]

There are good reasons for this position. Courts apply the choice of law rules of their forum, and the function of modal choice of law is to supplement these rules and give effect to the forum's policies; so it is natural that courts would not look towards foreign modal choice of law rules. Because the choice of law contract is grounded in the choice of law rules of the forum, it is those rules, ordinarily, that should provide any additional criteria for enforcement of the contract. Reliance

[84] Magnus (n 24) para 35; von Bar and Mankowski (n 22) 603, para 85; E Jayme, 'Inhaltskontrolle von Rechtswahlklauseln in Allgemeinen Geschäftsbedingungen' in B Pfister and M Will (eds), *Festschrift für Werner Lorenz* (Tübingen, Mohr Siebeck, 1991) 435, 438; cp H Heiss, 'Inhaltskontrolle von Rechtswahlklauseln in AGB nach europäischem Internationalen Privatrecht' (2001) 65 *Rabels Zeitschrift für ausländisches und internationales Privatrecht* 634, 642–43; cp Dickinson (n 22) para 13.19.

[85] OLG Düsseldorf, NJW-RR 1994, 1132; Mankowski (n 55) 422–23.

[86] Convention 80/934/ECC on the law applicable to contractual obligations [1980] OJ L266/1 (opened for signature 19 June 1980, entered into force 1 April 1991).

[87] Collins (n 24) para 1-081; see also references by AH Robertson, *Characterization in the Conflict of Laws* (Cambridge MA, Harvard University Press, 1940) 107–08.

[88] See Davies, Bell and Brereton (n 58) ch 15.

[89] *Re Annesley* [1926] Ch 692, 703–04.

[90] ibid, 703, citing Lindley MR in *In re Martin* [1900] P 211, 227.

on the law of the forum is also a matter of convenience. In some cases, it is simply the only reasonable option available, because the applicable (substantive) law is yet to be identified.[91] Based on this reasoning, there can be no basis for a 'conflict of modal choice of law rules'.

There are, however, possible exceptions to the general principle. In some circumstances, it may be in the forum's interest to supplement its own choice of law rules with the modal choice of law rules of another country.[92] In particular, foreign modal choice of law rules may be applicable to a choice of law contract where they fall within the scope of an existing choice of law rule (and the forum has no interest in exercising control over the issue).

An example of such an approach is a dictum in *Dubai Electricity Co v Islamic Republic of Iran Shipping Lines (The Iran Vojdan)* that it is the proper law of a contract that determines whether parties may choose a floating law.[93] The Court did not justify its departure from the general principle that connecting factors must be determined by the modal choice of law rules of the *lex fori*. But the necessary implication is that modal choice of law rules on floating choice of law clauses fall within the ambit of the choice of law rule that identifies the law applicable to choice of law agreements. This proposition does not seem so farfetched if the purpose of such modal choice of law rules is to clarify the application of the general law of contract to choice of law agreements.[94]

A less controversial example might be application of a foreign modal choice of law rule that *replaces* a rule of the foreign law of contract, because here the court would simply substitute the modal choice of law rule for a rule of contract which would otherwise be applicable to the choice of law contract.[95] For example, if the putative chosen law applicable to a choice of law agreement is English, and a New Zealand court is required to apply English law (as the putative chosen law) to determine whether the choice of law agreement may be established by reference to subsequent conduct, then the court could reasonably apply the modal choice of law rule on evidence developed pursuant to Article 3 of Rome I. It is difficult to see the harm in this.

Finally, the forum may specify that a foreign rule of the law of contract be applied as a modal choice of law rule. Although, strictly speaking, such rules apply as modal choice of law rules of the forum, their purpose is to incorporate a foreign rule of contract and adapt it to choice of law contracts. Articles 15(3) and 14(4)

[91] Robertson (n 87) 111.

[92] Hook (n 2).

[93] *Dubai Electricity Co v Islamic Republic of Iran Shipping Lines* (The Iran Vojdan) [1984] 2 Lloyd's Rep 380 (QB) 385; see also Nygh (n 41) 100.

[94] See above, s IV.A; cp Art 3(5) of Rome I (n 23), which submits the formal validity of choice of law contracts to the same *favor validitatis* rule that also governs substantive contracts (Art 11). The intention behind this particular choice of law rule, however, remains unclear. Art 3 of Rome I does not impose any formality requirements on party choice, which seems to negate the need for a *favor validitatis* rule.

[95] See above, s IV.B.

of the German Einführungsgesetz zum Bürgerlichen Gesetzbuch (EGBGB) are an example of such a combined rule of contract and modal choice of law. These Articles provide that choice of law contracts that have been concluded outside Germany must comply with the formalities required for matrimonial property contracts by either the chosen law or the place of contracting.[96] So instead of providing for the application of foreign modal choice of law rules, they require particular rules of the law of contract (namely rules of formality for matrimonial property contracts), which would otherwise be inapplicable, to be adapted to the choice of law contract. Such a rule would be particularly useful where the applicable foreign law does not recognise the party autonomy rule and hence does not provide for modal choice of law rules.

V. Limitations on the Scope of the Party Autonomy Rule

Whether there is a need to regulate particular matters relating to the existence and validity of choice of law contracts will often depend on the scope of party autonomy granted to the parties. As discussed in chapter three, the conflict of laws can restrict the scope of party autonomy in various ways. It may restrict the choice being granted, by limiting the choice to certain issues or to a particular selection of laws; or it may restrict its effect, via overriding mandatory rules or the public policy exception. As a general rule, limitations on the scope of party autonomy will make parties less vulnerable to detrimental choice of law contracts. A spouse has little opportunity to exploit his partner through the selection of a particularly unfavourable law if their choice is limited to the laws of their respective nationalities; and a consumer who is still entitled to the application of his local consumer protection legislation despite a choice of foreign law, may have no need to rely on a modal choice of law rule requiring, for example, that choice of law contracts with consumers be drafted clearly.

But limitations on the scope of party autonomy are not a general substitute for regulating the existence and validity of choice of law contracts. They are a blunt tool whose primary role is to give effect to the public policies of objective choice of law rules.[97] The more we limit party autonomy (or freedom of contract, for that matter), the less is at stake, and the less we need to worry about ensuring free and informed agreement. But it is still necessary to establish a basic agreement conforming to the general law of contract; and where the primary purpose of the

[96] J Kleinheisterkamp, 'Rechtswahl und Ehevertrag: Zum Formerfordernis nach Art 15 Abs 3 EGBGB' [2004] *Praxis des Internationalen Privat- und Verfahrensrechts* 397; see also Hague Convention 1978 (n 45) Art 13.

[97] See ch 3, s IV.

limitation is to address contractual concerns (ie that a choice of law contract be the product of free and informed agreement), then direct regulation of the existence and validity of the choice of law contract would be a less intrusive alternative.

A. Overriding Mandatory Rules and Public Policy: *Lex Fori*

It is common for fora to provide for overriding mandatory rules and public policy exceptions to temper the effect of the applicable law. Where an overriding mandatory rule or public policy exception applies qua forum, it is not usually targeted at reducing the scope of party autonomy (or addressing concerns about the contractualisation of choice of law). Rather, its function is to reduce the scope of the applicable law more generally, whether the applicable law is the result of the party autonomy rule or an objective choice of law rule. But the general observations above still hold true. An overriding mandatory rule or public policy exception may reduce the need to regulate the existence and validity of the choice of law contract because it limits the scope of the applicable law, so less is at stake. Yet the two forms of regulation cover fundamentally different ground. Rules on the existence and validity of choice of law contracts are concerned with the quality of the parties' agreement on the applicable law. The forum's overriding mandatory rules or public policy exceptions are concerned to give effect to the forum's substantive policies (usually irrespective of the applicable law). They tend to offer piecemeal protection that is substantive in nature.

For example, an English party to an international sales contract who claims that the Danish seller misrepresented the quality of the product argues that it never properly agreed to a choice of Danish law buried within a standard terms contract.[98] The contract provides for an exclusion of liability clause. The English party is able to obtain some protection under the Unfair Contract Terms Act 1977 (UK), whose provisions on exemption clauses are given overriding force by virtue of section 27(2) where an attempt has been made to 'evade' the operation of the Act through a choice of foreign law. However, if the choice of law clause is given effect, the English seller is still required to establish that the seller misrepresented the quality of the goods in accordance with Danish law. The overriding mandatory provisions provide piecemeal protection that is aimed at the substance of the dispute.

Another reason why the forum's overriding mandatory rules and public policy exceptions are of limited usefulness to curb the vagaries of party autonomy is that they apply most often in cases that display a close connection to the forum.[99]

[98] cp *Kingspan Environmental Ltd v Borealis A/S* [2012] EWHC 1147: see ch 7, s VII.

[99] See, eg, Credit Contracts and Consumer Finance Act 2003 (NZ), s 137; Competition and Consumer Act 2010 (Aust), sch 2, s 67; Insurance Contracts Act 1984 (Aust), s 8(2); Unfair Contract Terms Act 1977 (UK), s 27(2); Collins (n 24) para 1-057.

This is true in particular—and perhaps ironically—for overriding mandatory rules of the forum that are targeted specifically at the party autonomy rule. For example, section 137(b) of the Credit Contracts and Consumer Finance Act 2003 (NZ) provides that the Act applies to a credit contract that would be governed by the law of New Zealand but for a choice of law agreement. Section 137 is relevant only where the parties have chosen the applicable law but the chosen law is foreign and the objective proper law is the law of New Zealand. Another example is section 27(2) of the Unfair Contract Terms Act 1977 (UK), referred to in the previous paragraph. The consequence is that parties whose dispute has no real connection to the forum (with the result that the objective proper law would be a law other than the law of New Zealand) are left without special protection.

This desire to confine the forum's protection to cases that are closely connected to the forum is taken to the extreme by rules excluding protective provisions of the chosen (forum) law for contracts that would otherwise be governed by a foreign law (so-called 'self-denying statutes').[100] These rules are the opposite of overriding mandatory rules and, perversely, are likely to increase the risk of an exploitative choice of law contract. For example, section 27(1) of the Unfair Contract Terms Act 1977 provides:

> Where the law applicable to a contract is the law of any part of the United Kingdom only by choice of the parties (and apart from that choice would be the law of some country outside the United Kingdom) sections 2 to 7 and 16 to 21 of this Act do not operate as part of the law applicable to the contract.[101]

The effect of section 27(1) is that parties are able to choose the law of England in order to avoid protective measures on unfair terms, as long as foreign law would be applicable but for the choice of English law.[102] Statutes that are territorially limited may have a similar effect.[103]

B. Overriding Mandatory Rules and Public Policy: Objective Applicable Law

Chapter three discussed in some detail the use of specific limitations on party autonomy that are imposed via the objective applicable law. Such limitations

[100] Collins (n 24) para 1-063.

[101] cp also Late Payment of Commercial Debts (Interest) Act 1998 (UK), s 12; Control of Exemption Clauses Ordinance 1989 (HK), s 17.

[102] FA Mann, 'The Proposed New Law of Exemption Clauses and the Conflict of Laws' (1977) 26 *ICLQ* 903, 908; see *Air Transworld Ltd v Bombardier Inc* [2012] EWHC 243, [2012] 1 Lloyd's Rep 349 [98]–[108]; *Surzur Overseas Ltd v Ocean Reliance Shipping Co Ltd* [1997] CLY 906 (QB); *Deutsche Bank (Suisse) SA v Khan* [2013] EWHC 482 [356]ff.

[103] eg Employment Rights Act 1996 (UK), s 94(1) and *Serco Ltd v Lawson* [2006] UKHL 3, [2006] 1 All ER 823.

reduce the scope of the chosen law by giving effect to mandatory rules or public policies of the objective applicable law. Examples of this approach are the principle of the more favourable law in Rome I, which subjects certain consumer and employment contracts to the mandatory rules of the objective applicable law where these offer more protection than the chosen law;[104] and section 187(2)(b) of the Restatement (Second), which provides that the chosen law will not be given effect if its application 'would be contrary to a fundamental policy of [the objective applicable law]', provided the state has a 'materially greater interest than the chosen state in the determination of the particular issue'. The principle of the more favourable law gives effect to simple mandatory rules that 'cannot be derogated from by agreement' as a matter of substantive law,[105] and the concept of 'fundamental policy' that is relied on in section 187(2)(b) is broader than the traditional notion of *ordre public*.[106]

These limitations are targeted at the party autonomy rule. As a result, they can respond more directly to the need (if any) to offer substantive protection to parties who have concluded a choice of law contract; and the objective applicable law can play a much more weighty role than the *lex fori*. The public policy exception can even be likened to a contractual rule on substantive unfairness, because it renders choice of law contracts unenforceable to the extent that they depart significantly from the rights and obligations conferred under the objective applicable law. This issue will be considered in more detail in chapter eight.

However, the primary purpose of such limitations should be to protect the public policies of the relevant objective choice of law rule,[107] and not to address concerns about the parties' capacity to enter into a free and informed choice of law contract. Rules on the existence and validity of choice of law contracts can target such concerns more specifically than mandatory rules or public policy exceptions, which usually impose significant limits on the scope of party autonomy enjoyed by the parties. For example, if objective choice of law rules submitted consumer contracts to the law most closely connected to the transaction, and if it was accepted that the rule did not serve a protective function or give effect to external interests, then reliance on the principle of the more favourable law would have to be justified on the decidedly paternalistic ground that consumers are simply incapable of contracting about choice of law.

Finally, even the principle of the most favourable law cannot replace rules on the existence and validity of choice of law contracts in their entirety. If the parties did not intend to choose the applicable law, the party autonomy rule can have no application, and reliance on the principle of the most favourable law would be based on a fictional agreement.

[104] Rome I (n 23), Arts 6(2) and 8(1).
[105] Rome I, Arts 6(2) and 8(1).
[106] *Restatement (Second)* (n 46) s 187, cmnt (g).
[107] See ch 3, s IV.

C. Limits on the Selection of Applicable Laws

A common practice to restrict party autonomy is to limit parties to a selection of applicable laws.[108] For example, Article 8 of the Hague Protocol on the Law Applicable to Maintenance Obligations provides that parties may select the law of either party's nationality or habitual residence, the law applicable to the parties' property regime, or the law applicable to their divorce or separation.[109] A choice of any other law will be ineffective. It is also possible to think of such rules as modal choice of law rules, because they go to the existence and validity of the choice of law contract.

The primary purpose of these limitations would appear to be to take account of the public policies of objective choice of law (for example, the protective function of Article 3 of the Hague Maintenance Protocol, which calls for application of the law of the creditor's place of habitual residence). But they also reduce the potential for exploitative choice of law contracts, because they reduce the pool of laws that would be particularly unfavourable to a weaker party. Whether they are more effective than rules that attempt to regulate the unfairness of choice of law contracts directly is another issue to be considered in chapter eight.

VI. A Cohesive Framework

The conflict of laws is the starting point for any regime on the existence and validity of choice of law contracts. This contractual regime is made up, in turn, of modal choice of law rules and the general law of contract, which applies by virtue of a choice of law rule of the forum. The regime operates in parallel to conflict of laws rules that exclude or limit the operation of party autonomy or that control the effect of the chosen law on an ad hoc basis through mandatory rules and public policy. But it is the latter form of regulation—and overriding mandatory rules and public policy, in particular—that is usually associated with the need to place controls on the exercise of party autonomy. It arguably overshadows the role played by rules on the existence and validity of choice of law contracts. Why worry about submitting the choice of law contract to contractual rules if a similar function is already served by, for example, the principle of the more favourable

[108] Art 5 of Rome III (n 45); Art 16 of the Proposal for a Reg on matrimonial property (n 20); Art 5 of Rome I (n 23) on contracts of carriage and Art 7 on insurance contracts; EGBGB, Art 15(2); Hague Convention 1978 (n 45), Art 3; but see the French approach prior to the coming into force of the Hague Convention 1978, as described in M Revillard, 'Premier bilan de la Convention de La Haye du 14 mars 1978 sur la loi applicable aux régimes matrimoniaux' in A Borrás et al (eds), *E Pluribus Unum. Liber Amicorum Georges AL Droz* (The Hague, Martinus Nijhoff, 1996) 369, 372; cp Collins (n 24) para 28-034.

[109] Hague Protocol on the Law Applicable to Maintenance Obligations (opened for signature 23 November 2007, entered into force 1 August 2013).

law? Because the chosen law may be more favourable to the weaker party than the objective law, it would not be in the interest of the weaker party to impose strict contractual rules on the choice of law contract.

Any regime on the existence and validity of choice of law contracts has to take account of the interplay between limitations on the scope of the party autonomy rule, and contractual rules that might be redundant as a result of these limitations or that might interfere with them. Limitations on the scope of party autonomy may decrease the need for contractual rules. However, the two types of regulation do not serve identical functions; they are not substitutable. Contractual rules will always be needed to establish a basic agreement on the choice of law contract; public policy and overriding mandatory rules tend to offer only piecemeal protection; and if limitations on the scope of party autonomy are not already applicable to protect the public policies of objective choice of law rules, their use may well be disproportionately invasive, because, unlike contractual rules, they cannot be targeted at specific concerns relating to the parties' capacity to enter into a free and informed choice of law contract.

For the purposes of regulating the existence and validity of choice of law contracts, the conflict of laws is tasked with (1) submitting the choice of law contract to the law of contract, by virtue of choice of law rules applicable to it (and where appropriate, by the application of overriding mandatory rules) and (2) providing modal choice of law rules that function as contractual rules. This chapter outlined the respective regulatory functions of each of these sources. What is needed is a regime that, in adhering to the principles of the law of contract, reflects the unique nature of the choice of law contract. The basic structures for this regime are already in place. The choice of law contract is largely accepted to have its own applicable law, and modal choice of law rules, too, are being employed to determine its existence and validity.

But, as was shown in chapter four and as will be shown in chapters six to eight, more can be done to ensure that these sources are used effectively. The following principles should guide interpretation and reform of existing regimes on the existence and validity of choice of law contracts:

(1) The existence, validity and interpretation of the choice of law contract are determined in accordance with the law of contract and modal choice of law rules.

(2) The choice of law contract is submitted to its own choice of law rules.
  (a) In most jurisdictions, the principal connecting factor for the law applicable to the choice of law contract is the putative chosen law.
  (b) The modal choice of law rules of legal systems other than the *lex fori* are not usually applicable to the choice of law contract.

(3) Modal choice of law rules are *lex specialis* and prevail over conflicting rules of the law of contract.

(4) Rules of the general law of contract are applicable to the choice of law contract unless:
   (a) they are applicable only to relationships of obligation;
   (b) they are clearly excluded by modal choice of law rules;
   (c) they encroach on the regulatory scope of modal choice of law.
(5) The function of modal choice of law rules is to provide rules specific to the choice of law contract and, in particular:
   (a) to supplement the law of contract, usually by importing principles of the law of contract that would not be given sufficient effect by rules of the law of contract directly applicable to the choice of law contract.
   (b) to replace rules of the law of contract where these are inconsistent with the needs of the conflict of laws.

6

Agreement to Choose the Applicable Law

I. Introduction

Chapters two to five outlined the parameters of a contractual framework for the regulation of the party autonomy rule. The purpose of chapters six to eight is to consider in more detail the content of this framework, insofar as it relates to the existence and validity of choice of law contracts. The question of the existence and validity of choice of law contracts raises many issues. In particular, rules must prescribe the standard of agreement that is sufficient to constitute a choice of law (chapter six); there are such issues as offer and acceptance, certainty, form and transparency (chapter seven), which may be referred to loosely as matters of 'formation'; and there is a need to regulate the kinds of circumstances in which a choice of law contract is not enforceable because it is the product of a defective or unfair agreement (chapter eight).

The task for chapters six to eight is two-fold: to evaluate the existing regime that determines the existence and validity of choice of law contracts and, where appropriate, to propose changes to the regime itself or to the way it is given effect. The chapters are not intended to provide an exhaustive analysis of every possible issue that may (or should) affect the existence or validity of a choice of law contract. Instead, they highlight issues that are likely to carry the greatest impact for the enforcement of choice of law contracts.

The first, and most fundamental, question when determining whether parties have entered into a binding choice of law contract is whether there was agreement, or consensus ad idem: was there a mutual intention to choose the applicable law, in sufficiently certain terms, accompanied by an intention to be bound?[1] The purpose of the current chapter, therefore, is to delineate the meaning of a mutual intention to choose the applicable law. While such an intention is not usually difficult to determine where the parties' intentions are clearly evidenced

[1] See O Lando and H Beale (eds), *Principles of European Contract Law (PECL): Parts I and II* (The Hague, Kluwer, 2000) Art 2.101. As has already been discussed in ch 2 at s III.A.ii, consideration is not a requirement of choice of law contracts, even though it is central to the common law notion of contract.

in fact, in the form of an express choice of law contract, there are cases in which it is necessary to rely on contractual rules to determine whether the parties have made a choice.

In particular, there are three interrelated matters that require consideration here: first, the role of the parties' expectations as to the applicable law (see section II); second, the distinction between subjective and objective intention (see section III); and third, the role of hypothetical reasoning in inferring or interpreting a choice of law (see section IV). The focus of this chapter is on implied choice of law contracts. It is a general principle of the law of contract that, unless otherwise provided, contracts need not be concluded in express terms and parties are free to manifest their intentions through conduct.[2] The same principle applies to choice of law contracts. Unless otherwise provided, choice of law contracts need not be based on an express agreement to choose the applicable law. But this is not to say that implied choice of law contracts need not meet the same standard of agreement as express choice of law contracts. On the contrary, as will be argued in this chapter, it should be very difficult ordinarily to imply a choice of law contract *because* it has to meet a certain standard of agreement. Section II of this chapter argues that a mere expectation or assumption that a certain law will be applicable is not sufficient; and, as will be explained in section IV, nor is a hypothetical intention by the parties to choose the applicable law.

Because terms such as 'objective', 'subjective' or 'hypothetical' intention are often used inconsistently in the law of contract, both within and across jurisdictions, it is helpful at this point to provide short definitions for the purposes of this book. A 'subjective' theory of contract is founded on a subjective meeting of the minds, while an 'objective' theory of contract looks to acts that can reasonably be interpreted as manifestations of intent. Other terms that are sometimes used to denote this concept of subjective intention are 'actual' or 'real' intention. In this book, however, the term 'real' intention will be reserved to describe the opposite of 'hypothetical' or 'presumed' intention, an intention that a party would have had, had it turned its mind to the question. The term 'objective' intention is also not to be confused with the expressions 'objective' connecting factor or 'objective' law, which are here used to refer to connecting factors or applicable laws that are not based on, or derived from, a choice of law by the parties.

II. Intention or Expectation?

Party A and party B, who are both based in country C, enter into a contract for the sale of movable property situated in country D. Both parties assume that

[2] See, eg, H Beale (ed), *Chitty on Contracts* 31st edn (London, Sweet & Maxwell, 2012) para 1-096.

their relationship is governed by the law of country C. Have they reached an agreement to choose country C's law? It is submitted that they have not, because an expectation that a certain law will be applicable is not the same as an intention to choose the applicable law. Every choice of law contract requires a mutual intention to choose the applicable law.[3] Based on ordinary principles of contract, an intention to agree that something will happen is not the same as an expectation or assumption that something will happen. The same principle applies to choice of law contracts. At the very least, 'intention' requires an awareness that a law other than the chosen law may potentially be applicable, even if the existence of such an awareness is measured by objective standards.[4] This conclusion remains unaffected by modal choice of law rules like Article 3 of Regulation (EC) 593/2008 on the law applicable to contractual obligations (Rome I), which requires that the parties' choice be 'clearly demonstrated'.[5] If rules like Article 3 were interpreted as calling for anything less than intention, this would have the effect of eroding the very foundation of the party autonomy rule. An agreement to choose the applicable law requires more than just coinciding expectations as to the applicable law.[6]

Nonetheless, the distinction between intention and mere expectation or assumption is not always appreciated in practice, and it is not unusual for courts to infer a choice of law even though the only evidence available is that the parties expected or assumed the law to be applicable. These inferences, which are not contractually sound, tend to be drawn in either of two types of cases: where the parties conducted their affairs with the supposedly chosen law in mind (see section A below); and where the parties do not insist, before court, on the application of the law that would ordinarily be applicable (see section B).

A. Acting with a Legal System in Mind

There are several reasons why parties might regulate their relationship on the footing of a particular legal system without actually intending it to be applicable. The parties may simply be unaware of the choice of law dimension of their relationship, or of their power to choose the applicable law; or the facts giving rise to the issue of choice of law may not yet have occurred. It is also conceivable that the

[3] See ch 2.

[4] See below, s III.

[5] Reg (EC) 593/2008 on the law applicable to contractual obligations [2008] OJ L177/6 (Rome I).

[6] *Marubeni Hong Kong v Government of Mongolia* [2002] 2 All ER (Comm) 873 (QB) [42]; BGH NJW-RR 2000, 1002; U Magnus (ed), *Staudingers Kommentar zum Bürgerlichen Gesetzbuch: Rom I-VO Art 3* (Berlin, Sellier, 2011) para 72; T Rauscher (ed), *Europäisches Zivilprozess- und Kollisionsrecht* (Berlin, Sellier, 2011) Art 3 Rom I-VO, para 12; F Vischer, L Huber and D Oser, *Internationales Vertragsrecht* 2nd edn (Berlin, Stämpfli, 2000) 78; H Honsell et al (eds), *Basler Kommentar* 3rd edn (Basel, Helbing Lichtenhahn, 2013) 996–97; R Fentiman, *International Commercial Litigation* 2nd edn (Oxford, Oxford University Press, 2015) para 5.65. In Germany the term 'Rechtswahlbewusstsein' is used to denote this requirement.

parties, though aware of the relationship's international character, are mistaken as to the governing law, or that they do not wish to broach the potentially contentious question of choice of law.

i. Distinction Between Expectation and Intention

While the lines between expectation and intention are often blurred, it is necessary at least to attempt an evaluation of the parties' conduct to determine whether they have made a choice. This is regularly neglected by German,[7] French[8] and common law courts.[9] Swiss courts, on the other hand, are much more careful to distinguish between a mere expectation that a law will be applicable and a real intention to choose that law;[10] and US courts seem to be very slow generally to find an implied choice of law.[11] The following two examples serve to demonstrate the differences in approach.

[7] KG Berlin, NJW-RR 2009, 195 (inferring a choice of German law based on the reasonableness of the German tourist's *expectation* that the agreement would be subject to German law, stating that the seller could have easily negated this expectation by providing for a Turkish choice of law clause); BAG NJW 1996, 741 (inferring a choice of German law from the parties' reliance on a German collective labour agreement); BAGE 100, 130 (2001) and BAGE 125, 24 (2007) (inferring a choice of US law from the parties' reliance on a collective agreement between United Airlines Inc and the Association of Flight Attendants); BGH NJW-RR 1999, 813 (inferring a choice of German law from the parties' incorporation of German construction contract procedures); BGH NJW-RR 2006, 1694 [15] (concluding that the parties to a contract of carriage had chosen German law because they were both based in Germany); BGH NJW 2009, 1482 [10] (concluding that the parties, German tourists in South Africa, had chosen German law to govern their joint travel arrangements because the agreement was in German and they had effectively taken their German legal relationship with them to South Africa); BGH, XII ZR 75/98 (20 December 2000) (concluding that the parties had chosen German law because the contract was in German and seemed to have been drafted on the basis of German law); OLG Hamm, II-3 UF 267/12 (7 May 2013) (finding an implied choice of Iranian law for the purposes of divorce on the basis of the Iranian parties' reliance on Iranian substantive law in the marriage contract, which was entered into in Iran).

[8] Cass soc, 27 May 2009, no 08-41908 (inferring a choice of US law from a reference in the parties' contract to the collective agreement of the Association of Flight Attendants); Cass soc, 29 November 2000, no 98-41724 (concluding that an employment relationship was governed by an implied choice of French law because the employer was French and the employee, who worked for the employer's Spanish subsidiary in Madrid, had completed a prerequisite course in France before commencing work in Spain); CA Paris, 10 November 1993, JDI 1994, 678 (inferring a choice of French law from a reference in the contract to French legislation); Cass soc, 4 December 2012, no 11-22166 (concluding that the parties had chosen French law to govern the employee's redundancy because the redundancy procedure was completed pursuant to French law).

[9] *Amin Rasheed Shipping Corp v Kuwait Insurance Co* [1984] 1 AC 50 (HL) (inferring a choice of English law from the parties' use of a Lloyd's standard form of marine policy); *Wahda Bank v Arab Bank Plc* [1996] 1 Lloyd's Rep 470 (CA) (inferring a choice of Libyan law to govern counter-guarantees on the basis that the parties would have expected the counter-guarantees to be governed by the same law as the performance bonds); *Gan Insurance Co Ltd v Tai Ping Insurance Co Ltd* [1999] ILPr 729 (CA) (concluding that a contract of reinsurance placed on the London market was impliedly governed by English law).

[10] This is made particularly clear in BGE 119 II 173; see Honsell et al (n 6) 996–97 more generally.

[11] For an example where mere expectation was not enough, see *Sonat Exploration Co v Cudd Pressure Control Inc*, 271 SW 3d 228 (Tex 2008); but cp *George K Baum & Co v Twin City Fire Ins Co*, 760 F3d 795 (8th Cir 2014).

In *Bergner v Nelis*, the New Zealand High Court noted obiter that it was

> an almost irresistible inference that [a matrimonial property agreement] executed in the Netherlands by two people living in that country, dealing with property situated in the Netherlands and registered in a Dutch Court in accordance with Dutch law was intended to be governed by Dutch law.[12]

The spouses in that case were Dutch and German respectively. It is unclear why a choice of Dutch law ought to be an 'irresistible inference' in these circumstances, in the absence of any evidence that the parties knew of the possibility that foreign law might apply. There was no evidence to suggest, for example, that the spouses were already contemplating a move to New Zealand. What may have been an irresistible inference was that the parties assumed Dutch law to be applicable, or even that they would have chosen Dutch law had they considered the matter.[13] However, neither of these inferences could qualify as an intention to choose the applicable law.

Faced with a similar fact pattern, the Bavarian Oberlandesgericht took a more differentiated approach to the question of implied choice.[14] The spouses had celebrated their marriage in Syria, where they also entered into a marriage contract. The contract was concluded 'in accordance with Islamic law and principles'.[15] It provided that the wife was to live with the husband in Germany. Both spouses were Syrian nationals, but the husband was also German. In determining whether the parties had impliedly agreed to the application of Syrian law to their marriage, the Court acknowledged that the parties' reference to Islamic law was open to interpretation: it could be understood as a mere declaration that the marriage had been celebrated in accordance with Muslim law, or it could have been intended to simply record the applicability of Syrian law to marriages concluded in Syria. However, based on the circumstances of the case and the wording of the contract, the Court concluded that the parties had in fact intended to choose Syrian law to govern their marriage. The stipulation in the contract that the wife was to move to Germany with her husband, combined with the fact that the husband was also a German citizen, indicated that the spouses were aware of the issue of choice of law and that their reference to Islamic law was thus to be understood as a choice of law contract.[16]

None of this is to say that choice of law should necessarily ignore the parties' expectations where they do not reach the threshold of agreement. Such inflexibility could cause injustice in cases where parties have acted in reliance on the law that they assumed to be applicable. The alternative is not, however, a fiction of

[12] *Bergner v Nelis* HC Auckland CIV-2004-404-149, 19 December 2005 [24]. It is likely that a similar approach was followed in *Harley v Harley* [2004] NZFLR 1096 (FC), but the relevant facts are not set out in the judgment.

[13] On hypothetical reasoning, see below, s IV.

[14] BayObLGZ 1998, 103.

[15] ibid, 104 ('gemäß den islamrechtlichen und gesetzlichen Grundsätzen geschlossen').

[16] ibid, 107.

implied choice—or even a fictional matrimonial contract, which was the solution adopted by the New South Wales Court of Appeal in *Murakami v Wiryadi*.[17]

Here, Spigelman CJ inferred the existence of an Indonesian matrimonial property contract, with the effect that Indonesian law applied to the spouses' immovable property in New South Wales rather than the *lex situs*, on the basis that the parties had a 'reasonable expectation' that the Indonesian property regime would apply.[18] The couple's matrimonial domicile was Indonesia, and the parties had not opted out of the default regime at the time of marriage. The Court relied on the controversial case of *De Nicols v Curlier*[19] and, citing the following passage from an article by AM Gleeson,[20] concluded that an implied contract governed by Indonesian law would give effect to the parties' expectation that their matrimonial property relationship would be determined in accordance with the Indonesian default regime:

> The chief merit of the *De Nicols v Curlier* approach is that in most cases it will give effect to the intention of the parties. It is reasonable to assume, for example, that a husband and wife whose domiciliary law provides for a system of community of property would regard their dealings with all their property, including foreign immovables as operating within that system.[21]

But mere expectations are never sufficient to amount to a contract.[22] In effect, the Court sought to remedy the inflexibility of objective choice of law by creating a substantive matrimonial property contract whose proper law was Indonesian law.[23]

ii. Choice of Law Alternatives

There are two broad options that would allow courts to take account of the parties' expectations as to the applicable law. First, if the parties' expectations are to be relevant in the determination of the applicable law, the principal way to achieve this is through objective choice of law rules.[24] The law that the parties

17 *Murakami v Wiryadi* [2010] NSWCA 7, (2010) 268 ALR 377 [121].

18 ibid, [121], see also [118] and [119].

19 *De Nicols v Curlier* [1900] AC 21 (HL). For a discussion of this case and the controversy it has given rise to, see *Murakami* (n 17) [98]–[118].

20 AM Gleeson, 'Community of Property and the Conflict of Laws' (1962) 4 *Sydney Law Review* 139, 143.

21 ibid, 143, cited with approval in *Murakami* (n 17) at [118].

22 The previous edition of *Dicey, Morris and Collins* thus referred to a 'fictitious' contract (L Collins (ed), *Dicey, Morris and Collins on the Conflict of Laws* 15th edn (London, Sweet & Maxwell, 2012) para 28-023), but Spigelman CJ considered that this term was inappropriate, and that the contract was a contract inferred from conduct: at [122]. The current edition of *Dicey* seems to welcome this decision because it eliminates the 'supposed distinction between contractual and non-contractual matrimonial property regimes' (para 28-029). The issue was left open by the Court of Appeal in *Slutsker v Haron Investments Ltd* [2013] EWCA Civ 430 [37].

23 cp BGH NJW-RR 2011, 1225, referred to below in n 30.

24 cp P North, *Private International Law Problems in Common Law Jurisdictions* (Dordrecht, Martinus Nijhoff, 1993) 106.

subjectively expected to apply will also often be the law that, on objective grounds, is the law most closely connected. Hence, in New Zealand, the unilateral application of the Property (Relationships) Act to matrimonial property would have to give way to an open-ended connecting factor based on close connection, or at least to specific connecting factors based on common nationality or domicile; and in Australia and England, it would be necessary to reconsider the rationale for applying the *lex situs* to matrimonial property in the absence of a matrimonial property contract. But even a direct designation of the parties' expectations as a connecting factor is conceivable. In fact, both Germany and Austria once followed this approach,[25] even though propositions of a more general connecting factor based on good faith have had little success.[26] A transitional provision of the German Einführungsgesetz zum Bürgerlichen Gesetzbuch (EGBGB) on matrimonial property thus provided for the law that the spouses assumed to be applicable.[27] In the United States, section 188 of the Restatement (Second) of Conflict of Laws enables courts to take direct account of the parties' legitimate expectations.[28]

The second option is to address the parties' error at a substantive level, within the scope of the *lex causae*. This is a strategy employed in particular in German law. It aims to give meaning to acts that were addressed to an inapplicable law, by translating them into the language of the *lex causae*.[29] For obvious reasons, this strategy works best where the relevant legal systems are similar in nature.

For example, the German Bundesgerichtshof converted a choice of the Mauritian matrimonial property regime of separation of goods into the equivalent option of *Gütertrennung* under German law.[30] The parties, who lived in Germany, were married in Mauritius. The law of Mauritius provided for a choice of two matrimonial property regimes—community of goods or separation of goods. The regime of community of goods was the default regime, but spouses could opt into the regime of separation of goods by declaring that regime to be applicable at the time of their marriage. A separate marriage contract was not necessary to do so. Under the heading 'matrimonial regime/regime matrimonial', the parties' marriage document stated that they had chosen the 'legal system of separation of goods' to be applicable. The husband was a German citizen, the wife Mauritian. The Court held that German law was applicable, as the law of the couple's habitual place of residence. German law requires parties to have entered into a contract

[25] Einführungsgesetz zum Bürgerlichen Gesetzbuch (EGBGB), Art 220(3)(2) (this was a transitional provision); Art 35(1) of the Austrian Gesetz über das Internationale Privatrecht (BGBl 304/1978), which has since been amended.

[26] See generally M-N Jobard-Bachellier, *L'Apparence en Droit International Privé* (Paris, LGDJ, 1984) pt 2; P Grolimund, *Vertrauensanknüpfung im Internationalen Privat- und Zivilverfahrensrecht* (Zurich, Dike, 2008).

[27] EGBGB, Art 220(3)(2).

[28] By reference to the s 6 principles: American Law Institute, *Restatement (Second) of Conflict of Laws* (1971), s 188; see, eg, *Sonat Exploration Co v Cudd Pressure Control Inc*, 271 SW 3d 228 (Tex 2008).

[29] H-J Sonnenberger (ed), *Münchener Kommentar zum BGB: Band 10, EGBGB Art 1-24, Einleitung IPR* 5th edn (Munich, CH Beck, 2010) paras 611–12, 637.

[30] BGH NJW-RR 2011, 1225.

if they wish to opt out of the default regime of community of goods. But the Court was able to translate the parties' choice of the Mauritian regime of separation of goods into a valid contract, under substantive German law, to adopt the regime of *Gütertrennung*.

B. Procedural Choice of Law

Another issue that arises relatively frequently is whether parties made an implied choice of law because they relied on a particular law in the course of proceedings. There ought to be no difference in principle between a choice inferred from the parties' relationship and the circumstances of their case, and a choice inferred from the parties' conduct once proceedings have commenced. In particular, a mere failure to plead foreign law, or to insist on the application of the law designated by the relevant choice of law rules, cannot be equated with an implied choice of law.[31] As in any other case, the question is whether the parties intended by their conduct to choose the applicable law; so a mere assumption that a given law is applicable is not enough.[32]

i. Distinction Between Expectation and Intention

This distinction is often neglected. German courts, in particular, have regularly found exclusive reliance on forum law to be a sufficient indicator of an implied choice, without questioning whether the parties simply assumed forum law to be applicable.[33] There are also US cases that have followed this approach;[34] while Swiss courts have been predictably clear-headed.[35]

Of course it is possible to argue that exclusive reliance on forum law could reasonably be understood as an intention to choose the law of the forum.[36] However, such reasoning ought not to be cut short and must depend on the facts of each case. Relevant factors would be whether the parties referred to the law of the forum or foreign law (a reference to foreign law being an indication that the

[31] But cp Fentiman (n 6) para 5.80. It may, however, be evidence of a previous choice of law: see ch 7, s II.

[32] J Fawcett and JM Carruthers, *Cheshire, North & Fawcett: Private International Law* 14th edn (Oxford, Oxford University Press, 2008) 694; D Czernich and H Heiss (eds), *EVÜ—Das Europäische Schuldvertragsübereinkommen* (Vienna, Orac, 1999) 39; P Mankowski, 'Stillschweigende Rechtswahl und wählbares Recht' in S Leible (ed), *Das Grünbuch zum Internationalen Vertragsrecht* (Munich, Sellier, 2004) 63, 71, 73–74; see P Mayer and V Heuzé, *Droit international privé* 10th edn (Paris, LGDJ, 2014) 123.

[33] BGH NJW 1994, 187, referring to BGHZ 103, 84 (1988); BGH NJW 1991, 1292; BGH NJW 1992, 1380; see also BGH NJW 1993, 385; references cited by Mankowski (n 32) 71, 73; but see BGH NJW-RR 2000, 1002; BGH NJW 2009, 1205 [20]–[21]; see generally Magnus (n 6) [82] and [84].

[34] eg *Celle v Filipino Reporter Enterprises Inc* 209 F 3d 163 (2nd Cir 2000); *Motorola Credit Corp v Uzan* 388 F 3d 39 (2nd Cir 2004) 61.

[35] eg BGE 130 III 417; BGE 119 II 173; BGE 91 II 442; BGE 89 II 265; BGE 88 II 325.

[36] See below, s III.

parties had thought about the issue of choice of law), whether only one or both of the parties referred to it,[37] whether the parties had previously concluded a choice of law contract, whether the court raised the issue of choice of law and, more generally, whether the issue of choice of law was likely to have been in the parties' minds.

ii. Preclusion

This does not mean that procedural conduct that does not amount to a choice of law contract could not still be relevant for the purposes of choice of law or, more specifically, for the law of procedure. Whenever there are preclusionary principles at work, a mere failure to act is ordinarily sufficient to lead to the application of a law that would not otherwise be applicable. In relation to choice of law, these principles can be generally grouped under the concept of 'facultative choice of law'.[38]

In common law jurisdictions, for example, a failure to plead foreign law simply does away with the question of choice of law and results in the application of the *lex fori*.[39] In France, too, a court is not required to apply foreign law ex officio, provided the dispute concerns *droits disponibles*, rights of which the parties are free to dispose (but neither is the court bound to apply domestic law unless the parties have reached an agreement to that effect).[40] Even in Germany, which has no doctrine of facultative choice of law and follows the principle of *iura novit curia*,[41] some authors have argued that parties could be precluded from arguing that a different law is applicable under the ordinary rules of preclusion of the German Zivilprozessordnung (ZPO);[42] but there is little support for this view.

While there may be some overlap in practice between facultative choice of law and implied choice, it is important not to conflate the two concepts. There are two reasons for this. First, if choice of law is not 'facultative', then a mere failure to plead foreign law will not produce an effect. Article 3(2) of Rome I, which provides that the parties may at any time agree on a change in the applicable law, cannot be used to justify reliance on facultative choice of law under the Regulation.[43]

[37] See Magnus (n 6) para 83.

[38] See generally ThM de Boer, 'Facultative Choice of Law: The Procedural Status of Choice-of-Law Rules and Foreign Law' (1996) 257 *Recueil des Cours* 223.

[39] R Fentiman, *Foreign Law in English Courts* (Oxford, Clarendon Press, 1998) 3–4.

[40] Mayer and Heuzé (n 32) 118–24, citing Cass civ 1ère, 26 May 1999, RCDIP 1999, 707 (*Mutuelles du Mans*), and criticising the Cour de Cassation for its liberal notion of what constitutes agreement. To the extent that this second rule is still based on the freedom to conclude procedural agreements contained in Art 12(3) of the Code de Procédure Civile, it seems that an express agreement would be necessary: see generally B Fauvarque-Cosson, *Libre Disponibilité des Droits et Conflits de Lois* (Paris, LGDJ, 1996) 245ff.

[41] C von Bar and P Mankowski, *Internationales Privatrecht*, vol 1 (Munich, CH Beck, 2003) 393–96, paras 66–70; see also Swiss Bundesgesetz über das Internationale Privatrecht (IPRG), Art 16.

[42] B von Hoffmann and K Thorn, *Internationales Privatrecht* 9th edn (Munich, CH Beck, 2007) 437; see also the summary by G Wagner, 'Fakultatives Kollisionsrecht und prozessuale Parteiautonomie' [1999] *Zeitschrift für Europäisches Privatrecht* 6; contrast von Bar and Mankowski (n 41) 396ff; Mankowski (n 32) 73–74.

[43] But cp Collins (n 22) para 9-011 and fn 46; Fentiman (n 39) 95 and Fentiman (n 6) paras 5.77–5.81.

Second, opting out of a country's system of choice of law, or failing to plead choice of law in time, is, by definition, a procedural matter, even where the parties are agreed that this is the best course of action.[44] It is not a choice of law rule that leads to the application of the law of the forum in these circumstances, and its potential scope is much wider than that of the party autonomy rule.

There seem to be very few examples of choice of law rules that are based on preclusion rather than agreement. Dutch law provides that a spouse's unilateral choice of the law of common nationality is effective to govern divorce proceedings unless the other spouse contested this choice;[45] and Article 5 of the Hague Protocol on the Law Applicable to Maintenance Obligations states that the objective law 'shall not apply if one of the parties objects and the law of another State … has a closer connection with the marriage'.[46] But such rules are examples of unilateral party choice and have little in common with a bilateral party autonomy rule.

A conceptually different question is whether an estoppel can be created by a party's failure to challenge (or even by its unknowing acquiescence in) the application of a foreign law that would not be the governing law under the applicable choice of law rules. Here, the doctrine of facultative choice of law, which can only lead to the law of the forum, is of no relevance. But it is quite possible that such conduct would give rise to an implied choice of law contract—the reference to foreign law indicating an awareness by the parties of the matter of choice of law.[47]

C. Conclusion

There are a variety of circumstances that may create an expectation or assumption that a certain law will be applicable without also giving rise to an agreement on the applicable law. Whether such an expectation or assumption ought to be protected is not a matter for the party autonomy rule, which is concerned only with the enforcement of the parties' mutual intention to choose the applicable law. Instead, the answer is to be found in principles of good faith and estoppel, and objective choice of law or procedural rules of preclusion more generally.

One of the key considerations in this context must be the justification for holding parties to a law that they did not freely choose. Are spouses to be held to an expectation, based on misinformation by a notary, that the law of the husband's nationality would govern their matrimonial property relationship? Is a German tourist in Turkey entitled to expect that German law will govern an agreement for the purchase of rugs because the agreement is in German and partly executed in Germany?[48] These are not straightforward cases because, unlike mutual intentions,

[44] de Boer (n 38) 355.

[45] Dutch Burgerlijk Wetboek, Art 10: 56(2)(a).

[46] Hague Protocol on the Law Applicable to Maintenance Obligations (opened for signature 23 November 2007, entered into force 1 August 2013) (Hague Maintenance Protocol).

[47] Magnus (n 6) para 83.

[48] See KG Berlin, NJW-RR 2009, 195 (n 7).

expectations are not usually in themselves sufficient to give rise to a protected interest.[49]

Nevertheless, courts commonly conflate the concepts of 'intention' and 'expectation', enabling them to apply the law that they consider most appropriate in the circumstances. This approach provides relief where objective choice of law rules or preclusionary principles are too inflexible to yield the desired result; but it is inconsistent with the principle of party autonomy and the law of contract.[50] Courts should follow the example of the Swiss Bundesgericht and, in each case, evaluate carefully whether the facts manifest an intention to choose the applicable law.

III. Subjective or Objective Intention?

Once it is accepted that party autonomy requires an intention to choose the applicable law, the next step is to determine which kind of intention is necessary or sufficient to establish agreement: subjective, objective or even—as will be discussed in section IV—hypothetical? Most legal systems follow an objective approach to contractual intention, whereby a party's conduct is given the meaning that the other party would have reasonably understood it to have.[51] This does not mean that subjective considerations are entirely irrelevant in these legal systems. For example, the parties' mutual subjective intentions will usually be given effect, even if they do not accord with the agreement's objective meaning.[52] Conversely, the subjective approach, which requires a subjective meeting of the minds, is shaped to a significant degree by objective considerations.[53]

Ordinarily the parties' intention to choose the applicable law will be free from doubt, and the distinction between subjective and objective intention will not assume any relevance. But there are some cases in which the distinction has the potential to be determinative. For example, is party A bound by a choice of law inferred from its mistaken reliance, before court, on the law of the forum, in circumstances where party B could reasonably understand party A's conduct to manifest an intention to choose the law of the forum? What if party B knew that

[49] See generally J Cartwright, 'Protecting Legitimate Expectations and Estoppel in English Law' (2006) 10(3) *Electronic Journal of Comparative Law*; B Fauvarque-Cosson, 'La confiance légitime et l'estoppel' (2007) 11(3) *Electronic Journal of Comparative Law*.

[50] See ch 5, s VI: 'The existence, validity and interpretation of the choice of law contract are determined in accordance with the law of contract and modal choice of law rules'.

[51] H Kötz and A Flessner, *European Contract Law* (Oxford, Clarendon Press, 1997) 109ff; C-W Canaris and HC Grigoleit, 'Interpretation of Contracts' in A Hartkamp et al (eds), *Towards a European Civil Code* 4th edn (Alphen aan den Rijn, Kluwer, 2010) 587, 595ff.

[52] Kötz and Flessner (n 51) 108–09; Canaris and Grigoleit (n 51) para 2.3; but see *Byrnes v Kendle* [2011] HCA 26, (2011) 243 CLR 253 [98]–[101] (Heydon and Crennan JJ), criticised by D McLauchlan, 'The Contract That Neither Party Intends' (2012) 29 *Journal of Contract Law* 26.

[53] W Barnes, 'The French Subjective Theory of Contract: Separating Rhetoric from Reality' (2008) 83 *Tulane Law Review* 359.

party A did not intend the law of the forum to be applicable? Is party C bound by a choice of law clause included in a pre-negotiation document even though party C did not intend the document to be legally binding?[54] Provided there is evidence of the parties' subjective intention, these questions cannot be answered without at least implicit reference to the type of agreement—subjective or objective—that is considered relevant.

A. Relevance of the Law of Contract

The law of contract is an appropriate source of regulation to determine which kind of intention is necessary to establish agreement. Whether the applicable law is the putative chosen law, or the law of the challenging party's place of habitual residence because the party seeks to establish that it did not consent, or even the *lex fori*:[55] there will be rules of contract that give meaning to the requirement of 'agreement'.[56]

Thus, in a decision of 1965, the Oberlandesgericht Saarbrücken decided that it was immaterial whether a party, in relying on the application of forum law during the proceedings, subjectively intended to choose German law or merely mistakenly assumed it to be applicable.[57] What mattered, based on Article 133 of the Bürgerliches Gesetzbuch (BGB), was whether the other party was reasonably entitled to interpret the party's reliance on German law as a manifestation of intent. The parties were both Polish nationals who, while resident in Poland, had entered into an agreement whereby the plaintiff was to guarantee the defendant's liability. When the guarantee was called upon, the plaintiff sought to recover against the defendant, who had moved to Germany. At first instance both parties supported their arguments in German law. When the Court raised the issue of choice of law on appeal, the defendant claimed that Polish law was applicable. The Court rejected this argument. It found that express reliance on a particular law in proceedings would usually reasonably be understood as an intention to choose that law, and concluded that this case was no exception. There was nothing reasonably to indicate that the defendant had mistakenly 'submitted' to German law.

It may well be that the Court's assessment of reasonableness was too sweeping in the circumstances. In fact, this seems to be another case in which the parties had simply failed to consider the issue of choice of law. There is much scope for discussion here. An interesting question, for example, is whether an objective intention ought to be inferred more readily where a party is known to be in

[54] cp Cass soc, 24 November 2004, no 02-42660 (*Hoegaerden v Horphag Research (UK) Ltd)*.

[55] See ch 5, s III.C.

[56] See also I Schwander, 'Subjektivismus in der Anknüpfung im internationalen Privatrecht' in C Dominicé et al (eds), *Etudes de droit international en l'honneur de Pierre Lalive* (Basel, Helbing & Lichtenhahn, 1993) 181, 183–84, in relation to IPRG, Art 116.

[57] OLG Saarbrücken, OLGZ 1966, 142.

receipt of legal advice.[58] But the important point to take away from this case is that the distinction between objective and subjective intention may play a crucial role, and that the law of contract will be able to provide the relevant standards of intent.[59] This point is also borne out by Swiss jurisprudence, which sees courts apply the *Vertrauensprinzip* as a matter of routine to determine the existence of an agreement on the applicable law.[60]

B. Regulation Through Modal Choice of Law?

One of the advantages of relying on the law of contract instead of modal choice of law is that, where the challenge relates to both the choice of law contract and an underlying contract, and the putative chosen law is self-validating, it is more likely that the effect of the challenge on the two contracts will be the same. However, modal choice of law rules are not necessarily inappropriate to regulate the matter, particularly if the forum wishes to ensure that the standard of agreement that is imposed on the choice of law contract is not too restrictive. The Privy Council in *Vita Food Products Inc v Unus Shipping Co Ltd*, for example, noted that the intention to choose the applicable law is 'objectively ascertained'.[61]

What is inappropriate, however, is to adopt an exclusive interpretation of general modal choice of law rules that do not regulate the matter at all.[62] There are thus varied interpretations of Article 3(1) of Rome I, which provides only that the choice 'shall be made expressly or clearly demonstrated by the terms of the contract or the circumstances of the case'. While some German authors have interpreted Article 3(1) as giving rise to a subjective approach,[63] the English Court of Appeal recently concluded that 'The test whether an implied choice of law has been established is objective', and that evidence of subjective intention would be inadmissible.[64]

[58] In *Bank of Credit and Commerce International SA (in liq) v Ali* [2001] UKHL 8, [2002] AC 251 [39], for example, Lord Hoffmann said that the relevant admissible background includes anything which a reasonable man would have regarded as relevant, including 'the state of the law'. But see OLG Cologne, VersR 1992, 1527, where the Court considered that parties relying on German law in proceedings could not simply be assumed to have chosen German law because generally people's awareness of private international law was low (as cited by W-H Roth, 'Zur Stillschweigenden Rechtswahl in einem Künftigen EU-Gemeinschaftsinstrument über das Internationale Schuldvertragsrecht' in M Stathopoulos (ed), *Festschrift für Apostolos Georgiades* (Munich, CH Beck, 2006) 905, 912).

[59] See also KG Berlin, NJW-RR 2009, 195 (but see n 7 above); BGH NJW-RR 2000, 1002 (where the Court left open whether the issue was to be determined by the *lex causae* or the *lex fori*); D Henrich (ed), *Staudingers Kommentar zum Bürgerlichen Gesetzbuch: Art 13–17b EGBGB* (Berlin, Sellier, 2011) Art 14, para 143.

[60] eg BGE 123 III 35; BGE 119 II 173; BGE 117 II 490.

[61] *Vita Food Products Inc v Unus Shipping Co Ltd* [1939] AC 277 (PC) 290 (Lord Wright for the Court).

[62] See ch 5, s III.A.ii.

[63] HG Bamberger and H Roth, *Beck'scher Online-Kommentar BGB: VO (EG) 593/2008, Art 3* 24th edn (Munich, CH Beck, 2011) para 19; Rauscher (n 6) Art 3, para 12: both authors seem to conclude that a 'potentielles Erklärungsbewusstsein' is not enough.

[64] *Lawlor v Sandvik Mining and Construction Mobile Crushers and Screens Ltd* [2013] EWCA Civ 365, [2013] 2 Lloyd's Rep 98 [31]. The Court seemed to apply Art 3 to this issue, rather than English

This confusion is not helped by the emphasis that the Giuliano-Lagarde Report places on the need for a 'real' choice by the parties[65]—terminology that is often equated with 'subjective' intention in the law of contract.[66] In *British Arab Commercial Bank Plc v Bank of Communications*, the English High Court even noted that it was 'unnecessary to distinguish between objective or subjective intention', because the 'fundamental question' was whether the parties had made 'a real choice'.[67] In the Report, however, the references to 'real' intention appear to have been used as a juxtaposition to hypothetical intention—an intention that the parties would have had if they had turned their minds to the matter of choice of law. In fact, there is no indication in the Report that the distinction between subjective and objective intention was contemplated.

The key to resolving such confusion is to recognise that, just like any other contract, the choice of law contract must be regulated in accordance with either a subjective or objective theory of contract. Modal choice of law rules calling for the choice to be 'clearly demonstrated',[68] or to be expressed with 'reasonable certainty',[69] or to 'appear clearly'[70] from the contract are an unhelpful substitute.[71] Instead, modal choice of law could provide, for example, that the parties' intention to choose the applicable law is 'to be determined from the party's statements or conduct as they were reasonably understood by the other party'.[72]

IV. A Real or Hypothetical Agreement?

This chapter has argued that an expectation or assumption that a particular law will be applicable is not enough to found a choice of law agreement; and that the parties' intentions must meet the standard of agreement prescribed by the

law as the law applicable to the alleged choice of law contract, because it had just referred to the need for a consistent interpretation and application of the Rome Convention in the previous paragraph. On the admissibility of evidence, see ch 7, s II.

65 M Giuliano and P Lagarde, *Report on the Convention on the Law Applicable to Contractual Obligations* [1980] OJC 282/1 (*Giuliano-Lagarde Report*).

66 eg *Sirius International Insurance Company (Publ) v FAI General Insurance Ltd* [2004] UKHL 54, [2004] 1 WLR 3251 [18]; and the concept of *volonté réelle* in France.

67 *British Arab Commercial Plc v Bank of Communications* [2011] EWHC 281, [2011] 1 Lloyd's Rep 664 [29].

68 Rome I (n 5) Art 3.

69 Convention 80/934/ECC on the law applicable to contractual obligations [1980] OJ L266/1 (opened for signature 19 June 1980, entered into force 1 April 1991) (Rome Convention), Art 3.

70 Hague Conference on Private International Law, *Principles on Choice of Law in International Commercial Contracts* (approved on 19 March 2015), Art 4.

71 But cp BA Marshall, 'Reconsidering the Proper Law of the Contract' (2012) 13 *Melbourne Journal of International Law* 1.

72 See *PECL* (n 1) Art 2:102; Study Group on a European Civil Code and Research Group on the Existing EC Private Law (eds), *Draft Common Frame of Reference (DCFR)* (Munich, Sellier, 2009) Art 4:102.

relevant law of contract or modal choice of law rule. So how does hypothetical choice fit into all of this? It is not difficult to find authority for the proposition that a presumed, or hypothetical, agreement on choice of law is not effective to trigger the party autonomy rule.[73] Nevertheless, some courts routinely infer choices of law not on the basis of the parties' real intentions, but on the basis of what their intentions would have been had they turned their mind to the matter, or on the basis of putative factors. The justification seems to be that implied choice of law contracts are a necessary tool to fill gaps in the parties' contractual arrangements.[74]

The purpose of the present section is to point out the fallacy of this approach. Because the choice of law contract is an independent contract, a hypothetical agreement on choice of law ought not to produce an effect under the party autonomy rule if the law of contract is applied correctly. To this end it is first necessary, in section A below, to distinguish the concept of hypothetical choice of law from an implied exercise of party autonomy, and to explain the relevance of hypothetical or presumed intention in the law of contract. Section B then argues that the law of contract will only find an implied choice of law contract if there is a convincing reason why the parties did not express their choice. This also means, as discussed in sections C and D, that courts are wrong to rely on presumptive or putative indicators of implied choice, and that they are wrong to give putative effect to ambiguous choice of law contracts whose meaning depends on a disputed fact.

A. Hypothetical Choice of Law, and Hypothetical Reasoning in Contract

Historically the party autonomy rule was preceded, and then often complemented, by a choice of law rule based on the parties' hypothetical (or fictional) intentions as to the applicable law.[75] This choice of law rule led to the application of the law that reasonable parties would have chosen if they had made a choice of law. For example, prior to the Hague Convention on the Law Applicable to Matrimonial Property Regimes,[76] French choice of law rules still provided for a presumption

[73] *Giuliano-Lagarde Report* (n 65) Art 3 (referring to the need for a 'real choice of law'); *Restatement (Second)* (n 28) s 187, cmnt (a) ('It does not suffice to demonstrate that the parties, if they had thought about the matter, would have wished to have the law of a particular state applied'); *Commentary to the Hague Principles on Choice of Law in International Commercial Contracts* (n 70) para 4.6; BGE 119 II 173 (see *Basler Kommentar* (n 6) 996–97 more generally).

[74] See N Joubert, 'Le Choix Tacite dans les Jurisprudences Nationales: vers une Interprétation Uniforme du Règlement Rome I' in S Corneloup and N Joubert (eds), *Le Règlement Communautaire 'Rome I' et le Choix de Loi dans les Contrats Internationaux* (Paris, LexisNexis, 2011) 229, 233ff.

[75] P Nygh, *Autonomy in International Contracts* (Oxford, Oxford University Press, 1999) 104–09; Collins (n 22) paras 32-005–32-007.

[76] Hague Convention on the Law Applicable to Matrimonial Property Regimes (1977) 16 ILM 14 (opened for signature 14 March 1978, entered into force 1 September 1992).

that the parties intended to choose the law of the couple's first common domicile.[77] The same rule is now expressed in purely objective terms in Art 4 of the Convention. In relation to contract, it was Convention 80/934/ECC on the law applicable to contractual obligations (Rome Convention) that finally put an end to hypothetical choice of law in European Member States.[78]

Leaving to one side any possible benefits of hypothetical choice of law, it is evident that choice of law should not provide for hypothetical choice under the guise of the party autonomy rule. This is because hypothetical choice is not founded on a manifestation of the parties' intentions, but relies on an entirely fictional choice of law agreement. If hypothetical choice is to play a role in choice of law, this must occur in the form of a separate choice of law rule that applies if the parties have not made an express or implied choice of law.

But what about circumstances where the law of contract itself calls for the parties' hypothetical intentions to be ascertained? If the parties' intentions as to choice of law are to be ascertained in accordance with the law of contract, then how can we reject entirely the relevance of hypothetical intention for the purposes of the party autonomy rule? In many legal systems courts are able to imply terms to which the parties have given no thought at all. They are not the result of the parties' real intentions. So why should this approach not also be applicable to choice of law contracts?

The reason why it is not applicable to choice of law contracts is that hypothetical reasoning in the law of contract applies only to implied terms, not implied contracts;[79] and choice of law contracts are not mere terms of the underlying contract. Hypothetical reasoning is an exercise in gap-filling, requiring 'an additional normative judgment with respect to the content of the agreement which goes beyond the reasonable recipient's perspective'.[80] By definition, an independent contract cannot be inferred to fill a gap. It would be wrong, therefore, to infer an independent contract, not on the basis of the parties' conduct as reasonably understood, but on the hypothetical conduct of a reasonable person.

In Germany, for example, the tool of supplementary interpretation (*ergänzende Vertragsauslegung*) allows courts to fill contractual gaps on the basis of the principle of good faith.[81] It is a tool of last resort: it applies only if ordinary interpretation cannot detect an agreement by the parties to regulate the issue and there is no existing rule of contract that could be used to fill the gap.[82] The position is not much different in common law jurisdictions, where terms are implied in order to

77 Mayer and Heuzé (n 32) 576.

78 Rome Convention (n 69); *Giuliano-Lagarde Report* (n 65).

79 See, eg, *Pagnan SpA v Feed Products Ltd* [1987] 2 Lloyd's Rep 601 (CA) 611 (Bingham J): 'The Court's task is to review what the parties said and did and from that material to infer whether the parties' objective intentions as expressed to each other were to enter into a mutually binding contract'; *The Aramis* [1989] 1 Lloyd's Rep 213 (CA) 224 (Bingham LJ).

80 Canaris and Grigoleit (n 51) 614; see *DCFR* (n 72) Art 9:101(3).

81 BGHZ 16, 71 (1954).

82 BGH NJW 1984, 1177.

give 'business efficacy' to the contract.[83] In *Philips Electronique Grand Public SA v British Sky Broadcasting Ltd*, the Court of Appeal considered that hypothetical intention played no role in the ordinary interpretation of contracts but fell instead within the domain of the law on implied terms:

> The courts' usual role in contractual interpretation is, by resolving ambiguities or reconciling apparent inconsistencies, to attribute the true meaning to the language in which the parties themselves have expressed their contract. The implication of contract terms involves a different and altogether more ambitious undertaking: the interpolation of terms to deal with matters for which, ex hypothesi, the parties themselves have made no provision.[84]

A similar view was taken by Mason J in the High Court of Australia, where he said:

> When we say that the implication of a term raises an issue as to the meaning and effect of the contract we do not intend by that statement to convey that the court is embarking upon an orthodox exercise in the interpretation of the language of a contract, that is, assigning a meaning to a particular provision. …
>
> [W]ith implication the term is one which it is presumed that the parties would have agreed upon had they turned their minds to it—it is not a term that they have actually agreed upon. Thus, … the deficiency in the expression of the consensual agreement is caused by the failure of the parties to direct their minds to a particular eventuality and to make explicit provision for it.[85]

While the distinction between real and hypothetical intention is rarely emphasised with such clarity,[86] the purpose of implied terms is always to resolve a problem that has not been expressly regulated in the contract, even if the parties themselves did not give any consideration to the problem.

On the basis of the conclusions reached in chapter four, it is clear that the choice of law contract is an independent contract and cannot be reduced to an implied term.[87] It follows that choice of law contracts should not be submitted to the

[83] *The Moorcock* (1889) 14 PD 64 (CA).

[84] *Philips Electronique Grand Public SA v British Sky Broadcasting Ltd* [1995] EMLR 472 (CA) 481 (Bingham MR); but cp *Attorney General of Belize v Belize Telecom Ltd* [2009] UKPC 10, [2009] 1 WLR 1988 [22]–[27] (Lord Hoffmann); *Trollope & Colls Ltd v North West Metropolitan Regional Hospital Board* [1973] 1 WLR 601 (HL) 609 (Lord Pearson).

[85] *Codelfa Construction Pty Ltd v State Rail Authority of NSW* (1982) 149 CLR 337, 347–48 (Mason J).

[86] Especially now that, in English common law, implication of terms is subsumed within ordinary principles of interpretation: *Attorney General of Belize v Belize Telecom Ltd* (n 84); see J McCaughran, 'Implied Terms: The Journey of the Man on the Clapham Omnibus' (2011) 70 *CLJ* 607. But cp the difference drawn between inferred and imputed intention, in relation to constructive trusts, by Lord Neuberger in *Stack v Dowden* [2007] UKHL 17, [2007] 2 AC 432 [126], and Glanville Williams' tripartite approach to implied terms, where only the first category of terms is concerned with real intention: G Williams, 'Language and the Law' (1945) 61 *LQR* 384, 401; *Attorney-General v Dreux Holdings Ltd* (1996) 7 TCLR 617 (NZCA) 632 (Thomas J); *Gibbons Holdings Ltd v Wholesale Distributors Ltd* [2007] NZSC 37, [2008] 1 NZLR 277 [96] (Thomas J).

[87] See ch 4, s III.B.iv. See also R Moser, *Vertragsabschluss, Vertragsgültigkeit und Parteiwille im internationalen Obligationenrecht* (St Gallen, Verlag der Fehr'schen Buchhandlung, 1948) 240, describing implied party choice as an implied contract ('konkludenter Vertrag').

rules on implied terms or supplementary interpretation.[88] There is no need for 'gap-filling':[89] the very purpose of choice of law rules is to anticipate choice of law problems and provide relevant 'gap-filling' connecting factors. A hypothetical choice is not, like the implication of an unspecified sale price or time of delivery, an ad hoc solution that is necessary to make the underlying contract workable, to a matter that would ordinarily be determined by the parties.

B. The Implied Choice of Law Contract

Because implied choices of law are implied contracts, not implied terms of a contract, a hypothetical or presumed mutual intention to choose the applicable law is not sufficient to found a choice of law agreement. Consequently the standard for inferring an implied choice of law is relatively high. It is submitted that, when determining whether parties reached an agreement on the applicable law, courts should be guided by one question in particular: why did the parties fail to express their choice? This approach will be explored in subsection i below. Subsection ii then goes on to demonstrate that in practice courts often apply a much lower standard to find an implied choice of law. English courts in particular appear to have been unduly influenced by the law on implied terms and tend to treat implied choice of law contracts as implied terms.

i. Why did the Parties not Express their Choice?

If hypothetical intentions have no place in determining the parties' agreement on the applicable law, the question that immediately presents itself is why the parties failed to make their agreement express.[90] Parties who turn their minds to the matter of choice of law and who intend to make a choice of law (whether this intention is ascertained objectively or subjectively) would usually conclude an express choice of law agreement. The Swiss Bundesgericht, who is generally careful to discount the parties' hypothetical intentions as to choice of law, homed in on this question in a case involving the law applicable to a guarantee.[91] The defendant, who was resident in Switzerland, entered into a guarantee to assume responsibility for contractual obligations that were clearly governed by German law. Both parties to the German contract were resident in Germany; and the contract concerned property situated in Germany and included a German jurisdiction clause. However, according to the Bundesgericht, these facts were not sufficient to suggest an intention to submit the guarantee to German law, because it was unlikely that

[88] cp MN Howard, 'Floating Choice of Law Clauses' [1995] *Lloyd's Maritime and Commercial Law Quarterly* 1, 5.

[89] Contrast A Steiner, *Die stillschweigende Rechtswahl im Prozess im System der subjektiven Anknüpfung im deutschen Internationalen Privatrecht* (Frankfurt, Peter Lang, 1998) 79.

[90] Roth (n 58) 910; Joubert (n 74) 245.

[91] BGE 119 II 173.

the defendant had even considered the question of choice of law when signing the guarantee. This reasoning must surely be correct. In the absence of a choice of law clause, there was no reason to think that the guarantor had turned her mind to the issue of choice of law, so there was no basis for inferring an implied choice of German law.

Another helpful example that supports a relatively rigorous approach to implied choice is *Lawlor v Sandvik Mining and Construction Mobile Crushers and Screens Ltd*.[92] In that case, the English High Court rightly reasoned that a choice of English law could not be inferred from the fact that 'in general terms [the respondent] would seek to have its contracts governed by English law', or that 'experience and commonsense' indicated that most companies in the respondent's position 'would seek to do the same'.[93] The claimant, an Irish citizen, sought compensation for termination of his commercial agency agreement with the respondent. He had acted as the respondent's agent for the sale of mobile screens and crushing equipment in Spain. The respondent appeared to be based mainly in Ireland and England. The respondent submitted that the agency agreement was governed by English law, pointing to evidence that its contracts would usually be governed by English law.[94] Judge Mackie accepted 'that if the parties had made a choice it would have been of English law', but concluded that this did not point to a choice of English law because 'Given the casual and informal circumstances in which the agency took effect', it was 'very unlikely that choice of law was considered, let alone discussed'.[95]

The respondent appealed, arguing that the Judge 'was wrong to require evidence of actual consideration and discussion of the choice of law in order to be able to conclude that there had been an implicit choice'.[96] The Court of Appeal upheld the decision.[97] Toulson LJ considered that it was necessary to draw a distinction between 'inferring an unexpressed intention and imputing an intention', and that only the former could amount to a choice of law under Article 3 of the Rome Convention.[98] He also considered that an objective standard had to be applied to determine whether the parties had made a choice,[99] and that the Judge had been 'right in holding that it was not enough to establish that if a choice of law had been made, it would in all probability have been English law'.[100]

[92] *Lawlor v Sandvik Mining and Construction Mobile Crushers and Screens Ltd* [2012] EWHC 1188, [2012] 2 Lloyd's Rep 25.

[93] ibid, [45].

[94] ibid, [45].

[95] ibid, [45].

[96] ibid, [18].

[97] *Lawlor v Sandvik Mining and Construction Mobile Crushers and Screens Ltd* [2013] EWCA Civ 365, [2013] 2 Lloyd's Rep 98.

[98] ibid, [29].

[99] ibid, [31].

[100] ibid, [34].

Confusingly, however, some of Toulson LJ's dicta seem to endorse exactly what he had set out to reject—a hypothetical approach to implied choice:

> Logically there may be a certain artificiality in attributing to the parties a tacit choice in circumstances which do not suggest that they gave actual thought to the matter ... However, one can see the justice of inferring a choice of law in circumstances where it would not reasonably have occurred to the parties to suppose that a different law might apply. It would lack practical sense to require that they should have contemplated that which would not reasonably have occurred to them.[101]

He then went on to conclude that the party asserting an implied choice has to 'satisfy the court that the only reasonable conclusion to be drawn from the circumstances is that the parties *should be taken* to have intended the putative law to apply' (emphasis added);[102] and that, if the parties' previous employment contract had been governed by an express choice of law, there 'would have been force in the argument that the same law should be *presumed to have been intended* to apply to the agency contract' (emphasis added).[103]

It is submitted that this approach confuses objective and hypothetical reasoning. Pursuant to an objective standard, the issue was whether the agent and the company could reasonably be understood to have made a choice of English law. Because there was no evidence indicating an intention to choose English law, there could be no English choice of law contract. In particular, a reasonable person in the agent's position would not have attributed to the company an intention to choose English law as the law governing the agency agreement. The fact that the company usually included English choice of law clauses in its contracts, and that it would have been reasonable for it to do so in its agency agreement with the plaintiff, could not be enough.

So if real intention is needed, the question that must be raised is why the parties did not bother to express their choice.[104] This is not a question that is usually addressed in cases on implied choice,[105] nor was it raised by the authors of the Giuliano-Lagarde Report;[106] but it provides a valuable benchmark that staves off the temptation of hypothetical reasoning. In most cases, the only reasonable answer to that question would be that the parties failed to consider, or agree on, the question of choice of law. This, as Judge Mackie pointed out, should be the end of the matter.

[101] ibid, [32].
[102] ibid, [33].
[103] ibid, [35].
[104] Roth (n 58) 910; Joubert (n 74) 245; contrast Mankowski (n 32) 66.
[105] But see *British Arab Commercial Plc v Bank of Communications* [2011] EWHC 281, [2011] 1 Lloyd's Rep 664 [30]; *Sapporo Breweries Ltd v Lupofresh Ltd* [2012] EWHC 2013 [40], upheld on appeal ([2013] EWCA Civ 948, [2014] 1 All ER (Comm) 484 [23]); see also *Brownlie v Four Seasons Holdings Inc* [2014] EWHC 273 [93] (reversed in part on other grounds).
[106] *Giuliano-Lagarde Report* (n 65).

ii. Choice of Law Contracts as Implied Terms

Courts rarely specify the test that they apply when inferring choice of law contracts: did the parties intend to make the choice, or is it merely the case that they would have made the choice had the matter been brought to their attention? It is not always easy, therefore, to assess the role that hypothetical reasoning has played in the courts' determination of implied choice. Nevertheless, it is fair to say that some courts have tended to adopt a low standard for the implication of choice of law contracts.[107] This has been particularly true of cases under the Rome Convention in Germany and the United Kingdom,[108] while French courts, on the whole, seem to have taken a more conservative approach.[109]

Although English courts have accepted in principle that hypothetical intention is not sufficient to establish an implied choice,[110] they appear to have been inspired by the law on implied terms to impute choice of law intentions to the parties. In fact, it is not unusual for English courts to refer to the law on implied terms when ascertaining the parties' choice of law intentions. In *Lawlor*, the Court of Appeal asked whether 'it went without saying' that the contract was intended to be governed by English law.[111] Similarly, in *American Motorists Insurance Co v Cellstar Corp*,[112] Mance LJ stated that Article 3 required a 'real' choice by the parties but also said that the provision brought to mind:

> [T]he test governing the implication of an implied term at common law, on the grounds that it must have been intended or was so obvious that it went without saying and was one to which the parties would have said 'of course' if anyone had suggested it.[113]

In *FR Lurssen Werft GmbH v Halle*, Aikens LJ found that 'if the parties had been asked at the time, they would have said "of course the [contract] is governed by English law"';[114] and Potter LJ in *Aeolian Shipping SA v ISS Machinery Services Ltd*, rejecting an implied choice, found that there was 'certainly no room … for the

[107] See also references above, nn 7, 8, 9.

[108] Joubert (n 74) 234; but cp R Plender and M Wilderspin, *European Private International Law of Obligations* 4th edn (London, Sweet & Maxwell, 2015) paras 6-024–6.025. The language of Art 3(1) has since been strengthened, and now provides that the choice must be 'clearly demonstrated' instead of being 'demonstrated with reasonable certainty'.

[109] Joubert (n 74) 234; see Cass civ 1ère, 12 July 2005, Bull civ I no 322, 267, where the Court required an 'explicite' agreement on the applicable law.

[110] *Hellenic Steel Co v Svolamar Shipping Co (The Komninos S)* [1991] 1 Lloyd's Rep 370 (CA) 374; *Egon Oldendorff v Liberia Corporation* [1996] 1 Lloyd's Rep 380 (QB) 387; *Samcrete Egypt Engineers & Contractors SAE v Land Rover Exports Ltd* [2001] EWCA Civ 2019, [2002] CLC 533 [27].

[111] *Lawlor v Sandvik Mining and Construction Mobile Crushers and Screens Ltd* [2013] EWCA Civ 365, [2013] 2 Lloyd's Rep 98 [33], [34]; see *BP Refinery (Westernport) Pty Ltd v Shire of Hastings* (1977) 180 CLR 266 (PC).

[112] *American Motorists Insurance Co v Cellstar Corp* [2003] EWCA Civ 206, [2003] ILPr 22.

[113] ibid, [44]. Plender and Wilderspin (n 108) para 6-038 note that 'This case goes to the limit' because 'Rather than interpreting the real intention of the parties, both the trial judge and the Court of Appeal were in fact themselves choosing the law applicable to the contract on the basis of what they thought the parties would have been likely to choose had they thought about the matter'.

[114] *FR Lurssen Werft GmbH & Co KG v Halle* [2010] EWCA Civ 587, [2011] 1 Lloyd's Rep 265 [21]; see also *Zebrarise Ltd v De Nieffe* [2004] EWHC 1842, [2005] 1 Lloyd's Rep 154 [33].

implication of such a term under the principles of English law applicable to the implication of contractual terms, whether on the basis of business efficacy or the "officious bystander" test'.[115]

For the reasons outlined in section IV.A, courts are wrong to apply the law on implied terms to implied choices of law. The cases just cited suggest that English courts do so as a matter of course, allowing inferences of choice of law in the absence of evidence that the parties even considered the matter.[116] A striking example of such an approach is *Zebrarise Ltd v De Nieffe*,[117] where the Court found that an English solicitor living and practising in Belgium and an Irish property dealer living in England had impliedly agreed on a choice of English law to govern a loan contract entered into in Switzerland. The solicitor claimed that the property dealer had defaulted under the loan and that, under Belgian law as the law most closely connected to the contract, the solicitor's claim was not statute barred. The Court disagreed. It considered that if the parties had been asked at the time they would both have preferred English law to apply. Both parties had connections to England, and the solicitor had no knowledge of Belgian law. There was therefore an implied choice of English law, and the solicitor's claim was statute barred as a result.

Hypothetical reasoning of this nature is not a new development. There has been much confusion in English common law over the role of hypothetical factors in the determination of implied choice.[118] In *Amin Rasheed Shipping Corp v Kuwait Insurance Co*,[119] for example, Lord Diplock stated that party choice was a matter of 'necessary implication',[120] and then went on to infer a choice of English law on the basis of business efficacy rather than the parties' real intentions.[121] The parties in that case, a Kuwaiti insurance company and a Liberian shipowner trading from Dubai, had agreed on a policy that was based on the Lloyd's standard form of marine insurance. The policy identified Kuwait as the place of issue and provided for claims to be payable there, but it was drafted in English and used English legal terms that had been identified in the Marine Insurance Act 1906. This was sufficient, in the House of Lords' view, to allow the inference of a choice of law:

> Except by reference to the English statute and to the judicial exegesis of the code that it enacts it is not possible to interpret the policy or to determine what those mutual legal rights and obligations are. So, applying, as one must in deciding the jurisdiction point, English rules of conflict of laws, the proper law of the contract embodied in the policy is English law. …

[115] *Aeolian Shipping SA v ISS Machinery Services Ltd* [2001] EWCA Civ 1162, [2001] 2 Lloyd's Rep 641 [15].

[116] But see J Hill, 'Choice of Law in Contract under the Rome Convention: The Approach of the UK Courts' (2004) 53 *ICLQ* 325, 347.

[117] *Zebrarise Ltd v De Nieffe* [2004] EWHC 1842, [2005] 1 Lloyd's Rep 154.

[118] Fawcett and Carruthers (n 32) 704, fn 320.

[119] *Amin Rasheed Shipping Corp v Kuwait Insurance Co* [1984] 1 AC 50 (HL).

[120] ibid, 61.

[121] ibid, 64; see Nygh (n 75) 107.

> To speak of English law and practice providing a useful source of *persuasive* authority on the construction of the policy wherever it may be used, begs the whole question: why is recourse to English law needed at all? The necessity to do so is common ground between the experts on Kuwaiti law on either side; it is because in the absence of an indigenous law of marine insurance in Kuwait English law was the only system of private law by reference to which it was possible for a Kuwaiti court to give a sensible and precise meaning to the language that the parties had chosen to use in the policy.[122]

In *Compagnie d'Armement Maritime SA v Compagnie Tunisienne de Navigation SA*,[123] Lord Diplock had previously suggested that parties entering into a contract 'must ex necessitate contemplate that there will be some system of law by reference to which their mutual rights and liabilities will be determined, ie, the substantive or "proper" law of their agreement', before noting that the parties' intention as to the applicable law was to be ascertained by applying the ordinary rules of the common law relating to the construction of contracts.[124] Although he subsequently clarified that the court would have to rely on the objective proper law unless there was a real or actual intention as to the applicable law,[125] his suggestion that parties would have *necessarily* contemplated the issue comes dangerously close to an imputation of awareness.

More principled guidance on this matter has come from the Australian High Court in *Akai Pty Ltd v People's Insurance Co Ltd*,[126] where the majority held that inferred choice was not a 'question of implying a term as to choice of law' but a matter of construction, referring to the principles of contractual construction as outlined by Mason J in *Codelfa Construction Pty Ltd v State Rail Authority of NSW*.[127] It has already been noted that, in that case, Mason J distinguished the implication of terms—and hypothetical reasoning—from orthodox principles of construction. Toohey, Gaudron and Gummow JJ considered that, in inferring a choice of law:

> [T]he court applies the ordinary rules of the common law relating to the construction of contracts. That requires consideration of the terms and nature of the contract and 'the general circumstances of the case', in the sense explained, with reference to contractual construction, by Mason J in *Codelfa Construction Pty Ltd v State Rail Authority of NSW*. … What is involved in inquiring whether the parties have exercised their liberty to select a governing law is the ascertainment of that which, in truth, the parties are to be taken to have agreed. … It is not a question of implying a term as to choice of law. Rather it is one of whether, upon the construction of the contract and by the permissible means of construction, the court properly may infer that the parties intended their contract to be governed by reference to a particular system of law.[128]

[122] ibid, 64–65 per Lord Diplock (Lord Wilberforce dissenting on this point).
[123] *Compagnie d'Armement Maritime SA v Compagnie Tunisienne de Navigation SA* [1971] AC 572 (HL).
[124] ibid, 603.
[125] ibid, 608.
[126] *Akai Pty Ltd v People's Insurance Co Ltd* (1996) 188 CLR 418.
[127] ibid, 441, citing *Codelfa Construction Pty Ltd v State Rail Authority of NSW* (n 85) 347–53 per Mason J.
[128] ibid, 441 (footnotes omitted).

Because the choice of law contract and its underlying contract form two separate contracts, it is submitted that the High Court was wrong in its view that inferred choice is a matter of 'construction of the [underlying] contract'. While the underlying contract clearly forms part of the matrix of facts in which an assertion of choice of law must be considered, the two contracts cannot be construed as one. But in refusing to apply the law on implied terms, on the basis of the distinction drawn by Mason J, the High Court properly excluded the application of hypothetical reasoning to choice of law contracts.

C. Indicators of Implied Choice of Law

Hypothetical reasoning is also encouraged by a formalistic application of so-called indicators of implied choice. There are three ways in which indicators of implied choice can be misapplied to establish an entirely fictional agreement on choice of law: use of presumptive indicators of implied choice (see subsection i below), use of putative indicators of implied choice (see subsection ii), and reliance on the rule of validation (see subsection iii).

i. Presumptive Indicators

There are a number of factors that may exceptionally indicate an implied choice of law, such as evidence of a previous course of dealings, jurisdiction and arbitration agreements, references to legislation, or choice of law clauses in related contracts.[129] These factors may be indicators of an implied choice, provided always there is a convincing reason why the parties did not make their choice express. It is neither necessary nor advisable to treat them as general rules that create a (rebuttable) presumption of implied choice.[130] But all too often this is what happens in practice.[131] Even the commentary to the Hague Principles on Choice of Law in International Commercial Contracts, after declaring that a 'presumed intention

[129] See *Giuliano-Lagarde Report* (n 65) para 3.3. cp also, in the context of the law applicable to the arbitration agreement, the role of a choice by the parties of the applicable substantive law, or of the seat: Collins (n 22) paras 16-017–16-018.

[130] But see Fentiman (n 6) para 5.70; Plender and Wilderspin (n 108) para 6-033; Mankowski (n 32) 66.

[131] For examples of the courts' presumptive reliance on jurisdiction and arbitration agreements, see: *Hellenic Steel Co v Svolamar Shipping Co (The Komninos S)* [1991] 1 Lloyd's Rep 370 (CA) 375–76 (Bingham LJ); *Compagnie d'Armement Maritime SA v Compagnie Tunisienne de Navigation SA* [1971] AC 572 (HL) 590 (Lord Morris) and 596 (Lord Wilberforce); *Egon Oldendorff v Liberia Corporation* [1996] 1 Lloyd's Rep 380 (QB) 390; CA Paris, 21 July 1950, Rev crit dip 1952, 706; cp Cass com, 8 June 2010, no 08-16298; BGH, II ZR 232/64 (5 December 1966). See also Cass civ 1ère, 3 December 1996, Bull civ I no 428, 300 (concluding that the parties could be presumed to have chosen the law of the contract of obligation to apply to their contract of guarantee); *Golden Ocean Group Ltd v Salgaocar Mining Industries Pvt Ltd* [2012] EWCA Civ 265, [2012] 1 WLR 3674 [49] (obiter, inferring a choice of English law to govern a presumed contract of warranty of authority, on the basis that it should be governed by the same law as the principal contract to which it is ancillary).

imputed to the parties does not suffice',[132] seems to suggest that certain factors—like use of a standard form that is based on a specific system of law, or use of legal language characteristic of a particular law—would commonly be enough to demonstrate an implied choice.[133]

It is submitted that these factors should be considered as part of a wider enquiry into the parties' intentions,[134] in accordance with the approach outlined above in section IV.B. For example, depending on the circumstances of the particular case, a jurisdiction clause may exceptionally be taken as evidence of a real intention to choose the applicable law.[135] Depending on the facts of the case, it may be possible to explain the omission of an express choice on the basis that the parties wrongly assumed the jurisdiction clause to also apply to choice of law. Conversely, such an explanation would not ring true where parties had previously made use of choice of law clauses, or where they had received advice from lawyers with experience in international contracting. The jurisdiction clause is nothing more than a fact that may provide part of the necessary evidence to establish an implied choice of law contract.

ii. Putative Indicators of Implied Choice

There is a subsidiary problem caused by reliance on presumptive indicators of choice of law, which is that courts sometimes rely on indicators that they merely assume to exist. They rely on putative indicators of implied choice whose existence, though disputed, may be crucial to the inference of a choice of law as a matter of logic. Logically it is impossible to infer a choice of law from the terms of a contract alleged not to have been agreed upon, if it is the parties' agreement on these terms that is said to give rise to the inference. Agreement on the disputed terms cannot be established twice—once for the purposes of the choice of law contract, and once for the underlying contract pursuant to the implied chosen law—because the terms do not form part of the choice of law contract. They are legally independent of the choice of law contract, and it is in that role as separate terms that they would provide evidence of an implied choice if they did exist.

Logic also dictates that an implied choice of law contract cannot usually be inferred from a jurisdiction agreement that has not been validly concluded.[136]

[132] *Commentary to the Hague Principles on Choice of Law in International Commercial Contracts* (n 70) para 4.6.

[133] ibid, paras 4.9–4.10; but cp para 4.11 on the effect of jurisdiction agreements.

[134] Roth (n 58) 910 and 916.

[135] cp *Hague Principles on Choice of Law in International Commercial Contracts* (n 70) Art 4; Rome I (n 5) Recital 12. For an overview of the divergent positions on this point, see MC Scherer, 'Le Choix Implicite dans les Jurisprudences Nationales: vers une Interprétation Uniforme du Règlement? L'Exemple du Choix Tacite Résultant des Clauses Attributives de Juridiction et d'Arbitrage' in S Corneloup and N Joubert (eds), *Le Règlement Communautaire 'Rome I' et le Choix de Loi dans les Contrats Internationaux* (Paris, LexisNexis, 2011) 253.

[136] Bamberger and Roth (n 63) para 21; Mankowski (n 32) 67; C Rühl, *Rechtswahlfreiheit und Rechtswahlklauseln in Allgemeinen Geschäftsbedingungen* (Baden Baden, Nomos, 1999) 92.

If the parties' implied choice depends on their agreement on jurisdiction, it is the jurisdiction agreement whose validity must first be determined. The implied choice stands and falls with the jurisdiction agreement. It would be wrong, therefore, to treat a contested jurisdiction agreement as the source of a putative implied choice of law in order to determine the validity of the jurisdiction agreement in accordance with that law. But this is exactly the approach that has been taken in a number of cases.[137]

In *The Parouth*,[138] for example, the Court of Appeal held, for the purposes of an application for leave to serve out of the jurisdiction, that there was a good arguable case that an alleged charterparty was, 'by its terms or implication, governed by English law', because the charterparty—whose existence the defendants disputed—included a London arbitration clause (which was also contested).[139] The Court rejected Bingham J's conclusion that the arbitration clause was to be treated as a neutral factor. Similarly, in *Egon Oldendorff v Liberia Corp (No 1)*, Mance J appeared to rely on an implied choice of English law, based on an alleged agreement for arbitration in London, to conclude that, under English law, the arbitration clause was validly incorporated in the parties' contract.[140]

An implied choice, like an express choice, should only be used to determine the validity of another agreement once its own validity has been determined—an impossible task where the agreement in issue provides the factual basis for the choice of law. This does not mean that the law of the contested jurisdiction is necessarily inappropriate to determine the validity of the jurisdiction agreement, particularly if synchronisation of the two agreements is considered desirable. But its application would have to depend on objective connecting factors rather than on the party autonomy rule.

It has been argued that a choice of law may still be inferred from an invalid jurisdiction agreement where the reason for its invalidity is one of mere formality.[141] The argument seems to be that a failure to comply with formality requirements does not, in substance, place in doubt the parties' intention to agree on jurisdiction. This argument is consistent with the point made in subsection i, that factors like jurisdiction agreements are nothing more than a *fact* that may indicate an implied choice of law. They cannot operate as legal presumptions. So it is necessary to determine exactly what it is about a jurisdiction clause that may support

[137] See also Fawcett and Carruthers (n 32) 744–45 ('[T]he question whether a clause providing for arbitration in England is validly incorporated into a contract is governed by English law (the arbitration clause being an inferred choice of the governing law)'); cp *Dornoch Ltd v Mauritius Union Assurance Co Ltd* [2005] EWHC 1887, [2006] Lloyd's Rep IR 127 [43]–[45]; aff'd [2006] EWCA Civ 389, [2006] 2 Lloyd's Rep 475 [17] (that the jurisdiction agreement will only give rise to an inference of choice of law if there is an agreement that is 'unarguably subject to' only 'one possible putative law').

[138] *Compania Naviera Micro SA v Shipley International Inc (The Parouth)* [1982] 2 Lloyd's Rep 351 (CA).

[139] ibid, 353.

[140] *Egon Oldendorff v Liberia Corp (No 1)* [1995] 2 Lloyd's Rep 64 (QB) 69–71; see also *Marubeni Hong Kong v Government of Mongolia* [2002] 2 All ER (Comm) 873 (QB) [42].

[141] Mankowski (n 32) 67; Magnus (n 6) para 77.

the finding of an implied choice, whether or not the clause was validly concluded. If there was evidence that the parties understood the jurisdiction clause to affect both jurisdiction and applicable law, the fact that the jurisdiction clause is formally invalid and thus unenforceable may not be inconsistent with an implied choice of law. But such a conclusion would be highly fact-dependent, and it would depend in part on the purpose of the alleged choice of law. If the purpose of the alleged choice of law was to avoid the application of a law other than the *lex fori*, any implied choice of law contract may have to be regarded as being conditional on an enforceable jurisdiction agreement.[142]

iii. Rule of Validation

Finally, there has been some support for submitting choice of law contracts to a 'rule of validation'. The rule calls for the application of the law that validates the underlying contract, on the basis that the parties must have intended to choose a validating law.[143] This presumption in *favorem negotii* has rightly been described as 'conceptually suspect' because it 'confuses the parties' intentions regarding a contract's governing law with their intentions concerning its effect'.[144] It relies on hypothetical intention and therefore must be rejected. The purpose of choice of law contracts is to choose the applicable law that will then govern the parties' relationship, including such matters as the existence and validity of contracts. It cannot be material that the parties would have chosen a different law if they had been aware of all of the facts.

Perhaps surprisingly, the Swiss Bundesgericht came close to adopting a rule of validation in a case where the parties had chosen Swiss law to govern a contract for the sale of a foreign immovable.[145] The contract did not comply with Swiss formalities. It was clear that the parties would not have chosen Swiss law if they had been aware of the relevant invalidating provision. The Court concluded that the parties could not have intended Swiss law to govern the formal validity of the contract, because they could not have intended the contract to be invalid from the outset. But the Court was careful not to rely on a general presumption of validation. Instead it highlighted the particular facts of the case, including a reference in the contract to the Spanish form *Escritura Publica*, and found that, based on the *Vertrauensprinzip*, the parties had agreed to exclude formal validity from the scope of the Swiss choice of law agreement. The real issue was whether a choice of law agreement that was expressed in unqualified terms could, in the circumstances, be interpreted to exclude matters of formality from its scope.

[142] See Mankowski (n 32) 67.

[143] E Jayme, 'L'autonomie de la volonté des parties dans les contrats internationaux entre personnes privées' (1991) 64-I *Annuaire de l'Institut de Droit International* 7, 71–72, Art 2(3); F Jünger, 'Parteiautonomie und objektive Anknüpfung im EG-Übereinkommen zum Internationalen Vertragsrecht: Eine Kritik aus amerikanischer Sicht' (1982) 46 *Rabels Zeitschrift für ausländisches und internationales Privatrecht* 57, 66; see more generally M Abend, *Die lex validitatis im internationalen Vertragsrecht* (Heidelberg, Winter, 1994).

[144] Fentiman (n 6) para 5.68; see also Joubert (n 74) 248; Mayer and Heuzé (n 32) para 747.

[145] BGE 102 II 143; see Honsell et al (n 6) 1000.

An alternative approach to the rule of validation is to hold the choice of law agreement invalid on the basis that the parties made a mutual mistake in choosing an invalidating law, and to apply the objective applicable law instead. This is the approach favoured by the Restatement (Second) of the Conflict of Laws and will be discussed further in chapter eight.[146]

D. Ambiguous Choice of Law Contracts

Like any other contract, a choice of law contract can come into existence only if it is sufficiently certain.[147] One of the reasons why a choice of law contract might be uncertain is that it is unintentionally ambiguous, because it fails to state clearly the law that has been chosen. Whether such an ambiguity can be resolved is a matter of interpretation. As with implied choice of law contracts, it is necessary to ascertain the parties' 'real' intentions. Ambiguities in express choice of law clauses will often be easy to resolve because the parties' intentions are nonetheless sufficiently clear in the circumstances. Thus, a choice of 'UK law' in an insurance contract concluded by reference to a standard Lloyd's form could hardly be construed as anything other than a choice of English law in the absence of any links to Scotland or Northern Ireland.[148]

More difficult are those cases where the chosen law is expressed to be dependent on a fact that is disputed, and the disputed fact forms part of the underlying relationship that is to be submitted to the chosen law. As has been explained in relation to putative indicators of implied choice of law, the (putative) chosen law cannot be used to determine the disputed fact if the choice of law contract depends on the existence of that fact. This is because it is logically impossible to apply the party autonomy rule to an issue that itself determines the existence of the choice of law contract. Failure to appreciate this distinction is likely to lead to the application of the putative chosen law to matters other than the choice of law contract.

Yet this was exactly the approach taken by the German Bundesgerichtshof in a shipping case.[149] The claimant had purchased 560 steel pipes from an English company, which arranged for an English charterer to ship the goods to Sweden. When the shipment arrived in Sweden, it was found the pipes had been damaged during transport, and the claimant brought proceedings against the German owner of the ship in Germany. The English charterer's details were included on the front page of the bill of lading. However, the bill of lading's standard conditions stated that 'Any dispute arising under this Bill of Lading shall be decided in the country where the carrier has his principal place of business, and the law of such country shall apply except as provided elsewhere herein'. The standard

[146] *Restatement (Second)* (n 28) s 187, cmnt (e); see ch 8, s II.C.

[147] On certainty, see Kötz and Flessner (n 51) 42.

[148] See *Catlin Syndicate Ltd v Adams Land & Cattle Co* [2006] EWHC 2065, [2007] Lloyd's Rep IR 96 [22] and [23].

[149] BGH NJW 2007, 2036.

conditions also included an identity of carrier (IOC) clause, providing that 'The contract evidenced by this Bill of Lading is between the Merchant and the Owner of the vessel named herein'. The claimant argued that, under the IOC clause, the owner of the ship was identified as the carrier, leading to German jurisdiction and the application of German law. The German shipowner disputed the jurisdiction of the German courts.

The Bundesgerichtshof rejected the claimant's argument and held that the English charterer was the carrier. There was, therefore, an English jurisdiction and choice of law clause. The Court reasoned that the identity of the carrier was to be established in accordance with the law applicable to the bill of lading.[150] The applicable law, however, was the law chosen by the parties. Assuming the IOC clause to be valid, the putative chosen law was German law (because the IOC clause identified the German shipowner as the carrier). German law, in turn, rendered the IOC clause invalid under Article 4 of the German law on standard terms, because the individually negotiated identification of the English charterer as carrier on the front of the bill of lading took precedence over the bill's standard terms (that is, the IOC clause).[151] Hence, English jurisdiction and choice of law were established. What was not clear, however, was whether these agreements also bound the German ship owner, and the matter was sent back to the Berufungsgericht.

The Bundesgerichtshof's reasoning boils down to a simple case of putativity. The Court used German law, as the putative chosen law, to determine the identity of the carrier for the purposes of establishing an English choice of law clause. But having established English law as the applicable law, it could hardly proceed to revisit the issue and apply English law—as the chosen law—to determine the identity of the carrier. The carrier could have only one identity. If English law had upheld the IOC clause (which, in fact, it would not have done[152]), the Court would have been faced with an English choice of law clause, entered into by the English charterer as carrier, and a bill of lading identifying the German ship owner as the carrier. The result was that German law, as the putative chosen law, provided the final determination on the issue of identity.

A more appropriate solution would have been to recognise that it is logically impossible to found a choice of law contract on 'external' disputed facts without first resolving this dispute pursuant to objective choice of law rules.[153] This approach would have also been much simpler to apply. The Court could have

[150] ibid, [21].

[151] ibid, [22].

[152] ibid, [22], referring to *Homburg Houtimport BV v Agrosin Private Ltd (The Starsin)* [2003] UKHL 12, [2004] 1 AC 715.

[153] cp *Kingspan Environmental Ltd v Borealis A/S* [2012] EWHC 1147 [542]ff, where the relevant choice of law clause referred to the law of the supplier's domicile, and it was unclear whether this was a reference to the supplier's domicile in the United Kingdom or Denmark. The Court concluded that the relevant domicile was Denmark, applying English law rules, before determining whether the choice of law clause had been properly incorporated under Danish law.

applied English law, as the likely objective law, to determine the effectiveness of the IOC clause and, having so established the identity of the carrier for the purposes of the choice of law contract as well as the parties' relationship more generally, could have proceeded to apply the chosen law (ie the law of the carrier) to the remaining issues. The identification of the objective law might have involved some arbitrariness. But application of German law as the putative chosen law was no less arbitrary, and undermined the principle of party autonomy.

V. Conclusion

Although the party autonomy rule calls for a mutual intention to choose the applicable law, courts do not always uphold this general principle of the law of contract, giving effect instead to the parties' expectations or hypothetical intentions. There seem to be two principal reasons for this. The first is a tendency to rely on the party autonomy rule to make up for perceived deficiencies of objective choice of law or of the law of procedure (insofar as facultative choice of law is concerned). The second is a misunderstanding of the function of the choice of law contract (and of its independent nature). Both factors have led to an over-enforcement of choice of law contracts in relation to implied choice of law. Parties who do not wish to make a choice of law would be well advised to make that intention express.

If general principles of the law of contract are applied to the choice of law contract, and if they are applied correctly, then neither expectation nor hypothetical intention is sufficient to meet the requirements of the party autonomy rule. The court should determine why, if the parties turned their minds to the matter of choice of law, they did not enter into an express choice of law agreement. If choice of law does, in fact, seek to protect the expectations or hypothetical intentions of individual parties, this cannot be achieved by distorting the party autonomy rule into a catch-all for difficult cases. To maintain the institutional boundaries of the party autonomy rule, and to protect parties from the enforcement of fictional agreements, a choice of law contract must only be given effect if it meets the requirements of an agreement under the law.

Finally, the failure to look to the law of contract has also created confusion whether objective or subjective intention is needed to form a choice of law contract. This confusion, which risks arbitrary and inconsistent decision-making, is unnecessary: either the law of contract is relied upon, or modal choice of law must impose an appropriate solution. Choice of law contracts, like all other contracts, must be formed in accordance with a set standard of agreement.

7

Formation of the Choice of Law Contract

I. Introduction

Chapter six dealt with the fundamental question of the standard of agreement that is required to establish a choice of law contract. It inquired into the relevance of hypothetical, objective and subjective agreement and concluded that, based on general principles of contract, hypothetical agreements or mere expectations are not sufficient to trigger the party autonomy rule (and hence should be accorded no weight in practice). The purpose of chapters seven and eight is to inquire more specifically into selected issues that affect or may affect the formation or validity of the choice of law contract, ranging from rules on the admissibility of extrinsic evidence to the regulation of unfair choices of law. They evaluate the existing regime that applies to the formation and validity of choice of law contracts and, where appropriate, propose changes to the regime or to the way it is given effect.

In doing so, the chapters seek to explore two key questions: when, and how, does the law of contract apply to determine the formation and validity of choice of law contracts; and what is the role that modal choice of law plays, or should play, in the regulation of these issues? On the first question, it is worth reiterating that rules of the general law of contract are not applicable to choice of law contracts if they are specific to relationships of obligation,[1] and that the way they are applied must take account of the independent nature of the choice of law contract (ie the choice of law contract is not an implied term).[2] On the second question, it is necessary to determine whether modal choice of law rules are needed (a) to supplement the law of contract, by importing principles of the law of contract that would not be given sufficient effect by rules of the law of contract directly applicable to the choice of law contract; and (b) to replace rules of the law of contract where these are inconsistent with the needs of the conflict of laws.[3]

[1] See ch 5, s III.B.ii.
[2] See ch 4; see also ch 6, s IV.B.
[3] See ch 5, s IV.

Chapters seven and eight do not purport to provide an exhaustive analysis of the formation and validity of choice of law contracts. The variability of the applicable law of contract alone would make this an impossible task. Instead, the analysis takes a broad-brushed approach, highlighting issues that are likely to carry the greatest impact for the enforcement of choice of law contracts. These issues are split into loose categories of 'formation' (chapter seven) and 'validity' (chapter eight), which are not intended to be scientific labels. The present chapter on 'formation' focuses on rules that must be satisfied before a choice of law contract can come into existence, while chapter eight focuses on rules that render a choice of law contract unenforceable because it is the product of a defective or unfair agreement. Thus, chapter eight is concerned mostly with rules that require an ex post evaluation of the particular choice of law contract, the circumstances that led to its conclusion and/or its effect; and chapter seven is concerned mostly with ex ante standards for contracting that may not require an inquiry into individual parties' circumstances or the quality of their consent. In particular, this chapter covers rules that regulate the admissibility of extrinsic evidence (section II); rules on offer and acceptance (section III); the requirement of certainty of terms (section IV); formalities (section V); capacity (section VI); and requirements of transparency or disclosure (sections VII and VIII).

II. Extrinsic Evidence

Chapter six was concerned with the task of ascertaining the parties' intentions on the applicable law. Closely related to this task is the question of evidence: is, or should, the choice of law contract be subject to rules that restrict the admissibility of evidence? Common law jurisdictions in particular provide for complex rules on the admissibility of extrinsic evidence to prove contractual intention. In principle, such rules are clearly applicable to choice of law contracts. For example, if evidence of post-contractual conduct is inadmissible, a party's conduct during proceedings cannot be relied upon to establish the meaning of an earlier choice of law contract.[4]

But there are two important considerations that should limit the relevance of these rules to choice of law contracts. The first is that exclusionary rules of evidence are typically concerned with evidence of terms that were not included in the written contract, or with evidence of the meaning of the words used in the contract. The choice of law contract is not a term of the substantive contract. Courts that do not properly appreciate the independent nature of the choice of

[4] On the distinction between procedural choice and procedural conduct as evidence of a prior choice, see more generally A Steiner, *Die stillschweigende Rechtswahl im Prozess im System der subjektiven Anknüpfung im deutschen Internationalen Privatrecht* (Frankfurt, Peter Lang, 1998) 110–11.

law contract are at risk of giving too much weight to exclusionary rules of evidence (see section A below). The second consideration is that modal choice of law may exclude the operation of such rules, as does, for example, Article 3 of Regulation (EC) 593/2008 on the law applicable to contractual obligations,[5] because modal choice of law rules may be better suited to regulate the matter (see section B).

A. Applying Rules of Evidence to Choice of Law Contracts

It is a long-standing common law rule that 'parol evidence cannot be received to contradict, vary, add to or subtract from the terms of a written contract, or the terms in which the parties have deliberately agreed to record any part of their contract'.[6] This rule is subject to many exceptions, but it has been applied to reject an implied choice of law where the parties' substantive contract was contained in a written document.[7] The question arises, therefore, whether this approach gives proper effect to the independence of the choice of law contract. Does the independence of the choice of law contract affect the way in which rules like the parol evidence rule apply to it? It is submitted that it does, and that such rules are of limited relevance to choice of law contracts as a result.

There are at least two ways in which the independence of the choice of law contract may affect the admission of evidence relating to the parties' intentions on choice of law. First, because ascertaining the existence of a mutual intention to choose the applicable law is a question of formation, as opposed to a matter of interpretation of any underlying contract, rules against the admissibility of extrinsic evidence that are applicable only to the interpretation of contracts (or the implication of terms) are not relevant to determining whether the parties have formed an agreement on choice of law. This includes the rule on subsequent conduct, which excludes evidence of subsequent conduct for the purposes of interpreting—but not establishing the existence of—the parties' agreement.[8] It follows, therefore, that there is no bar against the admission of evidence on the parties' intention to choose the applicable law that postdates the entering into of both the underlying contract and the choice of law contract.

This point was neglected in *Whitworth Street Estates (Manchester) Ltd v James Miller and Partners Ltd*,[9] where the House of Lords held that the parties' subsequent conduct could not be looked at to determine the proper law of the contract. The respondents, an English company, had entered into a construction agreement

[5] Reg (EC) 593/2008 on the law applicable to contractual obligations [2008] OJ L177/6 (Rome I).

[6] *Bank of Australasia v Palmer* [1897] AC 540 (PC) 545 (Lord Morris).

[7] *Whitworth Street Estates (Manchester) Ltd v James Miller and Partners Ltd* [1970] AC 583 (HL).

[8] See H Beale (ed), *Chitty on Contracts* 31st edn (London, Sweet & Maxwell, 2012) para 12-126; DW McLauchlan, 'Contract Formation, Contract Interpretation, and Subsequent Conduct' (2006) 25 *University of Queensland Law Journal* 77.

[9] *Whitworth Street Estates (Manchester) Ltd v James Miller and Partners Ltd* [1970] AC 583 (HL); see also *Amin Rasheed Shipping Corp v Kuwait Insurance Co* [1984] 1 AC 50 (HL) 69 (Lord Wilberforce).

with the appellants, who were building contractors registered in Scotland. The contract, which involved construction on a building located in Scotland, was in the form published by the Royal Institute of British Architects. A dispute between the parties was submitted to arbitration in Scotland. The issue before the Court was whether the arbitration was a Scottish or an English arbitration. In determining this issue, it was also necessary to consider the proper law of the contract.

The Court of Appeal held that the contract was most closely connected to English law. In coming to this conclusion, Lord Denning MR made express reference to subsequent conduct of the parties that indicated, in his view, an assumption that English law was applicable (namely, a writ issued in the English courts prior to the commencement of arbitration; and a reference to arbitration under the Arbitration Act 1950).[10] On appeal, the respondents argued that the parties intended English law to be applicable. In rejecting this submission, four members of the House of Lords also dismissed the relevance of the parties' subsequent conduct to ascertaining the proper law.[11] Lord Reid stated:

> Like any other agreement [the proper law] may be inferred from reading their contract as a whole in light of relevant circumstances known to both parties when they made their contract. …It has been assumed in the course of this case that it is proper, in determining what was the proper law, to have regard to actings of the parties after their contract had been made. Of course the actings of the parties (including any words which they used) may be sufficient to show that they made a new contract. … But with regard to actings of the parties between the date of the original contract and the date of [the arbitrator's] appointment I did not understand it to be argued that they were sufficient to establish any new contract, and I think they clearly were not. As I understood him, counsel sought to use those actings to show that there was an agreement when the original contract was made that the proper law of that contract was to be the law of England. I must say that I had thought that it is now well settled that it is not legitimate to use as an aid in the construction of the contract anything which the parties said or did after it was made. Otherwise one might have the result that a contract meant one thing the day it was signed, but by reason of subsequent events meant something different a month or a year later.[12]

This criticism was not well-founded, because the parties' subsequent 'actings' were not an 'aid in the construction of the contract', but were arguably relevant to the formation of an alleged agreement to choose English law. Whether the parties agreed on English law when they entered into the construction contract had nothing to do with interpretation of the construction contract or with inferring a term into the construction contract or, indeed, with *interpretation* of the alleged choice of law contract. This was not a situation where it was clear that the parties had made a choice of English law but it was unclear whether, for example, the choice

[10] *Whitworth Street Estates (Manchester) Ltd v James Miller and Partners Ltd* [1969] 1 WLR 377 (CA) 381 (Lord Denning MR).

[11] *Whitworth Street Estates* (HL) 603 (Lord Reid), 606 (Lord Hodson), 611 (Viscount Dilhorne) and 615 (Lord Wilberforce).

[12] ibid, 603.

could be interpreted to apply to matters other than the construction contract. The issue was whether they had made a choice at all. Thus, the parol evidence rule could not apply.

Second, because the parol evidence rule applies only to written agreements,[13] it will not apply to implied or oral choice of law contracts, even if the choice relates to an underlying contract that is contained in a written document. For example, if party A and B agreed, in oral negotiations, that the law applicable to their contract was English law, but failed to make reference to that agreement in the written contract ultimately entered into, the parol evidence rule would not preclude admission of evidence relating to the parties' oral choice of law contract. The fact that the parties entered into an underlying written contract could not limit the type of evidence admissible to establish an implied or oral choice of law contract.

It follows that exclusionary rules of evidence are less relevant to choice of law contracts than may appear to be the case at first sight. The House of Lords' reasoning in *Whitworth Street Estates (Manchester) Ltd v James Miller and Partners Ltd* should not be followed. The choice of law contract is an independent contract, and a failure to treat it as such undermines the consistent and coherent application of exclusionary rules of evidence. Why should evidence of subsequent conduct be admissible to establish formation of the construction contract, but not of the choice of law contract that provides the law applicable to the construction contract?

B. A Modal Choice of Law Rule on the Admissibility of Evidence?

The preceding analysis demonstrates that submitting choice of law contracts to evidence rules of the law of contract raises potentially complex issues. A foreign court (ie a court applying a foreign *lex causae* to the choice of law contract) in particular may struggle with the complexity of the task. There is also a real concern that restrictions on the admissibility of evidence are misplaced in the context of choice of law, where the need for flexible and efficient decision-making carries particular weight. It would seem entirely appropriate for a court to have regard to any facts that, in its discretion, evidence a mutual choice of law, provided it does so in accordance with the applicable standard of agreement (as discussed in chapter six).[14] The parties would not need to argue about the relevance or irrelevance of exclusionary rules of evidence; and the court, relieved from the burden of applying these often technical rules, could focus on the substantive questions at hand—the formation or interpretation of the choice of law contract in the individual case. This approach would also pay due regard to the international nature

[13] *Chitty* (n 8) para 12-095; cp the effect of the rule on collateral agreements at para 12-103.
[14] See, eg, UNIDROIT Principles 2010, Arts 4.3 and 1.2.

of the choice of law contract, offering an internationalist solution to a problem that knows varying practices across borders.[15]

So a modal choice of law rule on the admissibility of evidence may appear to be a more effective source of regulation than the law of contract. In fact, Article 3 of Regulation (EC) 593/2008 on the law applicable to contractual obligations (Rome I)[16] has been interpreted as doing away with rules excluding evidence of pre-contractual or subsequent conduct, on the basis that it requires the court to have regard to 'the terms of the contract or the circumstances of the case'.[17] English courts have relied on Article 3 to admit evidence that otherwise would have been (wrongly) construed as inadmissible evidence of pre-contractual or subsequent conduct under English law.[18] If the evidence rule in Article 3 is meant to serve as an exclusive modal choice of law rule, it should express this clearly. It could also state more specifically what type of evidence is admissible to establish the existence or the meaning of the choice of law contract;[19] and it could provide for a complementary rule on the relevant standard of intention to ensure consistency.[20]

The alternative approach would be to leave the question of evidence to the law governing the choice of law contract,[21] but to ensure that the independent nature of the choice of law contract is properly recognised.

III. Offer and Acceptance

Where agreement cannot be clearly established as a matter of fact, the law sometimes intervenes to define the type of conduct that is to constitute an agreement, or an offer or acceptance. It may provide, for example, that silence does not amount to acceptance, or that an offer must be accepted within a certain period, or that an offer may be withdrawn under specified circumstances. Even though these

[15] cp UNIDROIT Principles 2010, Arts 4.3 and 1.2.

[16] Rome I (n 5).

[17] See R Plender and M Wilderspin, *European Private International Law of Obligations* 4th edn (London, Sweet & Maxwell, 2015) para 6-045; L Collins (ed), *Dicey, Morris and Collins on the Conflict of Laws* 15th edn (London, Sweet & Maxwell, 2012) para 32-037 ('It is suggested, with some hesitation, that the English court should be entitled to take subsequent conduct into account, at least to the extent that it sheds light on the intention of the parties (or on the country with which the contract is most closely connected) *at the time the contract was concluded*.'). cp *Lupofresh Ltd* v *Sapporo Breweries Ltd* [2013] EWCA Civ 948, [2014] 1 All ER (Comm) 484 [17]. Another view is that the matter is excluded from the Reg as a question of evidence pursuant to Art 1(3).

[18] eg *Samcrete Egypt Engineers & Contractors SAE v Land Rover Exports Ltd* [2001] EWCA Civ 2019, [2002] CLC 533 [23], [29]; *Lawlor v Sandvik Mining and Construction Mobile Crushers and Screens Ltd* [2012] EWHC 1188, [2012] 2 Lloyd's Rep 25 [11]–[12], [47].

[19] cp O Lando and H Beale (eds), *Principles of European Contract Law (PECL): Parts I and II* (The Hague, Kluwer, 2000) Art 5:102.

[20] See ch 6, s III.

[21] But see Collins (n 17) para 32-036, where it is suggested that the *lex fori* should apply to determine this issue.

questions generally fall to be determined by the law of contract,[22] there are two particular matters that could be more appropriately regulated by modal choice of law: communication of an acceptance of a proposed choice of law (see section A below), and conflicting choice of law clauses (see section B). This is because the rules of contract that would otherwise govern these matters may not properly give effect to the function of the choice of law contract.

A. Communicating Acceptance

With the exception of the postal acceptance rule, it is generally the case that a contract is concluded when the acceptance reaches the offeror (unless the offer provides otherwise).[23] But it is surely wrong to assume that an offeror would always intend to receive communication of the offeree's acceptance of a proposed choice of law. On the contrary, it is likely that the offeror would intend the stipulated law to determine any issues of agreement, including the question of whether there was valid acceptance of the underlying offer. Thus, neither party ought to be able to disclaim the offeror's proposed choice of law on the basis that there has been no communication of acceptance.

In some cases, it may be possible to arrive at this result through purposive interpretation of the law of contract. But a court may be reluctant to engage in such interpretation where the applicable law is not the law of the forum. A modal choice of law rule would also be much easier to apply. It could provide that, in circumstances where a choice of law contract is concluded by correspondence, acceptance of a proposed choice of law need not be communicated in order to be effective. Had the Englishman's offer in *Albeko Schuhmaschinen AG v Kamborian Shoe Machine Co Ltd* included a choice of English law,[24] and had there been evidence of the Swiss party's acceptance of the letter, an English modal choice of law rule dispensing with the need for communication of acceptance would have led to the application of English law to determine formation of the underlying contract of agency.[25]

[22] As it did, for example, in *Lincoln National Life Insurance Co v Employers Reinsurance Corp* [2002] EWHC 28, [2002] Lloyd's Rep IR 835 [22]. cp BAGE 125, 24 (2007), where the question whether the plaintiff had accepted a choice of law clause in a pre-hire agreement was left open because the Court simply inferred a choice of the same law. cp also BGE 131 III 511, where the Bundesgericht did not refer to the law of contract to conclude that there was silent acceptance of a proposed choice of Swiss law ('Il se trouve que les demanderesses ont reçu ces garanties sans protester et les ont fait valoir dès que les conditions en étaient remplies, acceptant ainsi tacitement ces engagements.'). On the argument that the effect of silence is governed by general modal choice of law rules requiring an express or clear choice (H Honsell et al (eds), *Basler Kommentar* 3rd edn (Basel, Helbing Lichtenhahn, 2013) 996 and 1096), see ch 5, s III.A.ii.

[23] *PECL* (n 19) Art 2.205(1); H Kötz and A Flessner, *European Contract Law* (Oxford, Clarendon Press, 1997) 26.

[24] *Albeko Schuhmaschinen AG v Kamborian Shoe Machine Co Ltd* (1961) 111 LJ 519; see ch 4, s II.A.i.

[25] cp AJE Jaffey, 'Offer and Acceptance and Related Questions in the English Conflict of Laws' (1975) 24 *ICLQ* 603, 605.

Similar considerations apply to the revocation of offers and to time limits for their acceptance.[26] Ordinarily, an offeror would not wish to extend the revocation of an offer, or time limits for its acceptance,[27] to a choice of law contract included in the offer, because the offeror would intend that the clause be used to determine the effectiveness of the contract. But this particular matter could probably be accommodated within the law of contract as a matter of contractual interpretation.

B. Conflicting Choice of Law Clauses

Another problem that may arise in the formation of choice of law contracts is the so-called 'battle of the forms'. Where, in concluding the contract, each party has referred to its own standard conditions, a conflict between the parties' terms and conditions is variously decided by the 'first shot' rule,[28] the 'last shot' rule,[29] or the 'knockout' rule.[30] While the first and last shot rules treat as decisive either the first or the last reference to standard terms in the negotiation process, the knockout rule upholds only those terms that are 'common in substance'.[31] But what is a court to do where the parties have used conflicting choice of law clauses? Can, and should, this question be resolved by the law of contract?

i. Proposed Solutions

There are three potential outcomes to a 'battle of the choice of law clauses' pursuant to the law of contract. If an English purchaser, who includes in its order an English choice of law clause, takes delivery of a German supplier's goods, but this delivery is accompanied by a delivery notice providing for German law to be applicable,[32] then the parties may be considered to have chosen (a) English law under the 'first shot' rule, (b) German law under the 'last shot' rule because the purchaser's acceptance of delivery also constituted acceptance of the proposed choice of German law, or (c) no law under the 'knockout' rule. But conflicting choice of law clauses present a difficult problem for putative choice of law. Can either of the two putative choices—namely, English law or German law—be used to determine the issue of formation?

[26] See *PECL* (n 19) Arts 2.202 and 2.206.

[27] See, eg, *White Cliffs Opal Mines Ltd v Miller* (1904) 4 SR (NSW) 150.

[28] See, eg, Dutch Burgerlijk Wetboek, Art 6:225(3).

[29] *Butler Machine Tool Co v Ex-cell-o Corp* [1979] 1 WLR 401 (CA).

[30] *PECL* (n 19) Art 2:209; see G Rühl, 'The Battle of the Forms: Comparative and Economic Observations' (2003) 24 *University of Pennsylvania Journal of International Economic Law* 189 for a general overview.

[31] *PECL* (n 19) Art 2.209(1).

[32] cp *Ferguson Shipbuilders Ltd v Voith Hydro GmbH & Co KG* 2000 SLT 229 (Court of Session) and *Guiliani v Invar Manufacturing* (2007) 52 CPC (6th) 129 (Ont SCJ), where there was a battle of the forms, but no conflicting choice of law clauses.

Several solutions to this problem have been suggested.[33] Some argue that the *lex fori* or the objective applicable law must govern the issue;[34] others consider that each choice of law clause ought to be assessed under its own putative law, which might then eliminate one of the alleged choices of law and leave only one chosen law. This is, in essence, the solution adopted by Article 6(1)(b) of the Hague Principles on Choice of Law in International Commercial Contracts,[35] which provides that there is only a choice of law if the same standard terms prevail under both of the designated laws.[36]

None of these solutions is entirely satisfactory. The proposition that each potential choice ought to be determined under its own putative chosen law has (rightly) been criticised as unprincipled, because it sets out to establish two agreements where there ought to be only one.[37] This leaves the possible options of the *lex fori* or the objective law, both of which may be criticised as arbitrary fallbacks. More generally, there is an unanswered question whether application of the law of contract can really meet the needs of the conflict of laws in this instance.

ii. A Modal Choice of Law Rule Based on the Knockout Principle

A popular view amongst German scholars is that the matter must be resolved within the bounds of modal choice of law, on the basis that conflicting choice of law clauses do not give rise to an appearance of choice and therefore do not fulfil the choice of law requirement of 'consent'.[38] This reasoning—exclusion of the choice in reliance on general rules of modal choice of law—is unconvincing.[39] General rules on party autonomy do not purport to regulate conflicting choices of law. However, there is force in the argument that the knockout rule provides the most appropriate solution for choice of law contracts.

A modal choice of law rule providing for the knockout rule would not only be easy to apply; it would also reflect the function of the choice of law contract more accurately than the first or last shot rule. The purpose of these rules is to preserve the existence of the parties' overall contract despite an exchange of

[33] See A Dutta, 'Kollidierende Rechtswahlklauseln in allgemeinen Geschäftsbedingungen' (2005) 104 *Zeitschrift für vergleichende Rechtswissenschaft* 461 for an overview.

[34] Collins (n 17) para 32-067 and see also 32-116; referred to in *Whitworths Ltd v Synergy Food Ingredients & Processing BV* [2014] EWHC 4239 [38]; cp *Evialis SA v SIAT* [2003] EWHC 863, [2003] 2 Lloyd's Rep 377 [38].

[35] Hague Conference on Private International Law, *Principles on Choice of Law in International Commercial Contracts* (approved on 19 March 2015).

[36] See also G Dannemann, 'The "Battle of the Forms" and the Conflict of Laws' in F Rose (ed), *Lex Mercatoria: Essays on International Commercial Law in Honour of Francis Reynolds* (London, LLP, 2000) 199, 210.

[37] Dutta (n 33) 479; F Vischer, L Huber and D Oser, *Internationales Vertragsrecht* 2nd edn (Berlin, Stämpfli, 2000) para 156. cp D Martiny, 'Die Haager *Principles on Choice of Law in International Commercial Contracts*' (2015) 79 *Rabels Zeitschrift für ausländisches und internationales Privatrecht* 624, 643.

[38] U Magnus (ed), *Staudingers Kommentar zum Bürgerlichen Gesetzbuch: Rom I-VO Art 3* (Berlin, Sellier, 2011) para 174; C von Bar, *Internationales Privatrecht*, vol 2 (Munich, Ch Beck, 1991) 349, para 475; cp P Nygh, *Autonomy in International Contracts* (Oxford, Oxford University Press, 1999) 95–96.

[39] See ch 5, s III.A.ii.

inconsistent terms, particularly if obligations under the contract have already been performed.[40] This rationale is not relevant to choice of law contracts. Because a choice of law contract is not a term of the underlying contract, a failed party choice does not transform an acceptance of the underlying contract into a counteroffer;[41] and a failure to agree on the applicable law does not leave a gap in the parties' contract.[42]

The law of contract should give way, therefore, to a modal choice of law rule that provides that conflicting choices of law do not form a choice of law contract. This rule should apply only where there is an actual conflict of choices of law. Where the 'battle' is between a standard choice of law clause and a negotiated choice of law, it is the negotiated choice of law clause that should prevail.[43] The Hague Principles have taken a disappointingly cautious approach in this regard. There is no need to require parties to prove the content of two applicable laws when a direct application of the knockout principle would provide the more principled answer.

IV. Certainty and Floating Choice of Law Contracts

Every contract must be sufficiently certain before it can be given effect; and the choice of law contract is no exception. Chapter six already touched on the problem of ambiguous choice of law contracts.[44] There is no reason why, on a general level, the law of contract should not be an adequate source to regulate uncertain choice of law contracts. But the law of contract provides no direct solution where the issue is whether the parties may enter into a 'floating' choice of law contract. A floating choice of law contract is temporarily uncertain because the identity of the chosen law depends on a future act or event, such as a unilateral choice or the lodging of proceedings in a certain jurisdiction. The issue for the court here is one of enforceability: is it appropriate to subject the parties' relationship to a chosen law that was not previously identifiable by the parties?

This question must necessarily be resolved by modal choice of law, because it is a question that is specific to choice of law contracts. But the fact that the law of contract cannot provide a direct answer here does not mean that it is irrelevant. On the contrary, the law of contract supplies the relevant criteria for enforceability of such 'floating' choice of law clauses: predictability and unfairness.

[40] See generally AT von Mehren, 'The "Battle of the Forms": A Comparative View' (1990) 38 *American Journal of Comparative Law* 265.

[41] This does not mean, however, that the contract could not be conditional on a valid choice of law agreement: see ch 4, s IV.B.

[42] See ch 6, s IV.

[43] *PECL* (n 19) Art 5:104.

[44] See ch 6, s IV.D.

A. Predictability and Unfairness

The law of contract generally requires that there be agreement on the essential terms of the contract.[45] Parties should be in a position to predict the consequences of their dealings. Where a contract places the burden of uncertainty on only one of the parties, because the other party is given contractual power to decide the matter unilaterally, the contract holds real potential for exploitation or unfairness.[46] In common law jurisdictions, a contract may be void *ab initio* where 'the discretionary power is so broad as to reserve performance entirely to the discretion of one party'.[47]

These concerns are directly relevant to choice of law contracts.[48] The more uncertain it is what the chosen law will be, the more difficult it is for parties to assess and predict their (potentially conflicting) rights and obligations.[49] These difficulties are exacerbated where the applicable law is to be determined by unilateral choice. While, in the law of contract, a unilateral power to impose or vary obligations is usually tempered by duties of good faith or fairness, such 'content-controlling' duties would not usually be applicable to choice of law contracts.[50] What is needed, therefore, is a modal choice of law rule that defines clearly the permissible parameters of floating choice of law contracts.

B. A Modal Choice of Law Rule for Floating Choice of Law Contracts

It is usually recognised that regulation of floating choice of law contracts must fall within the realm of modal choice of law.[51] While floating choice of law clauses were

[45] See generally *PECL* (n 19) Art 2:103.

[46] S Kós, 'Constraints on the Exercise of Contractual Powers' (2011) 42 *Victoria University of Wellington Law Review* 17; H Collins, *The Law of Contract* (Cambridge, Cambridge University Press, 2003) 339–40; JM Paterson, 'Implied Fetters on the Exercise of Discretionary Contractual Powers' (2009) 35 *Monash University Law Review* 45; MB Jaspers, *Nachträgliche Rechtswahl im internationalen Schuldvertragsrecht* (Frankfurt, Peter Lang, 2002) 211; see also Kötz and Flessner (n 23) 49.

[47] Kós (n 46) 19; see *Placer Development Ltd v Commonwealth* (1969) 121 CLR 353, 356.

[48] An irrelevant consideration in this context, on the other hand, is the traditional objection raised against floating choice of law clauses in common law jurisdictions, which was that every contract must have a governing law at the time of its formation, and that this law cannot subsequently be changed: *Armar Shipping Co Ltd v Caisse Algérienne d'Assurance et de Réassurance* [1981] 1 WLR 207(CA) 215; A Briggs, 'The Validity of "Floating" Choice of Law and Jurisdiction Clauses' [1986] *Lloyd's Maritime and Commercial Law Quarterly* 508, 514–15.

[49] *Sonatrach Petroleum Corp (BVI) v Ferrell International Ltd* [2002] 1 All ER (Comm) 627 (QB) [28].

[50] See ch 5, s III.B.ii.

[51] But see *Sonatrach Petroleum Corp (BVI) v Ferrell International Ltd* [2002] 1 All ER (Comm) 627 (QB) [27] and *BP Plc v National Union Fire Insurance Co* [2004] EWHC 1132 [35]; cp *Dubai Electricity Co v Islamic Republic of Iran Shipping Lines* (*The Iran Vojdan*) [1984] 2 Lloyd's Rep 380 (QB) 385; Nygh (n 38) 100.

treated with suspicion under English common law rules,[52] Convention 80/934/ECC on the law applicable to contractual obligations (Rome Convention)[53] and Rome I have been interpreted as allowing such a choice.[54] It has even been argued that there can be 'no objection at all' to a floating choice of law that applies to the entire relationship of the parties, including any conduct taking place prior to the identification of the chosen law.[55] In *BP Plc v National Union Fire Insurance Co*, for example, the English High Court upheld a floating choice of English law with retrospective effect, on an application for leave to serve out of the jurisdiction.[56] The plaintiff, BP, sought to bring proceedings under an insurance policy that provided cover for BP's oil and gas extraction projects. The policy required BP to make declarations of the particular projects to be insured, but the insurer disputed the validity of BP's declarations. The policy provided that, 'At the Principal Insured(s) discretion', the insurance was 'subject to English law and practice or USA law and practice'. Wrongly equating this floating choice of law with an agreement to vary the applicable law,[57] Colman J concluded that BP's choice of English law would apply retrospectively to determine the validity of its declarations.[58] He concluded:

> There can be no doubt that parties to a contract can effectively agree to empower one of them to vary it without agreement of the other party or parties, although terms may be implied to limit the scope of the variation or the circumstances in which the option may be exercised … There can be no doubt, however, that if an option to vary the proper law is exercised in good faith in the commercial interests of an insured such as BP and if it is exercised with sufficient clarity, such a variation would be effective.[59]

Such unreserved enthusiasm for floating choice of law contracts is astounding.[60] Where the chosen law is determined by an unforeseen future event or by a third party, both parties will have to adjust their conduct to potentially conflicting applicable laws; and where the chosen law is determined unilaterally, the choice of law contract confers a largely unchecked power to select the law that suits the

[52] *The Iran Vojdan* [1984] 2 Lloyd's Rep 380 (QB); see Collins (n 17) para 32-054; M Davies, AS Bell and PLG Brereton, *Nygh's Conflict of Laws in Australia* 9th edn (Chatswood NSW, LexisNexis, 2014) para 19.9.

[53] Convention 80/934/ECC on the law applicable to contractual obligations [1980] OJ L266/1 (opened for signature 19 June 1980, entered into force 1 April 1991) (Rome Convention).

[54] Collins (n 17) para 32-055; see Plender and Wilderspin (n 17) para 6-019; Magnus (n 38) para 54; cp J Fawcett and JM Carruthers, *Cheshire, North & Fawcett: Private International Law* 14th edn (Oxford, Oxford University Press, 2008) 700; *CGU International Insurance Plc v Szabo* [2002] 1 All ER (Comm) 83 [37].

[55] A Briggs, *Agreements on Jurisdiction and Choice of Law* (Oxford, Oxford University Press, 2008) para 10.05; cp J Kropholler, *Internationales Privatrecht* 6th edn (Tübingen, Mohr Siebeck, 2006) 463.

[56] *BP Plc v National Union Fire Insurance Co* [2004] EWHC 1132; but cp *Sonatrach Petroleum Corp (BVI) v Ferrell International Ltd* [2002] 1 All ER (Comm) 627 (QB) [27]; *Mauritius Commercial Bank Ltd v Hestia Holdings Ltd* [2013] EWHC 1328 [29].

[57] See also Fawcett and Carruthers (n 54) 700.

[58] *BP Plc v National Union Fire Insurance Co* [2004] EWHC 1132 [34].

[59] ibid, [35].

[60] cp the debate surrounding one-sided jurisdiction clauses, sparked by the *Rothschild* decision, Cass civ 1ère, 26 September 2012, no 11-26.022: M-E Ancel, L Marion and L Wynaendts, 'Contentieux international: Réflexions sur les clauses de juridiction asymétriques' (2013) 148 *Banque & Droit* 3.

choosing party. It is 'unchecked' because, contrary to Colman J's suggestion that such a power is subject to a duty of good faith, there are no useful standards that a court could apply to determine whether the chosen law is fair or reasonable.

Careful consideration of the law of contract supports a more proactive approach to the regulation of floating choice of law contracts. At the very least it is not true that there can be 'no objection at all' to a hands-off approach to floating choices of law. Commentators on Regulation (EU) 1259/2010 implementing enhanced cooperation in the area of the law applicable to divorce and legal separation (Rome III)[61] have argued that Article 5 does not permit a floating choice of the *lex fori* because Recital 18 provides that 'The informed choice of both spouses is a basic principle of this Regulation' and 'Each spouse should know exactly what are the legal and social implications of the choice of applicable law'.[62] But the same conclusion is available by reference to principles of contract. The need for predictability and fairness is as relevant to choice of law contracts as it is to ordinary contracts. It could even be argued that the discretionary power conferred by floating choice of law contracts is so broad as to render the choice of law contract 'illusory'[63] and thus void *ab initio*. There must be some ex ante restrictions on floating choice of law contracts, and not just in the context of divorce.

An appropriate compromise for commercial parties may be to give retrospective effect to only those floating choice of law contracts that contain no more than two alternative applicable laws, to enable parties to gain some understanding of their potential rights and obligations.[64] Under this approach, BP's floating choice of law clause still would have been valid, because it provided for the application of either English or US law, but the dangers of a more open-ended clause would be avoided. Without such a restriction, on the other hand, parties could easily place themselves in a position where they are unable to determine the legal implications of their actions, which could hardly be considered a desirable use of the party autonomy rule.

V. Formal Validity

The law of contract does not usually impose formality requirements on general contracts;[65] so whether a choice of law contract must comply with formality

[61] Reg (EU) 1259/2010 implementing enhanced cooperation in the area of the law applicable to divorce and legal separation [2010] OJ L343/10 (Rome III).

[62] See H Rösler, 'Rechtswahlfreiheit im Internationalen Scheidungsrecht der Rom III-Verordnung' (2014) 78 *Rabels Zeitschrift für ausländisches und internationales Privatrecht* 155, 169–70 and the references cited in fn 87; C Schall and J Weber, 'Die vorsorgende Wahl des Scheidungsstatuts nach der Rom III-VO' [2014] *Praxis des Internationalen Privat- und Verfahrensrechts* 381, 384.

[63] *Placer Development Ltd v Commonwealth* (1969) 121 CLR 353, 360.

[64] cp Jaspers (n 46) 235; Rösler (n 62) 169–70.

[65] eg *PECL* (n 19) Art 2:101(2); cp Code Civil, Art 1341 (imposing formalities for transactions exceeding a certain value).

requirements is largely a matter for modal choice of law. There are some choice of law contracts that are valid only if they are signed, or concluded expressly or in writing. But does modal choice of law make effective and sufficient use of such formalities (see section B below)? This question can only be answered by reference to the purposes of formality requirements more generally (see section A). The role of notarisation or independent legal advice, which is treated as a matter of formality by some legal systems, will be considered separately in section VII.

A. Purpose of Formalities

The purpose of formality requirements is to evidence the parties' intention to be bound, in circumstances where such an intention may not otherwise be obvious, and to ensure that parties who enter into binding commitments are aware of the implications of their actions.[66] English law prescribes formalities for, for example, consumer credit agreements, the sale of land and bills of exchange.[67] Transfers of interests that are not supported by consideration must be conducted by way of deed, presumably to fulfil the 'cautionary' and 'evidentiary' role that would otherwise be performed by the requirement of consideration.[68] So where the transaction is 'of sufficient importance to support the use of a form', the need for formalities:

> [W]ill depend upon the extent to which the guaranties that the formality would afford are rendered superfluous by forces native to the situation out of which the transaction arises—including in these 'forces' the habits and conceptions of the transacting parties.[69]

Although formalities are the exception rather than the rule, they are often used in relation to contracts that are characterised by unequal bargaining power.[70] Employment contracts, for example, are often subject to formalities that are designed to protect employees: Article L 1242-12 of the French Code du Travail requires fixed term employment contracts to be in writing, and so does Article 14 of the German Teilzeit- und Befristungsgesetz; Article 623 of the Bürgerliches Gesetzbuch (BGB) requires written notice to end an employment contract; section 1 of the Employment Rights Act 1996 (UK) requires the employer to 'give to the employee a written statement of particulars of employment' at the

[66] See eg *Chitty* (n 8) para 4-001.

[67] Consumer Credit Act 1974, s 60; Law of Property (Miscellaneous Provisions) Act 1989, s 2(3); Bills of Exchange Act 1882, s 3.

[68] L Fuller, 'Consideration and Form' (1941) 41 *Columbia Law Review* 799.

[69] ibid, 805 (emphasis removed).

[70] See EA Farnsworth, 'Comparative Contract Law' in M Reimann and R Zimmermann (eds), *The Oxford Handbook of Comparative Law* (Oxford, Oxford University Press, 2006) 899, 914–15. In the EU see, for example, Art 10(1) of the Dir 2008/48/EC on credit agreements for consumers [2008] OJ L133/66, which states that 'Credit agreements shall be drawn up on paper or on another durable medium'; and Art 5(1) of the Dir 2008/122/EC on the protection of consumers in respect of certain aspects of timeshare, long-term holiday product, resale and exchange contracts [2009] OJ L33/10, which states that 'Member states shall ensure that the contract is in writing, on paper or on another durable medium'.

beginning of the employment;[71] and Article 321c(3) of the Swiss Obligationenrecht requires a written agreement if the parties wish to forego payment for overtime.

B. Formalities for Choice of Law Contracts

In light of the exceptional nature of formal requirements for contracts, it is not surprising that they are not usually imposed on choice of law contracts in international commercial transactions.[72] But different considerations apply to choice of law contracts involving non-commercial parties, such as consumers, employees and spouses, where formalities may perform a useful cautionary and evidentiary role. Choice of law is a technical area of law with which private individuals are unlikely to be familiar. A requirement that choice of law contracts be express and in writing may allow such individuals to consider more carefully their decision to enter into a choice of law contract. It would also provide evidence of the parties' intentions and, where it is not complied with, offer a shortcut to objective choice of law in circumstances where an implied choice of law contract would rarely be made out.[73]

So some choice of law contracts may well benefit from formalities. This is particularly true of choice of law contracts that are relatively unrestricted in scope and content, because the consequences of such contracts are largely uncontrolled and potentially wide-reaching. But despite their obvious benefits, lawmakers have been reluctant to make use of formalities for choice of law contracts; and where formalities do exist, they are not always drafted in effective terms.

i. Consumer and Employment Relationships

It is not common practice to use formalities for choice of law contracts governing consumer and employment relationships. Although Article 3(5) of Rome I does submit the formal validity of choice of law contracts to the choice of law rules in Article 11, which are applicable to all contracts, this reference is widely understood to be meaningless because the law of contract would not ordinarily contain formality requirements applicable to choice of law contracts.[74]

[71] cp also s 65 of the Employment Relations Act 2000 (NZ).

[72] See, eg, *Hague Principles on Choice of Law in International Commercial Contracts*, Art 5.

[73] See ch 6, s IV.

[74] E Jayme, 'Choice-of-Law Clauses in International Contracts: Some Thoughts on the Reform of Art 3 of the Rome Convention' in L de Lima Pinheiro, *Seminário Internacional sobre a Comunitarização do Direito Internacional Privado* (Almedina, Coimbra, 2005) 53, 59; P Mankowski, 'Stillschweigende Rechtswahl und wählbares Recht' in S Leible (ed), *Das Grünbuch zum Internationalen Vertragsrecht* (Munich, Sellier, 2004) 63, 103; but see Plender and Wilderspin (n 17) para 6-023; Magnus (n 38) para 70 (for the point that formality requirements applicable to consumer contracts would also be applicable to choice of law contracts relating to such contracts); cp W Meyer-Sparenberg, 'Rechtswahlvereinbarungen in Allgemeinen Geschäftsbedingungen' [1989] *Recht der Internationalen Wirtschaft* 347, 349 (who argues that Art 3(5) is wide enough to include a reference to modal choice of law rules on formality; see also ch 5, s IV.C).

Employees and consumers tend to be vulnerable parties who enter into contracts without giving much thought at all to their rights and obligations, or to the law applicable to their rights and obligations. Formalities would be an attractive way of introducing simplicity into the choice of law process: it is easier to apply a requirement that the choice be express than it is to ascertain the (objective) implied intention of a non-commercial party who is unlikely to have given the matter of choice of law any thought.

Imposing formalities on consumer and employment choice of law contracts would also serve an important cautionary function, particularly in jurisdictions where such groups may be left without much substantive protection to rein in the chosen law. A New Zealand consumer, for example, would be stuck with the chosen law if his claim falls outside of the geographical reach of the Consumer Guarantees Act 1993 (and the chosen law does not offend against public policy). Surely the least that the conflict of laws can do for him is to put him on notice by requiring the choice of law contract to be express and in writing, and perhaps even signed or acknowledged in some other form.

Within the framework of Rome I, the lack of formalities can be explained to some extent by the principle of the more favourable law.[75] Arguably there is no need to protect consumers and employees against rashly concluded choice of law contracts because the chosen law will only be applicable where it is more favourable to the weaker party. However, the principle of the more favourable law does not apply to all consumer contracts;[76] and, more fundamentally, the fact that an implied choice might favour a weaker party cannot in itself provide a reason for enforcement of a choice of law contract that does not meet the relevant standard of agreement.

ii. Matrimonial Relationships

Choice of law contracts relating to matrimonial property, divorce and maintenance must usually comply with some formalities. Article 7 of Rome III requires that the agreement 'be expressed in writing, dated and signed by both spouses', and so does Article 13 of the Hague Convention on the Law Applicable to Matrimonial Property Regimes.[77] In both cases, the rule imposes only a minimum requirement. Rome III also allows participating Member States to lay down 'additional formal requirements'; and the Hague Convention requires the designation to 'comply with the form prescribed for marriage contracts, either by the internal law designated by the spouses, or by the internal law of the place where it is made'. A similar approach is taken by Article 19 of the Proposal for a Council Regulation on jurisdiction, applicable law and the recognition and enforcement of decisions

[75] See ch 5, s V.B.

[76] See Art 6(1) and (2), Rome I (n 5).

[77] Hague Convention on the Law Applicable to Matrimonial Property Regimes (1977) 16 ILM 14 (opened for signature 14 March 1978, entered into force 1 September 1992).

in matters of matrimonial property regimes;[78] and by Article 15-04 of the new compromise text of the Proposal for a Council Regulation on jurisdiction, applicable law and the recognition and enforcement of decisions regarding the property consequences of registered partnerships.[79] Article 8 of the Hague Protocol on the Law Applicable to Maintenance Obligations simply requires that the 'agreement shall be in writing or recorded in any medium, the information contained in which is accessible so as to be usable for subsequent reference, and shall be signed by both parties'.[80]

Article 14 of the Einführungsgesetz zum Bürgerlichen Gesetzbuch (EGBGB) on the general effects of marriage requires the parties' choice to be notarised if the choice was entered into in Germany. If it was not entered into in Germany, it must be made in accordance with the formal requirements for marriage contracts imposed by the chosen law or by the law of the place where the choice was made. Article 46d of the EGBGB, too, requires choice of law agreements to be notarised for the purposes of Rome III.

Switzerland and New Zealand take a more relaxed approach to formalities. Article 53 of the Bundesgesetz über das Internationale Privatrecht (IPRG) (on matrimonial property) states that the choice must be 'in writing' or 'arise clearly from the matrimonial property contracts'; and section 7A of the Property (Relationships) Act 1976 (NZ) requires that the agreement be 'in writing' or that it be 'otherwise valid according to the [chosen law]'. Similarly, Articles 25(3) and 22(2) of Regulation (EU) No 650/2012 on jurisdiction, applicable law, recognition and enforcement of decisions and acceptance and enforcement of authentic instruments in matters of succession (Succession Regulation) simply provide that the choice 'shall be made expressly' or 'shall be demonstrated by the terms of [the disposition of property]'.[81]

This summary demonstrates that lawmakers on the whole have turned their minds to the formal validity of choice of law contracts governing family relationships. The two principal exceptions are the Restatement (Second) of Conflict of Laws[82] and English and Australian common law rules, which do not provide for

[78] Proposal for a Council Reg on jurisdiction, applicable law and the recognition and enforcement of decisions in matters of matrimonial property regimes (COM 2011, 126, 16 March 2011) and compromise text of the Proposal, annexed to Council of the European Union, 'Proposal for a Council Regulation on jurisdiction, applicable law and the recognition and enforcement of decisions in matters of matrimonial property regimes—Political agreement' (Note, 14651/15, Brussels, 26 November 2015).

[79] Compromise text of the Proposal, annexed to Council of the European Union, 'Proposal for a Council Regulation on jurisdiction, applicable law and the recognition and enforcement of decisions regarding the property consequences of registered partnerships—Political agreement' (Note, 14652/15, Brussels, 26 November 2015).

[80] Hague Protocol on the Law Applicable to Maintenance Obligations (opened for signature 23 November 2007, entered into force 1 August 2013) (Hague Maintenance Protocol).

[81] Reg (EU) No 650/2012 on jurisdiction, applicable law, recognition and enforcement of decisions and acceptance and enforcement of authentic instruments in matters of succession and on the creation of a European Certificate of Succession [2012] OJ L201/107 (Succession Reg).

[82] American Law Institute, *Restatement (Second) of Conflict of Laws* (1971).

any modal choice of law rules on formal validity.[83] But even where such modal choice of law rules exist, they may not go far enough. There are two reasons in particular why some of the existing rules may not be as effective as they ought to be.

First, a requirement that the choice be signed or in writing does not necessarily exclude an implied choice. Yet a writing requirement holds little 'cautionary' value if it does not affect the parties' ability to enter into an implied choice of law contract. It also holds no 'evidentiary' value, and introduces the risk that courts will find implied choice of law contracts based on the parties' expectations or hypothetical intentions.[84] So while Article 13 of the Hague Convention requires that an express designation of the applicable law be 'in writing, dated and signed by both parties', Article 11 also provides for implied choice of law where the designation 'arise[s] by necessary implication from the provisions of a marriage contract'. Article 53 of the IPRG and Articles 25(3) and 22(2) of the Succession Regulation, too, provide for an implied choice of law.

Even where there is no express provision retaining the power of implied choice, courts and authors have expressed doubt whether a writing requirement has the effect of doing away with implied choice.[85] For example, Article 5 of Rome III has been used to allow an implied choice of law despite the requirement in Article 7 that the agreement 'be expressed in writing, dated and signed by both spouses'. In a case involving two Iranian citizens, the OLG Hamm concluded that the spouses chose Iranian law when, at the time of entering into the marriage in Iran, they agreed that the wife would have limited rights to divorce her husband in accordance with Iranian law.[86] The Court came to this conclusion although the parties seemed to admit that they had not turned their minds to a possible choice of law governing their divorce.

This reasoning is doubly indefensible: first, because the parties' expectations or hypothetical intentions could not be enough to found an implied choice of law;[87] and second, because implied choice of law undermines the purpose of the formality rules in Article 7 (and is also inconsistent with Recital 18, which states that 'Each spouse should know exactly what are the legal and social implications of the choice of applicable law').[88] In these circumstances, it was encouraging to see the solution adopted by Article 19 of the Proposal for a Regulation on matrimonial property, which provides that, as a minimum, the choice must 'be made *expressly*

[83] But which, in limited circumstances, recognise the power to select the law applicable to family relationships: see ch 3, s V.C.

[84] See, eg, OLG Hamm, II-3 UF 267/12 (7 May 2013).

[85] E Jayme, 'Party Autonomy in International Family and Succession Law: New Tendencies' (2009) 11 *Yearbook of Private International Law* 1, 8; *Bergner v Nelis* HC Auckland CIV-2004-404-149, 19 December 2005 [23] (obiter) on s 7A; D Henrich (ed), *Staudingers Kommentar zum Bürgerlichen Gesetzbuch: Art 13–17b EGBGB* (Berlin, Sellier, 2011) Art 14, para 143 (but cp at Art 15, para 101).

[86] OLG Hamm, II-3 UF 267/12 (7 May 2013).

[87] See ch 6.

[88] T Helms, 'Konkludente Wahl des auf die Ehescheidung anwendbaren Rechts' [2014] *Praxis des Internationalen Privat- und Verfahrensrechts* 334.

in a document dated and signed by both spouses' (emphasis added). However, the new compromise text simply adopts the wording of Article 7.[89]

Another weakness of some of the formalities listed above is that the writing requirement sometimes forms part of a composite choice of law rule, the aim of which is to subject the formal validity of the choice of law contract to whichever law is more favourable to the agreement. Section 7A(2)(b) of the Property (Relationships) Act thus requires that 'the agreement is in writing or is otherwise valid according to the law of that [chosen] country'; and Article 14(4) of the EGBGB requires that a choice of law that has not been made in Germany comply with the formality requirements for a matrimonial property contract provided by either the chosen law or the law of the place where the choice was made.[90]

The effect of these composite choice of law rules is to favour the formal validity of choice of law contracts, which, in turn, weakens their protective function. In fact, the literal effect of section 7A is to liberate the choice of law contract from all formality requirements, because the chosen law would not contain formalities applicable to choice of law contracts unless section 7A's reference to the chosen law included modal choice of law rules.[91] Even if it was possible to interpret section 7A as a reference to foreign modal choice of law rules on formality, such a rule would be effective only in circumstances where the applicable law recognises the party autonomy rule. Alternatively, section 7A could be interpreted as a 'combined' modal choice of law rule in the nature of Article 14(4), which turns the *lex causae*'s formalities for matrimonial contracts into modal choice of law rules.[92] If section 7A was meant to operate as a combined modal choice of law rule, its effectiveness would depend on the content of the *lex causae*, which would have to provide for rules that are adaptable to the choice of law contract. In any case, a preferable approach would be to use the composite choice of law rule in conjunction with a modal choice of law rule that imposes minimum requirements of formality.[93]

VI. Capacity

Capacity, the ability to enter into legally binding relations, is not an issue that is usually discussed in relation to choice of law contracts.[94] There seems to be an unexpressed assumption that capacity to enter into a choice of law contract is a non-issue. But this assumption is misconceived (see section A below). What is

[89] Compromise text of the Proposal (n 78).

[90] See J Kleinheisterkamp, 'Rechtswahl und Ehevertrag: Zum Formerfordernis nach Art 15 Abs 3 EGBGB' [2004] *Praxis des Internationalen Privat- und Verfahrensrechts* 397.

[91] See ch 5, s IV.C.

[92] ibid.

[93] See the original Proposal for a Reg on matrimonial property (n 78) Art 19; Hague Convention 1978 (n 77) Art 13.

[94] But see Hague Maintenance Protocol (n 80) Art 8(3).

more, the capacity of a natural person to enter into a choice of law contract is best regulated by modal choice of law (see section B). Article 8(3) of the Hague Maintenance Protocol provides a useful precedent in this regard.

A. Relevance of Capacity to Choice of Law Contracts

There seem to be two reasons why so little attention has been paid to the capacity or incapacity of parties to choose the applicable law. The first reason—which is entirely legitimate—is that capacity is not usually considered to be governed by the party autonomy rule,[95] with the result that the validity of a choice of law contract is of no relevance if the only substantive matter to be determined is a party's capacity to enter into the underlying transaction. For example, a minor enters into a sales contract that is expressed to be subject to the law of country X, and then attempts to argue that the contract is unenforceable because he lacked capacity to contract. If the only issue in dispute is the minor's capacity to enter into the sales contract, it is unnecessary to determine the minor's capacity to agree on the application of the law of country X, because neither party seeks to rely on the choice of law contract.

The second reason—which is not a valid reason—is that a distinction is not usually drawn between a party's capacity to enter into a choice of law contract and the party's capacity to complete the underlying transaction.[96] As a result, the choice of law contract stands and falls with the underlying transaction. For example, if the minor lacked capacity to enter into the sales contract, a court would assume that any choice of law contract that would have otherwise been given effect to determine the legal effects of invalidity is equally unenforceable (based on the law governing incapacity). Similarly, if the minor did not lack capacity to enter into the sales contract, a court would assume that the minor also did not lack capacity to enter into the choice of law contract, and that the chosen law can be applied to determine other substantive matters in dispute.

Although this reasoning may seem intuitively correct, it is not true that the choice of law contract necessarily stands and falls with the underlying transaction. Depending on the applicable rules of incapacity, a party may lack capacity to enter into a sales contract but may be capable of entering into a choice of law contract (and vice versa). Not all rules on incapacity apply to choice of law contracts and their underlying contracts in equal measure. In New Zealand law,

[95] See Collins (n 17) para 32-176; P Mayer and V Heuzé, *Droit international privé* 10th edn (Paris, LGDJ, 2014) 379ff; Vischer, Huber and Oser (n 37) 411ff; Einführungsgesetz zum Bürgerlichen Gesetzbuch (EGBGB), Art 7. But see *Restatement (Second)* (n 82) s 198, cmnt (a).

[96] See J Foyer, 'Le Contrat d'Electio Juris à la Lumière de la Convention de Rome du 19 Juin 1980' in *L'Internationalisation du Droit: Mélanges en l'Honneur de Yvon Loussouarn* (Paris, Dalloz, 1994) 169, 176, who argues that there is no distinction to be drawn between the two; see also S Maire, *Die Quelle der Parteiautonomie und das Statut der Rechtswahlvereinbarung im internationalen Vertragsrecht* (Basel, Helbing & Lichtenhahn, 2011) 150.

for example, section 6 of the Minors' Contracts Act 1969 provides that a contract entered into by a minor is unenforceable against the minor unless the court considers that the contract was fair and reasonable at the time it was entered into.[97] This rule would not render a choice of law contract unenforceable simply because the underlying contract was unfair or unreasonable; and the chosen law could then apply to any restitutionary claims arising from the void contract—provided, of course, that there is not some other reason why the choice of law contract is unenforceable.[98]

It follows that there is no guaranteed synchronisation between the choice of law contract and the underlying contract, because the choice of law contract will not always be subject to the same capacity requirements that are imposed on the underlying contract. More generally, it goes without saying that the issue of incapacity may also arise where there is no underlying contract, and the only question is whether the parties had capacity to choose the law governing their non-contractual relationship.

B. A Modal Choice of Law Rule on Incapacity

The next question that arises, then, is whether it is substantive law or modal choice of law that is the more appropriate source to regulate capacity to enter into a choice of law contract. Insofar as capacity of natural persons is concerned, modal choice of law would seem to be the preferable option. This is because there is a real risk that incapacity rules of the law of contract would be inapplicable to choice of law contracts. They may have a content-controlling component, or they may be expressed to apply to particular contracts.

Section 6 of the Minors' Contracts Act 1969 (NZ), for example, which provides that a contract is unenforceable against a minor unless it was fair and reasonable at the time it was entered into,[99] is a content-controlling rule that would not be directly applicable to choice of law contracts.[100] The purpose of this rule is to protect minors against burdens and obligations that are considered unreasonable in the circumstances. But the choice of law contract does not give rise to burdens and obligations.[101] The same reasoning applies to section 5 of the same Act, on contracts concerning life insurance and contracts of service, which are to have effect unless they are unconscionable or oppressive. Moreover, section 5 could not be interpreted so widely as to include choice of law contracts relating to life insurance

[97] cp Bürgerliches Gesetzbuch (BGB), Art 107.

[98] cp *Credit Suisse International v Stichting Vestia Groep* [2014] EWHC 3103, [2015] Bus LR D5 [185].

[99] cp Bürgerliches Gesetzbuch (BGB), Art 107.

[100] See ch 5, s III.B.ii.

[101] cp P Stankewitsch, *Entscheidungsnormen im IPR als Wirksamkeitsvoraussetzungen der Rechtswahl* (Frankfurt, Peter Lang, 2003) 102ff in relation to BGB, Art 107.

contracts or contracts of service. The section applies only to these latter forms of contract.[102]

Neither content-controlling rules nor rules on specific forms of contract are directly applicable to choice of law contracts. Overall, the likely effect of such rules would be to leave the choice of law contract under-regulated and over-enforced. What is needed is a modal choice of law rule on incapacity.

The only example of such a rule seems to be Article 8(3) of the Hague Maintenance Protocol, which provides that the freedom to choose the applicable law 'shall not apply to maintenance obligations in respect of a person under the age of 18 years or of an adult who, by reason of an impairment or insufficiency of his or her personal faculties, is not in a position to protect his or her interest'. This rule, while being sufficiently broad to capture cases of real injustice, seems admirably straightforward. Similar solutions would also be appropriate for other non-contractual relationships.

However, slightly different considerations apply to a choice of law contract that purports to govern a *contractual* relationship. Here, one of the dangers of modal choice of law rules of incapacity is that they might have the effect of undermining the incapacity rules that apply to the underlying contract. For example, a modal choice of law rule might exclude a minor's capacity to enter into a choice of law contract even though, under section 6 of the Minors' Contracts Act 1969, the underlying contract would have been fair and reasonable despite being submitted to the chosen law. A possible solution may be to provide that a party's capacity to choose the applicable law is conditional on the party's capacity to enter into the underlying contract. The effect would be to limit the parties' power to choose the applicable law to a particular group of contracts—contracts that are not void or unenforceable on the grounds of incapacity.[103]

VII. Transparency in Standard Terms

Standard term contracts are a commonplace feature of international transactions. Standard terms are drafted by one of the parties—ordinarily the party who holds greater bargaining power—and they are used in circumstances where individual negotiation of terms would be inefficient or even impossible. The problem with standard term contracts is that they introduce information asymmetries. The party who is on the receiving end is less familiar with the content of the standard terms than the drafting party. He also often has limited incentive to familiarise himself with the standard terms, unless the terms are open to negotiation. Such information asymmetries, in turn, may lead to an imbalance of power. This concern

[102] See also Property (Relationships) Act (NZ), s 21I.

[103] cp OLG Hamm, 22 U 227/94 (23 November 1995).

is of particular relevance to choice of law contracts, which are often included in standard terms, and which have potentially wide-reaching consequences.

A. Relevance of the Law of Contract

The law of contract in many legal systems has sought to increase transparency in standard term contracting. Some of these rules are applicable to choice of law contracts.[104] They may provide, for example, that the drafting party must take sufficient steps to bring the terms to the attention of the other party, or that mere reference to the terms is not sufficient.[105]

However, the law of contract also often provides for rules of incorporation that exclude standard terms on the basis of their content.[106] For example, Article 305c of the German Bürgerliches Gesetzbuch (BGB) provides that terms that are so unusual that the recipient need not expect their inclusion in standard terms do not form part of the contract; the English Court of Appeal in *Interfoto Picture Library Ltd v Stiletto Visual Programmes Ltd* held that particularly onerous or harsh terms must be reasonably drawn to the attention of the other party;[107] and Article 4.110 of the PECL (Principles of European Contract Law) provides for avoidance of standard terms that cause a significant imbalance in the parties' rights and obligations. Even the *contra proferentem* rule, which provides that unclear terms are to be interpreted against the drafting party,[108] is necessarily focused on the content of the disputed term. Such rules are not usually applicable to choice of law contracts, for the reasons provided in chapter five.[109]

The case of *Kingspan Environmental Ltd v Borealis A/S* illustrates this point.[110] The plaintiff argued that a choice of law clause, which provided for the application of the law of the Danish supplier's domicile, was not incorporated into the contract because, under Danish law, a standard term is not binding if it is of such a character that it could not reasonably have been expected.[111] The plaintiff argued that the choice of Danish law could not reasonably have been expected because it was unclear whether the clause was to be understood as a reference to the supplier's domicile in the United Kingdom or in Denmark, and because it

[104] But cp *Puccini Festival Australia Pty Ltd v Nippon Express (Australia) Pty Ltd* [2007] VSC 288 [52], where the Court found it unnecessary to consider whether a choice of law clause in a bill of lading could be 'unconscionable' on the basis of 'an inequality of bargaining power, perhaps coupled with the fact that the plaintiff was not actually made aware of the existence or the terms and conditions of the bill of lading at any relevant time'.

[105] See BGB, Art 305(2); *PECL* (n 19) Art 2:104; see generally T Wilhelmsson, 'Standard Form Conditions' in A Hartkamp et al (eds), *Towards a European Civil Code* 4th edn (Alphen aan den Rijn, Kluwer, 2010) 571.

[106] See Farnsworth (n 70) 911–13.

[107] *Interfoto Picture Library Ltd v Stiletto Visual Programmes Ltd* [1989] QB 433 (CA).

[108] *PECL* (n 19) Art 5:103.

[109] See ch 5, s III.B.ii; see also ch 8, s III.

[110] *Kingspan Environmental Ltd v Borealis A/S* [2012] EWHC 1147.

[111] ibid, [559].

deprived the plaintiff of its protection under the UK Misrepresentation Act 1967 and the Unfair Contract Terms Act. The Court concluded that 'The fact that the contract was to be governed by the law of [the supplier's] domicile was apparent from a reading of the invoices and [the choice of law clause] itself', and that 'The differences between the two systems [were] not so egregious as to call for special notice'.[112]

The Court was right to reject the plaintiff's argument. However, differences between Danish and English law could not be a relevant consideration in determining whether there was an agreement on choice of law.[113] There may be rare circumstances in which content-controlling rules might support an argument that a particular choice of law was so unusual or surprising that the non-drafting party did not need to expect its inclusion in the standard terms, on the basis that the parties' relationship did not have an obvious international character, or that the choice was entirely unconnected to the relationship and not readily explainable.[114] But the content, or effect, of Danish law could not in itself be considered reasonable or unreasonable; and any substantive restrictions on the scope of the party autonomy rule would have to be imposed by modal choice of law.

B. A Modal Choice of Law Rule on Transparency in Standard Terms

The law of contract can offer only patchy protection to parties who have agreed to standard terms that contain a choice of law clause. But choice of law clauses in standard terms are in particular need of regulation: they have the potential to decide the outcome of a dispute, yet parties who are unfamiliar with the conflict of laws are unlikely to take notice of them. It would be beneficial, therefore, to have specific modal choice of law rules that provide additional regulation of standard choice of law contracts. Generic requirements such as those contained in Articles 3 and 14 of Rome I and Regulation (EC) 864/2007 on the law applicable to non-contractual obligations (Rome II) respectively,[115] which require the choice to be expressly made or clearly demonstrated, are unlikely to be of any help in this context.[116]

[112] ibid, [564].

[113] cp ibid, [568]; but see *Re Futures Transactions* [1998] ILPr 327 (OLG Düsseldorf) 335; OLG Düsseldorf, NJW-RR 1994, 1132.

[114] See Magnus (n 38) para 177; C Rühl, 'Rechtswahlfreiheit und Rechtswahlklauseln in Allgemeinen Geschäftsbedingungen' (Baden Baden, Nomos, 1999) 128; BGH NJW 1994, 262, 263; LG Bremen, 2 O 37-06 (7 December 2006); LG Hamburg, 327 O 187/14 (2 September 2014). But this approach probably interferes with the regulatory scope of modal choice of law: see ch 5, s IV.

[115] Reg (EC) 864/2007 on the law applicable to non-contractual obligations [2007] OJ L199/40 (Rome II).

[116] But cp W-H Roth, 'Rechtswahlklauseln in Verbraucherverträgen—eine schwierige Sache?' [2013] *Praxis des Internationalen Privat- und Verfahrensrechts* 515, 522.

Article 14(1) of Rome II also requires the parties' choice to have been 'freely negotiated'. Arguably, the rule amounts to a blanket rejection of choice of law contracts that are the product of standard form contracting,[117] although this view is controversial.[118] Standard choice of law contracts serve a legitimate function, so it is true that, depending on the circumstances, their wholesale exclusion may be a disproportionate response. Modal choice of law could impose much more subtle requirements, including that there was an 'exchange' between the parties on the choice of law;[119] that the terms were expressly accepted by way of signature[120] or separate initialling; that the proposed choice was drafted clearly and unambiguously, or that it was highlighted and formatted in a way that made it clearly visible or even stand out from the document. Article 185(3)(m) and (6) of the Directive 2009/138/EC on the taking-up and pursuit of the business of Insurance and Reinsurance,[121] for example, provides that the applicable law must be communicated to the policy holder 'in a clear and accurate manner' before the contract is concluded.

It is useful to return to the case of *Kingspan* at this point. How would a modal choice of law rule have assisted the plaintiff in arguing that the supplier's stipulation of Danish law was not sufficiently clear? While the supplier's general terms and conditions referred to the law of the supplier's domicile, the purchaser had dealings with the supplier's offices in the United Kingdom and Denmark, and both of these offices were referred to on the front page of the general terms. In these circumstances, a modal choice of law rule that a standard choice of law contract be clearly and unambiguously expressed no doubt would have been useful to the plaintiff. The Court could have used the rule to require an express reference

[117] S Leible, 'Rechtswahl im IPR der außervertraglichen Schuldverhältnisse nach der Rom II-Verordnung' [2008] *Recht der Internationalen Wirtschaft* 257, 260; P Mankowski, 'Ausgewählte Einzelfragen zur Rom II-VO: Internationales Umwelthalftungsrecht, internationales Kartellrecht, renvoi, Parteiautonomie' [2010] *Praxis des Internationalen Privat- und Verfahrensrechts* 398, 400.

[118] G Wagner, 'Die neue Rom II-Verordnung' [2008] *Praxis des Internationalen Privat- und Verfahrensrechts* 12, 13–14; A Junker, 'Der Reformbedarf im Internationalen Deliktsrecht der Rom II-Verordnung drei Jahre nach ihrer Verabschiedung' [2010] *Recht der Internationalen Wirtschaft* 257, 267; cp A Dickinson, *The Rome II Regulation: The Law Applicable to Non-Contractual Obligations* (Oxford, Oxford University Press, 2010) para 13.41 (arguing that a choice of law clause in standard terms is valid if 'every party had an opportunity to influence its terms, and in particular the choice of law provisions'); cp T Kadner Graziano, 'Freedom to Choose the Applicable Law in Tort—Articles 14 and 4(3) of the Rome II Regulation' in W Binchy and J Ahern (eds), *The Rome II Regulation on the Law Applicable to Non-Contractual Obligations: A New Tort Litigation Regime* (Leiden, Martinus Nijhoff, 2009) 113, 121 (arguing that pre-formulated conditions must be signed or expressly accepted by the other party for the choice of law clause to be effective); Plender and Wilderspin (n 17) para 29-022 (arguing that there must have been an exchange by the parties on the standard terms 'in the course of which attention' was given to the choice of law clause, and that either party 'must have been genuinely free to reject the law stipulated in the agreement'; see also Collins (n 17) para 34-045).

[119] cp Plender and Wilderspin (n 17) para 29-022.

[120] See Kadner Graziano (n 118) 121.

[121] Dir 2009/138/EC on the taking-up and pursuit of the business of Insurance and Reinsurance [2009] OJ L335/1; see also Dir 2002/65/EC concerning the distance marketing of consumer financial services, Art 3.1(3)(f) and Art 3.2 ('clear and comprehensible').

to the law of Denmark rather than the law of the place where the supplier was domiciled.[122]

There may also be benefit in a modal choice of law rule that targets misleading or confusing choice of law contracts, particularly in relation to consumer and employment relationships.[123] Let us assume, for example, that a consumer choice of law contract provides that all of the parties' rights and obligations are submitted to the law of the Netherlands exclusively. A German consumer who has entered into the choice of law contract interprets the choice of law clause to exclude all foreign (non-Dutch) law and, as a result, decides to forego legal action when faced with a dispute; but, in fact, there are important German overriding mandatory rules that a German court would apply to determine the parties' rights and obligations. In these circumstances, a modal choice of law rule that voids misleading or confusing choice of law contracts would encourage traders to draft their choice of law clauses in a more consumer-friendly manner. In a case involving similar facts, the German BGH used Article 307(1) of the BGB to conclude that a Dutch choice of law clause was misleading.[124] Article 307 provides for the invalidity of standard terms that disadvantage the non-drafting party unreasonably; and the fact that a provision is unclear or difficult to understand may amount to an unreasonable disadvantage. But it is questionable whether German law was even applicable (the putative chosen law being Dutch law).[125]

VIII. Informed Choice

Rules on transparency seek to ensure that parties are aware of choice of law agreements that they enter into (see section VII above). But mere awareness of an agreement does not ensure an understanding of its effect. Where a party is ill-informed about the implications of a contract, he is more likely to enter into a contract that is contrary to his interests. Again the risk of information asymmetries looms large. In some circumstances, the law of contract intervenes to mitigate that risk: it imposes obligations of disclosure, or it requires that the contract be notarised or that the parties obtain independent legal advice. Whether these options are, or should be, available for choice of law contracts will be considered in section A and B below. Another possible solution, in relation to non-contractual obligations in particular, is to limit party autonomy to post-dispute choice of law contracts (see section C).

[122] cp OLG Frankfurt, NJW-RR 1989, 1018, overturned on different grounds: *Re Purchase of Faulty Goods in Spain* [1992] ECC 87 (BGH).

[123] Another interesting issue is whether the choice of law clause should be expressed in a language that the receiving party is able to understand, but there is probably no need for a specific modal choice of law rule on this particular issue: cp *Weiss v La Suisse* 154 F Supp 2d 734 (SDNY 2001) 737–38.

[124] BGH, I ZR 40/11 (19 July 2012); see also OLG Oldenburg, 6 U 113/14 (23 September 2014).

[125] See Roth (n 116).

A. Pre-contractual Disclosure Obligations

Pre-contractual duties of disclosure come in many shapes and forms. They may result from a general duty of disclosure or the principle of good faith, or from targeted requirements of disclosure relating to specific contracts.[126] Because most lay people would be unfamiliar with rules of choice of law, as well as with the content of any foreign chosen law, a duty of disclosure may assume particular relevance in relation to choice of law contracts included in consumer and employment contracts.[127] Modal choice of law rules could impose more targeted requirements of disclosure than the law of contract, without necessarily replacing any general obligations of disclosure that may exceptionally be available under the law of contract.

For example, modal choice of law could require choice of law clauses to include a brief explanation of the meaning and effect of choice of law contracts and to refer to the most relevant sources on the chosen law.[128] The EC Green Paper on the conversion of the Rome Convention into a Community instrument even suggested that, if party autonomy in consumer contracts were not subject to a special regime but limited to the law of the country where the business is established, businesses be required to show that consumers 'made an informed choice' by providing 'advance information on all the rights and obligations conferred on him by that law'.[129]

It is debatable whether such stringent obligations of disclosure, which would leave the drafter in real doubt as to the level of disclosure that is required, are an effective means of encouraging informed decision-making.[130] This does not mean, however, that similar options are not worth exploring, particularly in relation to consumer and employment contracts, and particularly in jurisdictions like New Zealand, Australia and the United States that have not adopted the principle of the more favourable law in relation to such contracts. Modal choice of law rules would do away with potentially difficult questions as to the scope of general duties of disclosure under the law of contract, and they would also ensure that the weaker party is not dependent on the putative chosen law for protection.

In fact, a modal choice of law rule on disclosure could go some way to preventing the kind of situation that arose in the so-called *Gran Canaria* and *Timesharing* cases,[131] which led German courts to disapply the putative chosen law on dubious

[126] See generally R Sefton-Green (ed), *Mistake, Fraud and Duties to Inform in European Contract Law* (Cambridge, Cambridge University Press, 2005); cp ch 8, s II on mistake.

[127] See G Rühl, 'Der Schutz des "Schwächeren" im europäischen Kollisionsrecht' in H Kronke and K Thorn (eds), *Grenzen überwinden—Prinzipien bewahren: Festschrift für Bernd von Hoffmann* (Bielefeld, Gieseking, 2011) 364, 367.

[128] cp *Fricke v Isbrandtsen* Co 151 F Supp 465 (DCNY 1957): see ch 8, s III.D.

[129] Green paper on the conversion of the Rome Convention of 1980 on the law applicable to contractual obligations into a Community instrument and its modernisation (COM 2002, 654) 32.

[130] For a critical view, see Z Tang, 'Parties' Choice of Law in E-Consumer Contracts' (2007) *Journal of Private International Law* 113, 116.

[131] See A Baumert, 'Abschlusskontrolle bei Rechtswahlvereinbarungen' [1997] *Recht der Internationalen Wirtschaft* 805; D Coester-Waltjen, 'Der Eskimo-Mantel aus Spanien—Ist der kollisionsrechtliche Verbraucherschutz zu kurz gestrickt?' in B Pfister and M Will (eds), *Festschrift für Werner Lorenz* (Tübingen, JCB Mohr, 1991) 297. cp also BGH, I ZR 40/11 (19 July 2012).

grounds and distort the meaning of German principles of contract, in order to strike down foreign choice of law clauses. The Stuttgart Landesgericht held, for example, that a Spanish choice of law clause, included in a consumer contract that was otherwise more closely connected to Germany and was clearly aimed at German tourists, was invalid because it failed to disclose that, unlike German law, Spanish law did not provide for a right of cancellation in relation to door-to-door sales.[132]

While on holiday in Gran Canaria, the defendant, a German tourist, had attended a sales event for tourists and entered into a contract to purchase a cashmere duvet and pillow. The supplier was a German company that, with the help of a Spanish agent, marketed its products to German tourists in Spain. The contract provided for the application of Spanish law. When the defendant returned home, he sought to cancel the order, and the supplier brought proceedings against him for the purchase price. The principle of the more favourable law was not applicable. Instead, the Court concluded that the validity of the Spanish choice of law clause was to be determined in accordance with Article 9(1) of the German law on standard terms, because the contract was between German parties and was to be performed in Germany. Article 9 required that the detrimental effect of a standard term be made clear to the recipient of the document. The Court held that the defendant was entitled to assume that he would have a right of cancellation, and struck down the Spanish choice of law clause on the basis that the plaintiff had breached its obligation to inform the defendant of his inability to cancel the contract pursuant to Spanish law.

Article 9(1) was not an overriding mandatory rule, which means that the Court was wrong to apply German law to determine the validity of the choice of law clause. The Court was also wrong to rely on Article 9 to control the content of the choice: the choice of law contract could not be struck down on the basis that it had a 'detrimental' effect.[133] But if the Rome Convention had imposed a disclosure obligation on the plaintiff—requiring the company to explain the effect of the choice of Spanish law, including the irrevocable nature of the underlying contract—then the choice of law contract could have easily been struck down; and if the plaintiff had complied with this disclosure obligation, then the defendant would have had no cause for complaint.

B. Legal Advice

Transactions that are inherently susceptible to uninformed decision-making, bounded rationality and an imbalance in bargaining power are typically associated with a requirement to obtain independent legal advice or, in civil law countries, to have the agreement notarised.[134] For example, section 90G(1)(b)

[132] LG Stuttgart, NJW-RR 1990, 1394.

[133] See ch 5, s III.B.ii and ch 8, s III.

[134] In relation to matrimonial agreements, see J Scherpe (ed), *Marital Agreements and Private Autonomy in Comparative Perspective* (Oxford, Hart Publishing, 2012) 491–92.

of the Family Law Act 1975 (Aust) provides that financial agreements between spouses are binding only if 'each spouse party was provided with independent legal advice from a legal practitioner about the effect of the agreement on the rights of that party' as well as 'the advantages and disadvantages … to that party of making the agreement', unless it would be unjust if the agreement were not binding.[135]

As is the case with rules on informed choice more generally, choice of law contracts that are made in relation to such relationships should not be exempt from requirements to obtain legal advice.[136] On the contrary, due to their complex nature and potentially far-reaching consequences, choice of law contracts are exactly the kind of contracts that would benefit from the enforced provision of legal advice. Although courts have, in the past, relied on substantive law to determine whether parties had sufficient understanding of the effect of foreign law on their matrimonial obligations,[137] reliance on the law of contract is not enough, for the following reasons.

First, choice of law contracts would often fall outside the scope of substantive provisions on the provision of legal advice. Section 90G of the Australian Act, for example, applies to 'financial agreements' and does not expressly apply to choice of law contracts contained within such agreements.

Second, a modal choice of law rule would ensure that the forum court need not depend on the putative chosen law to apply a requirement of legal advice. In *Harley v Harley*,[138] the New Zealand Family Court was asked to set aside a South African couple's matrimonial property agreement, which was expressed to be subject to South African law. The agreement, which provided for complete separation of property, was valid under South African law. The spouses had not obtained independent legal advice, which was not a requirement in South African law.[139] At the time of entering into the contract, the couple was already contemplating leaving South Africa permanently, and they finally settled in New Zealand. Mrs Harley argued that the application of South African law, which seemed to offer less protection to her than New Zealand law, would be contrary to justice or public policy under section 7A(3) of the Property (Relationships) Act 1976. The Family Court upheld the choice of South African law, noting that 'the parties understood

[135] See also Property (Relationships) Act (NZ), ss 21F(3) and 21H.

[136] See Consortium Asser-UCL, *Étude sur les régimes matrimoniaux des couples mariés et sur le patrimoine des couples non mariés dans le droit international privé et dans le droit interne des États membres de l'Union* (Offre n JAI/A3/2001/03) 42.

[137] See *B v S* [2012] EWHC 265, [2012] 2 FLR 502 [20], where the Court concluded that, even though there was no requirement 'to have received specific advice as to the operation of English law on the [foreign matrimonial property] agreement in question', legal advice would usually be necessary to ensure that the parties understood the agreement to be operable wherever they might be divorced; *Murphy v Murphy* [2009] FMCAFam 270 [58]; cp *V v V* [2011] EWHC 3230, [2012] 1 FLR 1315 [50]; *Elgar v Elgar* 238 Conn 839 (Conn, 1996).

[138] *Harley v Harley* [2004] NZFLR 1096 (FC).

[139] It is not clear from the judgment whether South African law required the agreement to be notarised.

clearly the effect and implications of the [matrimonial property] agreement'. But the Court might have reached a different conclusion if the Act had provided for a modal choice of law rule requiring spouses to have obtained legal advice on the meaning and effect of their choice of law.

Third, a modal choice of law rule would ensure that advice is given not only on the effect of the chosen law on the matrimonial property relationship, but also, more fundamentally, on the choice of law effect of the choice of law contract. Spouses would need to be made aware that, in the absence of choice, a court would apply objective choice of law rules, which might lead to the application of a law other than the chosen law. It would not be sufficient that they understood the effect of their matrimonial obligations in accordance with the governing law.[140]

It is unclear whether Mrs Harley in *Harley v Harley* understood the effect of the South African choice of law contract (although there was evidence that she understood the effect of the matrimonial property agreement). If she had been advised that her choice of law contract would probably prevent her from relying on a forum's objective choice of law rules, and that the objective applicable law might offer her greater protection than South African law, then Mrs Harley would at least have been able to appreciate that there was some risk involved in entering into a choice of law contract. Because the Property (Relationships) Act allows the application of foreign law only where the parties have made a choice, the New Zealand Parliament should be especially concerned to ensure that the parties were fully informed and aware of the consequences of their choice.[141]

Fourth, the putative chosen law may be too inflexible to accommodate varying local practices on the provision of legal advice. A modal choice of law rule, on the other hand, could be drafted in a way that is sufficiently wide so as not to be exclusive or unduly parochial, while still giving effect to the need for informed choice of law. In *Murphy v Murphy*,[142] for example, the Court held that an Australian matrimonial agreement was invalid pursuant to section 90G of the Family Law Act because the section required legal advice to be given by a 'legal practitioner', which was to be interpreted to mean a person qualified to practice in Australia. When visiting his wife in the Philippines, the husband had agreed to marry her on the condition that she enter into a matrimonial agreement, which was expressed to be subject to Australian law. The couple visited a lawyer's office in the Philippines,

[140] As the Federal Magistrates Court of Australia seemed to consider in *Murphy v Murphy* [2009] FMCAFam 270, at [58], where it held that the requirement of independent legal advice in s 90G of the Family Law Act 'must refer to those interests which arise, exist or occur under the governing jurisdiction of the agreement, which in this case was stated to be the Commonwealth of Australia and Queensland'; cp *V v V* (n 137) [50], where the parties had entered into a matrimonial property agreement with a Swedish choice of law clause, and the Court did not accord any weight to the fact that the parties had not had advice on the effect of the agreement in Swedish or in English law, because even a legally unadvised reader would have understood the meaning of the matrimonial property agreement. cp *Elgar v Elgar* 238 Conn 839 (Conn, 1996).

[141] See ch 3, s II.B.iii.

[142] *Murphy v Murphy* [2009] FMCAFam 270; see also *Ruane v Bachmann-Ruane* [2009] FamCA 1101.

and the lawyer signed a certificate of legal advice that the husband had previously obtained from an Australian lawyer. The effect of the Court's interpretation is that any choice of Australian law would need to be concluded on the basis of an Australian practitioner's advice, even if the spouses are not, at the time, resident in Australia. A modal choice of law rule could adopt a more internationalised approach.

A good example is Article 8(5) of the Hague Maintenance Protocol,[143] which provides that, 'Unless at the time of the designation the parties were fully informed and aware of the consequences of their designation', the chosen law shall not apply where its application would lead to 'manifestly unfair or unreasonable consequences'.[144] The former part of this provision was clarified in the Explanatory Report to the Protocol:

> This phrase is intended to allow parties to reduce the risk of having their agreement set aside by seeking legal advice about the consequences of their choice prior to its conclusion. The requirement that the parties have to be 'fully informed and aware' signifies that parties must not only have received relevant information but also have been able to understand it; the expression is not redundant because someone can be fully informed without being aware of the consequences of his/her choice.[145]

A similar rule—that parties must have been fully informed and aware of the consequences of their designation—could be devised for other forms of matrimonial relationships. For reasons that have already been discussed, the rule is preferable to the solution adopted by Articles 14 and 15 of the German EGBGB, which require choice of law contracts that are entered into in Germany to be notarised, while submitting choices that are not made in Germany to the formality requirements imposed on matrimonial contracts by either the chosen law or the law of the place where the choice was made.[146] There is currently no express requirement of legal advice for choice of law contracts in New Zealand's Property (Relationships) Act, the Proposal for a Regulation on matrimonial property,[147] the new compromise

[143] But cp J Carruthers, 'Party Autonomy in the Legal Regulation of Adult Relationships: What Place for Party Choice in Private International Law?' (2012) 61 *ICLQ* 881, fn 106, where she notes, in relation to Art 8(5) of the Hague Maintenance Protocol, that 'Presumably the forum would apply its own law to assess whether either/both party(ies) was/were "fully informed" and aware of the consequences of their choice.' cp also M Esser, 'Der Erlass weitergehender Formvorschriften im Rahmen des Haager Unterhaltsprotokolls durch die Mitgliedstaaten der EU' [2013] *Praxis des Internationalen Privat- und Verfahrensrechts* 399, who argues that Art 8 does not go far enough and that EU Member States should provide for an additional requirement of notarisation.

[144] On this latter part of the rule, see ch 8, s III.

[145] A Bonomi, *Explanatory Report: Protocol of 23 November 2007 on the Law Applicable to Maintenance Obligations* (HccH, October 2009) para 150.

[146] See above, s V.B.ii.

[147] But see Recital 24 and the suggested amendments by the European Parliament's Committee on Women's Rights and Gender Equality: M Yannakoudakis (Rapporteur), *Opinion of the Committee on Women's Rights and Gender Equality for the Committee on Legal Affairs on the proposal for a Council regulation on jurisdiction, applicable law and the recognition and enforcement of decisions in matters of matrimonial property regimes* (2011/0059 CNS, 7 May 2012).

text of the Proposal for a Council Regulation on jurisdiction, applicable law and the recognition and enforcement of decisions regarding the property consequences of registered partnerships,[148] the Hague Convention, or Rome III;[149] although Recital 18 of Rome III provides:

> The informed choice of both spouses is a basic principle of this Regulation. Each spouse should know exactly what are the legal and social implications of the choice of applicable law. The possibility of choosing the applicable law by common agreement should be without prejudice to the rights of, and equal opportunities for, the two spouses. Hence judges in the participating Member States should be aware of the importance of an informed choice on the part of the two spouses concerning the legal implications of the choice-of-law agreement concluded.

It is not clear how judges are to give effect to this 'basic principle', in the absence of relevant modal choice of law rules or (potentially) applicable rules of the putative chosen law.[150]

C. Post-dispute Agreements

Parties' freedom to enter into post-dispute, or settlement, agreements tends to be greater than their freedom to enter into pre-dispute agreements that exclude or limit liability for future disputes.[151] The reasoning behind this is obvious. A party who is in possession of all relevant facts, including the nature of the dispute, the harm that has been suffered and the prospects of bringing a successful claim, is in a better position to enter into a contract that meets his or her interests than a party who is faced with only a vague risk of a dispute occurring.

While this rationale provides an argument in favour of a less restrictive approach to party choice in the course of proceedings,[152] the reverse is equally true: the ability to enter into a post-dispute choice of law contract is better than no party autonomy at all, and a post-dispute restriction could be imposed where concerns about the contractual weaknesses of parties would otherwise result in the exclusion of party autonomy. Article 14 of Rome II, which provides that non-commercial parties may choose the applicable law 'by an agreement entered into after the event giving rise to the damage occurred', can be explained on that basis.[153] However,

[148] But see Recital 18a of the compromise text of the Proposal (n 79).

[149] But see Recital 19 and Art 7(2), which provides that Member States may separately provide for additional formal requirements; and Art 46d of the EGBGB, which provides that choice of law agreements under Art 5 of Rome III must be notarised.

[150] See Rösler (n 62) 179–81 for a more detailed analysis.

[151] See, eg, Scherpe (n 134) 511–14.

[152] Hague Maintenance Protocol (n 80) Art 7; cp the concept of facultative choice of law: see ch 6, s II.B.ii.

[153] cp Bundesgesetz über das Internationale Privatrecht (IPRG), Art 132; in the United States, the question whether pre-dispute choice of law contracts for torts are enforceable remains unsettled: see P Hay, P Borchers and S Symeonides, *Conflict of Laws* 5th edn (St Paul, West Academic Publishing, 2010) 1141–46. See S Symeonides, *Codifying Choice of Law Around the World* (New York, Oxford University Press, 2014) 99–106 for a critical view of pre-dispute choice in relation to torts.

because this restriction constitutes a significant interference with the freedom to choose the applicable law, it should not be resorted to without good cause. After all, one of the main reasons why parties choose the applicable law is to improve the predictability of choice of law.

An interesting balance between pre- and post-dispute choice is struck by the Hague Maintenance Protocol, which provides for two different rules of party autonomy. Pursuant to Article 7, parties are free to choose the law of the forum 'for the purpose of a particular proceeding'; but pursuant to Article 8, parties are free to make a pre-dispute choice that is more limited than the 'procedural' choice in several respects. Article 8 does not, for example, extend to the question of whether the creditor can renounce the right to maintenance, and is not available to a person under the age of 18 or an adult who 'by reason of an impairment or insufficiency of his or her personal faculties, is not in a position to protect his or her interest'. It also protects the parties against a choice that is manifestly unfair.[154] The Explanatory Report explains the thinking behind these rules as follows:

> The choice of law is subject to several restrictions, designed to protect the parties (and in particular the maintenance creditor) against risks of abuse. This risk is more serious where the choice is made before the occurrence of a dispute. This is why the Protocol's system includes two variations for party autonomy, in two separate provisions; Article 7 governs the choice of law applicable for the purpose of a particular proceeding (procedural agreement), whereas Article 8 allows—on a more limited basis—a choice at any time. …
>
> It should be emphasised that the choice provided for under Article 7 is made for the purpose of a particular proceeding; … At the time of that choice, the parties have the opportunity to obtain information (or will sometimes be informed by the authority seized) regarding the existence and nature of the maintenance provided for under the law of the forum. The risk of abuse is accordingly low.[155]

While it is arguably optimistic to conclude that a procedural agreement under Article 7 is low risk and does not require any of the protections offered under Article 8, the Hague Maintenance Protocol demonstrates that the party autonomy rule need not follow a 'one size fits all' approach. Pre-dispute choice of law contracts are in need of greater protection than post-dispute choice of law contracts.

IX. Conclusion

Regulation of the formation of choice of law contracts must often go far beyond a simple reference to the general law of contract. Modal choice of law should play a role in the regulation of offer and acceptance, floating choice of law clauses,

[154] See ch 8, s III.
[155] Bonomi (n 145) paras 111 and 115.

formalities, capacity, and transparent and informed choice of law, because in relation to these matters, the law of contract either fails to reflect properly the function of the choice of law contract or is insufficient to ensure a free and informed agreement on choice of law. Existing modal choice of law rules on formation do not go far enough.

In particular, modal choice of law has not done enough to regulate the transparency of choice of law in standard terms, or to ensure that vulnerable parties such as consumers, employees and spouses are properly informed of the meaning and effect of their choice. Floating choice of law clauses, too, are under-regulated, because insufficient attention has been paid to the potential for uncertainty and abuse that arises from a largely unchecked power to choose the applicable law other than by way of agreement; and too little use has been made of formalities, which are absent from choice of law rules on consumer and employment relationships. Even where modal choice of law does provide for formalities (in relation to matrimonial relationships, for example), they are not always drafted in a manner that is effective. With the notable exception of the Hague Maintenance Protocol, no attention has been paid to capacity to enter into a choice of law contract even though the law of contract may well be unable to provide a solution to this issue. Finally, it would be useful to have modal choice of law rules on the admissibility of evidence, conflicting choice of law clauses and (perhaps) acceptance of a proposed choice of law.

8

Validity of the Choice of Law Contract

I. Introduction

A bilateral choice of law that meets the relevant standard of agreement (chapter six) and complies with additional requirements of formation (chapter seven) may still be unenforceable as a result of vitiating factors. A contract may be vitiated by mistake, misrepresentation, deceit or illegitimate pressure; or it may be considered unfair in substance, or on account of a change in circumstances (this is not an exhaustive list, of course). Many of these grounds of invalidity are relevant to choice of law contracts. For example, a choice of law contract that was entered into under duress is as liable to be avoided as any other contract; and the law of contract will ordinarily be an appropriate source of regulation. To make out a case of duress, a claimant must typically show that he was subjected to illegitimate pressure which left him with no practical option but to enter into the contract.[1] This rule is applicable to any agreement regardless of its subject, including choice of law agreements; so there is no need to rely on modal choice of law to provide relief in such a case.[2]

But there are some challenging questions that arise in this context. In what circumstances will—or should—a contract be unenforceable on grounds that relate to the content of the chosen law? In particular, what is the effect of a mistake or a misrepresentation as to the content of the chosen law (see section II below); is a choice of law contract capable of being unfair in substance, or should regulation of the choice of law contract be focused on procedural fairness (see section III); what is the effect of a change in the chosen law on the choice of law contract (see section IV); and what is the role of modal choice of law in all of this? These questions strike at the heart of the choice of law contract. Where a choice of law contract is found to be void or invalid as a result of such vitiating factors, the only appropriate remedy, ordinarily, is to refuse enforcement of the choice of law (see section V).

[1] See, eg, H Beale (ed), *Chitty on Contracts* 31st edn (London, Sweet & Maxwell, 2012) para 7-008.
[2] eg *Dunes Hospitality LLC v Country Kitchen International Inc* 623 NW 2d 484 (SD 2001).

II. Mistake and Misrepresentation

Party A and party B enter into a choice of law contract under the mistaken assumption that the chosen law provides for a particular right or obligation; or party B makes false claims that the chosen law provides for a particular right or obligation and party A enters into the choice of law contract on the basis of those claims. Would, or should, the choice of law contract be enforceable? For example, what if the parties in *The Hollandia*[3] had chosen Dutch law in the mistaken belief that Dutch law incorporated the amended Hague Visby Rules of 1968, rather than the unamended Hague Rules of 1924? The plaintiffs claimed that a road-finishing machine that they had shipped on board the defendant's Dutch vessel was damaged in the course of discharge from the vessel. The bill of lading included a Dutch choice of law clause, and provided that the defendant's maximum liability was about £250. The damage to the machine was estimated to be £22,000. The Hague Visby Rules of 1968 rendered null and void any agreement purporting to reduce the maximum limit of liability below £11,000. The House of Lords held that the choice of Dutch law was invalidated by the Hague Visby Rules as enacted in the United Kingdom.[4] But could the choice of law clause have been void or voidable for mistake, if both or one of the parties had been mistaken as to its effect?

There are three broad categories of mistake: those that are caused intentionally by one of the parties, and thus amount to deceit or fraudulent misrepresentation; those that are caused by negligent misrepresentation; and simple mistakes, including common, mutual and unilateral mistakes, that are not the result of misrepresentation.[5] Not every contract that is entered into under a mistake is void or voidable. The further removed a mistake is from fraudulent misrepresentation, the more difficult it usually is to establish an actionable mistake. This is because a party's reliance on the validity of a contract deserves less protection where the party is to blame for causing the mistake,[6] and the mistaken party deserves less protection where the mistake is the result of his or her own carelessness.[7] There are many different approaches to mistake across jurisdictions. Generally, however, the purpose of the law on mistake is to recognise that a party's intention to enter into a contract may be vitiated by mistake while also protecting the other party's reliance on the contract.[8]

These considerations are just as relevant to choice of law contracts as they are to ordinary contracts. Thus, where a party has made a mistake as to the content

[3] *The Hollandia* [1983] 1 AC 565 (HL).
[4] See ch 5, s III.B.ii.
[5] See H Kötz and A Flessner, *European Contract Law* (Oxford, Clarendon Press, 1997) chs 10 and 11.
[6] ibid, 172 and 186.
[7] ibid, 185.
[8] ibid, 172.

of the chosen law, one of the principal considerations against avoidance of the choice of law contract must be that the mistake is—at least on the face of it—a mistake of law. Because mistakes of law are less likely to amount to an actionable mistake, the applicable law of contract may well operate so as to enforce the choice of law contract (see section A below). However, this is not necessarily the case in common law jurisdictions, which treat foreign law as fact and, as a result, may not treat a mistake as to the content of the chosen law as a mistake of law (see section B). Under this approach, a claimant's chances of avoiding a choice of law contract would be much higher. Even more claimant-friendly is the view that the doctrine of mistake applies to choice of law contracts that invalidate the parties' underlying contract, which raises more generally the role of modal choice of law in regulating mistakes (see section C).

A. Mistake of Law

A mistake of law is less likely to amount to an actionable mistake because a party who makes such a mistake tends to be less deserving of protection. Parties can research the law before entering into a contract; and a mistake of law will often amount to no more than a 'mistake in motive', that is, an expectation or supposition which, although it induced the party to enter into the contract, did not form part of the basis of the contract.[9] It follows that, depending on the applicable law of contract, an error as to the content of the chosen law will not ordinarily provide grounds for avoidance of the choice of law contract.

Cases of deceit or fraudulent misrepresentation would have the greatest chance of success. Article 4:107(1) of the Principles of European Contract Law (PECL) provides that a party may 'avoid a contract when it has been led to conclude it by the other party's fraudulent representation';[10] and even English law, which has traditionally rejected avoidance for mistakes of law,[11] has always offered protection against fraudulent statements of law.[12] If the carrier in *The Hollandia* had intentionally misinformed the shippers that Dutch law incorporated the amended Hague Visby Rules, Dutch law of contract may well have set aside the choice of law contract for fraudulent misrepresentation. The carrier's reliance on the choice of law contract would not have been deserving of the law's protection.

The position would be less clear in the case of negligent misrepresentation and simple mistakes. Article 4:103(1) of the PECL recognises mistakes of fact or law if

[9] On mistakes in motive, see H Beale, *Mistake and Non-Disclosure of Facts* (Oxford, Oxford University Press, 2012) 86; Kötz and Flessner (n 5) 179ff.

[10] O Lando and H Beale (eds), *Principles of European Contract Law (PECL): Parts I and II* (The Hague, Kluwer, 2000).

[11] But see *Kleinwort Benson Ltd v Lincoln City Council* [1999] 2 AC 349 (HL) and *Brennan v Bolt Burdon* [2004] EWCA Civ 1017, [2005] QB 303.

[12] Beale (n 1) para 6-016.

these were 'caused by information given by the other party';[13] if 'the other party knew or ought to have known of the mistake and it was contrary to good faith and fair dealing to leave the mistaken party in error';[14] or if 'the other party made the same mistake'.[15] However, such mistakes provide grounds for avoidance only if 'the other party knew or ought to have known that the mistaken party, had it known the truth, would not have entered into the contract or would have done so on fundamentally different terms'.[16] Moreover a party may not avoid the contract if 'in the circumstances its mistake was inexcusable' or 'the risk of the mistake was assumed, or in the circumstances should be borne, by it'.[17]

It is conceivable, but unlikely, that a mistake as to the Hague Visby Rules would have satisfied these requirements. For example, if Dutch law had, in fact, incorporated the amended Hague Visby Rules, but the parties had negotiated their choice of Dutch law on the basis of a mistaken belief that the stipulated maximum liability of £250 was in accordance with Dutch law, then the carrier would have had to show that the shippers knew or ought to have known that the carrier would not have entered into the Dutch choice of law contract if it had been aware that the unamended Hague Rules no longer formed part of Dutch law. In addition, the carrier would have had to argue that its mistake was excusable, or that the risk of the mistake should not be borne by it, even though it was in the position to obtain legal advice on the state of the Hague Rules in Dutch law prior to entering into the contract.

B. Foreign Law as Fact

This analysis changes dramatically if a mistake or misrepresentation as to foreign law is treated as fact, not law. It has long been the case that common law jurisdictions treat foreign law as fact. Foreign law is fact because it is a matter of proof, and it has to be pleaded. A court will only decide a case pursuant to a foreign applicable law if one of the parties pleads the foreign law to be applicable and the party adduces evidence of the content of that law.[18] The same reasoning has been extended to mistakes and misrepresentations involving foreign law. In *Andre & Cie SA v Ets Michel Blank & Fils* the Court held that an English agreement between traders could be rescinded because the seller had misrepresented the effect of US export regulations and 'a representation of foreign law is to be

[13] Lando and Beale (n 10) Art 4:103(1)(a)(i).

[14] ibid, Art 4:103(1)(a)(ii).

[15] ibid, Art 4:103(1)(a)(iii).

[16] ibid, Art 4:103(1)(b).

[17] ibid, Art 4:103(2).

[18] There are, of course, exceptions to this principle: L Collins (ed), *Dicey, Morris and Collins on the Conflict of Laws* 15th edn (London, Sweet & Maxwell, 2012) ch 9.

regarded here as a matter of fact';[19] and in *The Amazonia*,[20] the Court held that an ad hoc arbitration agreement was vitiated by a mistaken belief that an earlier arbitration clause was valid pursuant to the Australian Sea-Carriage of Goods Act 1924, concluding that 'in an English forum, only English law can be the subject-matter of a mistake or misrepresentation of law, and any other is a mistake or misrepresentation of fact'.[21]

In light of these authorities, it would be surprising if English courts were to treat a mistake as to the content of a foreign chosen law as a mistake of law. When applied to mistakes of foreign law, the 'foreign law as fact'-maxim creates the fiction of a mistake of fact that, in substance, is a mistake of law. A mistake as to the effect of the Australian Sea-Carriage of Goods Act 1924—a quintessential mistake of law—turns into a mistake of fact, attracting a different set of rules that may well lead to avoidance of the contract. There is no indication that this modal choice of law rule would not also be applied to choice of law contracts.

A possible justification for this position is that the contract rationale for distinguishing between mistakes of law and mistakes of fact does not apply in equal measure to mistakes of foreign law, because parties cannot be expected to be familiar with foreign law. In other words, mistakes of foreign law are more excusable and should be treated as mistakes of fact on that basis. However, if this were the true justification, there would be scope to discard the fiction where the parties happen to be familiar with the foreign law. Counsel in *The Amazonia* pursued an argument along these lines, submitting that a mistake of foreign law does not vitiate a contract if the party resides in the foreign country, because people are presumed to know the law of their country of residence.[22] Counsel further submitted that 'a person who makes a contract is presumed to know the law which is the proper law of that contract'.[23] Following *Andre*, the Court felt bound to reject these arguments, even though this led to the 'somewhat artificial conclusion' that a mistake as to section 9 of the Australian Act, whose effect was summarised in a textbook to which the parties had ready access, was a mistake of fact. A mistake of foreign law was *categorically* a mistake of fact.

Once this justification—that a lack of familiarity with foreign law requires the lesser standard of mistake of fact—is taken out of the equation, there is little support in principle for departing from the law of contract. It is true, of course, that foreign law is treated as fact for the purposes of pleading and proof, but this does not mean that foreign law must also be treated as fact for the purposes of mistake and misrepresentation. There is no logical nexus between the two, and there is no

[19] *Andre & Cie SA v Ets Michel Blanc & Fils* [1979] 2 Lloyd's Rep 427 (CA) 430 (Lord Denning MR), 434 (Geoffrey Lane LJ).

[20] *Furness Withy (Australia) Pty Ltd v Metal Distributors (UK) Ltd (The Amazonia)* [1990] 1 Lloyd's Rep 236; see also *PT Royal Bali Leisure v Hutchinson & Co Trust Company Ltd* [2004] EWHC 1014 [123].

[21] *The Amazonia*, ibid 246 (Staughton LJ).

[22] ibid, 245–46.

[23] ibid, 246.

benefit in the categorical application of the 'foreign law as fact'-maxim to mistaken choice of law contracts.

On the contrary, conflicts interests would point firmly in favour of abandoning the maxim for mistake and misrepresentation. Treating a mistake of foreign law as a mistake of fact jeopardises uniformity of decision-making, encourages forum shopping,[24] and leads to absurd results. It is absurd, for example, that parties who are mistaken as to the incorporation of the Hague-Visby Rules in Dutch law would be able to avoid the Dutch choice of law contract in an English court on the basis that there was a mistake of fact; when parties who are mistaken as to the incorporation of the Hague-Visby Rules in English law would be stuck with the contract rules on mistake of law.

In essence, the argument boils down to this: there is a reason why the law of contract distinguishes between mistakes of law and mistakes of fact. There is no reason to depart from the distinction for the purposes of choice of law. So common law jurisdictions should not treat mistakes as to the content of the foreign chosen law as mistakes of fact. Even if it was accepted that a lack of familiarity with the foreign law is a valid concern, parties who choose a governing law can surely be expected to be familiar with the content of that law.[25] Common law jurisdictions would therefore benefit from a modal choice of law rule that clarifies the effect of mistakes of foreign law on choice of law contracts (ie that a mistake of foreign law should be treated as a mistake of law for the purpose of determining the validity of the choice of law contract).

C. A Modal Choice of Law Rule on Mistake?

This last point raises more generally the question whether there is a need for a modal choice of law rule on mistake. The Restatement (Second) of Conflict of Laws proposes such a rule, stating that 'the chosen law will not be applied by reason of the parties' choice' if the parties choose a law 'that would declare the contract invalid'.[26] The reason for the rule is that it would 'defeat the expectations of the parties', and that 'The parties can be assumed to have intended that the provisions of the contract would be binding upon them'. Hence, if the parties choose a law that would invalidate the contract, 'it can be assumed that they did so by mistake'.

Apparently US courts do not usually apply this rule where the chosen law would invalidate only a part of the contract, because invalidating a part of the contract

[24] See also ibid, 246.

[25] cp counsel's argument in *The Amazonia* (n 20) 246.

[26] American Law Institute, *Restatement (Second) of Conflict of Laws* (1971), s 187, cmnt (e); see also Art 3(3) of the resolution by the Institut de Droit International,'L'autonomie de la volonté des parties dans les contrats internationaux entre personnes privées (session de Bâle, 1991)' (1992) 64-II *Annuaire de l'Institut de Droit International* 382. cp BGE 102 II 143, discussed in ch 6, s IV.C.iii.

is not inconsistent with the parties' expectation to create a binding contract.[27] But even then it is not clear why there should be a need for this particular rule. The law of contract does not automatically rectify a contract on the basis of a mutual mistake of law which has the effect of invalidating the contract; and it does not automatically void contracts that produce unexpected legal results. So why should modal choice of law automatically invalidate a choice of law contract that has the same effect? Legal certainty would seem to require the opposite result. Perhaps a more appropriate approach would be to ask whether the parties' choice of law contract was conditional on creating a valid substantive contract.[28] The answer to this question is not a foregone conclusion. The parties might have chosen to enter into a different substantive contract (or they might have chosen not to enter into a contract at all) if they had been aware of the invalidating effect of the chosen law; and the reason for, and timing of, the invalidity must be relevant factor, too.

None of this is to say that a modal choice of law rule that clarifies the effect of an invalidating choice of law contract would not be beneficial. On the contrary, modal choice of law rules on mistake would offer a useful alternative to the law of contract if the forum sought to define clearly the meaning of an actionable mistake as to the chosen law. A well drafted modal choice of law rule may avoid unnecessary litigation and expense because courts would not have to engage in the potentially difficult process of determining the law of contract (and its effect on the choice of law contract). Yet unlike the Restatement's approach to invalidating choice of law contracts, any modal choice of law rule on mistake should still be sufficiently nuanced to reflect the relevant principles or policies of the law of contract. Such a rule would work particularly well in the context of the Restatement, which already applies the *lex fori* to determine whether a choice of law contract is vitiated by mistake.[29]

Finally, there is another reason why a modal choice of law rule on mistake may be advisable, which is that the law on mistake sometimes contains content-controlling elements. An admittedly unusual example is section 6(1)(b) of the New Zealand Contractual Mistakes Act 1977,[30] which provides that the mistake must have resulted 'in a substantially unequal exchange of values' or 'in the conferment of a benefit, or in the imposition or inclusion of an obligation, which was, in all the circumstances, a benefit or obligation substantially disproportionate to the consideration therefor'.[31] As will be discussed in more detail in the following section, this content-controlling provision would not be applicable to choice of

[27] S Symeonides, *Codifying Choice of Law Around the World* (New York, Oxford University Press, 2014) 124; but see, eg, *Kipin Industries v Van Deilen International Inc* 182 F 3d 490 (6th Cir 1999).

[28] cp *CS-Lakeview at Gwinnett Inc v Simon Property Group Inc* 659 SE 2d 359 (Ga 2008) 362 ('It is not possible to conclude that the parties clearly and unequivocally intended the choice-of-law provision to fall whenever it would invalidate any provision of the contract').

[29] *Restatement (Second)* (n 26) s 187, cmnt (b).

[30] See Beale (n 9) 77.

[31] cp Contractual Remedies Act 1979 (NZ), s 7(4).

law contracts, with the likely result that a mistake as to the chosen law would not be actionable under New Zealand law.

III. Fairness in Substance

Most of the contractual rules that have been discussed so far are of a 'procedural' nature, in the sense that they focus on the process of contracting. The purpose of these rules is to prevent, rather than control, substantive unfairness. A consumer who has been made aware of a choice of law contract in standard terms, or a spouse who has been advised by her lawyer not to enter into a choice of law contract, is less likely to enter into a choice of law contract that is against her interests. The law on mistake, too, has the effect of protecting parties from contracts that, as a result of a mistake or misrepresentation, do not reflect their intentions.[32] But what if, despite all these rules, the choice of law contract is still somehow unfair? Is it necessary to tackle substantive unfairness in choice of law contracts and, if so, how could this be done?

Content-controlling rules of the law of contract are generally inapplicable to choice of law contracts, but they provide insights into the kinds of considerations that may support a modal choice of law rule on substantive unfairness (see section A below). Although devising a meaningful modal choice of law rule has proved to be a challenge (see section B), a rule that assesses unfairness by comparing the chosen law to the objective applicable law, while also taking account of the parties' conflicts interests, could still play a useful role in relation to particular relationships (see section C). Where rules on substantive fairness are too cumbersome or interventionist, rules on procedural unfairness may be a valid alternative (see section D).

A. Substantive Fairness and the Law of Contract

Although there are great discrepancies between legal systems on the extent of judicial control of the content of agreements, substantive fairness is now generally accepted to be a valid concern of the general law of contract.[33] Even common law systems, which have traditionally been reluctant to embrace substantive contractual fairness, have recognised the need to impose substantive standards in some cases. This was already acknowledged by Atiyah, when he said that it was 'no longer possible to accept without serious qualification the idea that the law is today solely concerned with the bargaining process and not with the result'.[34]

[32] See Beale (n 9) 77–78.
[33] See Kötz and Flessner (n 5) 130ff.
[34] PS Atiyah, *Essays on Contract* (Oxford, Clarendon Press, 1986) 346.

It is sometimes suggested that relief from unfair choice of law clauses could be obtained under such rules targeting substantive unfairness;[35] and courts have, in some cases, made use of them to avoid the application of laws that were considered unfavourable to the weaker party.[36] This approach must be rejected.[37] Rules on substantive fairness are concerned with the parties' rights and obligations, but the sole function of the choice of law contract is the selection of the applicable law. Although the applicable law in turn affects the parties' rights and obligations, the selection of the applicable law itself can hardly be considered unfair, particularly if the law governing the choice of law contract is the putative chosen law. For example, if a chosen law had the effect of excluding assets held in a sham trust from a couple's shared matrimonial property, the fairness of the chosen law could only be assessed by reference to other legal systems. There are no standards or reference points within the law of contract that could help to determine whether a chosen law is fair.[38]

At the same time, the content of choice of law contracts falls clearly within the regulatory scope of modal choice of law, because it is a matter that defines, to a significant extent, the scope of party autonomy permitted by the forum.[39] For example, a choice of Italian law to govern a contract of carriage was not 'abusive' for the purposes of French consumer law simply because Italian law imposed a much shorter limitation period.[40] Such a conclusion would have been inconsistent with the principle of free choice in Article 3 of the Convention 80/934/ECC on the law applicable to contractual obligations (Rome Convention).[41]

So rules of contract on substantive fairness should not usually be applied to choice of law contracts. Instead, it is necessary to determine whether there is a need for modal choice of law to regulate unfair choice of law contracts in order to protect vulnerable parties. The law of contract provides guidance on the kind of circumstances in which a choice of law contract would most benefit from a modal choice of law rule on unfairness. Substantive protection is offered primarily to

[35] eg J Camarote, 'A Little more Contract with my My Contract Please: The Need to Apply Unconscionability Directly to Choice-of-Law Clauses' (2009) 39 *Seton Hall Law Review* 605, 631; H Rösler, 'Rechtswahlfreiheit im Internationalen Scheidungsrecht der Rom III-Verordnung' (2014) 78 *Rabels Zeitschrift für ausländisches und internationales Privatrecht* 155, 181; cp M Davies, AS Bell and PLG Brereton, *Nygh's Conflict of Laws in Australia* 9th edn (Chatswood NSW, LexisNexis, 2014) para 19.10.

[36] eg LG Stuttgart, NJW-RR 1990, 1394 (see ch 7, s VIII.A); *Re Futures Transactions* [1998] ILPr 327 (OLG Düsseldorf) 335; OLG Düsseldorf, NJW-RR 1994, 1132.

[37] See ch 5, s III.B.ii.

[38] C Rühl, 'Rechtswahlfreiheit und Rechtswahlklauseln in Allgemeinen Geschäftsbedingungen' (Baden Baden, Nomos, 1999) 204–05; P Stankewitsch, *Entscheidungsnormen im IPR als Wirksamkeitsvoraussetzungen der Rechtswahl* (Frankfurt, Peter Lang, 2003) 313–14; see C von Bar and P Mankowski, *Internationales Privatrecht*, vol 1 (Munich, CH Beck, 2003) 603, para 85; cp H Stoll, 'Internationalprivatrechtliche Probleme bei Verwendung Allgemeiner Geschäftsbedingungen' in O Sandrock (ed), *Festschrift für Günther Beitzke* (Berlin, de Gruyter, 1979) 759, 770.

[39] See ch 5, s IV.

[40] CA Bastia, 2 February 2011, no 08-00291.

[41] Convention 80/934/ECC on the law applicable to contractual obligations [1980] OJ L266/1 (opened for signature 19 June 1980, entered into force 1 April 1991) (Rome Convention).

parties whose bargaining power is likely to be compromised, whether through an economic imbalance, information asymmetries, bounded rationality or emotional pressure. Parties who are seen as in need of protection include consumers, employees, spouses and commercial parties contracting under standard forms.[42] It will thus be necessary to consider whether such parties would also benefit from a modal choice of law rule on unfairness (see section C below), after discussing in more detail the meaning of substantive unfairness in the choice of law context (see section B). What is a substantively unfair choice of law contract?

B. What is an Unfair Choice of Law Contract?

A South African couple decides to move to New Zealand. Before leaving South Africa, they enter into a matrimonial agreement providing for complete separation of assets. They also choose South African law as the law governing their respective rights and obligations. In New Zealand, the husband earns a substantial income while the wife works part time and takes care of their children. After a few years, the marriage breaks down. Unlike his wife, the husband has amassed significant assets. Assuming the spouses' matrimonial agreement to be valid and enforceable under South African law,[43] can the choice of law contract be considered unfair by a New Zealand court?

There are two principal considerations that must inform any inquiry into the substantive fairness of choices of law. On the one hand, substantive control of choice of law contracts stands in direct conflict with the very purpose of party autonomy, which is to choose a system of law that the parties deem appropriate to govern their legal relationship. A choice of law cannot be disregarded simply because the content of the chosen law is not to the court's liking. On the other hand, the chosen law is undeniably capable of affecting parties' rights and obligations in ways that differ fundamentally from other legal systems, and it may thus amount to a tool of exploitation against vulnerable parties.[44] How are these considerations to be reconciled?

i. Existing Modal Choice of Law Rules

The few modal choice of law rules that deal with substantive fairness have done little to clarify this point. The common law rule on party autonomy, for example,

[42] See T Wilhelmsson, 'Standard Form Conditions' in A Hartkamp et al (eds), *Towards a European Civil Code* 4th edn (Alphen aan den Rijn, Kluwer, 2010) 571.

[43] This is a hypothetical example.

[44] MM Mohamed Salah, 'Loi d'autonomie et méthodes de protection de la partie faible en droit international privé' (2005) 315 *Recueil des Cours* 141, 164; U Magnus (ed), *Staudingers Kommentar zum Bürgerlichen Gesetzbuch: Rom I-VO Art 3* (Berlin, Sellier, 2011) para 31.

requires the choice to have been made in good faith.[45] But the rule is little used and extremely uncertain in scope. It is not even clear whether it is concerned with the content of the chosen law,[46] or whether it might be confined to such circumstances:

> [W]here the choice of law was imposed by one party, not as a real solution to the conflicts problem, but to oppress the other, eg by selecting the jurisdiction and law of a distant State plagued by civil war and anarchy, or where litigation is expensive and slow.[47]

More detailed is Article 8(5) of the Hague Protocol on the Law Applicable to Maintenance Obligations,[48] which provides that the chosen law will not apply where its application would lead to 'manifestly unfair or unreasonable consequences', unless the parties were fully aware of the consequences of their choice. The following clarification is offered in the Explanatory Report:

> This escape clause is based on considerations of substantive justice and corresponds to the powers that several national laws confer on courts to amend, or even set aside, maintenance agreements made between the parties when they lead to unfair or unreasonable results. However, delegations were also concerned that an unlimited power of the court to set aside the chosen law would completely undermine the possibility of the parties to conclude choice of law agreements under Article 8. It was therefore agreed to limit the mitigating powers of the court by providing that paragraph 5 would not apply if the parties were fully informed and aware of the consequences of their designation.[49]

But this explanation sheds no light on the circumstances in which the parties' choice may produce results that are 'manifestly unfair or unreasonable'. If the South African couple's agreement had also purported to limit the wife's right to maintenance to a sum barely sufficient to make ends meet, and if this agreement were valid under South African law, could the choice of South African law be considered manifestly unfair? In Article 8(4), the Protocol already excludes party autonomy in relation to 'the question of whether the creditor can renounce his or her right to maintenance'.

The Restatement (Second) of Conflict of Laws also seems to propose an unfairness rule when it states that 'the forum will scrutinize [adhesion contracts] with care and will refuse to apply any choice-of-law provision they may contain if to do so would result in substantial injustice to the adherent'.[50] It is difficult not to interpret this statement as a modal choice of law rule (on both procedural and

[45] *Vita Food Products Inc v Unus Shipping Co Ltd* [1939] AC 277 (PC) 290 ('the intention expressed [must be] bona fide'); cp more generally the doctrine of 'evasion of law' and *fraude à la loi*: J Fawcett, 'Evasion of Law and Mandatory Rules in Private International Law' (1990) 49 *CLJ* 44, 51; P Mayer and V Heuzé, *Droit international privé* 10th edn (Paris, LGDJ, 2014) 191ff.

[46] Fawcett (n 45) 51.

[47] P Nygh, *Autonomy in International Contracts* (Oxford, Oxford University Press, 1999) 68.

[48] Hague Protocol on the Law Applicable to Maintenance Obligations (opened for signature 23 November 2007, entered into force 1 August 2013) (Hague Maintenance Protocol).

[49] A Bonomi, *Explanatory Report: Protocol of 23 November 2007 on the Law Applicable to Maintenance Obligations* (HccH, October 2009) para 150.

[50] *Restatement (Second)* (n 26) s 187, cmnt (b).

substantive fairness). In *Washington Mutual Bank v Superior Court*,[51] the Supreme Court of California noted that 'the weaker party to an adhesion contract may seek to avoid enforcement of a choice-of-law provision therein by establishing that "substantial injustice" would result from its enforcement';[52] and where parties do raise the matter of 'substantial injustice', courts tend to treat it as an independent element of section 187.[53] Yet the California Court of Appeal in *Discover Bank v Superior Court* adopted a different interpretation,[54] concluding that 'substantial injustice' is merely one of the factors in determining whether a choice of law agreement came about by improper means or mistake:

> Read as a whole, then, the comment does not create a separate rule requiring invalidation of choice-of-law provisions in adhesion contracts if, upon careful scrutiny, they appear to work a substantial injustice. Rather, the comment explains that a choice-of-law provision—like any other contractual provision—will not be enforced if it was included because of improper means or mistake, and the comment further observes that the adhesive nature of a consumer contract may be a relevant factor in analyzing whether a provision was included by improper means or mistake.[55]

This view is unconvincing. The Restatement submits the issue of material consent—whether consent was obtained by improper means or by mistake—to the *lex fori* (more specifically, it provides that the issue 'will be determined by the forum in accordance with its own legal principles'). Presumably, this is a reference to the *lex fori*'s general law of contract. But even though the doctrine of unconscionability is well-established in US contract law, the general law of contract cannot apply to determine whether a choice of law contract causes 'substantial injustice'. This, by definition, is a matter for modal choice of law.

In any case, the proposed rule is no more illuminating than Article 8(5) of the Hague Maintenance Protocol, and few courts have made use of it.[56] When determining whether a choice of the law of Texas would result in substantial injustice, the California District Court noted that 'it is not clear exactly how that standard is to be applied … [t]he California Supreme Court refers generally to this standard in *Washington Mutual* and *Discover*, but provides no meaningful guidance as to its application'.[57] The Court then found that the fact that the law

[51] *Washington Mutual Bank v Superior Court* 24 Cal 4th 906 (Cal 2001).

[52] ibid, 918.

[53] eg *Omstead v Dell, Inc* 473 F Supp 2d 1018 (2007 DC) 1025; *Sall v GH Miller Co* 612 F Supp 1499 (DC Colo 1985) 1506.

[54] *Discover Bank v Superior Court* 134 Cal App 4th 886 (Cal App 2 Dist 2005).

[55] ibid, 896–97. cp *Samaniego v Empire Today LLC* 205 Cal App 4th 1138 (Cal App 2 Dist 2012) 1148–49.

[56] See, eg, *Carideo v Dell* 492 F Supp 2d 1283 (WD Wash 2007) 1287 ('Plaintiffs do not cite nor is the court aware of any instance in which a Washington court has invoked this "substantial injustice" standard to invalidate a choice-of-law clause'); Camarote (n 35), who argues that US courts should—but do not currently—apply the doctrine of unconscionability to choice of law contracts directly; cp ZS Tang, *Electronic Consumer Contracts in the Conflict of Laws* 2nd edn (Oxford, Hart, 2015) 202–06.

[57] *Omstead v Dell, Inc* 473 F Supp 2d 1018 (2007 DC) 1025 (reversed on different issue).

of Texas would deprive the plaintiffs of their right to bring a class action was not sufficient to amount to substantial injustice. Guidance has since been provided by the California Court of Appeal, in the shape of this astonishing proposition: 'When the weaker party to an adhesion contract can show the contract is unconscionable under California law, a contractual provision requiring the application of a different state's law to enforce the contract is itself unenforceable'.[58] In other words: a court will not apply the chosen law to determine the conscionability of an adhesion contract, so there is really no need to determine the conscionability of the choice of law contract at all!

It may be this seeming indefinability of substantive fairness that has led to the popularity of restricted party choice, which, by limiting the parties' choice to laws that are closely connected to their relationship, reduces the potential for exploitation;[59] though the (primary) purpose of such provisions is not necessarily substantive protection.[60] However, although the fairness of a choice of law contract cannot be measured in the same manner as that of an ordinary contract,[61] a meaningful modal choice of law rule on substantive fairness is not impossible. There are two factors that, together, may produce a workable solution.

ii. Comparing the Chosen with the Objective Law

The first is that, because the purpose of the choice of law contract is to contract out of the objective choice of law rule, the effect of the chosen law can only be considered unfair by reference to the position that would have obtained under the objective law. It is not necessary to rank legal systems in accordance with their relative 'fairness',[62] or to compare the chosen law to that of the forum; and it is certainly unnecessary to treat the chosen law as inherently unfair. What ought to count is the position that either party gave up, indirectly, by agreeing to the chosen law. In the case of the South African couple, this would require a comparison between South African law, as the chosen law, and New Zealand law, as the law that would apply to the parties' relationship property in the absence of choice. An unfairness rule of this nature would be particularly appropriate where

[58] *Pinela v Neiman Marcus Group, Inc* 238 Cal App 4th 227 (Cal App 1 Dist 2015) 246–47, applying *Samaniego v Empire Today LLC* 205 Cal App 4th 1138 (Cal App 2 Dist 2012).

[59] eg Reg (EC) 593/2008 on the law applicable to contractual obligations [2008] OJ L177/6 (Rome I), Arts 7(3) and 5(2) (insurance contracts and contracts of carriage); Reg (EU) 1259/2010 implementing enhanced cooperation in the area of the law applicable to divorce and legal separation [2010] OJ L343/10 (Rome III), Art 5(1); Proposal for a Council Reg on jurisdiction, applicable law and the recognition and enforcement of decisions in matters of matrimonial property regimes (COM 2011, 126, 16 March 2011) (Proposal for a Reg on matrimonial property), Art 16; Einführungsgesetz zum Bürgerlichen Gesetzbuch (EGBGB), Arts 14 and 15; Hague Maintenance Protocol (n 48) Art 8(1).

[60] See ch 3, s IV.A; G Rühl, 'The Protection of Weaker Parties in the Private International Law of the European Union: a Portrait of Inconsistency and Conceptual Truancy' (2014) 10 *Journal of Private International Law* 335, 349–51.

[61] See Rühl (n 38) 205.

[62] ibid, 207.

the objective connecting factor serves a protective function, like section 7 of the Property (Relationships) Act 1976.[63]

The proposed approach might achieve similar results to the public policy limitation in the Restatement, which states that the chosen law will be applied unless 'application of the law of the chosen state would be contrary to a fundamental policy of [the objective applicable law]', provided that state 'has a materially greater interest than the chosen state in the determination of the particular issue'.[64] The rule does not provide directly for a *comparison* between the chosen law and the objective applicable law; and determining whether the chosen law is 'contrary to a fundamental policy' is different, conceptually, from an assessment of substantive fairness (there are circumstances in which a choice of law contract could be unfair even though it does not offend a 'fundamental policy', and vice versa). But the rule does require an evaluation of the chosen law by reference to the objective applicable law. It allows courts to conclude, for example, that a choice of New York law in an adhesion contract is unenforceable because, unlike the objective applicable law of the state of Washington, New York law gives effect to class action waivers.[65] An unfairness rule might lead to the same conclusion.

The proposed approach also is not dissimilar from the principle of the more favourable law that is applied to consumer and employment contracts under Regulation (EC) 593/2008 on the law applicable to contractual obligations (Rome I).[66] Both evaluate the chosen law by reference to the objective applicable law. However, while the principle of the more favourable law leads to the application of any mandatory provisions that offer protection to the weaker party, unfairness could not arise simply because the chosen law is less favourable than the objective law. A more serious discrepancy would be needed. For example, if a New Zealand court were unable, pursuant to South African law, to take account of the South African wife's non-financial contribution to the relationship, even though New Zealand law would have required the court to do so, then this might render the South African choice of law contract unfair.

A possible criticism of the proposed approach is that 'to look to the end result of the dispute would be to involve the court in an expensive and time consuming mini-trial'.[67] The Australian Law Reform Commission in its report on choice of law considered accordingly that a comparison between the chosen law and the objective applicable law would not be feasible,[68] and relied only on procedural considerations when it recommended an unconscionability rule for choice of law contracts. In particular, the Commission referred to such factors as 'the relative

[63] See ch 3, s II.B.iii.

[64] *Restatement (Second)* (n 26) s 187(2)(b). cp s 7A(3) of the Property (Relationships) Act, which simply provides for an exception to the application of the chosen law where this would be 'contrary to justice or public policy'.

[65] *McKee v AT & T Corp* 164 Wash 2d 372 (2008).

[66] Rome I (n 59), Arts 6(2) and 8(1); see ch 5, s IV.C.ii.

[67] Australian Law Reform Commission, *Choice of Law* (Report 58, 1992) para 8.22.

[68] ibid, para 8.22.

strength of the bargaining position of the parties, the inability by one party to understand the documents involved, undue influence or unfair tactics'.[69] However, because substantive unfairness would arise only in the most glaring of cases where the objective applicable law is clearly more favourable to the disadvantaged party than the chosen law, it is unlikely that a 'mini-trial' would usually be necessary to determine whether a choice of law contract is unfair.

iii. Conflicts Interests in the Application of the Chosen Law

An assessment of fairness cannot be based entirely on the content of the chosen and objective laws. The second factor that ought to be reflected in any rule on substantive fairness is that parties may have an interest in the application of a particular law that is not derived primarily from its content. This means that a serious discrepancy caused by a choice of law may potentially be mitigated by the parties' 'conflicts' interests in the application of the law,[70] including their familiarity with the law, the connection of the law to the relationship, the benefits of choosing the law of the forum, or even the fact that the chosen law has developed a sophisticated set of rules dealing specifically with the subject-matter of the parties' relationship.

While such interests could, if they are attributable to the disadvantaged party, offset an otherwise unfair discrepancy between the chosen and the objective law, they might also be relied upon by the favoured party—as interests that, despite the discrepancy, are worth protecting, because their loss under the objective choice of law rule would constitute an undue burden on the favoured party. The South African husband could argue, for example, that the choice of South African law was in both his and his wife's interest, because this was the country with which they were most closely connected.

It should not be the case, as has been suggested in the past,[71] and as is still common practice in the United States,[72] that the parties must have a legitimate interest or reasonable basis for the choice, or that a choice that is driven purely by substantive reasons is inherently suspect. Rather, the absence of conflicts

[69] ibid, para 8.20.

[70] cp the concept of 'conflicts justice' in ch 3, s II.

[71] See BGE 91 II 44, 51 (which, since the IPRG, no longer represents the law), requiring a 'reasonable interest' in the application of the chosen law; FA Mann, 'The Proper Law of the Contract' (1950) 3 *International Law Quarterly* 60, 66–67, considering that a 'capricious' choice, or a choice that 'lack[ed] reality', was not available; Gesetz zur Regelung des Rechts der Allgemeinen Geschäftsbedingungen (AGBG), s 10 (BGBl 1976 I 3317, repealed in 1986), requiring a 'recognisable interest' ('anerkennenswertes Interesse') for choices of law in standard term contracts; G Kegel, *Internationales Privatrecht* 7th edn (Munich, CH Beck, 1995) 483, also requiring 'some recognisable interest' ('irgendein anerkennenswertes Interesse') in the applicable law for contracts more generally, as cited by Nygh (n 47) 57; O Lando, 'The Conflict of Laws of Contracts' (1984) 189 *Recueil des Cours* 225, 293, arguing that a choice of law which 'would violate a strong public policy of the otherwise applicable law' and which would not be 'supported by the interests of international trade' should not be recognised; cp generally the doctrine of 'evasion of law' and *fraude à la loi* (see above n 45); see ch 3, s IV.A.

[72] *Restatement (Second)* (n 26) s 187(2)(a).

interests should strengthen a claim of discrepancy because there are no countervailing interests to be taken into account. If the South African spouses had chosen Australian law to govern their matrimonial relationship, in the absence of a connection to Australia, then any substantive unfairness would have been enough to strike down the choice of law contract under the proposed unfairness rule. A parallel can again be drawn with the public policy limitation in the Restatement.[73] Under this rule, the relevant public policy threshold changes depending on the connection of the transaction with the chosen state. If the transaction has significant contacts with the chosen state, the public policy threshold must be higher than in a case involving only few contacts with the chosen state.[74]

C. The Rule on Substantive Fairness and its Potential Role

Generally, it seems preferable to rely on rules of formality, transparency, disclosure and procedural fairness instead of a rule on substantive fairness to protect vulnerable parties to a choice of law contract (on procedural fairness, see section D below). A substantive fairness rule would have the potential to restrict significantly the parties' freedom to choose the applicable law and, because of its open-ended nature, would introduce a substantial discretionary element into the court's decision-making. Whether an unfairness rule is necessary depends largely on the purpose of objective choice of law—that is, whether objective choice of law serves a protective purpose—and on the risk of exploitation inherent in the choice of law contract.[75] So if at all, it should be applied to only those relationships that are particularly prone to contractual imbalance, including family, consumer and employment relationships. It could also be accompanied by a requirement of procedural defects or injustice to ensure that its effect is not unduly restrictive, such as a lack of transparency or disclosure, a failure to obtain advice or undue pressure.[76]

An example of a prime candidate for such a rule may be section 7A of the Property (Relationships) Act 1976 (NZ), which allows parties to select the law applicable to their relationship property in circumstances where the objective applicable law would be the *lex fori*. Matrimonial relationships are prone to irrationality and contractual imbalance; and it is likely that the *lex fori* rule pursues—at least in part—a protective function.[77] In these circumstances, an unfairness rule may provide an appropriate safeguard. Section 7A(3) does provide for an exception to the application of the chosen law where this would be 'contrary to justice or

[73] ibid, s 187(2)(b).
[74] ibid, s 187(2)(b), cmnt (g): 'The more closely the state of the chosen law is related to the contract and the parties, the more fundamental must be the policy of the state of the otherwise applicable law to justify denying effect to the choice-of-law provision'.
[75] See ch 3, ss II and III.
[76] cp Hague Maintenance Protocol (n 48) Art 8(5); *Restatement (Second)* (n 26) s 187, cmnt (b).
[77] See ch 3, s II.B.iii.

public policy'. But this exception is a poor substitute for an unfairness rule. Under section 7A(3) a court is required to conclude that it is the application of the chosen law itself that produces injustice. No such value judgment is needed if it is the difference between the chosen law and the objective applicable law that determines the fairness of a choice of law contract.

A similar observation applies to the public policy limitation in section 187(2)(b) of the Restatement (Second). This rule also requires that the application of the chosen law be contrary to policy. What is more, the rule requires that application of the chosen law be contrary to 'a fundamental policy' of the objective applicable law, and that the state of the objective applicable law have a 'materially greater interest' in the determination of the issue. Neither of these requirements would form part of an unfairness rule, which is concerned not with the interests of connected states but with fairness between the parties.[78] For example, an employee lives and works in California for an employer headquartered in New York. He wants to leave the company and work for a Californian competitor. The employment agreement is expressed to be governed by New York law and contains a non-compete clause, which is valid pursuant to the chosen law (New York law) but not the objectively applicable law (Californian law). Even though non-compete clauses in employment contracts are contrary to a 'fundamental' Californian policy, section 187(2)(b) may not apply because California does not have a 'materially greater interest' in the determination of the issue.[79] The proposed unfairness rule, on the other hand, does not require the state of the objectively applicable law to have a 'materially greater interest' in the issue. Instead, it allows the parties' conflicts interests—and not the states' conflicts interests—to be taken into account, with the result that the employee may have to meet a higher threshold of substantive unfairness because New York law has a close connection to the employment relationship. Moreover, California's prohibition of non-compete clauses would not have to amount to a 'fundamental' policy to lead to an unfair discrepancy between Californian law and New York law (and hence an unfair choice of law contract).

More generally, an unfairness rule would operate so as to complement the forum's overriding mandatory rules and the traditional doctrine of public policy. The unfairness rule would be able to offer relief in circumstances where the chosen law, but not the objective applicable law, is the law of the forum. It would be based on a relative assessment of the fairness of the choice of law contract, and would require neither an evaluation of the chosen law itself nor a unilateral application of forum laws. It might also decrease the forum's need to rely on overriding mandatory rules or on the public policy exception, which would be of particular benefit in circumstances where the forum has no real connection to the dispute. Overall, the unfairness rule would be better suited to reflect considerations of comity and internationalism. But it could not replace—and indeed would conflict with—the

[78] cp Camarote (n 35). On the role of the public policy limitation, see ch 3, s IV.C.ii.

[79] See *Estee Lauder Co Inc v Batra* 430 F Supp 2d 158 (SDNY 2006).

principle of the more favourable law, whose purpose is to favour identified groups of vulnerable parties in order to maximise the level of protection afforded to them.

Finally, an unfairness rule would provide an alternative to choice of law rules that limit the parties to a selection of applicable laws—provided their purpose is in fact to prevent unfairness.[80] While such choice of law rules reduce the potential for exploitation, they do not exclude the possibility of unfair choice of law contracts and, even more so than the unfairness rule, amount to a significant restriction of party autonomy. For example, a couple of German and New Zealand nationality living in England and France respectively wish to select the law of Sweden to govern their matrimonial property, where they were both resident before they met. If the party autonomy rule limits the parties' selection of applicable laws, Swedish law is unlikely to be available to them—it is neither the law of their nationality nor the law of their current domicile. But Swedish law might achieve a distribution of assets that is quite similar to the legal position that would obtain under English or French law. So why should the parties not enjoy the power to select Swedish law? A modal choice of law rule on unfairness could manage any risk of hardship.

D. Procedural Fairness

The exceptional nature of the substantive fairness rule should prompt lawmakers to give careful consideration to a modal choice of law rule on procedural fairness, which may often be a less cumbersome and interventionist alternative. It has been suggested, for example, that choice of law clauses in electronic consumer contracts are unconscionable 'when the choice of law clause (1) has not been clearly presented, (2) has not been required to be read by the consumer, or (3) has not been unambiguously assented to by the consumer'.[81] In *Fricke v Isbrandtsen*,[82] the New York District Court found that a choice of US law in a steamship ticket was unenforceable against the German plaintiff, because 'unilaterally imposed provisions of this nature should not be enforced unless the party urging enforcement provided the other, illiterate in the language of the contract, with knowledge of what was intended'. However, the Court also gave significant weight to the connections of the case with Germany and considered that a choice of law agreement was 'but one element' in the determination of the applicable law.

Another reason why such an approach may be beneficial is that the law of contract often combines rules of procedural fairness with content-controlling elements, with the result that they may be inapplicable to choice of law contracts. The common law doctrine of presumed undue influence is an example of this.[83]

[80] See above nn 59 and 60, and ch 3, s IV.A.

[81] Tang (n 56) 205.

[82] *Fricke v Isbrandtsen* Co 151 F Supp 465 (DCNY 1957) 468.

[83] cp Art 138(2) of the Bürgerliches Gesetzbuch (BGB).

In order to establish a presumption of undue influence, the claimant must show that there was a relationship of trust and confidence, and that the transaction was one which cannot be readily explained by the relationship of the parties.[84] The factors which are relevant to this latter inquiry are not confined to—but include—the advantages and disadvantages arising from the transaction. If a court were to apply this doctrine to a choice of law contract, it would have to presume the exertion of illegitimate pressure by reference to the content of the chosen law—which, arguably, is not possible.

Although cases of *actual* undue influence do not require a manifestly disadvantageous transaction (or a transaction that cannot be readily explained),[85] actual undue influence requires proof of illegitimate pressure or control,[86] and courts have imposed a high threshold on the type of conduct that will amount to illegitimate pressure or control. A spouse who has lost the ability to exercise independent judgment and agrees to a choice of law to govern matrimonial property may struggle to demonstrate that the choice of law contract was entered into under undue influence.[87] In these circumstances, modal choice of law could usefully intervene by imposing additional requirements of formation, of the nature discussed in chapter seven, or by introducing a more claimant-friendly threshold for proof of actual undue influence.[88]

A more general consideration that could weigh in favour of a modal choice of law rule on procedural fairness is that the conflict of laws may not wish to leave this issue to the law applicable to the choice of law contract. Most jurisdictions do not submit the existence and validity of the choice of law contract to the *lex fori*. So to exercise control over the question of procedural fairness, the conflict of laws would have to submit the choice of law contract to the *lex fori* by way of exception or—the easier option—rely on modal choice of law.

IV. Changes in the Chosen Law

The focus of this chapter so far has been on grounds of invalidity that in some way implicate the content of the chosen law. The issue considered in this section is the quintessential example of this problem: what happens to choice of law contracts if their chosen law undergoes significant changes? Do, or should, courts have the power to void the parties' contract due to changes in the chosen law?

[84] *Royal Bank of Scotland v Etridge (No 2)* [2001] UKHL 44, [2002] 2 AC 773.

[85] *CIBC Mortgages v Pitt* [1994] 1 AC 200 (HL).

[86] See generally Beale (n 1) paras 7-067–7-069.

[87] eg *Elgar v Elgar* 238 Conn 839 (Conn 1996).

[88] cp *Dunes Hospitality LLC v Country Kitchen International Inc* 623 NW 2d 484 (SD 2001), where the Court struck down a choice of law clause based on duress, by imposing a comparatively low threshold for a finding of duress.

The law of contract recognises that there are some situations in which a change in circumstances may render a contract unenforceable, but the effect of a change in circumstances on a choice of law contract is a matter for modal choice of law, and modal choice of law must take a more conservative approach than the law of contract (see section A below). There are, however, a number of alternative options for parties who are concerned about future changes to their chosen law (see section B).

A. Change in Circumstances

There is no uniform approach to the principle of *clausula rebus sic stantibus* ('things thus standing') in the law of contract.[89] While some legal systems provide for a general power to modify a contract in case of hardship, others offer relief only by way of narrow exceptions to the obligation to perform the contract. The rationale underlying these rules, however, remains the same: to address injustice arising from an unforeseeable change in circumstances that fundamentally alters the equilibrium of the parties' contract or that renders it impossible to perform.[90] The common law doctrine of frustration, for example, allows the court to intervene in the case of a supervening act:

> [W]hich so significantly changes the nature … of the outstanding contractual rights and/or obligations from what the parties could reasonably have contemplated at the time of its execution that it would be unjust to hold them to the literal sense of its stipulations in the new circumstances.[91]

It seems that the only change in circumstances that might so affect a choice of law contract that relief is warranted would be a change within the chosen law. The law of contract recognises that changes in the law may result in the frustration of a contract or in actionable hardship.[92] A change in the law might render a contract illegal and therefore impossible to perform, or it might fundamentally alter the parties' rights and obligations. The same reasoning can be applied to choice of law contracts. For example, if a couple selects the law of country X to govern their matrimonial property relationship, but then the matrimonial property regime of country X undergoes fundamental changes, the choice of law contract may no longer represent the parties' original intentions and could be considered unjust.

Based on these general principles of contract, there may well be a need to regulate the effect of changes in the chosen law on choice of law contracts. But there

[89] See generally E Hondius and HC Grigoleit (eds), *Unexpected Circumstances in European Contract Law* (Cambridge, Cambridge University Press, 2011); M Mekki, 'Hardship and Modification (or "Revision") of the Contract' in A Hartkamp et al (eds), *Towards a European Civil Code* 4th edn (Alphen aan den Rijn, Kluwer, 2010) 651.

[90] See Mekki, ibid para 1.2.1.

[91] *National Carriers Ltd v Panalpina (Northern) Ltd* [1981] AC 675 (HL) 700 (Lord Simon).

[92] Mekki (n 89) 672.

are a couple of reasons why—if at all—any form of regulation should come in the form of a modal choice of law rule. The first reason is that the law on frustration and hardship is concerned primarily with the substantive fairness of parties' contracts. Whether it is unfair or inequitable to enforce a choice of law contract despite a fundamental change within the chosen law is a question that can only be answered within the specific context of choice of law.

The second—but related—reason is that the standards provided by the law of contract would be too intrusive when adapted to choice of law contracts, because the impact of a change in the law is measured by reference to the parties' rights and obligations. A choice of law contract ought not to be terminated simply because a change in the chosen law renders performance of the underlying contract illegal. A change in circumstances resulting from illegality of performance is not obviously relevant to the choice of law contract. Instead, it ought to be considered in relation to the underlying contract, by reference to the chosen law. The function of the choice of law contract is the selection of a living body of law, and the selection may be motivated by considerations other than the content of the chosen law at the time of contracting.[93]

A modal choice of law rule on changes in the chosen law must strike an appropriate balance: while recognising the chosen law as a living legal system, it should be available to strike down a choice of law that fundamentally differs from the law that was originally chosen. For choice of law contracts governing commercial relationships, the rule could apply only in truly exceptional cases. A feasible solution is offered by German law. Here, the established position seems to be that relief will be available in cases where the chosen law has undergone fundamental changes as a result of events such as a revolution or a change in regime.[94] A more interventionist solution may be appropriate for choice of law contracts governing non-commercial relationships.

B. Freezing Clauses and Other Options

There are a number of options for parties who are concerned about future changes to their chosen law. The most obvious option is to include a freezing clause in the choice of law contract. By agreeing that the law be applied as it existed at the time of contracting, parties may attempt to pre-empt the effect of undesired changes in the chosen law. Freezing clauses are common in state contracts, because private parties would otherwise be at the whim of the state's power to control the applicable law. The effect of freezing clauses in state contracts seems to be to make the state liable for any damage arising from a change in the chosen law.[95]

[93] cp ch 6, s IV.C.iii on the rule of validation.

[94] Magnus (n 44) para 53.

[95] H Honsell et al (eds), *Basler Kommentar* 3rd edn (Basel, Helbing Lichtenhahn, 2013) 991; F Vischer, 'Veränderungen des Vertragsstatuts und ihre Folgen' in P Forstmoser et al (ed), *Festschrift für Max Keller* (Zurich, Schulthess, 1989) 547, 550.

But freezing clauses are not generally considered enforceable as a matter of choice of law.[96] The established view is that choice of law rules require application of the applicable law as it stands at the relevant time, to mirror the way in which a local court of that country would apply the law.[97] Freezing of the applicable law would not sit well with this function.[98]

This position is undoubtedly correct; and as a result, freezing clauses are of limited value. But they do not have to be entirely ineffective. An appropriate compromise would be to allow freezing clauses insofar as they relate to dispositive rules of the chosen law, but to deny them any effect in relation to its (new) mandatory rules.[99] This approach would give effect to freezing clauses on the level of substantive law (and not on the level of choice of law). Alternatively, parties could specify that particular rules or provisions are to govern their relationship despite any subsequent changes to the law, which would then be given effect by way of incorporation—provided, again, that these rules or provisions are not inconsistent with new mandatory rules of the chosen law.[100]

Another option would be to make the choice of law contract conditional on the chosen law remaining unchanged, with the result that either a secondary chosen law or the objective applicable law would become applicable in case of change. This course of action may be worthwhile where the parties are concerned about possible reform of an area of law that is at the heart of their relationship. For example, the parties wish to select the law of country X to govern their construction contract, but the law commission of country X has proposed fundamental changes to the regulation of construction contracts. If the proposed changes are not to the parties' liking, they could agree that their choice of the law of country X is conditional on the changes not coming into effect and that, if the changes do come into effect, the law of country Y is to govern from that point in time.

V. Remedies

The final matter to be considered in this chapter—albeit very briefly—is that of remedies. Once a court is satisfied that the choice of law agreement was vitiated by mistake or misrepresentation, or by procedural or substantive unfairness, or by a change in circumstances, what is the appropriate remedy? This is perhaps a surprising choice of topic with which to end this chapter, because the answer seems painfully obvious: the agreement will be unenforceable, in the sense that the court

[96] See Nygh (n 47) 63ff; Collins (n 18) para 32-051; but cp Honsell et al, ibid 991 and P Hay, P Borchers and S Symeonides, *Conflict of Laws* 5th edn (St Paul, West Academic Publishing, 2010) 1133.

[97] See Nygh (n 47) 63; Vischer (n 95) 551; Mayer and Heuzé (n 45) para 746.

[98] But cp Nygh (n 47) 66.

[99] Magnus (n 44) para 51; cp Honsell et al (n 95) 991.

[100] On incorporation, see Collins (n 18) paras 32-056–32-057.

will not give effect to the choice of law. The court has ultimate control over the choice of law contract, because it is the court that has to 'perform' the contract. Any remedy other than avoidance or cancellation of the contract would be highly unusual in this context. In fact, the party autonomy rule does not envisage another remedy. For the purposes of the party autonomy rule, this is a binary issue: either the choice is given effect, or it is not.

But it is not unthinkable that some cases may be able to accommodate a different response. For example, if a party misrepresents the content of the chosen law and the misrepresentation does not conflict with any mandatory rules of the chosen law, then it may be more appropriate to incorporate the representation as a term than to refuse enforcement to the choice of law contract. Party A might have claimed that the chosen law provides for a 'cooling-off' period in which party B has the right to cancel its contract with party A; but the chosen law does not, in fact, provide for such a right. Party B cancels the substantive contract and party A seeks specific performance. Party B argues that it entered into the choice of law contract in reliance on party A's representation that the chosen law provided for a cooling-off period. Instead of striking down the choice of law contract, the court may be able to deal with the misrepresentation on a substantive level, by inferring an agreement that party B would be entitled to a cooling-off period.

These observations are highly speculative, and whether they hold any force would depend on the law applicable to the choice of law contract. The same goes for the possibility of damages: while it is not unthinkable that, in rare circumstances, a misrepresentation as to the chosen law could found an entitlement to damages, such a claim would be unorthodox and would require justification. The primary effect of vitiation is to render the choice of law contract unenforceable.

VI. Conclusion

Although the validity of choice of law contracts is still largely governed by the law of contract, modal choice of law is the only appropriate source to regulate the substantive fairness of choice of law contracts, as well as the effect of changes to the chosen law. Modal choice of law may also play a useful role in regulating procedural fairness; and it could define the meaning of an actionable mistake or misrepresentation as to the chosen law (common law jurisdictions should at least clarify that mistakes or misrepresentations as to the content of the chosen law do not fall within the 'foreign law as fact' maxim). So modal choice of law can play a potentially significant role where a choice of law contract is to be challenged on grounds that relate to the content of the chosen law. But lawmakers have made limited attempts to exploit the potential of modal choice of law in this context. This, by now, is a familiar story.

9

Conclusion

I. Contractualising Choice of Law: Unfinished Business

The party autonomy rule, 'one of the fundamental principles of private international law',[1] provides that the applicable law is the law the parties intended to govern. Where the party autonomy rule applies, and the parties have agreed on the applicable law, their choice is given effect by the court. The parties' agreement to choose the applicable law is crucial to the operation of the party autonomy rule: it is a choice of law contract—a contract to opt out of the applicable objective choice of law rule and to select the governing law.

However, the contractualisation of choice of law has never been taken to its logical conclusion. While the freedom to choose the applicable law has long been a mainstay of modern choice of law, the contractual function of the choice of law agreement has not been sufficiently recognised. The purpose of this book was to remedy this deficiency by providing a contractual framework for the regulation of the party autonomy rule. By fusing principles of contract and choice of law, the framework offers normative insights into the rationale for party autonomy, the relationship of the choice of law contract with the underlying dispute, as well as the regulation of its existence and validity.

This analysis revealed two principal but interrelated shortcomings in the approach that has traditionally been taken to party autonomy. The first is a false parallelism between the choice of law contract and the relationships it purports to govern (see section A below); the second is a reluctance to submit the choice of law contract to contractual rules to determine its existence and validity (see section B). These shortcomings result in a strange dichotomy between the underlying rationale for the party autonomy rule and the approach that is taken in practice to its enforcement (see section C). Interestingly, US and Swiss courts constitute an exception to some of these findings, to the extent that putative

[1] E Jayme, 'L'autonomie de la volonté des parties dans les contrats internationaux entre personnes privées' (1991) 64-I *Annuaire de l'Institut de Droit International* 7, 77, recital.

reasoning does not seem to be as well established in these jurisdictions,[2] and that they have largely resisted the pitfalls of implied choice.[3]

A. False Parallelism

What is meant here by false parallelism is the conceptualisation of the choice of law contract as a contract that, although it inhabits a higher legal plane than ordinary contracts because it affects even mandatory rules of the objective law, is just another transaction involving rights and obligations. This conceptualisation misconstrues the function of the choice of law contract, which is not to create or modify rights and obligations but to opt out of objective choice of law rules.[4] This misconception has manifested itself in several ways.

First, it is at least partly responsible for treatment of the choice of law contract as a term of the underlying contract, leading to putative reasoning,[5] the enforcement of hypothetical choices of law as implied terms,[6] and the misapplication of rules on the admissibility of extrinsic evidence.[7] If the choice of law contract is conceived as part and parcel of the parties' contractual bargain, any challenge affecting the underlying contract could not also logically be tested in relation to the choice of law contract; gap-filling rules would be applied to remedy the parties' failure to make an express choice of law; and evidence extrinsic to the underlying contract would be inadmissible to prove the existence or meaning of the choice of law.

Second, the conflation between the choice of law contract and its ultimate effect on relationships of obligation has led some courts to apply obligation-based rules to choice of law contracts,[8] and may have blinded lawmakers to the need for modal choice of law rules, which can fill regulatory gaps left by the general law of contract. It is simply assumed that, just like any other contract, a choice of law clause may be void because it is unreasonable, disadvantageous or unfair.

Finally, the power to choose the applicable law is often justified on the basis of substantive freedom of contract. In other words, party autonomy is seen as an extension of the parties' freedom to regulate their own affairs on a substantive level. This means that areas of law that leave little scope for self-ordering are less likely to be submitted to the party autonomy rule.[9] But because the function of the choice of law contract is to opt out of the applicable objective choice of law rule, party autonomy should primarily be evaluated against the policies of objective

[2] See ch 4, s II.
[3] See ch 6, ss II and IV.
[4] See ch 2.
[5] See ch 4.
[6] See ch 6, s IV.B.ii.
[7] See ch 7, s II.
[8] See, eg, ch 8, s III.A and ch 5, s III.B.ii.
[9] See ch 3.

choice of law. So it is possible that the scope of party autonomy has been unduly restricted.

B. Existence and Validity

Partly as a result of this parallelism between the choice of law contract and its underlying relationship of obligation, the task of determining the existence and validity of choice of law contracts has fallen by the wayside. Choice of law should lend its power of enforcement to only those agreements that do not undermine personal autonomy. Hence, the choice of law contract must be submitted to the law of contract and to modal choice of law rules, in a manner that properly reflects its function, to ensure effective agreement on the applicable law. That party autonomy requires a real, mutual intention to choose the applicable law is widely accepted in principle. But it is often neglected in practice.

First, courts frequently dispense with an assessment of the existence and validity of an alleged choice of law contract where the underlying contract is challenged on grounds that are factually relevant to both contracts. For example, a party who alleges that it did not sign a contract that also contains a choice of law clause is able to rely on the putative chosen law to support its claim.[10] Similarly, ambiguous and implied choices of law have been established in accordance with putative factors, such as disputed jurisdiction agreements.[11] The effect is that a potentially unilateral choice of law is sufficient to trigger the party autonomy rule.

Second, courts have been willing to infer choices of law on the basis of the parties' expectations and their hypothetical intentions.[12] This is particularly true of common law courts. Jurisdiction clauses, for example, are commonly considered to be reliable indicators of an implied intention as to the applicable law. Pursuant to ordinary principles of contract, neither expectation nor hypothetical intention is sufficient to found a contract.

Third, although modal choice of law rules are increasingly common to regulate the existence and validity of choice of law contracts, their contractual function has not yet been properly realised. The law of contract is not a sufficient source of regulation for choice of law contracts because it is geared towards relationships of obligation and does not contain norms specific to the choice of law contract.[13] Limitations on the party autonomy rule, too, are an insufficient source of regulation, because they do not target the existence and validity of the choice of law contract directly.[14] Of those modal choice of law rules that have been developed, many utilise terms that are so ambiguous as to be meaningless, referring, for example, to

[10] See ch 4.
[11] See ch 6, s IV.C.ii and D.
[12] See ch 6, ss II and IV.
[13] See ch 5, ss III and IV.
[14] See ch 5, s V.

a choice that must be 'clearly demonstrated',[15] or 'demonstrated with reasonable certainty',[16] or 'appear clearly' from the provisions of the contract or the circumstances of the case;[17] or a choice that must be 'freely negotiated'.[18]

C. Implications

These shortcomings result in a strange dichotomy between the reasons that are generally advanced to justify the party autonomy rule—that it gives effect to the parties' mutual intention, and that it produces predictable results—and the kind of circumstances that are sufficient, in practice, to lead to the application of the 'chosen' law: unilateral choices of law, choices of law based on expectation or hypothetical intention, and choices of law that fit vague standards of agreement and that are largely unregulated. Thus, the English High Court in *Egon Oldendorff v Liberia Corp* emphasised the need for 'real' intention under Article 3 of the Convention 80/934/ECC on the law applicable to contractual obligations (Rome Convention)[19] yet proceeded to draw 'the reasonable inference' that, having agreed a 'neutral' forum by way of a London arbitration clause for the determination of disputes 'arising out of a well known English language form of charterparty', the parties intended that forum to apply a 'neutral' law.[20]

Further, in *Navig8 Pte Ltd v Al-Riyadh Co*, a putative choice of law was enough to allow service out of the jurisdiction of a claim for negative declaratory relief, on the basis that the defendant's proceedings in Jordan would defeat the parties' agreement on English law.[21] The claimant disputed that it was a party to the bills of lading that provided for English law. The Court referred to Parker LJ's dictum in *Seashell Shipping Corp v Mutualidad e Seguros del Instituto Nacional de Industria (The Magnum)* that it would be unjust to prevent the plaintiff 'from proceeding in Courts where the result of his bargain would be to produce success and to force him to proceed in Courts where the result would or might be that the defendants escaped their bargain'.[22] It then concluded:

> [W]hat matters here, I think, is that (if Al-Riyadh's claim against Navig8 has any validity) not only is English the governing law of the putative bills of lading contracts but it was

[15] Reg (EC) 593/2008 on the law applicable to contractual obligations [2008] OJ L177/6 (Rome I), Art 3(1).

[16] Convention 80/934/ECC on the law applicable to contractual obligations [1980] OJ L266/1 (opened for signature 19 June 1980, entered into force 1 April 1991) (Rome Convention), Art 3(1).

[17] Hague Conference on Private International Law, *Principles on Choice of Law in International Commercial Contracts* (approved on 19 March 2015), Art 4(1); cp also Gesetz über das Internationale Privatrecht (IPRG), Art 116.

[18] Reg (EC) 864/2007 on the law applicable to non-contractual obligations [2007] OJ L199/40 (Rome II), Art 14(1)(b).

[19] *Egon Oldendorff v Libera Corporation* [1996] 1 Lloyd's Rep 380 (QB) 387–88; Rome Convention (n 16).

[20] *Egon Oldendorff*, ibid 390.

[21] *Navig8 Pte Ltd v Al-Riyadh Co* [2013] EWHC 328.

[22] ibid, [28], citing *Seashell Shipping Corp v Mutualidad de Seguros del Instituto Nacional de Industria (The Magnum)* [1989] 1 Lloyd's Rep 47 (CA) 53 (Parker LJ).

> chosen by the parties to them (by implication rather than explicit words, but that cannot be a significant distinction). This brings into play 'the fundamental principle of the English rule of conflict of laws that intention is the general test of what law is to apply'... and permits what would, in all probability, otherwise unacceptably defy comity.[23]

These examples demonstrate the lack of coherence that pervades the regulation of the party autonomy rule. The choice of law contract is a complex and unbreachable contract with potentially far-reaching consequences. It should not exist in a regulatory vacuum, as a contract that is given the force of law but is barely regulated in accordance with contractual rules—a real *contrat sans loi*.[24] Party autonomy has become an increasingly popular choice of law rule and, as was argued in chapter three, may not yet have reached its full potential. If it is to remain a popular choice of law rule both for lawmakers and parties, then a change in direction is needed to place the choice of law contract on a more principled footing.

There are two principal conclusions that must be drawn from all of this. The first is that, if the rigidity of objective choice of law rules has contributed to the erosion of the party autonomy principle, then they might need to be reassessed (see section II below). The second is that the party autonomy rule will need to be regulated in accordance with a contractual approach (see section III).

II. Reform of Objective Choice of Law Rules?

In jurisdictions other than the United States,[25] the pragmatic approach that has been taken by some courts to the party autonomy rule might be driven in part by a perceived failure of objective choice of law rules to provide a just outcome for individual parties. Thus, choice of law contracts might be inferred on the basis of the parties' expectations or hypothetical intentions because the applicable objective choice of law rule is not sufficiently flexible to take account of the individual parties' circumstances.[26] This would be the case in particular where the objective choice of law rule relies on fixed connecting factors such as the *lex situs*, the law of the place of habitual residence, the law of the place of nationality or the *lex loci delicti*. But even open-ended connecting factors, such as the law of the place of closest connection, may not be sufficiently wide to enable subjective (or 'pseudo-psychological')[27] factors to be taken into account.[28] If the law of the place of closest connection is derived from purely objective factors, it would be

[23] ibid, [35].

[24] cp V Heuzé, *La réglementation française des contrats internationaux* (Paris, Joly éditions, 1990) 111ff.

[25] See ch 3, s II.C on the United States' flexible approach to the objective applicable law.

[26] See ch 6, ss II and IV.

[27] F Juenger, 'Two European Conflicts Conventions' (1998) 28 *Victoria University of Wellington Law Review* 527, 539.

[28] See *Crédit Lyonnais v New Hampshire Insurance Co* [1997] 2 Lloyd's Rep 1 (CA) 5.

immaterial, for example, that the parties had acted with a certain legal system in mind.

Dissatisfaction with objective choice of law might also help to explain why there has been such limited reliance on modal choice of law rules. If the party autonomy rule is used as a tool to apply the law that the court considers most appropriate in the circumstances, having regard to the individual parties' expectations and circumstances, then a modal choice of law rule that, for example, requires the choice of law contract to be express and in writing would probably be considered counterproductive. In other words, modal choice of law rules would make it more difficult for courts to treat the party autonomy rule as a malleable standard that acts as a safety valve for rigid objective choice of law rules.

Whether a more individualised approach to objective choice of law is needed requires an evaluation of the aims and policies of choice of law.[29] If it is concerned primarily with the interests of the parties, its connecting factors need to strike an appropriate balance between predictability and justice in the particular case.[30] A connecting factor that is focused too heavily on individual parties' circumstances would make it more difficult for parties to predict what the applicable law will be, and would reduce the prospect of uniformity;[31] conversely, a connecting factor that is focused exclusively on objective factors might lead to injustice because of its rigidity. In the past, courts sought to address this tension by inquiring into the presumed intentions of the parties where they had failed to make a choice; but this second tier of presumed intention has since been rejected as unnecessarily artificial.[32]

Clearly, the role that subjective factors ought to play in choice of law, outside of the party autonomy rule, raises difficult questions. It is not the purpose of this book to answer these questions. If it is decided that choice of law rules should give effect to individual parties' expectations or hypothetical intentions, then this must occur in accordance with well-defined principles, by way of objective choice of law, or even by way of a secondary subjective choice of law rule that, unlike the party autonomy rule, does not require a mutual intention to choose the applicable law. But if it is decided that they should not, then it would be especially wrong to give effect to them under the guise of party autonomy.

[29] See ch 3, s II; see MP Fons, 'Commercial Choice of Law in Context: Looking Beyond Rome' (2015) 78 *MLR* 241 for the argument that the English courts' flexible approach to choice of law in contract is justified by particular policy objectives.

[30] On the need for an equilibrium between certainty and flexibility in objective choice of law generally, see PH Neuhaus, 'Legal Certainty Versus Equity in the Conflict of Laws' (1963) 28 *Law and Contemporary Problems* 795; S Symeonides, 'Codification and Flexibility in Private International Law' in K Brown and D Snyder (eds), *General Reports of the XVIIIth Congress of the International Academy of Comparative Law* (Dordrecht (New York), Springer, 2012) 167.

[31] See Recitals 6 and 16 of Rome I (n 15), which state that choice of law rules should be 'highly foreseeable' and that the outcome of litigation should be predictable, but that the courts should 'retain a degree of discretion to determine the law that is most closely connected to the situation'.

[32] See P Nygh, *Autonomy in International Contracts* (Oxford, Oxford University Press, 1999) 106–09; ch 6, s IV.A.

III. The Case for a Contractual Approach

The proposed contractual approach is built on the premise that, because the parties choose the applicable law by way of contract, choice of law must look to principles of contract to ensure an effective and coherent approach to party autonomy. It is necessary, therefore, to adapt contractual reasoning to choice of law. This requires an evaluation of the party autonomy rule against the policies of objective choice of law, which may have the effect of extending the reach of party choice.[33] More pressingly, it requires courts to give effect to basic principles of contract when establishing the parties' agreement on the applicable law (see section A below); and it also requires a more proactive use of modal choice of law (see section B).

These conclusions may seem contradictory. On the one hand, the normative vacuum of objective choice of law weighs in support of party autonomy. For example, if the *lex loci delicti* serves no external or protective interests, parties should be free to choose the law governing torts. On the other hand, it is imperative that we do more to scrutinise and regulate the existence and validity of choice of law contracts. So a choice of law contract governing torts should not be enforceable, for example, if it is based on putative consent, or if the parties were unable to make an informed choice. But this is not so much a contradiction as a reflection of the true nature of the party autonomy rule: it is a godsend for the conflict of laws, which seeks to produce predictable choice of law outcomes; but it is also based on a contract, so the usual concerns about freedom of contract apply.[34]

A. Establishing Agreement

Agreement on the applicable law must be established in accordance with basic principles of contract. This requires two principal changes to current practice in jurisdictions like England, France and Germany. The existence and validity of the choice of law contract must be determined before it is given effect (see subsection i below) and implied choice of law contracts must be based on conduct demonstrating a real agreement on the applicable law (see subsection ii). All that is needed to give effect to these proposed changes is a more functional interpretation of the choice of law rules that are already in place: the existence and validity of the choice of law contract must be submitted to the law of contract, by virtue of the law governing the choice of law contract; and general modal choice of law rules should not be interpreted to exclude application of the law of contract.

[33] See ch 3.
[34] See ch 5.

i. Putative Choice of Law Contracts are Ineffective

The party autonomy rule requires a mutual intention to choose the applicable law, which means that the existence and validity of the choice of law contract must be determined before the chosen law can be applied to the underlying relationship.[35] Putative reliance on the choice of law contract to determine the existence or validity of the underlying contract must be rejected. Thus, in those (few) cases where the putative chosen law invalidates the choice of law contract on grounds that also affect the underlying contract, those same grounds might then have to be reconsidered, in relation to the underlying contract, pursuant to the objective applicable law.

This approach is not inconsistent with the wording of Article 3 of Regulation (EC) 593/2008 on the law applicable to contractual obligations (Rome I)[36] or Articles 6 and 7 of the Hague Principles on Choice of Law in International Commercial Contracts.[37] On the contrary, the proposed interpretation of these provisions is the only interpretation that is logically available, because it is the only interpretation that will lead to the application of the law that the parties intended to be applicable.

ii. A Real Agreement on the Applicable Law

If the choice of law contract is to be established in accordance with the law of contract, this means that the parties' expectations or hypothetical intentions will not be sufficient to found an agreement on the applicable law. Where the parties have not expressed their choice, the court should ask why the parties failed to do so.[38] In most cases, the only proper explanation will be that the parties did not intend to make a choice of law: they might not have considered the question of choice of law, or they might not have wanted to raise it.

The proposed approach is not excluded by modal choice of law rules calling for the choice to be 'clearly demonstrated',[39] or to be expressed with 'reasonable certainty',[40] or to 'appear clearly'[41] from the contract, which are too vague to carry any real meaning. It also is not precluded by the more generous gap-filling rules that are often applied to the implication of terms, because these rules do not apply when determining the existence of an implied contract.

There has also been some unnecessary confusion whether the choice of law contract is established in accordance with objective or subjective intent, and whether this question is regulated by modal choice of law. If modal choice of law

35 See ch 4.
36 Rome I (n 15).
37 *Hague Principles* (n 17).
38 See ch 6, s IV.B.i.
39 Rome I (n 15) Art 3.
40 Rome Convention (n 16) Art 3.
41 *Hague Principles* (n 17) Art 4.

is to regulate this matter, then it needs to do so expressly. Otherwise, the court must find the answer in the applicable law of contract.

B. Reform of Modal Choice of Law

To achieve proper regulation of the choice of law contract, it is not sufficient to ensure more rigorous adherence to basic principles of contract. Modal choice of law rules are an indispensable yet under-utilised tool to regulate matters that are specific to the choice of law contract. The principal function of contractual modal choice of law rules is to supplement, and also sometimes to replace, rules of the general law of contract that govern the choice of law contract. Yet there are still many gaps for modal choice of law to fill (see subsection i below); and modal choice of law must do more to strike the right balance between principles of the law of contract and principles of the conflict of laws (see subsection ii). When properly used, modal choice of law rules can simplify the operation of the party autonomy rule, make the choice of law process more predictable and transparent for the parties, and reduce the need to rely on protective overriding mandatory rules or public policy exclusions.[42]

i. Gap-filling

Whether the law of contract creates a 'regulatory gap' for modal choice of law is not always a straightforward question. More often than not, the answer depends on an examination of the law of contract, including its underlying principles or policies, as well as an assessment of the needs of the conflict of laws. But there are some obvious gaps that scream out for a solution.

One such gap is the effect of floating choice of law contracts conferring a unilateral power of choice. There is currently no clear rule defining the parties' ability to provide for a unilateral power to choose the applicable law.[43] Modal choice of law could restrict the retrospective effect of floating choice of law contracts, to ensure that parties are capable of acting in accordance with the applicable law. Similarly, a modal choice of law rule is needed to regulate the effect of changes in the chosen law on the validity of the choice of law contract.[44] The rule could provide, for example, that the validity of the choice of law contract will only be affected by fundamental changes to the chosen legal system, and it could clarify that freezing clauses will ordinarily be limited to dispositive rules of law.

[42] See ch 5, s V.
[43] See ch 7, s IV.
[44] See ch 8, s IV.

Then there are gaps that modal choice of law should fill in order to give effect to well-established principles of the law of contract. Often, these principles assume particular importance in relation to the party autonomy rule, which is a both powerful and complex tool. For example, the law of contract in many legal systems has sought to increase transparency in standard term contracting, but there is a real risk that the relevant rules of contract would not apply to choice of law contracts in standard terms.[45] Without a modal choice of law rule on the matter, a party to a standard term contract who claims that it lacked proper notice of the choice of law clause may well be left without protection. Modal choice of law must also serve an educational function where non-commercial and potentially vulnerable parties are unlikely to understand the implications of their choice. Thus, choice of law contracts with consumers and employees should be required to comply with well-defined disclosure obligations concerning the meaning and the effect of the choice; and parties to family relationships should be required to obtain advice.[46]

Capacity is another example.[47] It can hardly be controversial to suggest that a party's capacity to enter into a choice of law contract must be subject to limitations. But the law of contract would not usually be applicable to deal with the issue, and Article 8(3) of the Hague Protocol on the Law Applicable to Maintenance Obligations (Hague Maintenance Protocol) seems to be the only example of a modal choice of law rule on incapacity.[48] Where the choice of law contract applies to an underlying contractual relationship, an appropriate solution might be to provide that a party's capacity to choose the applicable law is conditional on the party's capacity to enter into the underlying contract.

Finally, chapter seven argued that modal choice of law has made insufficient use of formalities.[49] In particular, a requirement that the parties' choice be in writing *and* express would act as a shortcut in cases involving non-commercial parties where an implied choice would in any case be extremely unlikely. It would also have the effect of cautioning such parties against entering into a choice of law contract without proper consideration.

ii. Striking the Right Balance

Modal choice of law must strike the right balance between principles of the law of contract and principles of the conflict of laws. In particular, modal choice of law must create modal choice of laws that give effect to the principles, needs or policies of the conflict of laws, where the law of contract fails to do so. For example, the law of contract does not offer an adequate solution to a proposed choice of law whose acceptance has not been communicated; or to conflicting choice of law clauses in a

[45] See ch 7, s VII.

[46] See ch 7, s VIII.

[47] See ch 7, s VI.

[48] Hague Protocol on the Law Applicable to Maintenance Obligations (opened for signature 23 November 2007, entered into force 1 August 2013).

[49] See ch 7, s V.

'battle of the forms'.[50] A modal choice of law rule could provide that acceptance of a proposed choice of law need not be communicated in order to be effective, which would give effect to the offeror's likely intention that the stipulated law should determine this particular issue of formation; and modal choice of law could adopt the knockout rule for conflicting choices of law, because the rationale for the 'first shot' and 'last shot' rules does not seem to be applicable to choice of law contracts (and the knockout rule would be much easier to apply).

The same reasoning applies to the drafting of modal choice of law rules more generally. For example, while principles of contract may exceptionally justify the creation of a modal choice of law rule on substantive fairness, the rule must also reflect the function of the choice of law contract. Existing modal choice of law rules on substantive fairness make no attempt to achieve this. The rule should provide for a comparison between the chosen law and the objective applicable law, because it is the objective choice of law rule that the parties' choice of law contract seeks to set aside, and it should also take account of conflicts interests.[51]

It goes without saying that any modal choice of law rule should be drafted as clearly as possible, to assist in the smooth and expedient operation of the party autonomy rule. Modal choice of law rules like Article 14(1) of Regulation (EC) 864/2007 on the law applicable to non-contractual obligations (Rome II),[52] which requires the parties' choice to have been 'freely negotiated', are bound to create unnecessary confusion;[53] and instead of ambiguous and potentially misleading requirements that a choice be 'clearly demonstrated' or 'demonstrated with reasonable certainty', or that it 'appear clearly' from the provisions of the contract or the circumstances of the case,[54] modal choice of law could clarify that a hypothetical agreement on choice of law is not sufficient—that courts should not infer a choice of law agreement on the basis of putative factors, or on the basis of what the parties' intentions would have been had they turned their mind to the matter.

Conversely, modal choice of law should not intervene in the application of the law of contract unless there is a reason to do so. An example of a modal choice of law rule that departs from the law of contract without apparent justification is the rule of invalidation that is proposed in the Restatement (Second) of Conflict of Laws in reliance on the law of mistake.[55] The law of contract would not automatically intervene to invalidate a contract with unexpected legal results, so neither should modal choice of law. Another example is the 'foreign law as fact'-maxim that is well established in common law jurisdictions. The maxim is not a convincing reason to depart from the distinction drawn in the law of contract between mistakes of fact and mistakes of law. Modal choice of law should instead clarify

[50] See ch 7, s III.
[51] See ch 8, s III.
[52] Rome II (n 18).
[53] See ch 7, s VII.B.
[54] See above, nn 15 to 17.
[55] American Law Institute, *Restatement (Second) of Conflict of Laws* (1971), s 187, cmnt (e); see ch 8, s II.C.

that a mistake of foreign law must be treated as a mistake of law for the purpose of determining the validity of the choice of law contract.

C. Implementing Reform

It has already been pointed out that some of the most fundamental changes proposed in this book—in particular, the need to establish the choice of law agreement in accordance with basic principles of contract—would not necessitate reform. The same cannot be said for modal choice of law. So it is fitting to conclude this book with a general observation about possible means of reform of modal choice of law. Such reform would have to take varied forms, of course, depending on the jurisdiction and the subject-matter involved. But it would be difficult to overemphasise the value of international unification or harmonisation in this regard. Uniform modal choice of law rules ensure that parties need not deal with potentially conflicting modal choice of law rules when entering into a choice of law contract; they serve to prevent forum shopping; and when drafted with an internationalist perspective, they are able to take account of divergent contractual practices.[56]

However, with the exception of the Hague Maintenance Protocol, international instruments have not yet recognised the importance of modal choice of law rules in the regulation of choice of law contracts. The Hague Conference, in particular, would be an appropriate forum to lead the way for a contractual approach to party autonomy—an approach that places the individual centre-stage of the choice of law process. To that extent, at least, the Hague Principles on Choice of Law in International Commercial Contracts are an opportunity missed. Party autonomy is no longer just a pragmatic tool that assists the court in ascertaining the applicable law, or a 'quick fix' for the failings or inadequacies of objective choice of law. It is an expression of the parties' power of self-determination on the international plane. So we should finally give it the attention that it deserves.

[56] See ch 5, s IV.

SELECT BIBLIOGRAPHY

Abend M, *Die lex validitatis im internationalen Vertragsrecht* (Heidelberg, Winter, 1994)
American Law Institute, *Restatement of Conflict of Laws* (1934)
—— *Restatement (Second) of Conflict of Laws* (1971)
—— *Uniform Commercial Code* (2008)
Ancel M-E, L Marion and L Wynaendts, 'Contentieux international: Réflexions sur les clauses de juridiction asymétriques' (2013) 148 *Banque & Droit* 3
Anton AE, *Private International Law: a Treatise from the Standpoint of Scots Law* (Edinburgh, Green, 1967)
Atiyah PS, *The Rise and Fall of Freedom of Contract* (Oxford, Clarendon Press, 1979)
—— *Essays on Contract* (Oxford, Clarendon Press, 1986)
—— *An Introduction to the Law of Contract* 5th edn (Oxford, Clarendon Press, 1995)
Australian Law Reform Commission, *Choice of Law* (Report 58, 1992)
Ayres I and R Gertner, 'Filling Gaps in Incomplete Contracts: An Economic Theory of Default Rules' (1989) 99 *Yale Law Journal* 87
Baldoni C, 'Il contratto di lavoro nel diritto internazionale privato italiano' (1932) 24 *Rivista di diritto internazionale* 1
Bamberger HG and H Roth, *Beck'scher Online-Kommentar BGB: VO (EG) 593/2008, Art 3* 24th edn (Munich, CH Beck, 2011)
Barnes W, 'The French Subjective Theory of Contract: Separating Rhetoric from Reality' (2008) 83 *Tulane Law Review* 359
Barnett R, 'A Consent Theory of Contract' (1986) 86 *Columbia Law Review* 269
Basedow J, 'Theorie der Rechtswahl oder Parteiautonomie als Grundlage des Internationalen Privatrechts' (2011) 75 *Rabels Zeitschrift für ausländisches und internationales Privatrecht* 32
Batiffol H, *Les conflits de lois en matière de contrats: Etude de droit international privé comparé* (Paris, Recueil Sirey, 1938)
—— and P Lagarde, *Droit international privé* 7th edn (Paris, LGDJ, 1981)
Baumert A, 'Abschlusskontrolle bei Rechtswahlvereinbarungen' [1997] *Recht der Internationalen Wirtschaft* 805
Beale H (ed), *Chitty on Contracts* 31st edn (London, Sweet & Maxwell, 2012)
—— Mistake and Non-Disclosure of Facts (Oxford, Oxford University Press, 2012)
Beatson J and D Friedman, 'Introduction: From "Classical" to Modern Contract Law' in J Beatson and Friedman D (eds), *Good Faith and Fault in Contract Law* (Oxford, Clarendon Press, 1995) 3
Beck A, 'Floating Choice of Law Clauses' [1987] *Lloyd's Maritime and Commercial Law Quarterly* 532
Benson P, 'The Unity of Contract Law' in P Benson (ed), *The Theory of Contract Law: New Essays* (Cambridge, Cambridge University Press, 2001) 118

Bird J, 'Choice of Law' in F Rose (ed), *Restitution and the Conflict of Laws* (Oxford, Mansfield Press, 1995) 64
Blackstone W, *Commentaries on the Laws of England, Book the Second* 16th edn by JT Coleridge (London, printed by A Strahan for T Cadell and J Butterworth & Son, 1825)
Bonomi A, *Explanatory Report: Protocol of 23 November 2007 on the Law Applicable to Maintenance Obligations* (HccH, October 2009)
Born G, *International Commercial Arbitration* 2nd edn (Alphen aan den Rijn, Kluwer, 2014)
Braucher J, 'Contract versus Contractarianism: The Regulatory Role of Contract Law' (1990) 47 *Washington and Lee Law Review* 697
Briggs A, *Agreements on Jurisdiction and Choice of Law* (Oxford, Oxford University Press, 2008)
—— 'The Formation of International Contracts' [1990] *Lloyd's Maritime and Commercial Law Quarterly* 192
—— 'The Validity of "Floating" Choice of Law and Jurisdiction Clauses' [1986] *Lloyd's Maritime and Commercial Law Quarterly* 508
Brulhart V, *Le choix de la loi applicable—questions choisies* (Bern, Stämpfli, 2004)
Bucher E, 'Was macht den Schiedsrichter?' in B Bachmann et al (eds), *Grenzüberschreitungen: Beiträge zum Internationalen Verfahrensrecht und zur Schiedsgerichtbarkeit—Festschrift für Peter Schlosser* (Tübingen, Mohr Siebeck, 2005) 97
Bureau D and H Muir Watt, *Droit international privé* 2nd edn (Paris, Presses Universitaires de France, 2010)
Camarote J, 'A Little more Contract with My Contract Please: The Need to Apply Unconscionability Directly to Choice-of-Law Clauses' (2009) 39 *Seton Hall Law Review* 605
Canaris C-W and HC Grigoleit, 'Interpretation of Contracts' in A Hartkamp et al (eds), *Towards a European Civil Code* 4th edn (Alphen aan den Rijn, Kluwer, 2010) 587
Carruthers J, 'Party Autonomy in the Legal Regulation of Adult Relationships: What Place for Party Choice in Private International Law?' (2012) 61 *ICLQ* 881
Cartwright J, 'Protecting Legitimate Expectations and Estoppel in English Law' (2006) 10(3) *Electronic Journal of Comparative Law*
Cavers D, *The Choice of Law Process* (Ann Arbor, University of Michigan Press, 1966)
—— 'The Common Market's Draft Conflicts Convention on Obligations: Some Preventive Law Aspects' (1975) 48 *Southern California Law Review* 603
Chen-Wishart M, Contract Law (Oxford, Oxford University Press, 2007)
Chong A, 'The Public Policy and Mandatory Rules of Third Countries in International Contracts' (2006) 2 *Journal of Private International Law* 27
—— 'Choice of Law for Void Contracts and Their Restitutionary Aftermath: The Putative Governing Law of the Contract' in P Giliker (ed), Re-examining Contract and Unjust Enrichment (Leiden, Martinus Nijhoff, 2007) 155
—— 'Void Contracts and the Applicability of Choice of Law Clauses to Consequential Restitutionary Claims' (2009) 21 *Singapore Academy of Law Journal* 54
Clarkson CMV, 'Matrimonial Property on Divorce: All Change in Europe' (2008) 4 *Journal of Private International Law* 421
Clay T, *L'arbitre* (Paris, Dalloz, 2001)
Coester-Waltjen D, 'Der Eskimo-Mantel aus Spanien—Ist der kollisionsrechtliche Verbraucherschutz zu kurz gestrickt?' in B Pfister and M Will (eds), *Festschrift für Werner Lorenz* (Tübingen, JCB Mohr, 1991) 297

—— 'Einige Überlegungen zur konkludenten Rechtswahl im europäischen Vertragsrecht' in M Coester, D Martiny and KA von Sachsen Gessaphe (eds), *Privatrecht in Europa—Festschrift für Hans Jürgen Sonnenberger* (Munich, CH Beck, 2004) 343

Collins H, *Regulating Contracts* (Oxford, Oxford University Press, 1999)

—— *The Law of Contract* (Cambridge, Cambridge University Press, 2003)

Collins L (ed), *Dicey, Morris and Collins on the Conflict of Laws* 15th edn (London, Sweet & Maxwell, 2012)

Consortium Asser-UCL, *Étude sur les régimes matrimoniaux des couples mariés et sur le patrimoine des couples non mariés dans le droit international privé et dans le droit interne des États membres de l'Union* (Offre n JAI/A3/2001/03)

Corbin A, *Corbin on Contracts* (St Paul, West Pub Co, 1952)

Crawford E, 'The Uses of Putativity and Negativity in the Conflict of Laws' (2005) 54 *ICLQ* 829

Czernich D and H Heiss (eds), *EVÜ—Das Europäische Schuldvertragsübereinkommen* (Vienna, Orac, 1999)

Dannemann G, 'The "Battle of the Forms" and the Conflict of Laws' in F Rose (ed), *Lex Mercatoria: Essays on International Commercial Law in Honour of Francis Reynolds* (London, LLP, 2000) 199

Davies M, AS Bell and PLG Brereton, *Nygh's Conflict of Laws in Australia* 9th edn (Chatswood NSW, LexisNexis, 2014)

Davis S, 'Same-sex Couples and the Harmonisation of EU Matrimonial Property Regimes: Unjustifiable Discrimination or Missed Opportunities?' (2013) 25 *Child and Family Law Quarterly* 19

de Boer ThM, 'Facultative Choice of Law: The Procedural Status of Choice-of-Law Rules and Foreign Law' (1996) 257 *Recueil des Cours* 223

—— 'Party Autonomy and its Limitations in the Rome II Regulation' (2007) 9 *Yearbook of Private International Law* 19

—— 'The Purpose of Uniform Choice-of-Law Rules: the Rome II Regulation' (2009) 56 *Netherlands International Law Review* 295

—— 'Living Apart Together: The Relationship between Public and Private International Law' (2010) 57 *Netherlands International Law Review* 183

Dickinson A, *The Rome II Regulation: The Law Applicable to Non-Contractual Obligations* (Oxford, Oxford University Press, 2010)

—— *A Note on the Autonomy of the Parties' Agreement on Choice of Law* (Legal Studies Research Paper No 12/83, Sydney Law School, October 2012)

Dutta A, 'Kollidierende Rechtswahlklauseln in allgemeinen Geschäftsbedingungen' (2005) 104 *Zeitschrift für vergleichende Rechtswissenschaft* 461

Eidenmüller H, 'Recht als Produkt' (2009) 64 *Juristenzeitung* 641

Einsele D, 'Rechtswahlfreiheit im Internationalen Privatrecht' (1996) 60 Rabels Zeitschrift für ausländisches und internationales Privatrecht 417

Esser M, 'Der Erlass weitergehender Formvorschriften im Rahmen des Haager Unterhaltsprotokolls durch die Mitgliedstaaten der EU' [2013] *Praxis des Internationalen Privat- und Verfahrensrechts* 399

European Parliament's Committee on Women's Rights and Gender Equality: M Yannakoudakis (Rapporteur), *Opinion of the Committee on Women's Rights and Gender Equality for the Committee on Legal Affairs on the proposal for a Council regulation on jurisdiction, applicable law and the recognition and enforcement of decisions in matters of matrimonial property regimes* (2011/0059 CNS, 7 May 2012)

European Union Agency for Fundamental Rights, *Opinion on the Proposal for a regulation on jurisdiction, applicable law and the recognition and enforcement of decisions regarding the property consequences of registered partnerships* (1/2012)
Farnsworth EA, 'Comparative Contract Law' in M Reimann and R Zimmermann (eds), *The Oxford Handbook of Comparative Law* (Oxford, Oxford University Press, 2006) 899
Fauvarque-Cosson B, *Libre Disponibilité des Droits et Conflits de Lois* (Paris, LGDJ, 1996)
—— 'Comparative Law and Conflict of Laws: Allies or Enemies? New Perspectives on an Old Couple' (2001) 49 *American Journal of Comparative Law* 407
—— 'La confiance légitime et l'estoppel' (2007) 11(3) *Electronic Journal of Comparative Law*
Fawcett J, 'Evasion of Law and Mandatory Rules in Private International Law' (1990) 49 *CLJ* 44
—— and JM Carruthers, *Cheshire, North & Fawcett: Private International Law* 14th edn (Oxford, Oxford University Press, 2008)
Fentiman R, *Foreign Law in English Courts* (Oxford, Clarendon Press, 1998)
—— *International Commercial Litigation* (Oxford, Oxford University Press, 2010)
—— *International Commercial Litigation* 2nd edn (Oxford, Oxford University Press, 2015)
Fisher R (ed), *Fisher on Matrimonial and Relationship Property* (online looseleaf ed, Butterworths)
Flessner A, *Interessenjurisprudenz im Internationalen Privatrecht* (Tübingen, JCB Mohr, 1990)
Fons MP, 'Commercial Choice of Law in Context: Looking Beyond Rome' (2015) 78 *MLR* 241
Foyer J, 'Le Contrat d'Electio Juris à la Lumière de la Convention de Rome du 19 Juin 1980' in *L'Internationalisation du Droit: Mélanges en l'Honneur de Yvon Loussouarn* (Paris, Dalloz, 1994) 169
Fuller L, 'Consideration and Form' (1941) 41 *Columbia Law Review* 799
Furmston MP, *Cheshire, Fifoot and Furmston's Law of Contract* 16th edn (Oxford, Oxford University Press, 2012)
Gal J, *Die Haftung des Schiedsrichters in der internationalen Handelsschiedsgerichtsbarkeit* (Tübingen, Mohr Siebeck, 2009)
Garner M, 'Formation of International Contracts—Finding the Right Choice of Law Rule' (1989) 63 *Australian Law Journal* 751
Gaudemet-Tallon H, 'Le Pluralisme en Droit International Privé' (2005) 312 *Recueil des Cours* 9
Gialdino C, 'La volonté des parties en droit international privé' (1972) 137 *Recueil des Cours* 743
Giuliano M, 'La Loi Applicable aux Contrats: Problèmes Choisis' (1977) 158 *Recueil des Cours* 183
—— and P Lagarde, *Report on the Convention on the Law Applicable to Contractual Obligations* [1980] OJC 282/1
Gleeson AM, 'Community of Property and the Conflict of Laws' (1962) 4 *Sydney Law Review* 139
Gothot P, 'La méthode unilatéraliste face au droit international privé des contrats' (1975–1977) *Travaux du Comité Français de Droit International Privé* 201
Gray K and S Gray, *Elements of Land Law* 4th edn (London, Oxford University Press, 2005)
Grigoleit HC, 'Abstraktion und Willensmängel—Die Anfechtbarkeit des Verfügungsgeschäfts' (1999) 199 *Archiv für die civilistische Praxis* 379

—— 'Mandatory Law: Fundamental Principles' in J Basedow et al (eds), *Max Planck Encyclopaedia of European Private Law* (Oxford, Oxford University Press, 2011)

Grolimund P, *Vertrauensanknüpfung im Internationalen Privat- und Zivilverfahrensrecht* (Zurich, Dike, 2008)

Habermaier S, 'Das Trennungsdenken: Ein Beitrag zur europäischen Privatrechtstheorie' (1995) 195 *Archiv für die civilistische Praxis* 283

Haftel B, 'Pour en finir avec le cercle vicieux du principe d'autonomie (ou presque)' in L d'Avout, D Bureau and H Muir Watt, *Mélanges en l'honneur du Professeur Bernard Audit: les relations privées internationales* (Paris, LGDJ, 2014) 409

Harris J, 'Contractual Freedom in the Conflict of Laws' (2000) 20 *OJLS* 247

—— 'Does Choice of Law Make Any Sense?' (2004) 57 *Current Legal Problems* 305

—— 'Mandatory Rules and Public Policy under the Rome I Regulation' in F Ferrari and S Leible (eds), *Rome I Regulation: The Law Applicable to Contractual Obligations in Europe* (Munich, Sellier, 2009) 269

Hartley T, 'Matrimonial (Marital) Property Rights in Conflict of Laws: A Reconsideration' in J Fawcett (ed), *Reform and Development of Private International Law: Essays in Honour of Sir Peter North* (Oxford, Oxford Univeristy Press, 2003) 215

Haudek W, *Die Bedeutung des Parteiwillens im internationalen Privatrecht* (Berlin, Springer, 1931)

Hay P, P Borchers and S Symeonides, *Conflict of Laws* 5th edn (St Paul, West Academic Publishing, 2010)

Heiss H, 'Inhaltskontrolle von Rechtswahlklauseln in AGB nach europäischem Internationalen Privatrecht' (2001) 65 Rabels Zeitschrift für ausländisches und internationales Privatrecht 634

Helms T, 'Konkludente Wahl des auf die Ehescheidung anwendbaren Rechts' [2014] *Praxis des Internationalen Privat- und Verfahrensrechts* 334

Henrich D (ed), *Staudingers Kommentar zum Bürgerlichen Gesetzbuch: Art 13–17b EGBGB* (Berlin, Sellier, 2011)

Henry D, *Kollisionsrechtliche Rechtswahl—eine Untersuchung ihrer Wirkungen und Grenzen* (Zurich/St Gallen, Dike Verlag, 2009)

Heuzé V, *La réglementation française des contrats internationaux* (Paris, Joly éditions, 1990)

Hill J, 'Choice of Law in Contract under the Rome Convention: The Approach of the UK Courts' (2004) 53 *ICLQ* 325

Ho LC, 'Anti-Suit Injunctions in Cross-Border Insolvency: A Restatement' (2003) 52 *ICLQ* 697

Hondius E and HC Grigoleit (eds), *Unexpected Circumstances in European Contract Law* (Cambridge, Cambridge University Press, 2011)

Honsell H et al (eds), *Basler Kommentar* 3rd edn (Basel, Helbing Lichtenhahn, 2013)

Hook M, 'The Choice of Law Agreement as a Reason for Exercising Jurisdiction' (2014) 63 *ICLQ* 963

—— 'The Concept of Modal Choice of Law Rules' (2015) 11 *Journal of Private International Law* 185

Howard MN, 'Floating Choice of Law Clauses' [1995] *Lloyd's Maritime and Commercial Law Quarterly* 1

Institut de Droit International, 'L'autonomie de la volonté des parties dans les contrats internationaux entre personnes privées (session de Bâle, 1991)' (1992) 64-II *Annuaire de l'Institut de Droit International* 382

Jacquet J-M, *Principe d'autonomie et contrats internationaux* (Paris, Economica, 1983)
—— 'La Théorie de l'Autonomie de la Volonté' in S Corneloup and N Joubert (eds), *Le Règlement Communautaire 'Rome I' et le Choix de Loi dans les Contrats Internationaux* (Paris, LexisNexis, 2011) 1
Jaffey AJE, 'Offer and Acceptance and Related Questions in the English Conflict of Laws' (1975) 24 *ICLQ* 603
—— 'The Foundations of Rules for the Choice of Law' (1982) 2 *OJLS* 368
Jaspers MB, *Nachträgliche Rechtswahl im internationalen Schuldvertragsrecht* (Frankfurt, Peter Lang, 2002)
Jayme E, 'Inhaltskontrolle von Rechtswahlklauseln in Allgemeinen Geschäftsbedingungen' in B Pfister and M Will (eds), *Festschrift für Werner Lorenz* (Tübingen, Mohr Siebeck, 1991) 435
—— 'L'autonomie de la volonté des parties dans les contrats internationaux entre personnes privées' (1991) 64-I *Annuaire de l'Institut de Droit International* 7
—— 'Identité culturelle et intégration: le droit international privé postmoderne' (1995) 251 *Recueil des Cours* 9
—— 'Choice-of-Law Clauses in International Contracts: Some Thoughts on the Reform of Art 3 of the Rome Convention' in L de Lima Pinheiro, *Seminário Internacional sobre a Comunitarização do Direito Internacional Privado* (Almedina, Coimbra, 2005) 53
—— 'Party Autonomy in International Family and Succession Law: New Tendencies' (2009) 11 *Yearbook of Private International Law* 1
Jessurun d'Oliveira HU, 'The EU and a Metamorphosis of Private International Law' in J Fawcett (ed), *Reform and Development of Private International Law: Essays in Honour of Sir Peter North* (Oxford, Oxford University Press, 2002) 111
Jobard-Bachellier M-N, *L'Apparence en Droit International Privé* (Paris, LGDJ, 1984)
Joubert N, 'Le Choix Tacite dans les Jurisprudences Nationales: vers une Interprétation Uniforme du Règlement Rome I' in S Corneloup and N Joubert (eds), *Le Règlement Communautaire 'Rome I' et le Choix de Loi dans les Contrats Internationaux* (Paris, LexisNexis, 2011) 229
Jünger F, 'Parteiautonomie und objektive Anknüpfung im EG-Übereinkommen zum Internationalen Vertragsrecht: Eine Kritik aus amerikanischer Sicht' (1982) 46 Rabels Zeitschrift für ausländisches und internationales Privatrecht 57
—— 'Two European Conflicts Conventions' (1998) 28 *Victoria University of Wellington Law Review* 527
Junker A, 'Der Reformbedarf im Internationalen Deliktsrecht der Rom II-Verordnung drei Jahre nach ihrer Verabschiedung' [2010] *Recht der Internationalen Wirtschaft* 257
Kadner Graziano T, 'Freedom to Choose the Applicable Law in Tort—Articles 14 and 4(3) of the Rome II Regulation' in W Binchy and J Ahern (eds), *The Rome II Regulation on the Law Applicable to Non-Contractual Obligations: A New Tort Litigation Regime* (Leiden, Martinus Nijhoff, 2009) 113
Kaye P, *The New Private International Law of Contract of the European Community* (Aldershot, Dartmouth Pub Co, 1993)
Kegel G, 'The Crisis of Conflict of Laws' (1964) 112 *Recueil des Cours* 92
—— 'Paternal Home and Dream Home: Traditional Conflict of Laws and the American Reformers' (1979) 27 *American Journal of Comparative Law* 615
—— *Internationales Privatrecht* 7th edn (Munich, CH Beck, 1995)
Kelsen H, *Pure Theory of Law* (Berkeley, University of California Press, 1978)
—— *General Theory of Law and State* (New Jersey, The Lawbook Exchange, 2009)

Keyes M, 'Financial Agreements in International Family Litigation' (2011) 25 *Australian Journal of Family Law* 167
Klass G, 'Three Pictures of Contract: Duty, Power, and Compound Rule' (2008) 83 *New York University Law Review* 1726
Kleinheisterkamp J, 'Rechtswahl und Ehevertrag: Zum Formerfordernis nach Art 15 Abs 3 EGBGB' [2004] *Praxis des Internationalen Privat- und Verfahrensrechts* 397
Knight CJS, 'The Damage of Damages: Agreements on Jurisdiction and Choice of Law' (2008) 4 *Journal of Private International Law* 501
Kós S, 'Constraints on the Exercise of Contractual Powers' (2011) 42 *Victoria University of Wellington Law Review* 17
Kost M, *Konsensprobleme im internationalen Schuldvertragsrecht* (Frankfurt, Peter Lang, 1995)
Kötz H and A Flessner, *European Contract Law* (Oxford, Clarendon Press, 1997)
Kropholler J, *Internationales Privatrecht* 6th edn (Tübingen, Mohr Siebeck, 2006)
Kuipers J, 'Party Autonomy in the Brussels I Regulation and Rome I Regulation and the European Court of Justice' (2009) 10 *German Law Journal* 1505
Lando O, 'Contracts' in K Lipstein (ed), *International Encyclopaedia of Comparative Law: Private International Law* (Tübingen, Mohr Siebeck, 1977) 14
—— 'The Conflict of Laws of Contracts' (1984) 189 *Recueil des Cours* 225
—— and H Beale (eds), *Principles of European Contract Law (PECL): Parts I and II* (The Hague, Kluwer, 2000)
Law Commission, *Unfair Terms in Contracts* (Law Com No 292, 2005)
Leible S, 'Parteiautonomie im IPR—Allgemeines Anknüpfungsprinzip oder Verlegenheitslösung?' in HP Mansel (ed), *Festschrift für Erik Jayme* (Munich, Sellier, 2004) 485
—— 'Rechtswahl im IPR der außervertraglichen Schuldverhältnisse nach der Rom II-Verordnung' [2008] *Recht der Internationalen Wirtschaft* 257
Levasseur AA, *Comparative Law of Contracts* (Durham, Carolina Academic Press, 2008)
Libling DF, 'Formation of International Contracts' (1979) 42 *MLR* 169
Lorenz E, 'Die Auslegung schlüssiger und ausdrücklicher Rechtswahlerklärungen im internationalen Schuldvertragsrecht' [1992] *Recht der Internationalen Wirtschaft* 697
Lorenz W, *Vertragsabschluss und Parteiwille im internationalen Obligationenrecht Englands* (Heidelberg, Winter, 1957)
Low, KFK 'Choice of Law in Formation of Contracts' (2004) 20 *Journal of Contract Law* 167
Magnus U (ed), *Staudingers Kommentar zum Bürgerlichen Gesetzbuch: Rom I-VO Art 3* (Berlin, Sellier, 2011)
—— and P Mankowski (eds), *Brussels I Regulation* 2nd edn (Munich, Sellier, 2012)
Maire S, *Die Quelle der Parteiautonomie und das Statut der Rechtswahlvereinbarung im internationalen Vertragsrecht* (Basel, Helbing & Lichtenhahn, 2011)
Mancini PS, 'De l'utilité de rendre obligatoires pour tous les États, sous la forme d'un ou de plusieurs traités internationaux, un certain nombre de règles générales du droit international privé pour assurer la décision uniforme des conflits entre les différentes législations civiles et criminelles' (1874) 1 *Journal du Droit International Privé* 221
Mankowski P, 'Unwirksame Vereinbarung englischen Rechts zwischen deutschen Anlegern und ausländischem Terminbroker' [1994] *Recht der Internationalen Wirtschaft* 420
—— 'Stillschweigende Rechtswahl und wählbares Recht' in S Leible (ed), *Das Grünbuch zum Internationalen Vertragsrecht* (Munich, Sellier, 2004) 63

—— 'Ist eine vertragliche Absicherung von Gerichtsstandsvereinbarungen möglich?' [2009] *Praxis des Internationalen Privat- und Verfahrensrechts* 23
—— 'Ausgewählte Einzelfragen zur Rom II-VO: Internationales Umwelthalftungsrecht, internationales Kartellrecht, renvoi, Parteiautonomie' [2010] *Praxis des Internationalen Privat- und Verfahrensrechts* 398
Mann FA, 'The Proper Law of the Contract' (1950) 3 *International Law Quarterly* 60
—— 'The Proposed New Law of Exemption Clauses and the Conflict of Laws' (1977) 26 *ICLQ* 903
—— 'Uniform Statutes in English Law' (1983) 99 *LQR* 376
—— 'The Proper Law in the Conflict of Laws' (1987) 36 *ICLQ* 437
Markesinis B, H Unberath and A Johnston, *The German Law of Contract: A Comparative Treatise 2nd edn* (Oxford, Hart Publishing, 2006)
Marshall BA, 'Reconsidering the Proper Law of the Contract' (2012) 13 *Melbourne Journal of International Law* 1
Marti H, 'Die Bedeutung des Parteiwillens im IOR'(1942) 77 *Zeitschrift des bernischen Juristenvereins* 97
Martiny D, 'Die Haager Principles on Choice of Law in International Commercial Contracts' (2015) 79 Rabels Zeitschrift für ausländisches und internationales Privatrecht 624
Matulionyte R, 'Calling for Party Autonomy in Intellectual Property Infringement Cases' (2013) 9 *Journal of Private International Law* 77
Maultzsch F, 'Rechtswahl und ius cogens im Internationalen Schuldvertragsrecht' (2011) 75 Rabels Zeitschrift für ausländisches und internationales Privatrecht 60
Mayer P, 'Les Limites de la Séparabilité de la Clause Compromissoire' [1998] *Revue de l'arbitrage* 359
—— and V Heuzé, *Droit international privé* 10th edn (Paris, LGDJ, 2014)
McCaughran J, 'Implied Terms: The Journey of the Man on the Clapham Omnibus' (2011) 70 *CLJ* 607
McLauchlan DW, 'Contract Formation, Contract Interpretation, and Subsequent Conduct' (2006) 25 *University of Queensland Law Journal* 77
—— 'The Contract That Neither Party Intends' (2012) 29 *Journal of Contract Law* 26
Mekki M, 'Hardship and Modification (or "Revision") of the Contract' in A Hartkamp et al (eds), *Towards a European Civil Code* 4th edn (Alphen aan den Rijn, Kluwer, 2010) 651
Merrett L, 'Article 23 of the Brussels I Regulation: A Comprehensive Code for Jurisdiction Agreements?' (2009) 58 *ICLQ* 545
Meyer-Sparenberg W, 'Rechtswahlvereinbarungen in Allgemeinen Geschäftsbedingungen' [1989] *Recht der Internationalen Wirtschaft* 347
Michaels R, 'The Re-state-ment of Non-State Law: The State, Choice of Law, and the Challenge from Global Legal Pluralism' (2005) 51 *Wayne Law Review* 1209
Mills A, *The Confluence of Public and Private International Law* (Cambridge, Cambridge University Press, 2009)
Mincke W, 'Die Parteiautonomie: Rechtswahl oder Ortswahl?' [1985] *Praxis des Internationalen Privat- und Verfahrensrechts* 313
Mohamed Salah MM, 'Loi d'autonomie et méthodes de protection de la partie faible en droit international privé' (2005) 315 *Recueil des Cours* 141
Morris JHC, 'The Proper Law of a Contract: A Reply' (1950) 3 *International Law Quarterly* 197
Mortensen R, 'Woodhouse Reprised: Accident Compensation and Trans-Tasman Integration' (2012) 9 *Journal of Private International Law* 1

Moser R, *Vertragsabschluss, Vertragsgültigkeit und Parteiwille im internationalen Obligationenrecht* (St Gallen, Verlag der Fehr'schen Buchhandlung, 1948)
Moyle JB, *The Institutes of Justinian* 5th edn (Oxford, Clarendon Press, 1913)
Muir Watt H, 'The Challenge of Market Integration for European Conflicts Theory' in AS Hartkamp and EH Hondius (eds), *Towards a European Civil Code* 3rd revised edn (The Hague, Kluwer, 2004) 191
—— 'European Integration, Legal Diversity, and the Conflict of Laws' (2004–2005) 9 *Edinburgh Law Review* 6
—— 'Concurrence d'ordres juridiques et conflits de lois de droit privé' in *Le droit international privé: esprit et méthodes, Mélanges en l'honneur de Paul Lagarde* (Paris, Dalloz, 2005)
—— "Party Autonomy" in International Contracts: from the Makings of a Myth to the Requirements of Global Governance' (2010) 6 *European Review of Contract Law* 250
Neuhaus PH, 'Legal Certainty Versus Equity in the Conflict of Laws' (1963) 28 *Law and Contemporary Problems* 795
—— *Die Grundbegriffe des Internationalen Privatrechts* 2nd edn (Tübingen, Mohr Siebeck, 1976)
Nishitani Y, *Mancini und die Parteiautonomie im Internationalen Privatrecht* (Heidelberg, Winter, 2000)
Nolan D, 'The Classical Legacy and Modern English Contract Law' (1996) 59 *MLR* 603
North P, *Private International Law Problems in Common Law Jurisdictions* (Dordrecht, Martinus Nijhoff, 1993)
Noyes H, 'If You (Re)Build It, They Will Come: Contracts to Remake the Rules of Litigation in Arbitration's Image' (2006–2007) 30 *Harvard Journal of Law and Public Policy* 579
Nygh P, *Autonomy in International Contracts* (Oxford, Oxford University Press, 1999)
O'Hara EA and LE Ribstein, *The Law Market* (New York, Oxford University Press, 2009)
Paterson JM, 'Implied Fetters on the Exercise of Discretionary Contractual Powers' (2009) 35 *Monash University Law Review* 45
Pierce DP, 'Post-formation Choice of Law in Contract' (1987) 50 *MLR* 176
Plender R and M Wilderspin, *European Private International Law of Obligations* 3rd edn (London, Sweet & Maxwell, 2009)
—— *European Private International Law of Obligations* 4th edn (London, Sweet & Maxwell, 2015)
Pontier JA, 'The Justification of Choice of Law: A Liberal-Political Theory as a Critical and Explanatory Model, and the Field of International Consumer Transactions as an Example' (1998) 45 *Netherlands International Law Review* 388
Prebble J, 'Choice of Law to Determine the Validity and Effect of Contracts: A Comparison of English and American Approaches to the Conflict of Laws' (1973) 58 *Cornell Law Review* 433
Püls J, *Parteiautonomie* (Berlin, Duncker & Humblot, 1995)
Rabel E, *The Conflict of Laws* 2nd edn (Ann Arbor, University of Michigan Law School, 1960)
Ranouil V, *L'Autonomie de la Volonté: Naissance et Évolution d'un Concept* (Paris, Presses Universitaires de France, 1980)
Rauscher T (ed), *Europäisches Zivilprozess- und Kollisionsrecht* (Berlin, Sellier, 2011)
Reithmann C and D Martiny, *Internationales Vertragsrecht* 7th edn (Cologne, Dr Otto Schmidt, 2010)
Resnik J, 'Procedure as Contract' (2004–2005) 80 *Notre Dame Law Review* 593

Revillard M, 'Premier bilan de la Convention de La Haye du 14 mars 1978 sur la loi applicable aux régimes matrimoniaux' in A Borrás et al (eds), *E Pluribus Unum. Liber Amicorum Georges AL Droz* (The Hague, Martinus Nijhoff, 1996) 369
Robertson AH, *Characterization in the Conflict of Laws* (Cambridge MA, Harvard University Press, 1940)
Rödl F, 'Private Law Beyond the Democratic Order? On the Legitimatory Problem of Private Law "Beyond the State"' (2008) 56 *American Journal of Comparative Law* 743
Rösler H, 'Rechtswahlfreiheit im Internationalen Scheidungsrecht der Rom III-Verordnung' (2014) 78 Rabels Zeitschrift für ausländisches und internationales Privatrecht 155
Roth W-H, 'Zur Stillschweigenden Rechtswahl in einem Künftigen EU-Gemeinschaftsinstrument über das Internationale Schuldvertragsrecht' in M Stathopoulos (ed), *Festschrift für Apostolos Georgiades* (Munich, CH Beck, 2006) 905
—— 'Rechtswahlklauseln in Verbraucherverträgen—eine schwierige Sache?' [2013] *Praxis des Internationalen Privat- und Verfahrensrechts* 515
Rudden B, 'Ius Cogens, Ius Dispositivum' (1980) 11 *Cambrian Law Review* 87
Rühl C, *Rechtswahlfreiheit und Rechtswahlklauseln in Allgemeinen Geschäftsbedingungen* (Baden Baden, Nomos, 1999)
Rühl G, 'The Battle of the Forms: Comparative and Economic Observations' (2003) 24 *University of Pennsylvania Journal of International Economic Law* 189
—— 'Party Autonomy in the Private International Law of Contracts: Transatlantic Convergence and Economic Efficiency' in E Gottschalk et al (eds), *Conflict of Laws in a Globalized World* (Cambridge, Cambridge University Press, 2007) 153
—— 'Rechtswahlfreiheit im europäischen Kollisionsrecht' in D Baetge et al (eds), *Die Richtige Ordnung: Festschrift für Jan* Kropholler (Tübingen, Mohr Siebeck, 2008) 187
—— 'Der Schutz des "Schwächeren" im europäischen Kollisionsrecht' in H Kronke and K Thorn (eds), *Grenzen überwinden—Prinzipien bewahren: Festschrift für Bernd von Hoffmann* (Bielefeld, Gieseking, 2011) 364
—— *Statut und Effizienz* (Tübingen, Mohr Siebeck, 2011)
—— 'Regulatory Competition in Contract Law: Empirical Evidence and Normative Implications' (2013) 9 *European Review of Contract Law* 61
—— 'The Protection of Weaker Parties in the Private International Law of the European Union: a Portrait of Inconsistency and Conceptual Truancy' (2014) 10 *Journal of Private International Law* 335
Salmond JW, *Jurisprudence or The Theory of Law* 2nd edn (London, Stevens and Haynes, 1907)
Sartor G, 'Legal Reasoning: A Cognitive Approach to the Law' in E Pattaro, *A Treatise of Legal Philosophy and General Jurisprudence*, vol 5 (Dordrecht, Springer, 2005)
Schall C and J Weber, 'Die vorsorgende Wahl des Scheidungsstatuts nach der Rom III-VO' [2014] *Praxis des Internationalen Privat- und Verfahrensrechts* 381
Scherer MC, 'Le Choix Implicite dans les Jurisprudences Nationales: vers une Interprétation Uniforme du Règlement? L'Exemple du Choix Tacite Résultant des Clauses Attributives de Juridiction et d'Arbitrage' in S Corneloup and N Joubert (eds), *Le Règlement Communautaire 'Rome I' et le Choix de Loi dans les Contrats Internationaux* (Paris, LexisNexis, 2011) 253
Scherpe J (ed), *Marital Agreements and Private Autonomy in Comparative Perspective* (Oxford, Hart Publishing, 2012)
Schlosser P, 'The Separability of Arbitration Agreements—a Model for Jurisdiction and Venue Agreements?' in T Einhorn and K Siehr (eds), *Intercontinental Cooperation*

Through Private International Law: Essays in Memory of Peter E Nygh (The Hague, Asser Press, 2004) 305

Schmeding J, 'Zur Bedeutung der Rechtswahl im Kollisionsrecht: Ein Beitrag zur funktionalen Methode nach von Mehren/Trautman' (1977) 41 Rabels Zeitschrift für ausländisches und internationales Privatrecht 299

Schwander I, 'Zur Rechtswahl im IPR des Schuldvertragsrechts' in P Forstmoser et al (ed), *Festschrift für Max Keller zum 65. Geburtstag* (Zurich, Schulthess, 1989) 473

—— 'Subjektivismus in der Anknüpfung im internationalen Privatrecht' in C Dominicé et al (eds), *Etudes de droit international en l'honneur de Pierre Lalive* (Basel, Helbing & Lichtenhahn, 1993) 181

Sefton-Green R (ed), *Mistake, Fraud and Duties to Inform in European Contract Law* (Cambridge, Cambridge University Press, 2005)

Silbermann L and F Ferrari, 'Getting to the Law Applicable to the Merits in International Arbitration and the Consequences of Getting it Wrong' in F Ferrari and S Kröll (eds), *Conflict of Laws in International Arbitration* (Munich, Sellier, 2011) 257

Smith ML, 'Contractual Obligations Owed by and to Arbitrators: Model Terms of Appointment' (1992) 8 *Arbitration International* 17

Smithdale J, 'Inference, Imputation, or Both? Confusion Persists over Beneficial Interests in the Family Home' (2011) 7 *Cambridge Student Law Review* 74

Sonnenberger H-J (ed), *Münchener Kommentar zum BGB: Band 10, EGBGB Art 1-24, Einleitung IPR* 5th edn (Munich, CH Beck, 2010)

Stankewitsch P, *Entscheidungsnormen im IPR als Wirksamkeitsvoraussetzungen der Rechtswahl* (Frankfurt, Peter Lang, 2003)

Steiner A, *Die stillschweigende Rechtswahl im Prozess im System der subjektiven Anknüpfung im deutschen Internationalen Privatrecht* (Frankfurt, Peter Lang, 1998)

Stoll H, 'Internationalprivatrechtliche Probleme bei Verwendung Allgemeiner Geschäftsbedingungen' in O Sandrock (ed), *Festschrift für Günther Beitzke* (Berlin, de Gruyter, 1979)

—— 'Das Statut der Rechtswahlvereinbarung—eine irreführende Konstruktion' in I Meier and K Siehr (eds), *Rechtskollisionen: Festschrift für Anton Heini zum 65. Geburtstag* (Zurich, Schulthess, 1995) 429

Study Group on a European Civil Code and Research Group on the Existing EC Private Law (eds), *Draft Common Frame of Reference (DCFR)* (Munich, Sellier, 2009)

Swadling WJ, 'Rescission, Property and the Common Law' (2005) 121 *LQR* 123

Symeonides S, 'Material Justice and Conflicts Justice in Choice of Law' in PJ Borchers and J Zekoll (eds), *International Conflict of Laws for the Third Millenium: Essays in Honor of Friedrich K Juenger* (New York, Transnational Publishers, 2001) 125

—— 'The American Choice-of-Law Revolution in the Courts: Today and Tomorrow' (2003) 298 *Recueil des Cours* 9

—— 'A New Conflicts Restatement: Why Not?' (2009) 5 *Journal of Private International Law* 383

—— 'Codification and Flexibility in Private International Law' in K Brown and D Snyder (eds), *General Reports of the XVIIIth Congress of the International Academy of Comparative Law* (Dordrecht (New York), Springer, 2012) 167

—— 'The Hague Principles on Choice of Law for International Contracts: Some Preliminary Comments' (2013) 61 *American Journal of Comparative Law* 873

—— *Codifying Choice of Law Around the World* (New York, Oxford University Press, 2014)

Takahashi K, 'Damages for Breach of a Choice-of-Court Agreement' (2008) 10 *Yearbook of Private International Law* 57
—— 'Damages for Breach of a Choice-of-Court Agreement: Remaining Issues' (2009) 11 *Yearbook of Private International Law* 73
Tang Z, 'Parties' Choice of Law in E-Consumer Contracts' (2007) *Journal of Private International Law* 113
—— *Electronic Consumer Contracts in the Conflict of Laws* 2nd edn (Oxford, Hart Publishing, 2015)
Thompson MP, 'Constructive Trusts, Estoppel and the Family Home' [2004] *Conveyancer and Property Lawyer* 496
Thomson A, 'A Different Approach to Choice of Law in Contract' (1980) 43 *MLR* 650
Tobin R and E Schoeman, 'The New Zealand Accident Compensation Scheme: The Statutory Bar and the Conflict of Laws' (2005) 53 *American Journal of Comparative Law* 493
Tomaszewski M, 'La désignation, postérieure à la conclusion du contrat, de la loi qui régit' [1972] *Revue critique de droit international privé* 567
Trakman L, 'Pluralism in Contract Law' (2010) 58 *Buffalo Law Review* 1031
van Vliet MPW, 'Iusta Causa Traditionis and its History in European Private Law' [2003] *European Review of Private Law* 342
Vischer F, 'Veränderungen des Vertragsstatuts und ihre Folgen' in P Forstmoser et al (ed), *Festschrift für Max Keller* (Zurich, Schulthess, 1989) 547
—— 'General Course on Private International Law' (1992) 232 *Recueil des Cours* 9
Vischer F, L Huber and D Oser, *Internationales Vertragsrecht* 2nd edn (Bern, Stämpfli, 2000)
Vogenauer S, 'Regulatory Competition through Choice of Contract Law and Choice of Forum in Europe: Theory and Evidence' (2013) 21 *European Review of Private Law* 13
von Bar C, *Internationales Privatrecht*, vol 2 (Munich, Ch Beck, 1991)
—— and P Mankowski, *Internationales Privatrecht*, vol 1 (Munich, CH Beck, 2003)
von Hoffmann B and K Thorn, *Internationales Privatrecht* 9th edn (Munich, CH Beck, 2007)
von Mehren AT, 'Civil-law Analogues to Consideration: an Exercise in Comparative Analysis' (1959) 72 *Harvard Law Review* 1009
—— 'The Contribution of Comparative Law to the Theory and Practice of Private International Law' (1977–1978) 26 *American Journal of Comparative Law (Supplement)* 31
—— 'The 'Battle of the Forms': A Comparative View' (1990) 38 *American Journal of Comparative Law* 265
von Savigny FK, *System des heutigen römischen Rechts*, vol 3 (Berlin, Veit, 1840)
—— *System des heutigen römischen Rechts*, vol 8 (Berlin, Veit, 1849)
Wagner G, *Prozessverträge: Privatautonomie im Verfahrensrecht* (Tübingen, Mohr Siebeck, 1998)
—— 'Fakultatives Kollisionsrecht und prozessuale Parteiautonomie' [1999] *Zeitschrift für Europäisches Privatrecht* 6
—— 'Die neue Rom II-Verordnung' [2008] *Praxis des Internationalen Privat- und Verfahrensrechts* 12
Wai R, 'Transnational Liftoff and Juridical Touchdown: The Regulatory Function of Private International Law in an Era of Globalization' (2001–2002) 40 *Columbia Journal of Transnational Law* 209
Wengler W, 'Rechtswahl unter Zwang' in C Dominicé et al (eds) *Études de droit international privé en l'honneur de Pierre Lalive* (Basel, Helbing & Lichtenhahn, 1993) 211

Westlake J, *A Treatise on Private International Law* 7th edn (London, Sweet & Maxwell, 1925)

Westrik R and J van der Weide (eds), *Party Autonomy in International Property Law* (Munich, Sellier, 2011)

Whincop M and M Keyes, 'Putting the "Private" Back into Private International Law: Default Rules and the Proper Law of the Contract' (1997) 21 *Melbourne University Law Review* 515

Whitecross Paton G, *A Text-book of Jurisprudence* 4th edn (Oxford, Oxford University Press, 1972)

Wilhelmsson T, 'Standard Form Conditions' in A Hartkamp et al (eds), *Towards a European Civil Code* 4th edn (Alphen aan den Rijn, Kluwer, 2010) 571

Williams G, 'Language and the Law' (1945) 61 *LQR* 384

Wolff M, 'The Choice of Law by the Parties in International Contracts' (1937) 49 *Juridical Review* 110

Woodward W, 'Finding the Contract in Contracts for Law, Forum and Arbitration' (2006) 2 *Hastings Business Law Journal* 1

Yeo TM, 'The Contractual Basis of the Enforcement of Exclusive and Non-Exclusive Choice of Court Agreements' (2005) 17 *Singapore Academy of Law Journal* 306

Yetano TM, 'The Constitutionalisation of Party Autonomy in European Family Law' (2010) 6 *Journal of Private International Law* 155

Yntema H, "Autonomy" in Choice of Law' (1952) 1 *American Journal of Comparative Law* 341

Youngs RH, 'Compulsory and Voluntary Law: Lessons in Categorization for English Law from Continental Models' (2012) 33 *Statute Law Review* 84

Zweigert K, 'Some Reflections on the Sociological Dimensions of Private International Law or What is Justice in the Conflict of Laws?' (1972–1973) 44 *University of Colorado Law Review* 283

INDEX

www.ingramcontent.com/pod-product-compliance
Ingram Content Group UK Ltd.
Pitfield, Milton Keynes, MK11 3LW, UK
UKHW020136290926
15471UKWH00003B/516

9 781509 926800

SOURCES OF BAILIFF LAW